Subjects unto the Same King

EARLY AMERICAN STUDIES
Daniel K. Richter and Kathleen M. Brown, Series Editors

Exploring neglected aspects of our colonial, revolutionary, and early national history and culture, Early American Studies reinterprets familiar themes and events in fresh ways. Interdisciplinary in character, and with a special emphasis on the period from about 1600 to 1850, the series is published in partnership with the McNeil Center for Early American Studies.

A complete list of books in the series is available from the publisher.

Subjects unto the Same King

Indians, English, and the Contest for
Authority in Colonial New England

JENNY HALE PULSIPHER

PENN

University of Pennsylvania Press

Philadelphia

10 9 8 7 6 5 4 3 2 1

First paperback edition 2007

Published by
University of Pennsylvania Press
Philadelphia, Pennsylvania 19104-4112

Library of Congress Cataloging-in-Publication Data

Pulsipher, Jenny Hale.
    Subjects unto the same king : Indians, English, and the contest for authority in colonial
New England / Jenny Hale Pulsipher.
        p.   cm. — (Early American studies)
    Includes bibliographical references and index.
    ISBN-13: 978-0-8122-1908-1 (pbk. : alk. paper)
    ISBN-10: 0-8122-1908-2 (pbk. : alk. paper)
    1. Indians of North America—New England—Government relations.   2. Indians of North
America—Government relations—To 1789.   3. Indians of North America—New
England—History—17th century.   4. New England—History—Colonial period, ca.
1600–1775.   5. Massachusetts—Politics and government—To 1775.   I. Title.   II. Series
E78.N5 P85   2005
974.4′02—dc22   005042213

For Mike

Contents

Note on the Text

To aid in understanding, I have standardized the spelling in quoted passages except for names and places. I have left capitalization as it appears in
the sources and have added punctuation only where clarity required it. I
have also shifted dates within the text to the modern Julian calendar, in
which the new year begins on January 1 rather than March 25. Within note
citations I have preserved old-style dates (where used) to allow interested
readers to more easily find archival sources.

We have subjected our selves, our lands, & possessions, with all the rights, & inheritances of us, & our people, either by conquest, voluntary subjection, or otherwise, unto that famous, & honorable government, of that royal King Charles, & that state of old England, to be ordered, & governed, according to the laws, & customs thereof, not doubting of the continuance of that former love, that hath been between you, & us; but rather to have it increased hereby, being subjects now, (& that with joint, & voluntary consent,) unto the same king, & state yourselves are.

—Pessacus and Canonicus, Narragansett Sachems, May 1644

Introduction

Land. A boundless canopy of forest shelters the soil of New England. Rock juts from the earth. Orange clumps of lichen blunt the sheer blocks of granite jumbled in crevices and tumbled down cliffs. White pines, thicker than a man can reach around, shoot to neck-craning heights, their roots clinging to stone up to the very edge of the shore. Cedars and spruces dot the coast as well, and "the scent of our Aromatic, and Balsam bearing pines, spruces, and Larch Trees with our Tall Cedars, exceeding all in *Europe*," wafts far out to sea.[1] At the feet of these giants, light filters green, dappling the forest floor, which is clear of all but berry brambles. These—hurtleberry, blueberry, checkerberry—grow in the ashes of last year's fires, set to nourish them and to clear a path for game by the people of the land: the Massachusetts, Nipmucks, Narragansetts, Pennacooks, Mohegans, Pequots, Wabanakis—great peoples, and great in number.[2] They plant, trap, fish, harvest, hunt, and dwell on the land, setting their wigwams streamside in fishing season, moving them inland when the cold winds of winter blow. Further west, large villages of Pocumtucks and Norwottocks tend rich fields of maize.[3]

Sea. The Atlantic stretches pale, gray, and endlessly eastward. Its waves fling clams and mussels along sandy shores. Natives skirt the coast in canoes whose bark sides are peeled from birches of the forest. From time to time whales beach themselves on the sand, offering unexpected bounties of meat that native leaders—sachems and sagamores—will distribute to their people.[4] What is not expected from the sea is men, and when they come they are hailed, up and down the coasts of the land as "manittóo," like gods.[5] Equally remarkable are the ships that bring them. Their unfamiliar construction and great size lead some natives to describe them as enormous birds, floating islands, or clouds.[6] The newcomers offer bright beads of glass, heavy cloth, metal pots, and knives. Natives accept the gifts and offer in exchange the rich furs of beaver, marten, fox, and deer.[7] Soon more men come from the sea, bearded and barking out short, harsh syllables of sound. Not all the newcomers are content with the peltry the natives offer. Some want captives and take them, luring them onto their ships with their tantalizing goods, then carrying them away as their kin's cries of loss ring from the shore.[8]

Death. What the travelers leave behind, other than their trinkets and copper kettles, is also unexpected at first, by either native or newcomer. In the wake of the traders and fishermen who appear off the shores of New England in the sixteenth century, natives begin falling sick. Isolated from the rest of humanity for centuries, they have no immunity to diseases that kill many even among long-exposed Europeans. Plagues here claim up to 90 percent of the men, women, and children. First along the shores, then in inland villages, hundreds, then thousands weaken and die.[9] Whole villages succumb, with none well enough to tend the stricken and none left to bury the dead. When only a handful survive the sudden and bewildering plague that strikes a village, they flee, finding new leaders and substitute families among Indians the plague has passed by. In the chaos of the epidemics, Indian polities form and reform, and familiar power relations shift.

Vacuum domicilium. For the earliest English who arrive to settle, not merely to trade, in New England, the land appears oddly empty. What seemed to be thriving villages from the shore turn out to be ghost towns upon closer inspection. Fields, cleared and planted, stand unharvested next to vacant houses. The land appears to be, as Massachusetts governor John Winthrop will later argue, a *vacuum domicilium*: stripped of its owners, lying waste, it is free for the taking by anyone who will fertilize, plant, fence, build upon, or otherwise "improve" it.[10] Patterning themselves after God's chosen people, the Israelites, the English arriving on Cape Cod in 1620 and Massachusetts Bay in 1630 see the vacant land as a "special providence of God."[11] It is what they have been looking for—a place free of the constraints placed on their religious worship in England, untroubled by the worldly attractions drawing too many of their children into sin, and unhampered by the increasing political conflict at home, where all the world seems hastening to destruction. Here they can begin their world anew and shape it to their own desires. Here, in this empty land, there will be no one to challenge their way of life.

Authority. English hopes to be free from challenge in New England are naïve. The land that appears empty is actually teeming with people. Although greatly reduced, Indians are still more numerous than the earliest English settlers. Many Indians, such as the powerful Iroquois of the future New York and the Narragansett of what will become Rhode Island, have yet to suffer significant impact from European diseases. As the English settlers well know, there are other Europeans in the region as well— English fishermen and coastal traders scattered from Cape Cod to northern Maine, the French of Canada, the Dutch of New Netherland. Each of these groups will challenge English colonial assumptions about their authority in the region. Challenges will come from within English colonies as well, from those who differ with colony leaders over religious and political practice. Intervention from the crown to revoke or restrict colony authority will remain a constant threat. Invoking the rights and obligations of subjects of the king will become a familiar tactic in colonial New

England, a way for English, Europeans, and Indians to bolster their own positions—or undercut those of colonial leaders—in a contest of authority that will play out over the next century and beyond.

The key player in the contest of authority in seventeenth-century New England was the Massachusetts Bay Colony, whose colonists arrived to settle the area in 1630. This colony was key not merely because of its large and rapidly growing population and central location relative to the other colonies and peoples of the region, but because of the position its leaders took on the question of authority. From the beginning of settlement, despite differing opinions within and outside governing councils, colony leaders maintained that the charter of government granted them by the crown gave them supreme authority over all the people—Indian and English—within their jurisdiction. To this authority there could be no appeal, not even to the king himself.

Newly settled in Massachusetts Bay, colony leaders found themselves confronted not only with Indians whose expectations of authority differed from their own, but with similar conflicts among their own people, between themselves and the crown, and with other competitors for the region. These leaders' insistence that they were the final authority powerfully shaped their relationship with all these people. As soon as they were well established in the region, Massachusetts officers insisted that Indians acknowledge their superiority and subject themselves to colony authority. This was a significant difference from the relationship that had been established between local Indians and Plymouth Colony. That relationship, codified in the 1621 league of peace, was described as a friendship and seemed to promise an alliance between fellow subjects of the distant English king rather than an unequal relationship of superiors and inferiors. The Indians responded in a variety of ways to colony leaders' demands. Some acquiesced, hoping for protection and benefit from the powerful colony. Others sought competing sources of power in rival colonies and nations, English or otherwise. Some resisted violently. These divergent choices created divisions among Indian groups that the English used to strengthen their own position.

The tensions between Indians and Massachusetts were evident to all, and surrounding colonies were quick to use them as a tool in their own struggles against the sometimes overbearing presence of Massachusetts in the region. By critiquing or distancing themselves from the interactions of Massachusetts with the Indians, they hoped to preserve or enhance their own power. Three English colonies—Plymouth, Connecticut, and New Haven—shared with Massachusetts a similar religious worldview, generally maintained friendly relations with each other, and offered fairly consistent mutual assistance. Rhode Island, New Hampshire, and Maine, on the other hand, were settled by many who were actively opposed to Massachusetts's political and religious authority or who had fled or been banished from the colony for religious or political offenses. The efforts of Massachusetts to exert authority in these regions met fierce, sometimes violent, resistance, and these conflicts would draw in both Indians and the authority of the English crown.

Non-European powers, too, influenced the tug-of-war over authority. Since the colony's establishment in 1614, Dutch settlers in New Netherland had forged strong trade ties with Indians of the region and the more northerly Mohawks. They followed native protocols in their diplomacy and trade, setting a pattern that Indians expected the French and English to observe as well. The persistent Dutch presence, as well as the more distant French one, provided competition for the trade and friendship of the Indians. This gave the Indians power—the ability to demand concessions and good treatment. Each nation had to work to please the Indians, often by criticizing and undercutting the others, thus diminishing them in the natives' eyes.

Within Massachusetts as well, different groups complicated the colony's efforts to build the stable government necessary to maintain authority with English and Indians. Not all agreed with the religious principles undergirding the colony government, and those whose beliefs disqualified them for participation in the political life of the colony frequently complained of their exclusion, both to colony authorities and to ready listeners across the Atlantic. Even among those who shared Puritan religious beliefs, some differed on the degree of dependence the colony should have on the crown, with some arguing that the colony was the final authority and others urging more acknowledgment of their duty to and dependence on the king.

Some who felt oppressed by Massachusetts leaders chose to go over their heads to the crown. Religious dissidents, colonists from Maine and New Hampshire brought under Massachusetts jursidiction against their will, and Indians who resented the colony's intrusion into their own governance all sent their complaints and appeals for assistance to the king, something Massachusetts leaders viewed and responded to as a direct attack on their authority. Although the king was generally preoccupied with more pressing and lucrative concerns, he did respond from time to time to the shrill protests of those trampled on by Massachusetts, as when Charles II sent royal commissioners to investigate the state of the New England colonies in 1664. Thus the threat of royal action was always present and invoked by rivals of Massachusetts to combat the colony's overreaching.

The crown's interest in and ability to intervene in its colonies depended on the political stability of England, and this stability—or lack of it—also had a powerful impact on the authority of the colonies. England was rent with political turmoil during the mid-seventeenth century, a fact well known to New Englanders. The Civil War, which raged between Parliament and the crown from 1642 to 1648, distracted the king from prosecution of charter violations, and the replacement of the monarchy with Oliver Cromwell's Commonwealth government, friendly to Massachusetts, gave it welcome respite from the critical scrutiny of the king and his advisors.

But the respite was only temporary. Wrenching divisions between factions in the Commonwealth government undermined its ability to rule, leading Parliament to invite Charles I's son to return from exile to restore the monarchy in 1660. This development revived the hopes of those with complaints against Massachusetts, and they renewed their petitions to the king. Other developments—the rise and fall of government ministers, the growing centralization of power in the crown, wars with neighboring European countries—also affected the crown's interest in and freedom to intervene in New England. Massachusetts colonists—those both in favor of and opposed to colony leadership—kept close watch on these events to gauge their ability to act in support of or resistance to the government. Indians, too, observed the ebb and flow of the colony's political fortunes, both locally and in the Atlantic world, and chose times when the colony was particularly vulnerable to target its leaders' authority directly or to appeal over their heads to the king. Thus, Massachusetts's conflicts with its own people, with neighboring colonies, with those over whom its jurisdiction was contested, and with the crown intersected with its dealings with Indians in ways that would bolster Indian resistance and hasten royal intervention in New England.

Throughout the seventeenth century, then, Indian, English, Dutch, and French residents of the region worked to secure their own authority and to create relationships with the other parties that would serve their own interests. This often meant maintaining a precarious balance, tolerating affronts to their authority because of the benefits each was able to gain from relationships with the others. Over time, this balance became increasingly difficult to achieve. All were interested in preserving their authority according to their own interpretation of it. None were interested in going to war over their disagreements, and there were almost always other options available. Indians could appeal to the French or Dutch, or to Indian nations outside the region. English and Indians could appeal to the crown, or threaten to do so. The crown itself could threaten intervention. Colonists or Indians could simply resist or ignore demands and hope, with good reason, that colonial authorities would lack the will or means to enforce their authority. But when these and other alternatives failed, there was the final option of violent resistance—going to war.

Many of New England's Indians chose that option in 1675. It was the culmination of years of bickering over whether the Massachusetts Bay government had final authority in New England. War was a way to throw off the yoke. As a direct challenge to Massachusetts, war brought the contest of authority between the colony and all the other parties in the region into stark relief. It also raised the profile of the region with the crown, creating a situation in which disgruntled citizens of both the colony and its disputed territories could declare their dissatisfaction with greater expectation that their pleas might win support from the king. For the Indians, war offered a final chance to preserve their belief that they were sovereign nations, not subject to local English colonial governments. Their decisive defeat in the war crushed that hope. Indians remaining in Massachusetts were forced to accept full submission. Many others fled the colony, taking refuge in New York or Canada, where they would join with the French in attacks against New England for years to come. In Maine and New Hampshire, where Indians were still a sizeable population relative to the English, the contest of authority would persist for nearly another century.

King Philip's War ended a period of tenuous balance between the various competitors for power in New England and began a painfully prolonged era of political, social, and religious instability. War, which dramatically weakened Massachusetts and stepped up the protests of disgruntled citizens, unhappy neighboring colonies, and Indians, gave the crown the opportunity and ability to intervene again, as it did repeatedly over the period from 1676 to 1691. These years saw the revocation of the colony charter, the establishment and fall of royal government under the Dominion of New England, a brief but impotent restoration of the charter government, the beginning of a new war with the French and with Indians fighting to defend their sovereignty, and, finally, the reestablishment of royal authority under the Massachusetts province charter of 1691. By the time this period of upheaval had drawn to a close, much of the English population of Massachusetts was prepared to surrender their long-cherished authority in return for some stability and peace.

This storyline—which reveals Indians being intimately involved in a power struggle that spanned the Atlantic—is one that has not been adequately told. Despite the growing appearance of Indians in the main narrative of early American history, too many students and readers still view that history in a simplified way, as the record of two monolithic cultures fighting it out in North America. As this brief account suggests, it is a much more complicated—and much more interesting—story. It *is* a tale of two (divided) cultures, but also of a host of other individuals, groups, colonies, and nations who used the struggle between and among the Indians and English for their own ends. That struggle would draw the attention of the crown and would by the end of the century result in a dramatic loss of authority for both Indians and English. This book traces that history. We begin at a time when the question of who would exercise supreme authority in New England was still open.

Spring 1621. English houses are rising on a hill overlooking Plymouth Bay. Indians are nearby, watching, wondering how and when to approach these people who apparently mean to stay. One morning an Indian man walks into the new village of Plymouth. He is alone. English settlers at work building shelters look up, alarmed, then "intercept" him before he can advance further. The man—Samoset is his name—greets them, using English words, and bids them welcome.[12] The contest begins.

Chapter 1
Models of Authority

Indians and English maintained a wary distance from each other in the months following the Plymouth colonists' arrival on the coast of New England in 1620. The newcomers had landed in the bitter cold of November, scouted the area for weeks, and at the end of December had chosen the site of their plantation, set high for defense and with fresh water nearby. English people had been there before, but not as settlers, and members of the Plymouth company knew of Indian violence toward previous visitors to these same shores. Some of those attacks, they also knew, were provoked.[1]

Throughout the first, cold months of the colony's existence, William Bradford noted Indians "skulking about them," but "when any approached near them, they would run away." Other ominous signs—cries and noises by day and night and "great smokes of fire" in the distance—alarmed the settlers. Frequent sightings and sounds confirmed English suspicions that the Indians were carefully watching them as they built, hunted, and explored the area around their new settlement. But when the English approached the sources of smoke or traveled to places where they had seen Indians far off, they found only empty houses. So it went, through the lean months of November, December, January, February, and early March. Fearing the worst, the English built stockades to defend against Indian attack and kept watch by night.[2]

The Indians—Wampanoags—had witnessed the power of English guns. So while they observed the English, they remained aloof, trying to judge their purpose and disposition. Previous contacts with European sailors had not inclined them to trust the newcomers. Six years earlier, Englishmen had arrived in ships, seized Indians after pretended overtures of friendship, and taken them away across the ocean, most never to return.[3]

But some had come back. Epenow, of Martha's Vineyard, had been to England and returned, bearing tales of English deception and cruelty that may have reached the Wampanoags on the coast. Squanto, who would be one of the first to approach the Plymouth settlers, had also been delivered from English capture. He had returned from captivity to find his village of Patuxet, where English houses were now being raised, empty and his people dead of European diseases brought by the fishermen and traders who

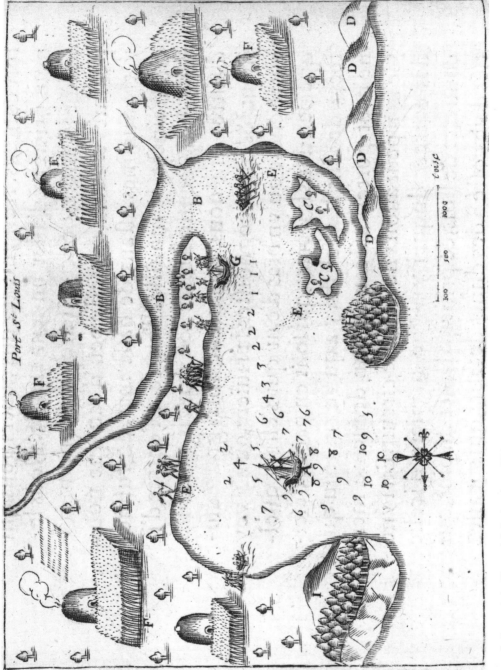

Figure 1. Samuel de Champlain's drawing of Wampanoag wigwams at Plymouth Bay, July 1605. Courtesy of the John Carter Brown Library, Brown University.

had frequented the coast for decades. Bereft of family and friends, Squanto joined Massasoit's people at Pokanoket.[4]

By March the Indians had watched long enough. On the morning of March 16, Samoset, a Wabanaki Indian staying with the Wampanoags, walked "boldly" and "all alone" into Plymouth and, to the amazement of the colonists, addressed them in English and bade them welcome.[5]

Over the next few days, Samoset remained in Plymouth, and other Indian men came also, bringing furs and indicating through signs their eagerness to trade, a desire the English shared. The winter months had been hard for Plymouth; nearly half the original hundred colonists had died of disease, hunger, and exposure by the end of February.[6] It was still too early for harvest of any but the earliest plantings. They needed corn. Too few and weak to defend against any sizeable attack, they welcomed peace.

On March 21, Samoset came to Plymouth yet again, this time with Squanto, who spoke better English. They told the colonists that the leader of the Wampanoags, the great sachem Massasoit, was nearby with his brother Quadequina and they wished to speak with the governor. Within an hour, the sachem appeared at the top of the hill, accompanied by sixty warriors. The sachem's appearance and bearing both proclaimed his authority. He was tall, like his men, "a very lusty man, in his best years, an able body, grave of countenance, and spare of speech." Dressed in skins like his followers, he was distinguished by "a great chain of white bone beads" around his neck and a pouch of tobacco hanging behind. After an initial parley between Massasoit and Edward Winslow, sent as the governor's messenger, the sachem and twenty of his men left their weapons on the ground and followed the English into the village.

Led by Winslow, Massasoit and his men entered a house "then in building" within the town. The English laid down a green rug and some cushions for seating; the sound of a trumpet and drums announced the arrival of the colony's governor, John Carver, accompanied by musketeers. Carver and the sachem greeted each other, "our governor kissing his hand, the king kissed him." The governor offered food and drink, which the sachem accepted and shared with his men. Then, as Winslow described it, "they treated of peace." Each leader promised that he and his people would not harm the other, that they would give warning of danger, that they would assist if the other were attacked, and that they would work to maintain order and peace between the two peoples.

This agreement, made in the earliest days of contact, was the 1621 league of peace between Plymouth Colony and the Wampanoags.[7] That agreement established expectations that would have a profound impact on relations between Indians and English throughout the remainder of the century. It would also affect the relationships among the English, Dutch, and French, the several English colonies, and the conflicting groups within each colony, all of whom used the Indian-English relationship as a tool to critique Massachusetts's exercise of authority and bolster their own. This critique, in turn, would help bring on the intervention of the crown, making the contest of authority span the Atlantic Ocean. Thus the Indian-English relationship is key to understanding the contest of authority in New England, which helped move both Indians and English from independence to dependence by the end of the century.

For the treaty of 1621 to have meaning and therefore power among the Indians and English, it was necessary for the two groups to have similar patterns of authority in their respective societies. There were similarities, but there were also differences that profoundly influenced how each interpreted what precisely was agreed to in 1621. To appreciate fully each party's understanding of this agreement as well as the larger context of the struggle over authority that lies at the center of this book, we need to know what came before contact.

For up to a century before English settlement, the Wampanoags and other Indians of the northeast had had sporadic contact and trade with Europeans. Trade introduced new materials, language, and ways of doing things into native cultures, but Squanto's experience demonstrates that European-borne diseases wrought the most dramatic change, killing up to 90 percent of Indians in some areas of New England, including many leaders, undermining the authority of the remaining sachems and religious leaders or powwows, and forcing realignments of Indian groups because of drastically reduced populations.[8] Much of this process took place before the first English Pilgrim set foot on Cape Cod.

Yet much of what we know of Indian government in seventeenth-century New England comes from our reading of English accounts that follow the Pilgrims' landing; they describe the customs and structure of already changed societies that continued to change, adapting to the English presence, seeking to turn it to benefit in their lives.[9] People poorly describe the unfamiliar; their natural tendency is to draw parallels with what they know. Early descriptions of Indian societies by English observers apply English labels such as "king" and "prince" to figures who seemed to fill similar roles in an unfamiliar culture. Recognizing the inherent bias of reports filtered through English observers, scholars of Indian North America of the last generation have shifted their emphasis to values and characteristics in various Indian cultures such as government by consensus and egalitarianism that are directly contrary to hierarchical European models.[10] Consensus operated when Indians "voted with their feet," for example, temporarily or permanently shifting allegiance to another community when they were displeased with a sachem's governance. Rhode Island colonist William Harris claimed that Indians' allegiance could not be determined by where they were born or resided, but only "by voluntary consent: they are: or are not: Such or such a Sachem's men."[11]

While consent was an important aspect of Indian governance, New England Indians were also much concerned with status and maintaining orderly, ranked societies.[12] Well before Europeans arrived in North America, Indian polities in the New England area were organized under sachems, hereditary political leaders acknowledged as superiors by their subjects. While English preconceptions of authority undoubtedly influenced their descriptions of these leaders, Indians themselves witnessed to the hierarchical nature of their societies. One sachem testifying before English magistrates claimed that "he doth know nothing unto what the great Sachems or company of the Indians know for he is a little Sachem and hath few men under him."[13] The very word "under"—"agwa" in the Massachusett language—demonstrates that these relationships were vertical, rather than equal. Indeed, "agwa" is at the root of the words for "subject" and "subjection" in Massachusett. Roger Williams's 1643 *Key into the Language of America* included the Narragansett phrases "Ntacquêtunck ewò" and "Kuttáckquêtous," which Williams translated as "He is my subject" and "I will subject to you."[14]

One way that sachems maintained the loyalty of their subjects and demonstrated their power was through generosity, by redistributing goods they received through tribute or by virtue of the trade routes they controlled. Gift-giving, in addition to solidifying a sachem's power and prestige, helped demonstrate friendships, establish obligations, and renew alliances, playing a vital role in the social life and rituals of Indian societies throughout the northeast.[15] Sachems also offered their subjects protection from enemies. In return, subjects had obligations to sachems, such as the payment of tribute. Sachems themselves sometimes paid tribute to higher sachems they recognized as more powerful and from whom they desired protection. Sachems likewise expected payment of tribute from people they had conquered, as the Pequots did from the Montauks of Long Island. Tribute was paid with a number of goods, including deerskins and, increasingly with the arrival of Europeans, wampum—shell beads manufactured by the Indians, which became the chief source of currency for English and Dutch colonists.[16]

Indians of the northeast signaled the nature of their relationships with each other through the selective use of kinship terms: "fathers" were superiors, "friends" or "brethren" were allies or equals, "children" were inferiors.[17] These relationships were not permanent; they could shift from vertical to horizontal and back again. For instance, when the chief sachem of the Narragansetts, who received tribute from the Montauks, desired their support in a war, he raised their status, signaling the change by using terms that suggested a more equal relationship: "and instead of receiving

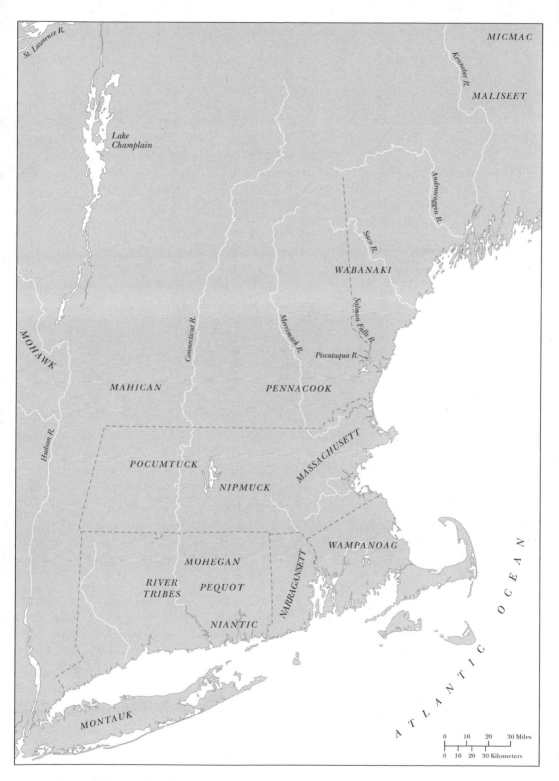

Map 1. Indians of the Northeast in the early seventeenth century.

presents, which they used to do in their progress, he gave them gifts, calling them brethren and friends."[18]

Relationships of superiors and inferiors among Indians varied in degree, just as they did among Europeans. For example, William Strachey recorded in 1612 that the Algonquian Chickahominies of Virginia paid "certain duties" to the great sachem Powhatan and agreed to be hired by him as warriors from time to time, but they maintained governmental independence: "they will not admit of any werowance [leader] from him [Powhatan] to govern over them but suffer themselves to be regulated and guided by their priests, with the assistance of their elders."[19] A similar relationship—an unequal alliance—seems to have existed between the Narragansetts and the more powerful Mohawks.[20] The Narragansetts sent them presents and sought their aid but governed themselves. The Pocumtucks of the Connecticut River also governed themselves but acknowledged that they needed the consent of the Mohawks, with whom they were "in confederacy," to take any significant action such as going to war.[21]

Among the English, both hierarchy and consent were present as well. Their kings, princes, and other royalty are evidence of English hierarchy, an order believed to be of divine institution. But, as among the Indians, hierarchy and consent were frequently—and increasingly—at odds with each other in government. Within a generation of the Pilgrims' settlement in New England, disagreements over the relative authority of king and Parliament would result in civil war in their home country, leaving England a parliamentary commonwealth under Oliver Cromwell, rather than a monarchy, for over a decade. The opposing imperatives of consent and hierarchy are evident in governments instituted in New England as well.[22]

The New England minister John Davenport laid out the model for government in an election sermon he preached in 1669: "The orderly ruling of men over men, in general, is from God, in its root, though voluntary in the manner of coalescing and being supposed that men be combined in Family-Society, it is necessary that they be joined in a Civil Society; that union being made, the power of Civil Government, and of making Laws, followeth naturally."[23] God was at the top of the hierarchical ladder implicit in Davenport's model, and on each descending rung stood leaders committed to acting out his will: king, governor, magistrates, deputies, town officers, fathers, and mothers. Children, women, and servants followed the lead of fathers and husbands in the family order, and the family was the model for civil government, which was "a great family."[24] Like the Indians, the English used family terminology to indicate superior rank: God, the king, and the magistrates, as well as literal parents, were "fathers." And the fifth commandment requiring children to honor parents was applied to all relationships of authority, between masters and servants, parents and children, rulers and ruled. Under the Puritans' peculiar interpretation of authority, subjection to these rulers was part of a covenant relationship and thus voluntary.[25] But it did not follow that people were at liberty to disobey. They had the right to choose, not the right to govern. Once chosen, leaders, good or bad, must be obeyed.

Plymouth Colony offers a good example of the operation of both hierarchy and consent in English society. The Plymouth Company patent gave the colonists the right to settle the land, but they lacked a charter with authority and guidelines for government. The Mayflower Compact of 1620, a voluntary agreement for government, is evidence of both the colonists' lack of any regular authority for their enterprise and their acknowledgment that government by consent could help fill that gap. Although it was a model of government by consent, the compact invoked the highest earthly authority it could name to lend weight to its binding promises, declaring the signatories "loyal subjects of our dread sovereign Lord, King James" and avowing that, even without a charter of government, their colony was undertaken for "the honor of our King and country."[26] Plymouth's colonists would follow the same pattern in their dealings with the Indians, invoking the king's name as a way of underlining their own strength and authority.

English political and cultural thinking predisposed the English to believe that they had the right to exercise authority over the natives of the land the king had granted them by patent. According to the English, when Indian nations compacted with them and acknowledged themselves subjects of the English king, they placed themselves on the same hierarchical ladder as the English, with the king at the top, followed by magistrates, deputies, town selectmen, fathers, mothers, and finally servants and children. While the English used the term "subject" for both themselves and the Indians, they insisted that subject status was mediated through them, making them superior to the king's Indian subjects. Furthermore, many English believed that the Indians were at a lower level of civilization than themselves and therefore deserved, even needed, subjection. Englishmen of the time saw wealth—particularly as embodied in clothing—as a gauge of status. The Indians displayed their lack of status—their incivility—by their "nakedness." Hence the 1664 royal gift of two sumptuous coats to the Narragansett sachems was viewed by some of Rhode Island's leaders as "most unfitting and improper."[27] Royal gifts might be appropriate honors for English governors, not for "naked" Indian sachems.

This judgment about social standing or rank went hand-in-hand with English views of how much weight Indian authority could or should carry and with their belief that Indians needed the English example and benevolent guidance to rise to civility. The first governor of the Massachusetts Bay Company, Matthew Cradock, saw this as a natural progression. The Indians were uncivil, but the English had once been equally so, and, "but for the mercy and goodness of our good God, might have continued to this day."

Figure 2. The seal of the the Massachusetts Bay Colony. Courtesy of the American Antiquarian Society.

As missionaries had brought the civilizing light of the gospel to England, English colonists should "omit no good opportunity that may tend to bring [the Indians] out of that woeful state and condition they now are in" and raise them to a higher state.[28]

While the idea of paying tribute was familiar to the English from their reading of the Bible and European history, only vague, symbolic remnants of the practice persisted among them, such as the king's requirement, traditionally listed on colony charters, that one fifth of the gold discovered in the colonies be paid to him.[29] This—in addition to the obvious weakness of the fledgling colonies—may account for the fact that none of the early English colonies in North America initially demanded tribute from surrounding Indians. Another reason may also have discouraged the practice: tribute was strongly associated with the Spanish conquest of America. Bartolomé de las Casas's *The Destruction of the Indies,* reprinted in English several times during the sixteenth century, condemned the cruelty of the Spanish toward the Indians, including the heavy tributes laid on them.[30] This and other writings helped create the "Black Legend" of Spanish cruelty toward the Indians, which English adventurers and promoters of colonization were determined not to emulate. On the contrary, they held up the Spanish example as the dark mirror to their own benevolent intentions. Writing in 1585, Richard Hakluyt the Elder, the leading English promoter of colonization, declared that, though trade was desirable and conquest might be necessary, the primary purpose and goal of colonization should be

to plant Christian religion. . . . In regard whereof, many circumstances are to be considered, and, principally, by what means the people of those parties may be drawn by all courtesy into love with our nation, that we become not hateful unto them as the Spaniard is in Italy and in the West Indies and elsewhere by their manner of usage: for a gentle course without cruelty and tyranny best answereth the profession of a Christian, best planteth Christian religion, maketh our seating most void of blood, most profitable in trade of merchandise, most firm and stable, and least subject to remove by practice of enemies.[31]

New England planters made similar professions. In a letter of instructions to John Endicott, sent to prepare for the first wave of settlement at Massachusetts Bay, Cradock urged him not to forget the "main end of our Plantation . . . to bring the Indians to the knowledge of the Gospel" and reminded him that that aim would be seriously hindered by a bad English example. Endicott must ensure that the English "live unblameable and without reproof, and demean themselves justly and courteous towards the Indians, thereby to draw them to affect our persons, and consequently our religion."[32] That same year the governor and council, still in England, ordered that a seal be cast for the new colony. On its face it bore the image of a nearly naked Indian standing, holding a spear, with these words emerging from his mouth: "Come over and help us." Company leaders wrote to Endicott in New England and asked him to publish a proclamation directing the English settlers to offer no injury or offense to the Indians, stipulating that punishment would follow any who did. This proclamation was to be "fixed under the Company's seal in some eminent place, for all to take notice at such time as both the heathen themselves, as well as our people, may take notice of it." They wanted the seal, and its message, to be "noticed" and understood by Indians and English alike.[33]

Englishmen such as Massachusetts minister Thomas Shepard took pride in this benevolent approach, this care to avoid offense. They deplored the Spanish example; Shephard noted that nineteen million Indians had died under Spanish oppression. And they believed that the English were more benevolent than the Indians' own rulers as well. Shepherd eagerly recorded an early Indian convert's declaration to his fellows: "All the time you have lived after the Indian fashion under the power and protection of higher Indian Sachems, what did they care for you? They only sought their own ends out of you, and therefore would exact upon you, and take away your skins and your kettles & your Wampum from you at their own pleasure, & this was all that they regarded: But you may evidently see that the English mind no such things, care for none of your goods, but only seek your good and welfare, and instead of taking away, are ready to give to you."[34] Demanding tribute could not help but discourage such hopeful beginnings.

While the English understanding that Indians stood beneath them on the hierarchical ladder informs the dealings of Plymouth and, later, Massachusetts with the Indians in seventeenth-century New England, there is evidence that the Indians did not see their position in relation to the English as inferior at all. Plymouth, established ten years before the larger and stronger Massachusetts Bay Colony, was the first colony to treat with the Indians, and the terms of their 1621 league of peace did not make the Plymouth colonists' assumptions of superiority over the Indians clear. It could as easily be read as an alliance of equals as a submission of one people to another. In fact, an alliance is how the Wampanoags seem to have interpreted it, and this initial interpretation, or, as the English might argue, misinterpretation, reverberated through their dealings with the English for generations.

In that first treaty between Indians and English in New England, Plymouth leaders addressed the Wampanoag sachem Massasoit as "friend" and "ally" of King James, a signal to the Indians that their relationship with the English was one of equality.[35] The Plymouth colonists further reinforced this perception among the Indians by their choice of language and their actions in dealing with the Indians in the years after the treaty. Its original stipulations were, for the most part, reciprocal, implying equality, though one notable exception existed—the clause that demanded that Indians send any offender to the English "that we might punish him" but failed to offer to send offenders to the Indians in return. The historical record makes it clear, however, that Massasoit assumed reciprocity applied to every aspect of the treaty, whether it was stated or not. When Squanto was suspected of wronging the Wampanoag people, for example, Massasoit demanded the English turn him over to the Indians for judgment. When Plymouth's governor resisted, Massasoit protested vehemently, "demanding him . . . as being one of his subjects, whom, by our first Articles of Peace, we could not retain."[36] And when the English displayed guns—to honor their visitors, they said—the Indians protested that it went against the treaty.[37]

It is also significant that the English demanded no tribute of the Indians, thus demonstrating that they were not seeking subjection, but friendship. Indeed, when Edward Winslow and several other Plymouth colonists set out to visit Massasoit four months after the treaty conference, they took gifts, as allies would, and they acknowledged that they did so "to bind him the faster unto them."[38] Notably, throughout this period, Winslow and other Englishmen in contact with the Indians used the term "friend," not "subject," to describe their relationship with the Indians.[39]

Plymouth's failure to demand tribute may have encouraged some Indians to assume that only the king, not the local English, had the right to anyone's subjection. Consider this incident: in the midst of the Pequot War of 1637, the Montauks volunteered to switch their subjection from the Pequots, who had formerly conquered them, to the English and to pay tribute to them instead. Narragansett sachem Miantonomi protested strongly against this, telling Montauk sachem Waiandance that he "must give no more wampum to the English, for they are no Sachems, nor none of their children shall be in their place if they die; and they have no tribute given them; there is but one king in England, who is over them all."[40] Miantonomi was openly denying English settlers' assumptions of superiority, declaring that English leaders neither received tribute from their own people nor had a right to demand it of the Indians, as did a true sachem. Judged against the pattern of the Indians' past political relationships, English actions and expressions gave the Indians good reason to judge their relationship with the English as one of friendship and alliance rather than subjection. That Plymouth gave gifts and did not demand tribute of the Indians, that they called them *friends*, sent the signal that what was being set up was an *alliance* of peoples.

If Massasoit did not see himself as submitting to English authority in the 1621 treaty, what do we make of the fact that when Winslow visited him a few months later, the sachem proclaimed himself "King James his man" and said that his land was "King James his country," or that within the next year, many surrounding sachems openly acknowledged themselves "subjects" of King James?[41] It may have been connected to traditional Indian understandings of unequal alliances. Just as the Narragansetts sent gifts to the Mohawks and acknowledged their superior strength but governed themselves, the Wampanoags and surrounding Indians who acknowledged themselves as subjects of the distant king could, simultaneously, have viewed themselves as sovereign peoples. The English may have solidified the impression that the Indians were allies, not inferiors, by using the term "subject" for both themselves and the Indians. They proclaimed their own subjection to the king far across the ocean. If the Indians, too, were subjects of the king, that placed them on the *same* level with the local English, not a lower one. The use of kinship terms of equality in two Native American sources also suggests that Massasoit and his heirs saw their relationship with the king as an alliance, rather than a subjection. Zerviah Mitchell, who claimed direct descent from Massasoit, recorded that one of that sachem's prized possessions was a silver pipe sent to him by King James, "his white brother over the sea."[42] And in 1671, when Metacom, or Philip, defied the authority of the United Colonies, he declared that he "would not Treat except his Brother King Charles of England were there."[43]

News of the friendship and alliance between the Wampanoags and English of Plymouth spread quickly to other Indian groups in the region, including the Narragansetts. Indeed, the English encouraged spreading the news, placing a clause in the 1621 treaty enjoining the Wampanoags to inform their friends and neighbors of their new ties to the English. One of the most numerous and powerful New England Indian groups, the Narragansetts had somehow escaped the epidemic that decimated the Wampanoags before the Plymouth colonists arrived. A compelling reason for Massasoit's alliance with the English was, in fact, to obtain an ally against his threatening neighbors.[44] The two Indian groups knew each other well, and, whether in hostility or friendship, their interaction is well documented throughout the seventeenth century. Thus, while there is no proof that the Narragansetts understood the exact terms of Plymouth's treaty with the Wampanoags, it would be surprising if they did not have at least a general understanding of the nature of the relationship.

One incident shortly after the treaty was signed suggests that the Narragansetts quickly recognized the threat of the new Wampanoag-English alliance and sought to advertise their own claims to dominance in the region. In January 1622, Canonicus, chief sachem of the Narragansetts, sent a gift to Governor William Bradford of Plymouth, a snakeskin stuffed full of arrows, which the governor's Indian interpreters assured him was "a threatening and a challenge." Bradford observed that the Narragansetts, "since the death of so many of the Indians" in the devastating epidemics before the Pilgrims arrived, "thought to domineer and lord it over the rest, and conceived the English would be a bar in their way, and saw that Massasoit took shelter already under their wings." According to native practice, accepting the gift would be accepting both its symbolic message, that the Narragansetts were the dominant power in the region, and the obligation to submit to Narragansett authority. Instead, Bradford added a pile of bullets and gunpowder to the bundle and sent it back to Canonicus. This was his own assertion of dominance, and Canonicus refused it, sending it away immediately. Thus "through this mutual act of rejection, each party signalled its refusal to submit to the other."[45]

Given this prickly beginning, it is not surprising that the Narragansetts made their first overtures of friendship to the English of Massachusetts rather than to Plymouth. As in Plymouth, Massachusetts leaders began interacting with local Indians soon after their settlement in 1630, and, again as in Plymouth, alliance rather than subjection seemed to characterize their initial meetings. In March 1631, Massachusett sachem Chickatabut came to Boston with a large party and bestowed on Governor Winthrop a hogshead of Indian corn. In turn, Winthrop gave each of the Indians there a "small cup of sack and beer, and the men tobacco." After staying the night, Chickatabut and two others dined with Winthrop "at his own table," where, Winthrop observed, "he behaved himself as soberly . . . as an Englishman." When the sachem departed the next day, Winthrop gave him still more presents—cheese, peas, a rug, "and some other small things."[46] This mutual exchange of gifts and the seating at the governor's table were clear signals of friendship and equality. Just four months after this meeting, Canonicus's son, accompanied by a local Massachusett sachem, visited Winthrop as well. He brought an animal skin as a gift for the governor, and Winthrop "requited him with a fair pewter pot, which he took very thankfully, and stayed all night."[47] Thus with another mutual exchange of presents and hospitality, the Narragansetts and English of Massachusetts sealed their friendship.[48]

The Narragansetts' first treaty with the English, a 1636 compact with the Massachusetts government made in the days leading up to the Pequot War, also indicates a relationship of friendship rather than subjection. Most of the treaty's articles concerning mutual protection, giving notice of war, trade, and so forth, are reciprocal; there is no mention of submission to government or king and no mention of tribute to be paid by either party. And, as before, there is a ritual exchange of presents—wampum and a Pequot hand from the Narragansetts (signaling their willingness to help the English fight the Pequots) and four English coats from the Massachusetts government, all sent well after the agreement, "according to [the Indians'] manner."[49] It is striking that Winthrop here makes a point of accommodating Indian custom. That effort would be short-lived.

Like the Narragansetts, the Pequot Indians of Connecticut had established dominance over many Indian groups in the region, exacting tribute even from the Narragansetts for a time. Their proximity to the coast allowed them to share with the Narragansetts a monopoly on making and trading wampum, which the Dutch colonists used as currency in their extensive fur trade. But by 1634 the Pequot relationship with the Dutch had disintegrated into war. The Pequot relationship with the Narragansetts was also strained and frequently violent. In this quandary, the Pequots sought an alliance with the Bay Colony. Massachusetts leaders were willing to consider a relationship, but only on their own terms, which included the Pequots turning over the men who had earlier killed two English traders. The Pequot sachems ignored this demand. Tensions escalated over several years and finally broke into open violence between Pequots and English settlers in the Pequot War of 1637.[50]

The Pequot War fundamentally altered the structures of authority between the English and surrounding Indians that had been established in the treaty of 1621 and subsequent agreements. Abandoning a short-lived treaty of peace with Massachusetts, the Pequots sought an alliance with the Narragansetts against the English. Ironically, the Pequots' arguments "to move them thereunto" would prove to be prophetic. They declared that "the English were strangers, and began to overspread their country, and would deprive them thereof in time, if they were suffered to grow and increase; and if the Narragansetts did assist the English to subdue them, that did but make way for their own overthrow; for if they were rooted out, the English would soon take occasion to subjugate them."[51] Still smarting from their former subjection to the Pequots, however, the Narragansetts rejected this plea. They chose instead to ally themselves with the English. On May 25, 1637, Narragansett and English warriors attacked a large Pequot fort at the mouth of the Mystic River in Connecticut. In the course of the fight, the English set fire to the wigwams within the fort, and hundreds of Pequots inside, including old men, women, and children, died in the flames. The massacre at the Pequot fort essentially ended both the war and Pequot power in the region. In the aftermath, the Pequot survivors were subjected to English authority and forced to pay the English tribute as a conquered people.[52]

The victory in the Pequot War was a dramatic demonstration of English power, and its impact rippled through the Indian governments of the region. The Montauks, also former subjects of the Pequots, sought the protection of the demonstrably powerful English by offering to shift their subjection and their tribute to them. Other Indian groups sought English protection as well. In a letter to Plymouth Governor William Bradford, Massachusetts governor John Winthrop reported "the Indians in all quarters so terrified as all their friends are afraid to receive them. Two of the Montauk sachems came to Mr. Stoughton and tendered themselves to be tributaries under our protection. And two of the Nipmuck sachems have been with me to seek our friendship."[53] Even Massasoit, long on good terms with Plymouth colony leaders, brought a gift of eighteen beaver skins to the Massachusetts governor: "The occasion was, (as he said,) it was reported, that we were angry with him, and intended to war upon them; so they came to seek peace."[54]

At the same time the Indians were seeking English friendship, the English, determined to prevent future uprisings, moved to solidify their authority over surrounding Indians. At first, their efforts were uncoordinated. In 1638 Connecticut called the Mohegans and Narragansetts to Hartford and made a "tripartite" treaty of peace with them. Under the terms of the treaty, the two Indian parties agreed to pay a yearly tribute for

Figure 3. The English and Narragansett Indian attack on the Pequot fort at Mystic, Connecticut, from John Underhill's *Newes from America; or a new discoverie of New England* (1638). Courtesy of the New England Historic Genealogical Society.

each male Pequot captive under their supervision and to "resign and yield up the whole Pequot country, and every part of it to the English colonies as due to them by conquest." The Narragansetts and Niantics were ordered to give hostages—four children—until 2000 fathoms of wampum due as tribute were delivered to the English.[55] What is most striking about this treaty is who is missing from it. Connecticut did not invite an obvious and interested power—Massachusetts—to participate, in spite of the fact that Massachusetts officials had asked to be included. By excluding Massachusetts, Connecticut officials revealed to the Indians the intercolonial conflict over who should wield authority over the Mohegans and Narragansetts. Massachusetts leaders felt the slight keenly. Governor Winthrop complained that Connecticut officials had undermined Massachusetts's authority with the Narragansetts by "disclaiming to their Narragansetts to be bound by our former agreement with them," the treaty of 1636, and by requiring all the Indians who had Pequots under their supervision to pay their tribute "at Connecticut," not Massachusetts. Given both this intercolonial confusion and the Narragansetts' dissatisfaction with the growing Massachusetts dominance over them, it is not surprising that such sachems as Ninigret repeatedly refused to pay this tribute.[56] By demonstrating that the colonies were divided, the tripartite treaty may also have encouraged the Indians in continued resistance to the demands of individual colonies and nourished their hopes of overthrowing English power, evident in the increasingly frequent rumors of Indian uprisings against the English.

The demonstrated power of the English and the rush of Indian groups to secure friendships with them after the Pequot War threatened Narragansett power in the region. And there is reason to believe that English actions after the war betrayed Narragansett expectations of a relationship of equality with the English. Although the English had made a treaty with the Narragansetts agreeing to mutual assistance in the war, they did not share with their allies the fruits of war—tribute from the conquered Pequots. The English also claimed exclusive rights to the Pequots' conquered lands.[57] That this angered the Narragansetts is evident in Nathaniell Morton's description of Narragansett service in the Pequot War. They were, he claimed, "very cold or backward in the business, either out of envy, or that they thought the English would make more profit of the victory than they were willing they should, or else deprive them of that advantage that they desired in making the Pequots become tributaries unto them, or the like."[58] Ninigret, sachem of the Niantics, who lived near the Narragansetts and had close ties with them, was particularly angered by English behavior following the war. His response was to ignore English demands and to behave as if the conquered Indians were his own subjects, not English ones. He repeatedly refused to turn over Pequots who had surrendered to him, and in August 1638 he traveled to Block Island and "rifled some of those Indians, which were tributaries to [the English]," apparently seeking the tribute the English thought was theirs alone. Called to account for his misdeeds by the English, Ninigret alternately refused to appear, delayed, or gave grudging satisfaction.[59]

Miantonomi, who shared leadership over the Narragansetts with his uncle Canonicus, was also disturbed by the changed relationship and by English behavior during and after the war. Miantonomi was a powerful man, "very stern, and of a great stature." His authority and bearing were such that it caused "all his nobility and such as were his attendants to tremble at his speech."[60] He expected to be treated with the deference due a great sachem. English behavior in the aftermath of the war was far from deferential, however, and English descriptions of Miantonomi highlight the sachem's growing anger and offended pride. Tensions between Narragansetts and English suggest that the English had promised them both Pequot lands and authority over the Pequots, particularly the women and children, who Miantonomi specifically requested would be spared in any attacks. The massacre at the Pequot fort did not discriminate by gender or age, and the Narragansetts' protest that the attack was "naught, because it is too furious, and slays too many men," reflects their anger at both the manner of warfare and the loss of subjects.[61] Highlighting his sense that English treatment had fallen far below his expectations of mutuality, Miantonomi complained, "Did ever friends deal so with friends?"[62]

This phrase, "Did ever friends deal so with friends," highlights the Indians' persistent expectations of equality and reciprocity and their growing alarm at English violation of those expectations. Before the war, both Massachusetts and Plymouth officials had made a point of accommodating Indian custom, participating in gift exchange and following the traditional protocols and timing of gift-giving "according to [the Indians'] manner." After the war, Massachusetts leaders showed a distinct reluctance to continue these patterns, insisting that the Indians follow theirs. An exchange between Miantonomi and Governor Thomas Dudley in 1640 demonstrates this shift. The English had called Miantonomi to court to answer for rumors that he was involved in a conspiracy against them. The court provided Miantonomi a Pequot woman as an interpreter, which the sachem viewed as an insult to his honor. Miantonomi left the court in protest, and Dudley insisted that, before he was admitted again or allowed to dine with the English as before, he must apologize. Miantonomi did so, but John Winthrop, who recorded the exchange, noted that it rankled Miantonomi deeply to have to give "satisfaction" "for not observing our custom in matter of manners, for he told us that when our men came to him, they were permitted to use their own fashions, and so he expected the same liberty with us."[63] Reciprocity between the two peoples had slipped substantially. The following year, when Miantonomi was called to court again to answer for another rumor, he was seated at a table set apart for Indians, rather than with the governor and magistrates. Offended, Miantonomi "would eat nothing, till the governor sent him meat from his table."[64]

Miantonomi's growing dissatisfaction led him to push back against English control in a way that would lead not only to his own downfall, but to increased English interference in Indian affairs. Miantonomi showed his resistance initially by failing to deliver the tribute due from Pequots under his care or to bring his fellow sachem Ninigret into line with English demands. Massachusetts's interference in Miantonomi's sale of land, and thus in his authority over the sub-sachem who lived on it, led to even greater resistance and a distinct falling out between the English and himself. Miantonomi had sold the land to Samuel Gorton of Rhode Island. Gorton, considered a heretic by his Puritan neighbors, practiced a radical strain of Christianity and managed to tangle with civil authorities in every place he lived.[65] Banished from Massachusetts, Plymouth, and two Rhode Island towns, he finally decided to set up his own kingdom by purchasing land for his town of Warwick from Miantonomi. Pomham, the subsachem who actually held the land, signed the deed under duress but immediately fled to Massachusetts and submitted himself and his lands to the colony's authority, begging their aid against Gorton and Miantonomi. Massachusetts officials accepted Pomham's submission, acknowledged his rightful sachemship and ownership of the lands, and asserted the colony's authority over the area. By submitting to the English, Pomham hoped not only to preserve his land and authority, but to gain English protection and raise himself to an equal level of authority with the sachem who had been his overlord.[66] Furious, Miantonomi attacked one of Pomham's men "and then bid him go and complain to the Massachusetts."[67]

These affronts to Miantonomi's authority led him, finally, to act on the very suggestion the Pequots had made to him before the war, to drive the English out of the country before they "[took] occasion to subjugate them."[68] In 1642 he met with Waiandance, the Montauk sachem, and urged him to join the Narragansetts and "all the Sachems from east to west, both Moquakues and Mohauks joining with us" in an uprising against the English. He warned them that the consequences of not doing so would be disastrous: "otherwise we shall be all gone shortly, for you know our fathers had plenty of deer and skins, our plains were full of deer, as also our woods, and of turkeys, and our coves full of fish and fowl. But these English having gotten our land, they with scythes cut down the grass, and with axes fell the trees; their cows and horses eat the grass, and their hogs spoil our clam banks, and we shall all be starved."[69] Sachems loyal to the English revealed Miantonomi's plans for an uprising, however, before he could bring it about.

Miantonomi's obvious displeasure with the English and his demonstration of his willingness to resist English authority openly made him a dangerous threat to English security. In 1643, when war erupted between the Narragansetts and their longtime enemies the Mohegans, the English found an opportunity to rid themselves of a nettlesome problem. The Mohegan sachem Uncas captured Miantonomi and sent messengers to English officials asking what should be done with him. English officials conferred with local ministers and concluded that the "safest" course would be to have Uncas execute Miantonomi. Their reasons? They now had proof that Miantonomi was at the head of the long-rumored Indian uprising against the English. And, even if that uprising had failed, Miantonomi was not a man the English could trust for long: "He was of a turbulent and proud spirit, and would never be at rest."[70] Mohegan Indians retrieved Miantonomi from the jail where he was being held in Hartford, and then, on the march to their own country, tomahawked him from behind and buried him on the trail. This execution—or murder, as the Narragansetts saw it—cemented the enmity between Mohegans and Narragansetts that would lead to continuous tension and increased English interference in the region.

This near uprising of 1643 may have awakened the English colonies to the need for a united front against the Indians and a single agency for negotiating and communicating with them. Later the same year the colonies finalized a union long in preparation—the United Colonies of New England, a compact including Massachusetts, Plymouth, Connecticut, and New Haven that was intended to be a means of mutual defense against, and a diplomatic arm to, the Indians. The union pointedly excluded both Rhode Island and Maine, colonies that, Winthrop argued, "ran a different course from us both in their ministry and civil administration."[71] The United Colonies demanded that the Indians submit all their grievances with other Indians to them and receive their permission before going to war with any Indians "in friendship with or subject to" any member of the compact. The right to give or withhold permission for war was wielded only by chief sachems in Indian society, so by assuming this right, the United Colonies Commissioners were presenting themselves as superiors—as chief sachems.[72]

In the wake of the establishment of the United Colonies, a number of New England Indian groups moved to establish closer ties with the most powerful English government in the region, the Massachusetts Bay Colony. While we cannot know what kind of relationships these Indians hoped for, Bay Colony leaders made it clear to the Indians that submission to their government entailed subjection, not alliance. Pomham's submission in 1643 set the pattern for future submissions. Before accepting it, the Massachusetts magistrates questioned Pomham extensively about his understanding of submission, making sure that he accepted the English view of it: Did he honor "parents and superiors"? The sachem replied, "It is our custom so to do, for inferiors to be subject to superiors." Then, the magistrates explained, they would understand "that we did not receive them in as confederates but as subjects." In a pointed demonstration of the Indians' inferior status, the discussion was followed by a banquet at which Pomham and his men dined at a separate table from the governor.[73]

A number of other Indian groups soon followed Pomham's example, seeking the good favor and protection of the Massachusetts Bay Colony. In 1644 five Massachusett Indian sachems around Boston submitted to the English government. At the colony's urging, the sachems agreed to "put ourselves, our subjects, lands, and estates under the government and jurisdiction of the Massachusets" and to "be true and faithful to the said government."[74] Passaconnaway, sachem of the Pennacooks, submitted later that year, on terms the colony's leaders later described as "friendship, Amity & subjection."[75] In 1668, ten Nipmuck sachems from western Massachusetts likewise submitted to Massachusetts's authority, seeking protection and agreeing to be "ruled" by colony leaders. Like Pomham, their submission came in the immediate aftermath of conflict with the Narragansett sachems who had attacked and seized their property because of failure to pay overdue tribute. By submitting to Massachusetts, the Nipmucks hoped to escape this subjection in return for one less burdensome.[76]

These submissions to Massachusetts's authority omitted any reference to the king, as did, by 1643, all other oaths and treaties used by Massachusetts or its sister colony of Connecticut. This omission reflected the ongoing turmoil of the English Civil War. Massachusetts leaders, who saw Parliament's struggle as their own, justified striking the king's name from official colony oaths because the king had "violated the privileges of parliament, and made war upon them, and thereby had lost much of his kingdom and many of his subjects."[77] Massachusetts leaders' own political struggles with royal government encouraged them to assert a relationship of direct rule over the Indians, making the Indians' inferior status explicit in their treaties with them, something that Plymouth had been attempting to do in practice, if not in the actual wording of treaties. Massachusetts leaders were determined to make their position as the final authority in the region clear to Indians as well as English.

While Pomham, Passaconnaway, and other Indian sachems worked to turn English authority to their benefit, either by ensuring good relations with the English or by using them to escape Indian authority, the chief sachems of the Narragansetts continued to resist English dominance in the region. The newly established United Colonies had bound the Indians to seek their permission before going to war with any Indians "in amity and subjection" with the English. The successors to Miantonomi's authority, his aged uncle Canonicus and twenty-year-old brother Pessacus, sought that permission in 1643, wanting to revenge the Mohegans' murder of Miantonomi. Massachusetts governor Winthrop refused to give it, and when Pessacus sought the same permission six months later, the governor sent a stinging rebuke, declaring that "if they sent us 1000 fathom of wampum and 1000 skins, yet we would not do that which we judged to be unjust, viz. to desert [the Mohegan sachem] Onkus, but our resolution was, and that they must rest upon, that if they made war upon Onkus, the English would all fall upon them." [78] Frustrated and angry, the sachems made a fateful decision: they appealed directly to the king.

Their decision—and the resentment of Massachusetts's dominance that prompted it—was shared, and perhaps guided, by a group of English settlers in Rhode Island with similar complaints. Like Plymouth, Rhode Island was much weaker than Massachusetts and lacked a charter early in its settlement. More significantly, the chief founders of the colony were exiles from Massachusetts, and their relationship with that colony continued to be troubled. Rhode Island had been excluded from the 1643 establishment of the United Colonies, and it was derided by leaders of the other English colonies as a cesspool of religious and political radicalism that overflowed far too often for the safety and comfort of its neighbors. Locked in disputes with Massachusetts, Plymouth, and Connecticut, leaders of the isolated and despised colony had little choice but to appeal to outside powers for help. Roger Williams traveled to London in 1643 and succeeded in obtaining a parliamentary patent for the colony of Rhode Island and Providence Plantations. And John Greene, who obtained a royal charter for the colony in 1663, made a point of securing the right to appeal to the king over any disputes with neighbor colonies. This clause implicitly forced the other colonies to recognize royal appeals, a direct challenge to Massachusetts officials' insistence that their own charter allowed no appeal over their own authority.[79]

Such insistence on supremacy, and past punishment of its own colonists' appeals to the king, had made Massachusetts the subject of numerous complaints, leading in 1637 to a royal attempt to revoke the colony's charter, a process cut short by England's domestic upheavals. Rhode Island officials were keenly aware of Massachusetts's political troubles and were not above highlighting its colonists' bad behavior—and their own comparative loyalty—to incline the king to favor their petitions. One of the ways they kept this comparison before the king, and before Massachusetts, was through their styling of their authority. Rhode Island leaders, like those of Plymouth, cited their connection to the king at every opportunity, both to bolster their own authority and to highlight their loyalty in comparison to that of the Massachusetts government. Both colony governments dated their judicial proceedings according to the "Year of the Reign of our Sovereign Lord, Charles by the Grace of God King of England, Scotland, France & Ireland, Defender of the Faith, &c."[80] Both summoned people to court "in his Majesties name." And Rhode Island officials made a point of attaching the king's name to their government's official title: "the Governor and Company of his Majesties Colony of Rhode Island and Providence Plantations."[81] Rhode Islanders with complaints against Massachusetts frequently inserted pointed comparisons of the two colonies into their letters and petitions to the crown, such as the claim that the Rhode Island government was "ready to assent and yield all obedience to [the king's] supreme authority, not making our Patents a cloak for contempt, or warrant to disobey and oppose his Royal commands."[82]

One Rhode Islander who took undisguised glee in goading the Massachusetts government's precarious claims to independence was Samuel Gorton, who targeted its pretensions to authority in the subtitle of a tract he published in London, "The Combat of the United Colonies, not only against some of the Natives and Subjects, but against the authority also of the Kingdom of England."[83] Gorton's purchase of Pomham's land from Narragansett sachem Miantonomi and Pomham's subsequent submission to the Massachusetts government brought Gorton and colony leaders into direct conflict. After Pomham petitioned the Massachusetts government to take him under the colony's protection and help him get his land back, Massachusetts leaders sent an armed band to root the Gortonists out (thus dispossessing both Gorton and Miantonomi). With no local recourse against this attack, the Gortonists sailed for London to appeal to the king, and they arranged to take the Narragansett sachems' protests along with them. The Narragansetts had their own grievances with Massachusetts. The colony had consistently sided with their enemies, the Mohegans, had refused to allow either Indian people to go to war, had fined the Narragansetts heavily for disobeying its orders, and then had consented to—even urged—the Mohegans' execution of captured Narragansett sachem Miantonomi.[84] The Narragansett sachems' complaints against Massachusetts would bolster Gorton's argument that Massachusetts was exceeding its authority, and dispossessing Pomham would ensure that the land sold to Gorton would stay sold. Thus what started as a minor intercolonial dispute soon leapt the Atlantic, drawing in Indians, English, and royal government and powerfully influencing the course of Massachusetts's relations with the Narragansetts and the crown ever after.

On April 19, 1644, in a letter delivered to King Charles I of England by Samuel Gorton and three of his associates, Narragansett sachems Canonicus and Pessacus made the impact of this international dispute apparent. The sachems were Miantonomi's uncle and brother, and his death rankled them deeply. Seeking relief for their grievances, they appealed to the king in what would become the first of many future Indian appeals to royal authority. They submitted themselves, their land, and their possessions to the king, "upon condition of His Majesties' royal protection," his righting whatever wrong might be done to them, and his overthrowing their enemies. And who might those enemies be? The sachems asserted that they did not need the king's assistance against "any of the natives in these parts, knowing ourselves sufficient defence." But they had "just cause of jealousy and suspicion of some of His Majesty's pretended subjects"—a pointed jab at Massachusetts. "Nor can we yield over ourselves unto any, that are subjects themselves in any case; having ourselves been the chief Sachems, or Princes successively, of the country, time out of mind."[85]

The consequences of this submission became apparent the following month, when the Massachusetts General Court sent a letter to the Narragansett sachems ordering them to come and take counsel over their ongoing war with the Mohegans. Pessacus and Canonicus sent a letter in reply, declining to come. They informed the magistrates that they had "subjected our selves, our lands, & possessions" to "that royal King Charles, & that state of old England to be ordered, & governed, according to the laws, & customs thereof." More pointedly, they noted their status of equality with the English, "being subjects now, (& that with joint & voluntary consent,) unto the same king, & state yourselves are." As equal subjects of the king,

Figure 4. Charles I, 1600–1649 (r. 1625–1649). Courtesy of the Library of Congress.

disputes between the English and Indians could no longer be mediated by English colonial officials, but only by a higher power. Both must "repair, unto that honorable, & just government" of the king in England.[86] Ending on a conciliatory note, the sachems expressed their willingness to remain in "friendly correspondency" with the colony—as friends, not subjects.

Massachusetts officials responded to this letter with a collective gasp of outrage. Having effectively kicked out the highest rung on their own hierarchical ladder, the colony leaders found it a direct challenge to their authority to have the king's preeminence pointed out to them, by English or Indian. In his journal, John Winthrop noted the receipt of the letter from Pessacus and Canonicus but insisted it was actually "written by Gorton's company." The General Court was then in session, and it immediately directed two messengers to the Narragansetts to ask them "whether they did own that letter . . . and by whose advice they had done as they wrote, and why they would countenance and take counsel from such evil men, and such as we had banished from us, and to persuade them to sit still, and to have more regard to us than such as Gorton." When the messengers arrived in Narragansett country, Canonicus refused to let them in to speak with him, leaving them to stand soaking in the rain for two hours. Later, when Pessacus arrived, he led the messengers not to the sachem's residence but to an "ordinary wigwam" (a slight comparable to not seating Miantonomi at the governor's table) and insisted that, rather than obeying the Massachusetts government, his people would do as they pleased.[87]

This tangled situation was the result of power struggles on several levels: local, intercolonial, and across the empire. In 1644 the conflict became a vehicle not only for Gorton's aspirations, but for Indian aspirations as well. The sachems' submission to Charles I was the first recorded example of Indian appeal to royal authority in New England, but it would by no means be the last.

Indians in the New England area responded in different ways to English dominance. In addition to the kind of resistance Miantonomi and Ninigret offered the English, Indians could counter English demands by playing the colonial powers off against each other, offering their trade or friendship to the nation that treated them best or seemed likeliest to triumph in the latest European war. A measure of the Indians' ability to play the various powers in the region against each other is Long Island sachem Yougheo's declaration that he wished to maintain good relations with both the Dutch and the English, with its implicit threat that he could turn to one if the other offended him. A certain menace also lies behind his assurance to United Colonies officials that he had not sent any wampum to the Mohawks to persuade them to attack either European power. Clearly, though he had not done so, the option was available, and saying so would likely persuade the English to treat him well.[88]

Evidence that Indians were well informed about European affairs appears in Niantic sachem Ninigret's report that a group of Indians were discussing a ship that had just arrived from Holland bearing the news that English and Dutch were at war "in their own country." They also reported, ominously, that the Dutch were sending ships of war, which would give a "great blow" to the English in the colonies.[89] The English were well aware of the potential danger posed by both the Dutch and French colonies and by Indian nations—the Mohawks and more local Indians in alliance with English enemies. The United Colonies commissioners repeatedly discussed their fears that French or Dutch colonists would sell powder and ammunition to the Indians, and they issued orders banning any such sales from the English to Indians, or from English to French or Dutch, who might then trade them to the Indians.[90]

The first of the seventeenth-century Anglo-Dutch wars brought English anxieties over the Indians' recourse to competing authorities to a crisis.

In 1653 the commissioners of the United Colonies called an extraordinary session to discuss rumors that the Dutch were engaging Indians to fight against the English. The commissioners sent a messenger to Narragansett and Niantic sachems Ninigret, Pessacus, and Mixam to demand their appearance before them. All denied that any such plot existed. And both Pessacus and Mixam urged Thomas Stanton to "inform the Sachems in the Bay that the child that is now born or to bear shall see no war made by us against the English."[91] Testimony from other Indians, including the Mohegan sachem Uncas and the Montauk Indians, contradicted these avowals. They claimed Ninigret had taken a gift of wampum to Dutch governor Peter Stuyvesant as a token of their alliance, that he had been closeted with Stuyvesant and his financial officer for two days and had made "ample Declamation against the English and Uncas and what great Injuries he had sustained by them." These witnesses were, admittedly, enemies of the Niantic sachem, but testimony from less interested parties also reported Stuyvesant's efforts to recruit Indians to his cause. Indians from Rhode Island relayed the news that Pomham and Soconoco were reconciled with the Narragansetts and spoke of the Indians' new league with the Dutch, getting goods at half the price of English goods, plentiful powder, "wildfire from the Dutch which being shot with their Arrows will kindle and burn any thing," and unlimited alcohol. Nine Indian sagamores from Manhatoes testified that the Dutch had solicited them to join with them against the English, promising guns and coats. If promises of a "shipful of powder," other goods, and the entire Dutch trade were not enticing enough, Stuyvesant's financial officer added this threat: the English would cut off, or kill, the Indians, if the Indians did not cut them off first.[92]

This damning evidence led the United Colonies commissioners to call for an immediate expedition against the Narragansetts. The Massachusetts General Court, however, refused to go along, protesting that it did not "see sufficient grounds" for a just offensive war.[93] When the other colonies challenged this refusal as destructive to the league of United Colonies, the Court replied "It can be no less than a contradiction to affirm the supreme power (which we take to be the General Courts of each jurisdiction) can be commanded by others."[94] Not surprisingly, a colony resistant to interference from its king was unwilling to yield its sovereignty to other colonies. For over a year, Massachusetts held out against the other United Colonies. Finally, in 1654, the General Court agreed to join the expedition, but only after insisting that all acknowledge the principle that, if a General Court did not consider the United Colonies decision in harmony with principles of godly justice, it was bound to withhold its assistance.[95] The colonies began preparations to march on the Narragansetts, but they were halted by word that peace had been declared in Europe. So there was no war, but great costs had already been incurred. The United Colonies passed these on to the Narragansetts and Niantics in the form of a heavy fine, which the Indians paid begrudgingly and infrequently.

The Massachusetts leaders' denial of assistance shook the intercolonial union deeply. While the principle that sovereignty rested in each General Court was widely accepted, this was the first time any member of the United Colonies had insisted on it to the exclusion of group action, and it led to an immediate weakening of the confederation. Governments more protective of their own sovereignty than communal goals could not act decisively or quickly, something the Indians were quick to notice. Lion Gardiner reported in 1660 that the Indians "say to our faces that our Commissioners meeting once a year, and speak a great deal, or write a letter, and there's all, for they dare not fight."[96] The United Colonies' failure to join together at this crisis undermined their joint authority with the Indians and set a precedent that would have a profound impact on later conflicts.

The Narragansetts' apparent involvement in a plot with the Dutch shows that they were casting about for any lever against the overbearing weight of the English, using in turns the power of the king, rival European colonies, and outside Indian powers, such as the Mohawks, to challenge English authority. When pressed to submit, Indians repeatedly protested that the English had no right to interfere in Indian affairs and invoked the relationship that had originally been established between Indians and English— friendship, not subjection. For instance, when United Colonies commissioners charged the Narragansett sachems with plotting with the Dutch, Pessacus declared, "Do you think that we are mad and that we have forgot our writing that we had in the Bay which doth bind us to the English our friends in a way of friendship? Shall we throw away that writing and ourselves too; Again have we not Reason in us; how can the Dutch shelter us being so Remote against the power of the English our friends."[97] In little more than two sentences, Pessacus described his relationship with the English as a friendship three times.

English assumptions of superior authority, such as the United Colonies' insistence that sachems seek their permission before going to war with other Indians, were repeatedly violated by Narragansetts, Mohegans, Pocumtucks, and others, not because they did not wish the relationship preserved, but because they did not accept the inferior position the English had assigned them on their hierarchical ladder. In spite of treaty obligations to refer conflict to the English, disputes continued between Narragansetts and both Mohegans and Montauks. When Indians attacked each other without notifying the English first, the United Colonies commissioners summoned them and reproached them. Again and again, they reprimanded Niantic sachem Ninigret for breaches of covenant: failing to deliver the tribute due from Pequots placed under his supervision after the Pequot War, and attacking the Montauks without first obtaining United Colonies approval. Ninigret's response was to chide the English for interference: he wished "the English would let him alone" instead of bidding him to appear before the commissioners. Why should he explain his quarrel with the Montauks to the English, who knew it well, "adding if your Governors son were slain and several other men would you ask Counsel of another Nation how and when to Right your selves. . . . I do but Right my own quarrel."[98] The Niantics were "another Nation." They, too, desired friendship with the English, but they resented English involvement in Indian quarrels.

As English settlement expanded, other Indian groups came into the English orbit and they, like the Narragansetts, maintained models of authority that preserved their independence, directly contrary to the model of subjection inherent in United Colonies dealings with Indians. In 1659 the Pocumtuck sachems of western Massachusetts politely declined to come to a meeting of the United Colonies commissioners to discuss their ongoing hostilities with the Mohegans. In doing so, they drew explicit comparisons between themselves and the English. They were, they pointed out, preparing for a large meeting of their own, "it being all one with the Commissioners meeting." Like the United Colonies, the Pocumtucks had obligations to allies that must be respected: "They are in confederacy with many others as with the Souquakes and Mowhawkes and others and can do nothing without them," or without informing them and receiving their consent. In the same message, the Pocumtucks chided the commissioners for demanding that they attend their meeting: "Neither do they know any engagement that lies on them to come to the meetings of the English Sachems; and they do not send for the English Sachems to their meetings." The Pocumtucks desired English friendship and trade ("They say that as friends they come to the English for victuals"), but they would not accept the English assumption of authority over their dealings with other nations: "They are Resolved not to be beginners of any breach with the English; and will yield to the English in any thing but in making peace with Uncas; and that they would not have the English to persuade them to it; for they can not have peace with him."[99] It is striking that the Pocumtucks used English examples to make their case. They understood the hierarchical system and how the English expected them to fit into it, but they insisted on a dual model. The Pocumtucks saw English and Indian authority as parallel, but separate. They were not a rung in an English ladder. They were another ladder entirely.

The English had shifted the basis of their relationship with the Indians considerably in the first decades of settlement, from expectations of reciprocal friendship to demands of subjection. While a more "gentle course," drawing the Indians "by all courtesy into love with our nation" had been hoped for, had even been seen as the most likely approach to ensure "firm and stable" English settlement, even the idealistic Hakluyt had admitted conquest might be necessary.[100] In the wake of the Pequot War, the leaders of English government felt impelled to assert their authority over the Indians, by virtue of conquest or through relationships of subjection in which the English clearly stated their position of superiority. Despite this change, which was clearly unwelcome to many Indians, English trade and protection continued to be compelling reasons for New England Indians to forge or maintain relationships with the increasingly powerful English. Many Indians continued to resist the English view of the relationship, however, holding to the pattern of equal alliance that their initial treaties, their own past experience with other Indian nations, and English wording and behavior had originally established.

But resistance had its price. The United Colonies' continued insistence on the right to disallow war and the Indians' continued disobedience had resulted in multiple English missions to try to prevent conflict. All these were charged to the offending native parties and finally resulted in the Narragansetts being forced to ransom and then lose their land to English creditors to pay their debt.[101] Their dismay at this turn of events was not simply over their material loss, but over their loss of position. From the dominant power in New England, the Indians had been reduced, in a matter of decades, to the status of children at the mercy of English interlopers who the Indians believed had no right to such authority. In the judgment of one Narragansett leader, the English were "no sachems." The Indians had good reason to seek the king's aid to "right their wrongs" and "protect them from their enemies." And there were others in the region—Gorton of Rhode Island, the Quakers, the non-Puritan settlers of Maine, and more—who would borrow the Indians' example in their own quests to free themselves of Massachusetts interference. In 1664, all of them would get their chance.

Chapter 2
Massachusetts Under Fire

Colonists of Massachusetts Bay looked to the eastern horizon with both anticipation and dread early in 1664. Ships were coming from England bearing representatives of the newly restored king, Charles II, that much was certain. Only four years after the king's restoration in 1660 the backlog of petitions against Massachusetts had turned his attention to New England. Now he had sent agents to ensure that they had abandoned allegiance to the Christian Commonwealth, a dream that had come to an end in England after little more than a decade. It was well known that New England colonists had supported Oliver Cromwell's rule and that they had given refuge to men who had helped murder the last king. Royal commissioners would judge the colonies' loyalty and obedience to the crown and assure them of the king's desires for their welfare. It was a promise that daunted some and raised the hopes of others. In Ipswich, mounting tensions exploded. Major Daniel Denison ordered the men of his county regiment to clear stumps from a field in preparation for the next day's militia training exercises. Already disgruntled because the General Court had curtailed their freedom to choose their own officers, several men in the group refused to follow Denison's orders.[1] Colonist Samuel Hunt backed them up, complaining that Denison went beyond his authority in requiring the work, and then declared that if they did not have greater liberty in the choice of their officers, they would "divide the company and train by themselves." Simon Tuttle, standing on the green and watching the showdown, snarled out his contempt for the colony's laws and leaders: "If he were in England again, he would soon have our laws and law makers laid neck and heels, and further said if we cannot have the liberty the King gave us, we would win it by the edge of the sword." Then, referring to the rumor that the king planned to impose a royal governor on Massachusetts with an armed frigate to back him up, Tuttle added, "We have lost our opportunity, but we hope we shall gain it again, though the Frigates be stopped for the present. And that the Government of the Country, was in a few sneaking fellows' hands, and hoped we should have a turn and upon a brush would soon be cut off and have our necks from under the yoke."[2] For his fiery words, the county court charged Tuttle with sedition and sent him on to the General Court. Hunt, too, was arrested, disfranchised, and fined. Dis-

Figure 5. Charles II, 1630–1685 (r. 1660–1685). From Thomas Babbington Macauley, *The History of England from the Accession of James II* (New York: A. L. Burt Co.), 148 interleaf. Courtesy of the J. Willard Marriott Library, University of Utah.

satisfaction with the country's "yoke" was widespread, at least according to
Hunt, who claimed there were "hundreds in the country of his mind."[3]

The royal commissioners' visit to New England in 1664 would have a powerful impact on both those who resisted Massachusetts's authority and those
who worked to uphold it, intensifying existing divisions in society, reviving
dormant disputes with neighboring regions, and challenging English
authority over Indians in a way that would hasten a conflict long held at
bay. The list of those who, like Tuttle, believed Massachusetts had exceeded
its authority in its dealings with them was long and spanned the Atlantic:
colonists of Maine and New Hampshire over whom Massachusetts had
imposed its jurisdiction, Quakers and Baptists who were excluded from full
participation in the public life of the colony, English merchants who
believed Massachusetts was flouting the king's Navigation Acts to their det-
riment, Indians defending their rights to land and authority, among others. The visit of the royal commissioners gave these people an opportunity
to air their grievances, to appeal to the king to right their wrongs. The commissioners represented a supreme authority that Massachusetts leaders
only reluctantly acknowledged and usually ignored. Their presence was a
direct challenge to the colony's authority that its leaders felt impelled to
resist, almost at the cost of losing that authority.

The colony was never free of the kinds of discontent that led to Tuttle's
passionate outburst. Even the first decade of settlement saw challenges to
the colony's interpretation of its authority. So threatening were the protests of such men as Dr. Robert Child, Samuel Gorton, and the young minister Roger Williams that colony magistrates ordered them banished to
prevent their poisoning others, but these self-protective measures backfired when the protestors published their complaints to the king.[4] Such
complaints fueled Charles I's decision to rescind the Massachusetts charter
in 1637, an action cut short only by the English Civil War and Charles's loss
of his throne. The years between the 1649 execution of the king and the
restoration of his son Charles II to the throne in 1660 brought the colony
welcome respite from royal pressures. With the governments on both sides
of the ocean in general agreement on principles of godly rule, Massachusetts was insulated from many of the complaints and charges of people
opposed to its government.[5]

That did not mean that there were no complaints. Maine, where Massachusetts officials had assumed jurisdiction in the 1650s, was a reliable
source, and as word of the royal commissioners' impending visit spread
across the Atlantic, many Maine residents increased their protests over the
intrusion and their resistance to Massachusetts's authority. Maine's tumultuous political history dated back to 1607, when the ill-fated Popham Colony was founded in the Sagadahoc region. From then to 1652, when the
first Maine towns submitted to Massachusetts jurisdiction, the governments

of Maine and New Hampshire changed hands repeatedly, reflecting the shifting fortunes of their distant proprietors in England.[6] The most consistent sources of government for the two regions were John Mason, who received grants to Maine and New Hampshire in 1622 and 1629, and Ferdinando Gorges, granted patents to Maine in 1622, 1631, and again in 1639.[7] Neither man spent more than a year in his patent, and the various relatives they appointed as governors spent little more. Instead, government fell to local residents appointed by the patent-holders. The political upheaval of the English Civil War cut off communication and political favor from both proprietors for long periods of time. The ebb in their personal fortunes distracted them from their colonial business, leaving governors with little direction or funding to maintain order.[8]

Dissatisfied with the lax order in the region, some immigrants from Massachusetts who had moved to Maine to supervise fishing, trade, or timber enterprises appealed to their home colony to take over jurisdiction of Maine, as it had of New Hampshire in the 1640s. Massachusetts leaders' reasons for doing so were directly linked to the colony's explosive growth.[9] Their growing trade could benefit from control of the "commodious" Piscataqua River, and the merchants plying that trade could benefit from more protection than the unstable governments of the region could offer. But the Massachusetts Council justified its move chiefly as a preemptive strike against hazard to its own authority. In 1651, word had reached the colony magistrates that a group of Maine residents, frustrated with the unsettled government, had entered into a "combination" for self-government styled the "Keepers of the Liberties of England." This group was collecting support to petition Parliament to transfer the grant of Maine to them so they would not have to wait for Gorges to improve local administration.[10] The Council received this news with alarm, declaring "how prejudicial it would be to this government if the aforesaid place and river should be possessed by such as are no friends to us."[11] If Maine became self-governing by men hostile to Puritan rule, it would not only threaten Massachusetts's trade and the well-being of citizens who had transported their enterprises there, but it could become, like Rhode Island, a magnet for Quakers and other discontents, threatening the religious mission of the colony. Finding (rather fortuitously, as these discoveries go) that the line of their patent took in Kittery "and many miles to the northward," Massachusetts leaders appointed representatives to travel to Kittery with a letter "acquainting them with our foresaid right."[12]

The shift to Massachusetts government in Maine was neither immediate nor easy, a fact witnessed by the Maine towns' sluggardly pace in officially submitting. Kittery and Agamenticus (later renamed York) took over a year; Wells, Saco, and Cape Porpoise waited a year longer, sending their agreements to the change on July 4 and 5, 1653.[13] Inhabitants of towns farther north, in the region dubbed Lygonia under one of Maine's short-lived governments, held out much longer, perhaps hoping for some relief from England. When none had come by 1658, they, too, sent in their submissions.[14]

Recognizing the different character of the settlers to the northeast, Massachusetts did not require men from Maine or New Hampshire to meet the requirements for freemanship (full political rights) that prevailed in the Bay Colony. Every man signing the submission to the new government was automatically a freeman.[15] However, anticipating a gradual transition in both society and government, Massachusetts stipulated that anyone applying for freeman status in the future would fall under the church membership and property requirements that held in Massachusetts. While this initial leniency allowed for widespread participation in public affairs, the new order also brought enforcement of such requirements as attendance at public worship and payment of taxes, or rates, to support the officers and courts attending the change in government.

Maine's court records bear witness to the reluctance of many in the region to either accept new restrictions or new government. One of most adamant resisters was John Bonithon. In May 1656 the Massachusetts General Court sent the constable of Saco a warrant for Bonithon's arrest for refusing to pay the new rates and sending an "abusive letter" to the Court. Bonithon was ordered to appear in Boston to answer for his abuse of authority. The Court sent warrants for his arrest again and again, but, whether because Bonithon was remarkably hard to find or because of local reluctance to enforce the warrant, Saco authorities utterly failed to comply. Bonithon still had not reported for trial in Boston by 1658, when the last Maine towns finally sent in their submissions to Massachusetts government, with Bonithon as one signatory. As a condition of his submission, the Massachusetts magistrates insisted that he report to answer for his offense. There is no record that he ever did. Massachusetts was by no means exempt from similar cases of flagrant abuse of authority, but none of its colonists were able to persist in their belligerency so long and with so few consequences.

Bonithon was not alone in resisting the new government. In the first three years following Kittery and York's submission, five men and one woman, in addition to Bonithon, were brought to court for "laying some aspersions" upon Massachusetts court officers.[16] There were also clear signs of antagonism between long-time residents of the area and newcomers from Massachusetts. Some of the latter, such as Joseph Phippeny, lorded it over the old settlers, boasting of personal acquaintance with Deputy Governor Richard Bellingham, who, Phippeny alleged, had advised him on how to deal with his overbearing neighbor Richard Foxwell: "beat the said Foxwell & Manacle him, & carry him down to his door in a rope."[17] Following—or inventing—that advice landed Phippeny before the local court.[18]

Hoping to avoid such conflicts, Massachusetts had appointed to its own administration in Maine many of those who formerly held office under Gorges's government. But the magistrates clearly believed—or hoped—that the transition would be brief, culminating in the creation of a sort of "Massachusetts downeast." To speed the change, officials could not resist urging the election of pro-Massachusetts officers in succeeding elections. Governor Endicott's letter to that effect caused a minor uproar in the election of 1659. Henry Watts responded to the governor's suggestions with contempt, "saying he thanked him for his letter of Advice & making a sign with his hand, saying I have seen him do thus." George Cleeves, formerly an officer in Lygonia, refused to cast his vote for any Massachusetts magistrates, particularly Captain Thomas Clark, whom the governor apparently urged on him. Clark, a recent immigrant from Massachusetts, was rapidly monopolizing the local fur and fishing trade and antagonizing his neighbors in the process.[19] Cleeves, like Henry Watts, was called to court for his contempt of authority.[20] Cleeves's fine was not recorded, but Watts escaped with nothing more than court costs, a punishment in striking contrast to the fifty-pound bond the Massachusetts magistrates laid on Kittery's constables for failing to bring in the names of town residents who voted for a Quaker, contrary to law. Clearly, regardless of the source of their authority, Maine judges had no intention of punishing Maine residents with any kind of severity for abuse of Massachusetts's authority.

The source of the political strife and its negative impact on Massachusetts's authority was a conflict of cultures. Nearly everyone who described seventeenth-century Maine noted its "scattering" pattern of settlement, with houses strung along coasts and rivers for miles and no clear centers of towns.[21] The scattering reflected a political and spiritual reality as well as a physical one, at least according to those viewing the colony from the south. Massachusetts minister William Hubbard noted of "these Scattering Plantations in our Borders, that many were contented to live without, yea, desirous to shake off all Yoke of Government, both sacred and civil, and so transforming themselves as much as well they could into the Manners of the Indians they lived amongst."[22] Increase Mather expressed "sad Apprehensions concerning the Inhabitants in those parts of the Country, in that they were a scattered people, and such as had many of them Scandalized the Heathen, and lived themselves too like the Heathen, without any *Instituted Ordinances.*"[23] Maine and New Hampshire were in fact notoriously remiss in establishing churches or hiring settled ministers. And the ministers they did have showed a more than common tendency toward moral laxity.[24] The lack of a suitably inspiring shepherd may partly explain the region's staggering number of complaints for neglect of public worship.

Given the apparent resistance of many, manifested in individual as well as community actions, why did the eastern towns submit? They probably had little choice. The onset of the Protestant Interregnum had removed their proprietors from political favor, and before Massachusetts took possession of Maine in the 1650s, both Mason and Gorges were dead, neither with heirs of sufficient age to take charge effectively.[25] Massachusetts was close and insistent and the order it imposed may have appeared better than the alternative disorder, even to those who preferred government from another source. Those deprived of their political offices by Massachusetts's intrusion bided their time, hoping for relief should their masters' political fortunes improve.

The authority of the Massachusetts Bay Colony was questioned not only by the residents of Maine. Quakers and Baptists, too, were openly resistant during this time period. Men and women opposed to the Puritans' manner of religious worship and civil government had troubled the colony since its beginnings, but the cases were sporadic and few. Beginning in the late 1650s, however, Quakers began entering the colony, and Baptists increased in numbers. For Rhode Island, which tolerated religious differences, the increase in Quakers was annoying but bearable. Quakers were, in fact, well represented in the colony's leadership. For Massachusetts, whose very being required the preservation of one true form of worship, the Quakers were a mortal threat to both spiritual and civic life.

Knowing how religious and civil authority entwined in Massachusetts, the Quakers challenged both from the very start, being "open enemies to government itself . . . malignant assiduous promoters of doctrines directly tending to subvert both our churches & state."[26] When called to answer for attendance at Quaker meetings, men refused to doff their hats in respect for the magistrates and had them forcibly removed by court officers, and Quakers insisted on using the familiar form in addressing a superior, "thee-ing & thouing of him & many other abusive speeche[s]."[27] The root of these and more flamboyant abuses was, the magistrates believed, a rejection of all order. The Quakers were a people "whose design it is to overthrow the order established."[28] The Society of Friends of this period had not yet adopted the public persona of passive resistance and gentleness by which they are known today and which they were actively cultivating by the 1670s.[29] They took the offensive and did offend. They burst into worship services naked and smeared with ashes to testify against the "nakedness" of Puritan doctrine. They paraded through the streets unclothed and interrupted sermons and sessions of court, "belch[ing] out railing & cursing speeches," denouncing the authority of the country and the purity of its religion.[30] The colony's college was, they said, a "Cage of unclean birds."[31]

The colony passed its first laws against the Quakers in 1656, imposing fines and whipping for any who "shall revile the office or persons of magistrates or ministers, as is usual with the Quakers."[32] But ordinary members of the colony protested the Quaker presence as well. In 1658 many inhabitants of Boston presented a petition against the sect; another petition beseeching protection from Quaker rantings came from New Hampshire.[33] The magistrates increased the severity of their penalties, but this only seemed to spur the Quakers to greater protests. Finally, the colony passed capital sentence against any Quakers who, having been banished on pain of death, willfully returned to the colony. William Robinson and Marmaduke Stephenson were hanged after violating their banishment in 1659; Mary Dyer followed them to the gallows in 1660.[34]

In justifying the executions, the magistrates painted the Quakers as virtual suicides: "Their wittingly [returning for execution] was their own act, & we, with all humility, conceive a crime, bringing their blood on their own head." Defending themselves against obvious charges of religious persecution, the magistrates also insisted that contempt of authority was a crime that not only merited punishment but needed to be rooted out to protect the health—even the life—of the colony: "The Quakers died, not because of their other crimes, how capital soever, but upon their superadded presumptuous & incorrigible contempt of authority.. . . . Had they not been restrained, so far as appeared, there was too much cause to fear that we ourselves must quickly have died, or worse."[35] With these executions, the magistrates succeeded in providing an unquenchable fuel for Quaker and other religious dissent, as well as for political protest against Massachusetts's authority.

Quakers were quick to pounce on the executions as examples of the colony's flagrant violation of its charter, which forbade any laws contrary to English law. Quakers such as Philip Veren, Samuel Shattock, and Edward Wharton flung the executions in the magistrates' faces, accusing them of being "guilty of innocent blood."[36] Others took ship to England to present their petitions for relief to the king, who responded in September 1661 by requesting that Massachusetts immediately cease any corporal punishment of Quakers and that any offenders be sent to England for trial.[37] The colony had already suspended capital punishment; it discontinued other corporal punishments for a brief period but continued to impose fines. By October 1662, however, Quaker protests had increased, spreading to the settlements in New Hampshire and Maine, to the point that the Court reimposed the vagabond law, which required that Quakers be whipped at the end of a cart's tail and transported from town to town until out of the colony.[38]

The Quakers were joined by Baptists in resisting the religious hegemony of the colony. Baptist sentiments, most typically an opposition to infant baptism, had been present in the colony for years but had generally kept within the bounds of religious orthodoxy. But by the early 1660s many Baptists had carried their convictions to the point of turning their backs on the ordinance of baptism or leaving church meetings in the middle of the service, affronting the minister and congregation. In Charlestown Christopher Goodwin offered "violence . . . to the public dispensation of the ordinance of baptism, . . . throwing down the Basin of Water in the meeting house, & striking the constable in the meeting House, & kicking Him on the Lord's day & Expressing himself in Court, with High contempt of that Holy ordinance."[39] Such outrageous behavior would have been troubling under any circumstances, but pressure from the restored king to tolerate such displays turned them into painful reminders of the colony's precarious political standing.

Not only Quakers and Baptists but many others drew encouragement in their resistance to Massachusetts from the 1660 restoration of Charles II to the throne. The return of royal government unleashed a torrent of pent-up petitions and complaints against Massachusetts. First in line were the heirs and employees of Mason and Gorges, protesting Massachusetts's usurpation of the government of New Hampshire and Maine. Others punished or antagonized by Massachusetts rule also presented their cases: investors in a Massachusetts mining enterprise bewailed proceedings against them for debt. Non-Puritans such as Samuel Maverick and Samuel Gorton complained of their lack of religious liberties or of legal injustices. Petitions from Indians complaining of abuses from Massachusetts found their way to the king as well.[40]

Thomas Bredon, a New England royalist, summed up the litany of Massachusetts abuses as disloyalty, writing that "They look on themselves as a free state . . . sat in council December last, a week, before they could agree in writing to His Majesty, there being so many against owning the King or having any dependence on England."[41] Massachusetts leaders had, indeed, long delayed public acknowledgment of the restored king, divided over how—and whether—to recognize and respond to the change in government. While the General Court finally sent its written acknowledgment of the king's authority in December 1660, it did not get around to proclaiming the same publicly until August 8, 1661.[42] On June 19 of that same year, thirty-six freemen from Boston petitioned the General Court, pleading with its members to publish their loyalty to the king by publicly proclaiming his restoration to the throne, as had their neighbor colonies. They also urged them to delay no further in following the king's orders about apprehending men "attainted of high treason" for the murder of Charles I who had fled to New England for refuge. Recognizing the impasse in the Court between the governor, who had already taken steps to apprehend these suspected traitors, and many magistrates and deputies, the petitioners urged the Court to approve the governor's obedience to the king's command. "A Loyal, and Religious compliance with our Royal King in all Lawful Commands," they argued, would "conduce to the Establishment of our Ancient Liberties, the Omission whereof (we fear) will give too great occasion both to Himself and to our Enemies to question the Integrity of the Late Address and to brand us as infamous for hypocrisy."[43] The Court had already received three similar petitions from "freemen & others" from Ipswich, Newbury, and Sudbury and had given them a testy answer: "We must let them understand that this Court hath not been altogether negligent to provide for their & our own safety." They sent the same bristling reply to the Boston petitioners, but they also officially proclaimed the king before the summer was out.[44] These petitions provide explicit evidence of the tensions between the General Court and members of the colony, as well as between the Court and its chief member, the governor. Clearly, all were concerned over preserving the colony's authority—their "Ancient Liberties"—but whether resistance or accommodation to the king's demands was the best method of doing so was an open debate.[45]

One reason for the Court's long delay in proclaiming the crown may have been a hope for a swift answer to its December letter to the king, one that would assure members of the Court that he did not intend to alter their way of government. Their letters to king and Parliament, drafted December 19, 1660, as well as their instructions to their agents to England, directly addressed those fears. In both letters, the Court members begged for the confirmation of their charter and the continuation of religious liberties. Only the compelling need to worship free from legal constraints could have made them depart their dear native country for this "desert wilderness," they wrote, noting that, "We could not live without the public worship of God."[46] Their instructions to the Massachusetts agents made this point even more explicit. The agents should seek from the king all that had been previously granted by patent, "without any other power imposed over us, or any other infringement of them which would be destructive to the ends of our coming hither; as also that no appeals may be permitted from hence in any case, civil or criminal, which would be such an intolerable & unsupportable burden as this poor place (at this distance) are not able to undergo, but would render authority & government vain & uneffectual."[47] Massachusetts insisted on having the final word, vested with royal authority by charter, to answer all complaints and petitions, above which there could be no appeal, even to the king himself.[48]

On June 28, 1662, the king replied to the colony, thanking it for its somewhat belated expressions of duty, loyalty, and good affection, confirming its charter and patent, and making a number of small requests. First, he asked that any laws made during the Protestant Interregnum that were "contrary and derogatory to our authority & government" be repealed. Second, he asked that the oath of allegiance to the king be administered, as stipulated in the charter, and that all administrations of justice be in the king's name.[49] The Court immediately gave orders for these requests, as well as for the king's final stipulation that his letter be published, so that all his subjects might know of his favor toward them.[50] The king went on to state that since "freedom & liberty of conscience" were the "principal end & foundation" of the charter, such rights should be admitted and allowed to all. He directed that the Church of England's Book of Common Prayer be permitted and that no prejudice be offered to those who used it as long as they did not disturb others. In addition, all persons "of good &

honest lives & conversations" should be admitted to the sacrament of the Lord's Supper and their children baptized. The king agreed that strict measures might have to be taken against the Quakers, there as in Old England, but had asked in a previous letter that corporal punishments be stopped.[51] Finally, all freeholders not vicious in conversation and orthodox in religion though of different "persuasions concerning church government" (meaning Anglicans and other non-Puritan Protestants) should be allowed to vote for civil and military officers.[52]

The king couched these requests in gentle, reasonable terms, demonstrating his desire to persuade the colony to comply, rather than to impose change by force. This was consistent with his approach to other colonies in the post-Restoration period and with contemporary political thought about the relationship between the king and his subjects. Both Connecticut and Rhode Island wrote new charters after the Restoration and then sent agents to the king to ask for his confirmation. Both received what they asked for. Massachusetts, too, had had its original charter confirmed by the king, as had every other English colony not seeking a new charter. This was a clear illustration of the king's desire to reassure the colonies, to confirm the idea of the charter as a contract between subjects and sovereign, with rights on each side. The Declaration of Breda, which preceded the Restoration, also conveyed this idea of mutual rights and obligations: "The Breda letters . . . posit an organic affinity between the [king's] prerogative and subjects' liberties and rights," or, as the king himself explained in several letters, his subjects' rights would be protected if his own were.[53] These were the terms that had made a return to monarchy in England possible, and the king had no intention of violating them, at least not immediately.

Despite the clearly ameliorative intent of the king's letter, it must have come as a blow to the leaders of Massachusetts. It is easy to imagine the consternation in the General Court as the letter was being read. Only someone who knew nothing of the congregational way could order that all honest persons be admitted to the Lord's Supper, a privilege few Puritans felt worthy to accept. And the king would have the vote extended to all freeholders, not just church members, thus opening the door for the transformation of the colony's godly government.[54] On November 25, 1662, the General Court sent the king its response, and judging by the king's great dissatisfaction with it, we can guess that colony leaders protested his suggestions vigorously.[55] These leaders were still mulling over the king's demands the following May, when they sent for church elders to counsel them on how to proceed and invited any freemen of the colony to send in their written suggestions as well.[56]

Even a completely conciliatory letter from the Massachusetts government might not have made much of a difference. The king's decision to investigate abuses of authority in New England had been made shortly after his restoration. The string of protests and complaints coming before him

from petitioners from the trade centers of England to the coastal settlements of Maine must have confirmed that resolve. Definitive plans for the
royal commission had been made as early as November 1662;[57] by February
1664 orders had been given to supply the ships that would be carrying
the commissioners with arms and ammunition for a planned expedition
against the Dutch of New Netherland. Their convoy would include four
ships, all fitted with guns and carrying three to four hundred soldiers.[58]
By the end of April the commissioners had departed, letters and instructions in hand, for New England, where they were to safeguard his majesty's
interests.

News that the commissioners' arrival was imminent prompted panic
among Massachusetts leaders and colonists. The magistrates ordered that
all copies of the charter be entrusted to the safekeeping of chosen men.
Next, they alerted the commander of the Castle—a fortress in Massachusetts Bay—of the impending visit and ordered him to limit the access to the
town of the troops on board the royal ships and to restrict their behavior
while in it.[59] Inhabitants of Boston, Cambridge, and many other towns both
near Boston and on the western reaches of the colony sent lengthy petitions begging the General Court to preserve their liberties and expressing
their satisfaction with the present government.[60]

Anticipating such a response, the king's letter announcing the royal
commission assured the colony that his main end was to "better know how
to contribute to the further improvement of their happiness & prosperity."[61] That same declaration, however, included the alarming pronounce-
ment that the commissioners, contrary to all Massachusetts's former pleas,
had been invested by the king with "full power & authority to hear, &
receive, & examine, & determine all complaints & appeals in all causes and
matters, as well military as criminal & civil."[62] The magistrates read this
phrase as a direct contradiction of their charter, which granted them "full
power & authority, both legislative & executive, for the government of all
the people here . . . without appeal, excepting law or laws repugnant to the
laws of England."[63] By this interpretation of the charter, the royal commissioners should stay out of the colony's affairs unless colony law did, in fact,
contradict English law. They should certainly not intervene in "all causes
and matters," military, criminal, and civil. And, in fact, the commissioners
made a point of referring back to the general courts several cases appealed
to them in the colonies they visited before Massachusetts, "to the general
satisfaction of them all."[64] Massachusetts leaders, on the other hand, made
their opposition to the commissioners' acceptance of any appeals the focus
of their objections throughout the visit. As a result, they extinguished
any intention the commissioners may have had to deliver jurisdiction back
to the colony after first obtaining acknowledgement of their superior
authority.

In August 1664 the General Court met to consider its official response to the king's letter, which gave six reasons for the commissioners' visit. One reason, phrased to seem simultaneously threatening and reassuring, was the crown's desire to extinguish "unreasonable jealousies & malicious calumnies" constantly being spread "that our subjects in those parts do not submit to our government, but look upon themselves as independent upon us & our laws." The commissioners were also to assure the colony that the king had no intent to infringe on its charter, would settle differences between the colonies concerning their boundaries, and would examine the condition of the Indian sachems of each colony, some of whom had complained to the king of injustice. Finally, and most pointedly, the commissioners would confer with Massachusetts leaders about the king's letter to them of June 28, 1662, concerning which he still had not received satisfaction.[65]

While the king's letter repeatedly assured the colony of his goodwill, to many in Massachusetts it seemed a sheathed sword. The General Court had made concessions to some demands of the 1662 letter earlier, but for the rest it had sent its excuses, protesting that its charter required nothing more. Now the king was again demanding compliance and enforcing it by his agents. After some debate, the Court passed several resolutions concerning administering the oath of allegiance to the king and broadening the franchise, but these were hedged with enough limitations to render them meaningless, a result the commissioners did not fail to notice.[66] Within weeks of the August meeting, the General Court took a series of actions almost martial in their effect. First, it drafted a declaration reasserting its final authority in the colony. Next, in order to defend against the commissioners' actions and any sympathy their presence might inspire, it passed a series of laws. One law forbade anyone from summoning an audience by beating of drum, sounding of trumpet, or other means, without the explicit license of the General Court. Others declared the penalty—death—for any attempt to overthrow the government and gave notice that the laws against sedition would be enforced.[67]

This siege response to any infringement on the authority of the General Court arose from impulses as closely tied to religion as to political power. Evidence of this appears in the Court's letter to the king asking—almost demanding—that he recall his royal commission. It was, Court members wailed, an infringement of their charter and a mortal threat to their civil liberties. By the charter (a point they returned to continually), they had been granted "full & absolute power of governing all the people of this place, by men chosen from among themselves, & according to such laws as they shall from time to time see meet to make & establish, being not repugnant to the laws of England." The king had empowered his royal commissioners to act not according to any "established law," but according to their own discretion, which could make the Massachusetts government "void & of none effect" and could "end in the subversion of our all." In stirring words, the Court declared, "let our life be given us at our petition, (or rather that which is dearer than life, that we have ventured our lives, & willingly passed through many deaths to obtain . . . at our request let our govenment live, our patent live, our magistrates live, our laws & liberties live, our religious enjoyments live" and then they would have cause to say "let the king live forever."[68] In Massachusetts the religious way of life and authority were inseparable. Allowing men not "among themselves" and averse to their religion to decide what the law of the colony would be would irrevocably change what the Massachusetts colonists had "ventured [their] lives" to preserve. "It is a great unhappiness," Governor Endicott wrote for the Court, "to be reduced to so hard a case as to have no other testimony of our subjection & loyalty offered us but this, viz, to destroy our own being." While they begged the king's intervention and confirmation of their rights, the Court members too had a sheathed sword: if they were forced to endure the changes the commissioners threatened to impose, it "should drive this people out of the country."[69]

The king responded to the panicky missive as a parent soothing a hysterical—and annoying—child. He and his secretaries assured colony leaders once again that they had only the colony's best interests at heart.[70] Massachusetts leaders begged others to intercede for them as well, including the king's secretary of state, William Morrice, and Robert Boyle, head of the Company for the Propagation of the Gospel in New England. After expressing his surprise that they would be so bold as to demand that the king recall his agents, Boyle, too, urged them to trust the king's goodwill, not to try his patience by their protests. All would be well, he argued, if they would be true and loyal subjects.[71] Word of the Massachusetts campaign against them reached the commissioners by way of their own correspondence with the king and his council and only increased their determination to humble the stubborn colony. Thus each side prepared for the approaching political conflict, one that would lay bare the divisions in Massachusetts society and severely weaken the colony's authority over its English and Indian subjects.

Who were the men so dreaded and hoped for in Massachusetts Bay? The chief of them was Colonel Richard Nicolls, a loyal attendant of the duke of York, the future King James II. He was considered an excellent choice by all who knew him. Even the anxious Puritans found no fault with him.[72] His letters to the other commissioners and to colonists such as John Winthrop, Jr., of Connecticut show him to be patient, judicious, and intelligent. Unfortunately, Nicolls played only a shadow role on the commission. Assigned to be governor of the colony of New York, formerly New Netherland, he remained in New York for all but a few weeks of the commissioners' visit. As head of the commission, Nicolls was supposed to have the deciding vote in all decisions; when only two were present, he was required to be one of them. To the dismay of Massachusetts, the royal commissioners disregarded this and other royal directives, including the king's private instructions that the commissioners take a conciliatory approach to the colony, "insinuating yourselves by all kind and dexterous carriage into the good opinion of the principal persons there" in order to encourage them to request a new charter with changes that "will appear necessary for their own benefit."[73] The commissioners were supposed to tread softly.

The men who carried out the work of the commission in Nicolls's absence were George Cartwright and Robert Carr, both of England, and Samuel Maverick, a longtime resident of Massachusetts. While we should not expect modern notions of disinterest to prevail in the selection of royal agents in seventeenth-century England, even the king's own advisers seemed alarmed at the choice of these men. Joseph Williamson, secretary to Lord Arlington, wrote that "Mavericke was of all men the worst to do it; debauched, idle, and under great prejudices." Maverick had been, with Robert Child, one of the remonstrants against the Massachusetts government in the early years of the colony and had spent the three years previous to his appointment to the commission shepherding petitions against Massachusetts through the royal bureaucracy in London.[74] Aware of his bias against Massachusetts, Lord Clarendon warned Maverick to behave circumspectly, "For if he should revenge any old discourtesies, the King would take it very ill and do himself justice accordingly."[75] Robert Carr was, in Williamson's estimate, "a weak man," preoccupied during his visit with acquiring new offices and lands for himself. While spoils were an expected perquisite of royal business, Carr's eagerness for them, and his resultant absence from the commission for long stretches of time, won him reprimands not only from his fellow commissioners but from the king himself.[76] Most unfit of all was George Cartwright, whose letters to fellow commissioners and officers in England drip with contempt for Massachusetts. One letter from Cartwright to Rhode Island gadfly Samuel Gorton suggests the two may have become acquainted earlier, perhaps during one of Gorton's petition-bearing visits to London.[77] Gorton may well have supplied the material that fueled Cartwright's scorn for Massachusetts, which would prove nearly to exceed his own. Massachusetts leaders had no experience with the other members of the commission, but Maverick's place on it drew their impassioned protest. He was their "professed enemy," and they were convinced by his inclusion that the mission was punitive, intended to strip them of their liberties.[78] The behavior of Maverick, Carr, and Cartwright after their arrival in New England would do nothing to dispel these apprehensions.

The commissioners confirmed the magistrates' preconception of them as enemies by refusing the accommodations arranged for them. Instead, they made their Boston residence with Captain Thomas Bredon, who had affronted the magistrates to the tune of a 200-pound fine for refusing to acknowledge their authority in 1662.[79] Holed up in their quarters, close to fellow royalists Thomas Kellond and Thomas Deane,[80] the commissioners received Quakers and other discontented persons who brought tales of abuses by Massachusetts leaders. What they failed to do was mingle with the orthodox, mainstream members of the colony, in spite of the king's explicit instructions that they do so.[81] Only Maverick, the longtime New Englander, spent any time visiting colonists.[82] Carr and Nicolls absented themselves from the colony on other business. Cartwright, on his own admission, had "not yet been to dinner with any townsman, suspecting them all."[83]

The commissioners were clearly predisposed to see Massachusetts as rebellious, and colony leaders did little to disabuse them. No other colony had been complained against so often and so strenuously in England.[84] No other colony, since the absorption of New Haven into Connecticut in 1663, was so rigidly Puritan, and the General Court's inflexibility over charter privileges set it up for continual conflict with the king's agents. The Massachusetts leaders presented an obdurate face, standing resolutely on their charter rights, which they believed forbade them from accepting any authority above their own, even if such a stand resulted in the charter's revocation. Better to be destroyed, they reasoned, than to commit suicide or "destroy our own being, which nature teacheth us to preserve."[85] Writing to Secretary Morrice, colonist Samuel Nadhorth expressed similar feelings: the "body of the people have a higher esteem of their liberties, sacred and civil, than of their lives; they well know they are such twins, as God & not nature have joined together & are resolved to bury their estates & liberties in the same grave."[86] Not all in Massachusetts looked for civil death, of course, by their own hand or otherwise. The conflict between those who would brook no challenge to the charter and those who favored appeasing the king would become increasingly evident in the duration and aftermath of the royal commissioners' visit.

The first two boats of the commissioners' convoy, bearing Samuel Maverick and Robert Carr, landed in Portsmouth, New Hampshire, in July 1664. Their presence revived the resistance to Massachusetts's authority that had existed since the colony's takeover but had dramatically increased since the king's restoration, and that resistance helped confirm the commissioners' belief that New Englanders were longing for relief from Massachusetts's oppression. While all the Maine towns had submitted to Massachusetts by 1658, Maine residents were quick to jump ship at the first word of active assistance from the Gorges heirs, who had petitioned Parliament for the restoration of their rights in New England at the first hint of the monarchy's restoration. They complained that Massachusetts had "by strong hand and menaces [brought] the most part of their vast country under their own power and subjection, depriving them of their privileges, patents, and interests, and imposing upon them an oath of fidelity to their state without any relation to England."[87] Ousted Maine officials and disgruntled settlers echoed these claims in their own petitions to the crown.[88] Such complaints had received little attention while the Cromwells held power, but they attracted immediate notice once Charles II was restored to the throne in 1660. Edward Godfrey, who had lost his place as governor of Maine when Massachusetts seized jurisdiction, was one of the first who took his grievances to England, where he, along with Samuel Maverick, the heirs of John Mason and Ferdinando Gorges, and others dissatisfied with Massachusetts, gave the king detailed accounts of the colony's usurpation. In response to their complaints, the king granted young Gorges a new commission, asserting his rightful claim to the province.[89]

As so many times before, news of royal proceedings far outpaced any significant royal action, leaving those who proclaimed their resistance to Massachusetts vulnerable. The king granted his commission to Gorges in May 1661. By December, Gorges's trustees had staged an "agitation" at Wells against the Massachusetts government. In the following months, Henry Jocelyn, Robert Jordan, Francis Champernowne, and Nicholas Shapleigh, all of whom had served under the Massachusetts government but now returned to their former positions as trustees of Gorges's government, called for delegates to Gorges's General Court to gather in May 1662 at Wells. When no deputies from Maine appeared at the Massachusetts General Court in Boston, that government launched an immediate inquiry, sending Daniel Denison, William Hathorne, and Richard Waldron to confer with Gorges's court at Wells. With delegates from ten Maine settlements present, the competing authorities asserted their claims. The Massachusetts agents were apparently more convincing, or perhaps more threatening. Nine of the ten towns voted to continue under Massachusetts's authority until the king had made his own will clear. In the absence of either official proclamation or royal agents, the king's will was still open to debate. To Massachusetts's satisfaction, the letter the colony received from the king in June 1662 announced the sovereign's intent to reconfirm its charter and said not a word about Mason, Gorges, New Hampshire, or Maine.[90]

Despite this setback, and despite Gorges stalwart Henry Jocelyn's election as an associate for the Massachusetts government in Maine in July 1662, he and the other Gorges commissioners continued to assert Gorges's rightful government. So confident of royal backing were these men that in 1662 Jocelyn publicly declared that Samuel Maverick and four other royal commissioners were "coming in two great frigates to countermand the authority of Massachusetts in Maine."[91] While they continued to express their firm belief that Gorges's royal commission to rule the province would arrive "by every ship," those expectations would be disappointed for years.

Under firm pressure from Massachusetts, the Maine towns settled back under Massachusetts governance, electing and sending deputies to the

Massachusetts General Court in May 1663. But resistance was far from over. That same month, Massachusetts stripped the intransigent Nicholas Shapleigh of his office as major in the county militia. Two months later, it issued indictments against Jocelyn, Jordan, Champernowne, and Shapleigh "for Acting against this Authority & so renouncing the authority of the Massachusetts, using means for the subverting thereof under pretence of a sufficient power from Esquire Gorges to take off the people, which is manifest to the contrary."[92]

Evidence of the strength of the continuing resistance to Massachusetts's authority in Maine was the indictment, in the same session, of 31 other men for "sundry political acts and neglects."[93] Several of those who resisted Massachusetts claimed royal warrant for doing so, asserting their own authority above that of the Bay Colony. Gorges commissioner (and sometime Anglican minister) Robert Jordan declared, "by their power they had they would Command the Governor of Boston to Assist them & if any did rebel against their power, that they would take them & hang them, or burn their houses." Doing so would be justifiable because "the Governor of Boston was a Rogue & all the rest thereof were Traitors & Rebels against the King."[94] Not surprisingly, at his court appearance Jordan was charged with breaching his oath of fidelity to Massachusetts. That oath, which Massachusetts gave in place of the oath of allegiance to the king, would, both during the royal commissioners' visit and through the following decades, be used as a chief justification for the king's revocation of Massachusetts's authority.

Such challenges as these multiple claims to authority in Maine confirmed Massachusetts's fears that the king meant to undermine its authority, as did the recent experience of the English colony of Barbados. Lord Willoughby had been sent there as governor in June 1663, directed, like New England's royal commissioners, to "defend, with force if need be, the rights, privileges, and prerogatives of the crown."[95] He had managed his task so harshly that several former officials fled the island, bearing tales of the governor's "rigorous dealing" that soon reached Massachusetts.[96]

The colony's first test of whether the royal commission to New England would echo Willoughby's severity came in July 1664, when the commissioners arrived in Boston. They stayed only long enough to deliver the king's letter and requests for assistance against the Dutch who had invaded English settlements on Long Island. The magistrates complied with the military requests, but only after a vote of the entire General Court, a bit of legalism the commissioners found irksome.[97] Nevertheless, the troops gathered and marched south, where the Dutch surrendered without a fight. Colonel Nicolls took over as governor of the renamed colony of New York, and the three remaining commissioners began their visits to the New England colonies, saving Massachusetts for last so that its expected resistance would not set a dangerous precedent for the other colonies.[98] As they waited for the commissioners' return, the members of the General Court perused the king's letter as well as his commission to Nicolls, Carr, Cartwright, and Maverick, and their anxiety increased.

The commissioners began their official visits with Plymouth, then progressed through Rhode Island, Connecticut, back to Rhode Island, and finally again to Massachusetts. In each colony, the commissioners asked officials to remove church membership restrictions, if any, from the franchise and to strike any laws repugnant to the laws of England. This process went smoothly in Plymouth, Rhode Island, and Connecticut, probably because the commissioners viewed them as underdogs to the overbearing Massachusetts and approached them sympathetically. Even when these colonies chose to object to particular matters, they did so in a way that maintained good relations between the parties.[99] In addition, these colonies greased the skids adeptly, something Massachusetts made no attempt to do. Connecticut, for example, sent a gracious letter of thanks to the king for his favors, even for "sending over your Majesty's Honorable Commissioners by whom we received your Majesty's Gracious Letter."[100] The letter breathed no hint of objection to any of the king's directions or the royal commissioners' actions. In recognition of these colonies' cooperation, the royal commissioners wrote letters commending them to the king, and they did so in terms that highlighted Massachusetts's obstinacy. "Your carriage," wrote the king to the Plymouth government after receiving the commissioners' report on that colony, "seems to be set off with the more luster by the contrary deportment of the colony of the Massachusetts, as if, by their refractoriness, they had designed to recommend and heighten the merit of your compliance."[101] The royal commissioners played on the contrast not only in their letters to the king and his officers, but also in letters between themselves. The other colonies, particularly Rhode Island, did their best to ensure that the contrast favored them.

Rhode Island, which had long had a troubled relationship with Massachusetts, was the site of several royal commissioners' proceedings that had a great impact on Massachusetts and on its relations with neighboring Indians. The commissioners' first order of business in Rhode Island was the settlement of a long-standing dispute over the Narragansett lands. They were responding directly to a recent Narragansett petition to the king that complained of "violence and injustice from the Massachusetts, amongst others that they had caused them to be fined, and then took their whole country in mortgage."[102] This complaint dated back over twenty years to the 1643 war between the Narragansetts and Mohegans, when the Mohegans, with United Colonies consent, executed captured Narragansett sachem Miantonomi. Even after Miantonomi's death, conflict between the Narragansetts and Mohegans remained heated. The United Colonies mediated a series of treaties between the two peoples, which both repeatedly violated. Finally, in response to the Narragansetts' last violation, the United

Colonies raised an expedition against them in 1645. Although it did not end in war, the expedition's costs were substantial, and the United Colonies had recouped them through a heavy fine against the offending Indians.[103] Unable to pay the fine, the Narragansetts mortgaged their land to a group called the Atherton proprietors, chiefly from Massachusetts, and lost the land by default in 1662. Massachusetts and Connecticut had claimed other sections of the Narragansett lands by conquest during the Pequot War, and all these lands were the subject of ongoing boundary and jurisdiction disputes between those colonies and Rhode Island.

The royal commissioners settled the dispute by removing Narragansett land and jurisdiction from colonial control, instead placing them directly under the protection of Charles II. Henceforward, the Narragansett lands would be known as the "King's Province." They voided the Atherton proprietors' deed, on payment of 750 fathoms of wampum by the Narragansetts, declared another deed held by the English illegal, and ordered English residents to remove themselves and all their improvements from the land by the following September.[104] The royal commissioners justified their action by the Narragansetts' earlier submission to Charles I, which legally voided all succeeding transactions. That submission, made in 1644, had probably been forgotten by everyone in New England but the Indians themselves and the man who had presented the petition for them, Samuel Gorton. He had kept the original deed in his possession for the last twenty years. When the commissioners made their way to Warwick, he retrieved it and gave it to Narragansett sachem Pessacus, who presented it, with other petitions, to the royal commissioners.[105]

Having received the Narragansetts' original deed of submission, the commissioners next visited them in their own lands, where the Indians again submitted themselves, their subjects, and lands to the "protection, government and dispose" of the king. They laid down their arms "as at his Majesty's feet" and presented gifts for the king and queen, "two caps of peag [wampum] and two clubs inlaid with peag for a present to the King, and a feather mantle and a porcupine bag for a present to the Queen."[106] The commissioners, in turn, had gifts to bestow. In acknowledgment of the great affection two Narragansett sachems had expressed for him after Rhode Island's 1663 charter was granted, the king sent them two luxurious coats.[107]

In all these doings, Massachusetts was the loser. The English had worked over the years to impose their model of a hierarchical ladder on the Indians, with sachems yielding subjection to the topmost rung, the government of the colony to which they had submitted themselves. King Charles, so distant as to be almost mythical, hardly counted in the hierarchy, certainly not for any practical purpose. By bringing the king back into the picture, the royal commissioners effectively kicked out the intervening rungs of the ladder, placing the sachems directly under the king. In theory, nothing had changed: the king was the head of the government, above his subordinate colonial governments. In practice, however, Massachusetts leaders had always resisted the royal hierarchical structure, protesting that appeals to England would undermine their ability to govern.[108] And they were right. The Narragansetts had gone over the heads of the United Colonies in appealing to England. They had, in fact, appealed directly to the king at least three times before the commissioners' visit, clear evidence that, even if Massachusetts disregarded the top rung of the ladder, the Narragansetts did not.

The hostility toward Massachusetts evident in the royal commissioners' letters to each other and to England must have come through very clearly to the Narragansetts, further undermining Massachusetts's authority. According to Massachusetts leaders, the Narragansetts' deportment took an alarming turn for the worse following the commissioners' visit to them. While the "savage natives bordering upon this & other his majesty's colonies . . . have beene principally awed by the Massachusets," the magistrates now found "that awe turned into contempt by their unwonted, proud, & insolent words & deeds" against persons and colonies. Travelers among the Indians reported such taunts as, "'Whence are you? Of the Massachusets?'" To the Narragansetts "Massachusets men are all but as a straw, blown away without breath . . . so that this bridle taken off, what else could be expected but trouble from them, especially seeing there were intimations that it was occasioned from some words & acting of the [royal] commissioners . . . wittingly or unwittingly, God knows."[109] In its letter to the king in July 1665, the Massachusetts General Court complained that the United Colonies, which had been the liaison to the Indians in surrounding areas, had been publicly derided and undermined by the royal commissioners as "that usurped authority." They lamented the "causeless complaints from Indians received & countenanced, in so much that the very carriage & deportment of many of the heathen is changed towards us."[110]

The Narragansetts were apparently the only Indian group to petition the king directly, helping to bring on the royal commission, but they were not the only Indian group the royal commissioners visited. Philip of the Wampanoags also received the royal agents, who listened to a dispute between the Wampanoags and the Narragansetts over land at Mount Hope and declared in Philip's favor, confirming the lands to him in the name of the king.[111] The records do not mention visits to other Indian groups, but several quickly saw the potential of appealing over the heads of local officials. When the Mohegan sachem Uncas complained to the Connecticut magistrates of a long-unsettled dispute over land, he warned, "Wherefore he is weary of such Court attendance, intimating that if . . . there be no effectual course taken for a fair & just issue, he then shall be enforced to apply himself unto King Charles his Commissioners for relief."[112] The visit of the royal commissioners likely influenced the actions of Massachusett sachem

Josiah Wampatuck as well. In 1657 the sachem had leased land on the south side of the Blue Hills to Richard Thayer. While Wampatuck claimed that this had been done "with the consent of my wisemen," later Indian testimony denied that any such consent was given. There was enough disagreement that the town of Dorchester ordered Thayer to leave the land after he had farmed it for three years. The visit of the royal commissioners in 1664–65 demonstrated the possibilities of appeal to higher authority; in 1666 Wampatuck made out a deed in Plymouth Colony Court conveying his land to Charles II, promising him a yearly payment of five pounds (collectible from Richard Thayer), and craving his protection.[113] Thus, like the Narragansetts in 1644, Wampatuck used direct appeal to royal authority to subvert both local English power and Indian authority for his own benefit. Maine Indians, too, saw advantage in appealing to the commissioners. George Cartwright reported to the king that an Indian sachem near the source of the Merrimack River had petitioned to be taken under the king's protection, like the Narragansetts.[114] While evidence is less clear, another document from the period suggests that Wampanoag sachem Philip used the authority of the king's agents as an effective tool in his power struggles with the Narragansetts. In a 1666 letter penned by Philip's scribe John Sassamon, Eliese Pokonoahkit (probably Philip) instructed the Montauk Indians not to pay tribute to Ninigret, who was coming to collect it, until the issue could be heard and determined by "the honored Commissioners."[115]

The royal commissioners' visit to Rhode Island severed ties between Massachusetts and the Narragansetts, overriding the 1636 treaty that Massachusetts leaders believed made the Narragansetts their subjects. The colony's protest was immediate. Those whose lands had been seized and who had been ordered peremptorily off of them, including such prominent men as Daniel Gookin, howled their outrage to the commissioners and to the king. Their anger may have been fueled by knowledge that the commissioners' decision to evict them from the Narragansett lands was contrary to royal instructions. In his directions to the commissioners, the king had ordered that any English people settled in Narragansett be left undisturbed, or that the land be granted to them, "we not having the least purpose to question or take advantage of their title, whatsoever our right shall fall out to be." In addition, the commissioners had directed that after their departure the Rhode Island government would serve in their place to represent the king, ignoring the wishes of the ousted Atherton proprietors that Connecticut have jurisdiction of the region. Thus the commissioners had given jurisdiction to a government disdained as lawless by the other English colonies of the region.[116] Within weeks, that order was revoked by Commissioner Nicolls, who directed instead that all present inhabitants be allowed to remain until the king made his wishes known.[117]

This turnabout could not have been welcome to the Narragansetts, who still held to the belief that their relationship with Massachusetts was a friendship or alliance. Massachusetts resumed its assumption of superiority over the Indians as soon as the commissioners were out of the way, but the Narragansetts were no more willing to relinquish their assumption of equality with the local English after 1664 than they had been in the twenty previous years.

The commissioners' visit to Rhode Island not only undercut Massachusetts's authority over the Narragansetts but helped further widen divisions between the Massachusetts government and the English residents of Rhode Island, who chafed under its intrusive authority. Eager to cooperate and prove their loyalty, Rhode Islanders flocked to the royal commissioners with petitions and appeals, demonstrating that they acknowledged the commission as the highest court in New England. One of these petitioners, longtime gadfly and religious dissident Samuel Gorton, addressed his petition of complaint against Massachusetts to "the high and honorable Court of Commissioners, appointed by the king's majesty as the supreme authority in these parts of America." The address, with its emphasis on the commissioners' role as the highest court of appeal—the "supreme" authority in New England—seems designed intentionally to goad Massachusetts for its insistence on the same privilege.[118]

The royal commissioners proved a magnet for the discontented in Massachusetts as well. Among those Massachusetts residents appealing to the commissioners were royalist Thomas Deane, whose case had been dismissed by the magistrates for lack of evidence several years before; John Hoar, who was dissatisfied with the magistrates' decision on a suit involving his brother's property; and John Porter, Jr., newly escaped from a Boston jail where he had been held on the capital charge of dishonoring his parents.[119] Porter's case was particularly irksome to the Massachusetts magistrates. Porter had abused the authority of those placed over him on every level: parents, local leaders, and colony magistrates. He derided his father and mother with names such as "simple ape," "shittabed," and "Gammar Pisshouse," threatened to burn down the family home, savagely beat family servants, and tried to stab his brother. When local magistrates tried to rein him in, he turned his tongue on them as well, telling Major Hathorne he was a "base, corrupt fellow" and that he "cared not a turd for him."[120] That the royal commissioners, who were infringing on charter authority, would offer such a "horrid unnatural malefactor" protection further convinced Massachusetts that the commissioners' intentions were hostile.[121]

May 1665 came, and with it the royal commissioners returned to Boston. In preparation for the visit, the commissioners had stopped by the governor's house in February, with the specific request that every inhabitant of the colony—then numbering about 25,000, though only ablebodied men were intended—gather on election day to hear the commissioners' address.[122] When the governor and several magistrates demurred, saying such a gathering would leave their families and property exposed to the "rage of the natives," Cartwright sputtered that the request was so reasonable that only a traitor would refuse it. The secretary recording the exchange duly noted the insult.[123] Blow for blow, every offensive word and act was recorded by each side.

Perhaps sensing the need to correct its dreadful start, the Massachusetts Council, following advice from the colony's elders that "all things should be carried on between his majesty's honorable commissioners & the honored Court . . . in an amicable or respectful way," prepared to give the royal commissioners an official welcome on their return. The commissioners, however, entered town separately and quietly, slipping back into the home of Captain Bredon. It is unclear whether the commissioners intentionally avoided the planned welcome, but the magistrates took it as a deliberate affront, and the commissioners' continual accommodation with Bredon, from whom they were sure to get an earful of Massachusetts's abuses against the crown, heightened colony leaders' distress.[124] It was a poor start to the official investigation.

The night before the May election of Massachusetts officers, the commissioners sent word to the colony leaders preparing for the vote that they wished to meet with them. The men replied that they were missing many members and thus were "no Court, not being orderly constituted by law," a legalistic point the royal commissioners chose to ignore. The commissioners arrived and delivered several papers that they desired them to consider, wished them well in their election, and reminded them that religion should play no part in their selection of the man to replace recently deceased Governor Endicott. (Colony leaders must have snorted at that suggestion.) The General Court members asked the commissioners to give them all the king's directions at once so they could have their "whole work before them." The commissioners declined; they would send more business as soon as they had received satisfaction on what had been presented already. The Court protested. The commissioners refused to budge.[125] Back and forth the papers went, with frustration mounting on both sides. Massachusetts leaders' responses to the king's letter of 1662 continued to be unsatisfactory, as was their response to the Narragansetts' complaints.[126] The Court's continued protest over the commissioners' hearing of appeals, particularly that of John Porter, Jr., finally led the commissioners to demand whether the Court acknowledged the royal commission "to be of full force to all the intents & purposes therein contained?"[127] The Court members refused to give a direct answer, saying they did not know what the real purpose of the commission was and were only trying to defend their charter, a response clearly indicating their continuing suspicion that the commissioners' secret purpose was to extinguish their authority, not to convey the king's goodwill.[128] After one more fruitless exchange, the commissioners shot back, "The little success of your late address might discharge you from a second, especially when you find his majesty so highly concerned for his prerogative, which he cannot be supposed to have parted withal by any privileges or immunities granted in your charter." They also wished the Court had "spared that salvo of your duty to God, & the privileges of your charter, whereby you would mysteriously insinuate that all your liberties, civil & ecclesiastical, were intended to be violated, which is so high an imputation to his majesty . . . that it ought not to be believed nor imagined by his good subjects."[129] They then announced their intention to hear the Thomas Deane case the next day at the home of Captain Bredon.

It was Massachusetts's turn to be furious. The commissioners had repeatedly ignored their objections to hearing appeals above their authority. Worse, they were accepting appeals right under their noses and in the home of a man who had publicly refused to acknowledge the colony's authority. The magistrates immediately composed and printed a declaration that the court being held was in violation of their charter and they could not consent to it. As the commissioners' court began its session the next day, three men on horseback arrived at Bredon's door. One, Thomas Bligh, carried a trumpet, which he sounded to call attention. The next, Oliver Purchase, unscrolled the General Court's declaration and read it to all within earshot, while the last, Marshall Richard Waite, stood guard. In a parting shot consistent with the Court's position that loyalty to the charter showed true loyalty to the sovereign, Purchase concluded his reading by declaring, in an "audible voice" as ordered, "God Save the King."[130]

It was the final straw for the commissioners. Since "you will make use of that authority which [the king] hath given you to oppose that sovereignty which he hath over you, we shall not lose more of our labors upon you, but refer it to his majesty's wisdom," they wrote. With what must have been grim satisfaction, they assured the Council that they would use the magistrates' own words to represent them to the king.[131] Finally, they presented a list of changes that they expected to be made in the colony's laws and declared their business concluded.[132]

The list of changes to be made to the colony's *Book of General Laws & Liberties* was delivered to the Court on May 24, 1665, and proved that legalism was not confined to the Massachusetts General Court. The royal commissioners demanded that the book's title page acknowledge that the king was the "fountain" of all the colony's liberties and insisted on a law stating that all writs, arrests, acts, and justice be in the king's name, that royal arms be set up in every court of justice, and that military companies and ships carry the king's colors.[133] They then made it clear that the persistent use of the term "commonwealth" was offensive, declaring that all such "undecent expressions & repetitions of the word 'commonwealth,' 'state,' & the like" should be removed from the law books and replaced by "his majesty's colony."[134] In addition, every reference to the General Court as the chief civil power in the colony must acknowledge that it was "under his majesty," and the coining of money must be halted, as that was a royal prerogative. Finally, the commissioners denied the right of Massachusetts to join with other colonies, as it had in the organization of the United Colonies, or to exercise any power through that means.[135]

The royal commissioners' list of changes to Massachusetts laws also contained many amendments that struck at the heart of the New England way. They asked that laws be removed that were prejudicial to ministers of the Church of England, that thanksgiving days be inserted celebrating the king's birth, his restoration to the crown, and the putting down of the gunpowder treason, and that a day of humiliation be ordered for the murder of Charles I. They ordered that fines for not attending public worship be eliminated (if at a Church of England service), that there be no penalty for keeping Christmas, that the heresy law be rephrased to not implicate the Church of England, and that the Quaker laws be softened so that they might "quietly pass about their lawful occasions, though in other cases they be punished." To colony leaders, this sounded like nothing less than transforming the colony into England, removing the very reason for coming to North America. They could not submit.

Massachusetts leaders saw these orders as a threat not only to their authority, but to their very being, a feeling accentuated by the king's agents' apparent hostility to their religious way of life.[136] The royal commissioners had made no secret of their contempt for the Puritans.[137] Rather than make any attempt to acquaint themselves with the orthodox members of the society, they had kept to their royalist, Anglican, and dissident companions and had received discontented persons who shared their suspicions of the disloyal behavior of the Massachusetts Puritans. Prompted as it was in part by Quaker petitions, the royal commissioners' visit gave tacit encouragement to Quakers in the colony, who freely visited the commissioners in Boston. One such visitor, a Quaker woman, carried tales of the colonists' slurs against the commissioners. She reported that colonists called Cartwright a "Papist" and that some whispered that Carr kept a "naughty woman."[138] Others brought news of lawsuits that seemed to prove the injustice—or the absurdity—of the colony's courts. A friend of Maverick claimed he had brought an obviously superior case to court during the commissioners' stay in Boston but lost to his opponent, a church member.[139] Another told of a current court proceeding between a married couple for the male partner's "insufficiency." To that, Cartwright crowed, "It will be worth the knowing what or how much is necessary for a holy sister."[140]

The composition of the commission, lacking a single Puritan, had given Massachusetts cause to suspect its religious practices were under attack. In old England, religious tensions between nonconformists and the state church had grown alarmingly since Charles II's restoration. His laws against nonconformists, persecution of nonconformists in Scotland, and sympathy toward his openly Catholic brother, the future King James II, had given New Englanders reason to be thankful they were on the other side of the ocean, where, Roger Williams opined, they received better care from the Indians than they had from their "native countrymen."[141] Instead of protecting their religious liberties, as Massachusetts had pleaded, the commissioners cited the colonists' religious persuasion as evidence of disloyalty. In his report before the king in 1665, Cartwright associated the Massachusetts Puritans with their counterparts of the deposed English government, noting that the colony had supplied Oliver Cromwell with "many instruments out of their Corporation and College" and had served as a refuge for many of those fleeing England from the restored monarchy. Cartwright reported that Massachusetts leaders had solicited Cromwell "to be declared a Free State, and many times in their laws style themselves this STATE, this COMMON-WEALTH, and now believe themselves to be so." Their resistance to the king, their insistence on the privileges of their patent, proved their disloyalty. Some colonists, the commissioners reported, even publicly hoped for "a change" in the government of England through Dutch victory in the war.[142] In the view of the commissioners, all these abuses demonstrated the colony leaders' unfitness to remain in authority, and the colony's desperate need for a firm governing hand from England.

When the royal commissioners left Massachusetts in disgust, Nicolls returned to New York, and Carr, Cartwright, and Maverick went to New Hampshire and Maine to begin settling disputes of jurisdiction.[143] Massachusetts had sent artists out to collect information and draw maps justifying the colony's claims to the region, but the commissioners refused to hear the colony's arguments before their departure.[144] They arrived in New Hampshire in June 1665, and it soon became very clear that what John Josselyn called the "topsy-turvy" nature of Maine government had left the people of both Maine and New Hampshire divided and fractious.[145]

So weary of the political tug-of-war were residents of both Maine and New Hampshire that some saw direct royal government as the only solution. In the weeks following the royal commissioners' departure from Boston, a large group, spurred by Abraham Corbett of Portsmouth, petitioned the commissioners to free them not only from the Massachusetts government, but from other claimants, such as the heirs of Gorges and Mason, as well. They requested direct royal government, with royal commissioner Robert Carr as governor. The commissioners received a similar request in Maine.[146]

Notwithstanding these petitions, others were just as adamant for Massachusetts control and still more felt torn by the competing demands. The dilemma of the dueling calls of authority emerges clearly in a letter from

Portsmouth's selectmen John and Nathan Pratt, Elias Stileman, and Nathaniel Fryer. Writing to the Massachusetts Governor and Council on July 10, 1665, they begged for their advice and counsel on "what Point of the compass it will be our safety to steer, so as not to hazard either our Allegiance to his Majesty or our oaths to the Government aforesaid under his Majesty's Authority [Massachusetts], each of which we are conscientiously solicitous about."[147]

The royal commissioners decided to leave the New Hampshire government under Massachusetts's authority until the king could determine matters. In Maine, however, they established a royal government, crushing the aspirations of both Massachusetts and the Gorges proprietors. Massachusetts's immediate response was to issue declarations that the commissioners' proceedings were a violation of their charter privileges and that the old government should continue to be obeyed. They sent three agents to convey these orders to the inhabitants. This, in turn, aroused a reproof from royal commissioner Robert Carr, who was still in the area. When the Massachusetts agents returned home, the newly appointed royal government resumed its duties, a situation that persisted, prompting disgruntlement and resistance to both claimants, for the next three years.[148]

On the eve of George Cartwright's December 1665 departure for England, he, Carr, and Maverick penned final letters, one to Massachusetts and another to Sir Henry Bennet, secretary of state, with an account of their actions in New Hampshire and Maine and their recommendations for reducing Massachusetts to obedience to the king. In the first letter, the commissioners chastised Massachusetts for its recalcitrance, being "so much misled by the spirit of independency." Referring to the constant insistence of Massachusetts leaders that their charter granted them final power to govern, the commissioners chided, "The King did not grant away his Sovereignty over you when he made you a Corporation." Pointedly, they reminded the colony of the "deserved punishment and destruction" of others who "of late made use of the King's authority to oppose His Majesty's power, and raised arms and fought against His Majesty and yet pretended the defense & safety of the King." If the Massachusetts leaders had any idea of taking a similar course, as some of their actions suggested, they should think better of it.[149]

In the letter to Secretary Bennet, the commissioners recommended that strong action be taken against Massachusetts without delay. Let the king take away its charter, they urged, as Charles I had intended to do in 1637, and bring out "visible force" against the colony. "If his Majesty should now let these people rest, having so much declared themselves against his authority over them, those that are well affected will never dare hereafter to declare themselves." They warned that Massachusetts would try to gain time by writing its objections: "They can keep the business in agitation, until the King and all his Secretaries there and all his good subjects here, be weary of it." If this were allowed, all the commissioners' work would "be undone" and petitioners against them left without redress.[150] The commissioners would prove to be excellent prophets.

Cartwright set sail for England, petitions and reports in hand, in the fall of 1665. On December 14 he made his report to the king, commending Plymouth, Connecticut, and Rhode Island for their faithfulness and cooperation and condemning Massachusetts for its unrelenting resistance to the royal commission. In response to Cartwright's list of charges, the king wrote to the leaders of the Massachusetts Bay Colony in April 1666, expressing his dissatisfaction with their reception of the royal commission, particularly their insistent belief that "his Majesty hath no jurisdiction over them, and no appeals against their judgments can be made to the King," an attitude "which would be a matter of such high consequence as every man discerns where it must end." He demanded that four or five agents be sent to England to answer directly to him and that these include two of the chief offenders: Major William Hathorne and the governor, Richard Bellingham.[151]

The colony's response to this demand shows how far the lines of division had widened during the commissioners' visit, further undermining colony leaders' authority with many of its citizens. The question of how divided they were was of great concern to the colony and the commissioners. "There have . . . been high representations of great divisions & discontents among us," the General Court complained in October of 1664, "& of a necessity of sending commissioners to relieve the aggrieved." Court members denied these rumors, claiming that "the body of this people are unanimously satisfied in the present government, & abhorrent from change."[152] If there were any divisions, they were caused not by the Massachusetts government, but by the visit of the royal commissioners, which had brought "sinking discouragements" and "distracting fears."[153] But Cartwright, as his report to the king illustrates, would have none of this. In his eyes, only a few rabble-rousers—eight at the most—were causing all the obstruction to the king's commission; the majority of Massachusetts residents were loyal to the king and longed for his more direct hand in their government.[154]

This opinion, repeatedly conveyed to the king and his counselors by the royal commissioners and petitioners against Massachusetts, is clearly reflected in Secretary Morrice's response to the Massachusetts General Court's October 20, 1664, letter protesting the royal commission. Although the entire Court had spent two months preparing and revising the letter, Secretary Morrice reported that the king thought it the "contrivance of a few persons who have had too long authority there." Governor Endicott, whose name was affixed to the letter, had been in office during "all the late revolutions," and Morrice declared that he was "not a person well affected to his Majesty's person." The king would be pleased if someone else were chosen as governor.[155] Endicott obliged the king by dying before the next election. In the person of Samuel Nadhorth, the Massachusetts government continued to protest the idea that the colony was divided. Writing in October 1666 in response to the king's demand that agents be chosen and sent to England, Nadhorth claimed that the idea that obstruction to the commissioners came from "the Magistrates & leading men & not the people" was demonstrably false. Yearly elections installed magistrates and governor; if the people were "diversely minded from their rulers, they have advantage enough to attain their desires." In fact, Nadhorth declared, the people had been so opposed to yielding to the commissioners that had the magistrates done so, the people would have united in protest, "some discontents, Quakers, and others, excepted."[156]

While the strength of Massachusetts's unity was debatable, the magistrates' argument that the commissioners' presence alone widened divisions in the colony was amply demonstrated. The commissioners' visit gave legitimacy to dissenters from the Puritan hegemony and gave them a stage on which to act out their protests. Simon Tuttle's quickly repented sedition was but one example of discontent vented by the impending visit. May of the same year saw the arrest of William Cotton, who later signed the petition for direct royal authority in New Hampshire, for "sinful and unjust reflections against the governor and freemen."[157] This, along with other disturbances and fears occasioned by the royal commissioners' visit, led to the General Court's framing a new law in September 1664 for the prevention of sedition and treason "against our commonwealth."[158] As the royal commissioners traveled from colony to colony, others discontented with Massachusetts flocked to them with their stories and petitions; Cartwright carried thirty petitions against Massachusetts with him on his return voyage to England.[159] While many of these people had protested to the Massachusetts authorities before, the commissioners' visit gave them a higher court of appeal and new language in which to couch their protests. When servant Hugh Hancock was fined 22 pounds for defying not only his master but the colony, he proclaimed, "he did not care a straw for the Governor and hoped he would see half of those in the country hanged within this half year."[160] John Hoar, disappointed in a previous debt case, carried his petition to the royal commissioners. After their departure, he again argued before the Massachusetts General Court and was disbarred for acting and speaking "to the scandal & reproach of several of our Courts, honored magistrates, & officers of Court."[161] Hoar's language at that juncture has not been preserved, but his language in a 1668 case does remain. In that case, he called the king's and commissioners' arguments to his own service, goading the magistrates with the king's June 28, 1662, directive that the stipulations of the "said Charter be henceforth strictly observed, and not swerved from as formerly."[162]

It cannot be coincidental that Boston's Baptists, subject to repeated fines for failing to attend public worship—by definition the Congregational Church—chose May 1665 to officially organize themselves as a church. And they, like John Hoar, challenged the colony's laws by citing the king's higher authority when they were again brought to court in October 1665: "His Majesty hath explained in his letter to the general Court, Saying that the principal end and foundation of that Charter was and is the freedom and liberty of conscience."[163]

There were, indeed, many who opposed the Massachusetts government and many more who, though generally supportive, thought that the colony's resistance to the king and royal commissioners went too far. But the magistrates were not alone in taking an inflexible stand against any royal exercise of authority. Hundreds of townsmen from all over the colony signed petitions in support of the Massachusetts government, filled with phrases just as passionate as any in the letters sent from the Court to the king. One Woburn constable refused to post the king's letter of 1662 as directed and returned it to the General Court. Essex minister William Gilbert, a Scottish immigrant, preached so frequently and passionately against royal government that he was finally admonished in open General Court. In notable contrast to Thomas Bredon, who was fined 200 pounds for his contempt of Massachusetts's authority, the sympathetic magistrates merely slapped Gilbert's wrist, charging him the costs of court—five pounds.[164]

Even after the commissioners' departure, the ranks remained split. Unsure of where power lay and when or whether royal government would be reasserted, competing interests freely launched accusations of treason. In one case in New Hampshire, Henry Greenland attempted to kidnap Richard Cutt and carry him to England for trial for speaking "treason, and the King's Commissioners were gone, nothing being Done." His recruited accomplice in the attempt warned Cutt of his danger, and Greenland was brought before the Massachusetts magistrates for trying to undermine the king's government—vested in Massachusetts—and for "making quarrels & contentions among the People, in a very perfidious manner."[165]

Similar divisions appear in the General Court's debate over whether to send agents in response to the king's command. Some argued that obeying the king and defending the charter were not necessarily contradictory: "our absolute power to determine must not abate the king's prerogative."[166] Others saw sending agents as abandoning the charter, a form of civil suicide. The Court acknowledged that the colony, too, was divided on the issue: "There is so much dissatisfaction, that men are not sent, that it will provoke and raise a tumult."[167] Both sending and refusing to send agents were seen as courses that were potentially ruinous to the colony, and colony leaders finally determined to take what seemed a middle course: they would not send agents but would send assurances of their loyalty, accompanied by the valuable gift of a shipload of masts for his majesty. (The shipmaster who carried the gift to England gave tongue-in-cheek names to the pine masts, "the one Governor Bellingham, the other Major Hathorne.")[168] In response to the Court's decision, men from Boston, Ipswich, Salem, and Newbury, making up over 150 signatures, submitted petitions urging the Court to comply with the king's demand for agents. Several signers were prominent men in the colony: Captain William Gerrish, Captain John Appleton, Edmond Batter, Captain Thomas Savage, Thomas Brattle, Habbacuck Glover, and Thomas Deane. The General Court ordered these "principal signers" to answer for their demands, which had, the Court complained, "a tendency to divide the Court & the Country; and to render the Court obnoxious to his Majesty for disloyalty, & to lay great reproach & ignominy upon the government."[169] Responding on behalf of the petitioners, John Appleton denied any ill intent, claiming rather that they had acted so out of their desire, like the Court, to preserve their charter liberties and to give "faithful advertisements of danger," and they begged the Court to consider them loyal.[170] Clearly, there were divisions within the colony over just how much authority colony leaders rightly held, with some fearing that their view of authority was dangerous to the continued existence of the colony.

Thus in the centers of power, as well as on the fringes of the colony, Massachusetts was divided over how to respond to the king—the final authority in the minds of some and a threat to the colony in the minds of others. The magistrates sent off boats laden with masts, hoping to stave off royal action, but many feared that, either way, disaster was assured: "Some fearing these actings will precipitate our ruin, and others apprehending that to act further, will necessitate our ruin."[171] What actually happened could hardly have been anticipated by the most optimistic among them. From 1665 through the end of the decade, a series of calamities befell many of the chief actors against them. George Cartwright, speeding to England with his papers and petitions against Massachusetts, was attacked by Dutch pirates and lost everything but his life, forcing him to report to the king with nothing but his memories of the commission. Robert Carr, returning to England early in 1667, became ill and died one day after disembarking in Bristol. Lord Willoughby of Barbados, whose example of "uncivilly & inhumanely carrying it towards" his council had made the "name of a Commissioner odious" to Massachusetts, drowned along with over a thousand soldiers in a hurricane off St. Christopher's Island. Lord Clarendon, Charles II's secretary who seemed hostile to Massachusetts, was ousted by Parliament, and a succession of reorganizations of the Council for Foreign Plantations so diluted its effectiveness that business against Massachusetts sifted into oblivion.[172] The newly restored king's reluctance to insist on his prerogative, evident in his instructions and reactions throughout the commissioners' stay, undoubtedly played a role in abating action against Massachusetts as well.[173]

In 1668, following a second shipment of masts from Massachusetts leaders to the king, intended as a "manifestation of their loyalty and good affection," the king sent a gracious letter in reply. He stated that he accepted the gifts as an expression of their loyalty and sincere affection and found both the masts and the colony's supplies to the royal fleet in the Caribbean "exceeding acceptable."[174] The royal commission and the king's request for agents to answer directly to him were not mentioned. This letter and the series of disasters must have seemed nothing less than miraculous providence to many in the colony.[175] The royal commissioners' visit had made it clear that Massachusetts's authority, imposed not only within the colony but on Indians and English outside the colony's jurisdiction, was insecure. When the king, through his commissioners, challenged that authority, it encouraged the resistance of many English and Indians in New England who had long resented Massachusetts's imposition. The Bay Colony came perilously close to losing its authority in the mid-1660s, but what colony leaders and many residents interpreted as providence intervened. Indians, religious dissidents and discontents might continue to chafe at the bit, but the General Court had held its ground; it had preserved the holy commonwealth. God still smiled on New England.

Chapter 3

Years of Uncertainty

Ever since the visit of the royal commissioners in 1665, the Massachusetts General Court lamented that the "savage natives bordering upon this & other his majesty's colonies" had traded their awe of the English for contempt. Freed of any direct ties to colonial governments, the Indians had repeatedly threatened the English in words and deeds, showing particular hostility toward any from "the Massachusets."[1] There had, of course, been similar flare-ups from time to time since the English colonists' first settlement. What is striking, however, is that almost all the explicitly stated resistance to English authority between the Pequot War and the royal commissioners' visit came from the Narragansetts, the only group that had submitted themselves directly to the king and thus most likely to resent local English assumptions of superiority over them. They made a point of stating their status as subjects of the king, hence equal to his English subjects, in their interactions with Massachusetts Bay government, and they renewed their submission to the king when the royal commissioners came in 1665. The Wampanoags under Philip, who would lead devastating attacks on the English in 1675, were virtually absent from United Colonies records in these years. That changed after 1665, when Philip met with the royal commissioners and received confirmation of his lands, as if from the king himself.[2] In the decade between 1665 and 1675, reports of Indian uprisings accompanied by Indian protests over English interference in their governance alarmed English colonists three times. And it was no longer just the Narragansetts but the Wampanoags as well who were suspected of intent to "cut off" the English.[3]

For both English and Indians, the years after the visit of the royal commissioners were filled with uncertainty, waiting to see what reprisals might come, what power would hold sway. The challenges to Massachusetts's authority that emerged during the royal commissioners' visit had not disappeared. In fact, divisions seemed to be widening as a new generation came of age, and political and religious strife undermined authority in a colony where governance rested on consent. The pressures of English growth, changes in the economy and politics of the region, and altered power structures within and outside of the colony were working great changes in native life as well, making the Indians increasingly dependent on—hence increas-

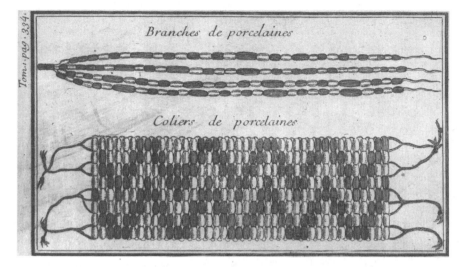

Tom.i.pag.334.

Branches de porcelaines

Coliers de porcelaines

Figure 6. Illustration of Iroquois wampum, in strings and belts, from Bacqueville de La Potherie's *Histoire de l'Amérique Septentrionale* (1722). Courtesy of the Robert Dechert Collection, Annenberg Rare Book and Manuscript Library, University of Pennsylvania.

ingly vulnerable to—the English. The choice of many Indians to adopt English religious beliefs and, to an extent, the English lifestyle challenged both English and Indian societies. The benefits of close association with the English, which had kept the Narragansetts, Pocumtucks, Wampanoags, and others in friendship with the English even when they rejected their interpretation of authority, were dwindling. But the potential to turn to other powers in the region was also diminishing. The English defeat of the Dutch and the animosity of the Iroquois decreased New England Indians' opportunity to appeal to outside powers to counterbalance the English. By the beginning of the 1670s, few options remained to the Indians other than to acknowledge submission to and dependence on the English or to throw off the yoke by going to war.

For the Indians, the transition to dependence on the English accelerated as the second generation of English colonists came of age. In the early years of English settlement, the Indians, particularly the Narragansetts, had become "rich and potent" through making and distributing wampum. In control of the fur trade as well, the Indians had been in a strong position to negotiate with the English and obtain goods and terms favorable to them. By 1665, however, hunting had drastically reduced the local numbers of beaver and deer, and wampum was slipping into disuse. Indians were forced to accept the position of middlemen for northern Indians who still had access to furs, and they were soon edged out of even this role by

Englishmen.[4] There was still land, of course, and many Indians sold their land to replace previous sources of income. Growth in the English population created ample demand for pastures and farms, and some English ignored General Court stipulations that all Indian land sales be approved by the magistrates.[5] By 1665 nearly fifty English towns had been settled in Massachusetts and Plymouth, with over thirty more in Connecticut, Rhode Island, New Hampshire, and Maine. Over fifty thousand English populated the New England colonies, compared to ten to fifteen thousand Indians.[6] This rapid growth pressed on Indian settlements, creating tension and conflict. The rapid creation of new towns was a source of conflict in English as well as Indian society, seen by some as threatening to the communal life and mission of the colony. Increase Mather clearly believed as much when he condemned land as the "Idol of many in New-England." Mather's condemnation did not imply that people should give up their land. It was, instead, directed at excess, men "being every where apt to engross more Land into their Hands than they were able to subdue." Where one man held more land than he could keep clear, it soon became overrun with saplings and weeds, "as if they were seated amidst of a Heap of Bushes."[7] It was a clear balancing act. Land fed the body, without which the soul would wither. But too eager pursuit of land led people away from gathered churches and the regular religious communion necessary for their own spiritual growth and that of their fellows. It also nurtured a contagious competition that undermined the unity held up as a model by the first settlers. Many new settlements continued without benefit of church or minister for years at a time, leading John Cotton to exclaim, "Let there then be no more Plantations erected in New England, where people professing Christianity shall live like Indians, without any solemn invocation on the name of God."[8]

Indians living "without any solemn invocation on the name of God" and free of the constraints of society were troubling to the English settlers, not only for the danger they posed (particularly for those English who had allowed their untended land to grow effective cover for an Indian attack), but for their physical reminder of the Puritans' responsibility to share the Christian message. While little was done in direct fulfillment of the "main end of [the] plantation . . . to bring the Indians to the knowledge of the gospel" in the first two decades of Massachusetts settlement, the language used in submissions of Indians to the colony clearly suggests that the responsibility was on the minds of the English.[9] Massachusett sachem Cutshamekin's 1643 submission to the Bay Colony included the promise to "from time to time" receive instruction in Christian beliefs.[10]

Within three years of that first submission, John Eliot, who would come to be known as the "apostle to the Indians," made his first, not very successful, attempt at preaching to Cutshamekin's people. Chastened by the Indians' resistance to his halting efforts to address them in their own language,

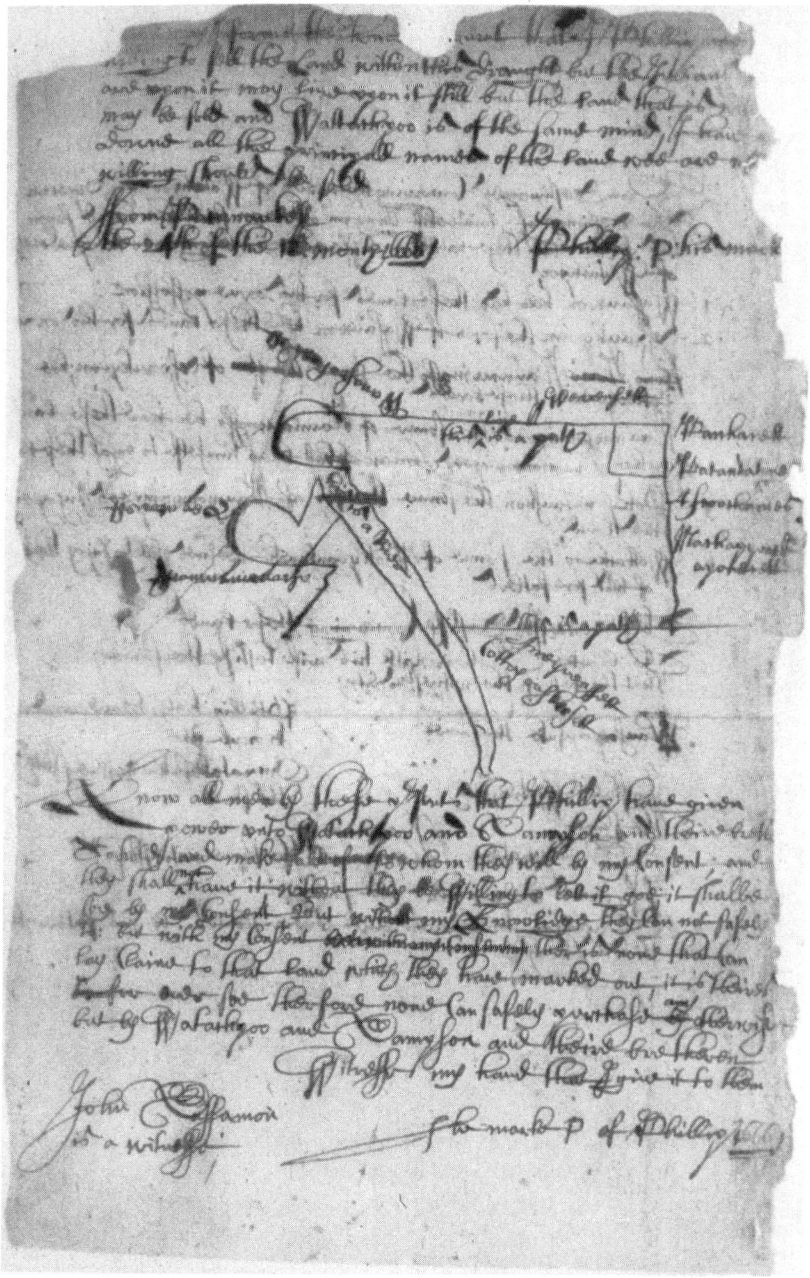

Figure 7. The 1666 deed and map of land sold to the English by Philip, sachem of the Wampanoags, evidence of the accelerating transfer of land from Indians to English in the decade before King Philip's War. Courtesy of the Plimoth Plantation and Plymouth County Registry of Deeds. Photograph by Gary Andrashko.

Eliot returned home and increased his efforts to learn Massachusett. His second attempt, addressing Waban and others at Nonantum, was well received.[11] By 1650, these Indians had accepted Eliot's proposal that they join in a Christian community where they could pray and work together, following the English model of communal living and worship. Natick, the first "praying town" in the Massachusetts Bay Colony, was established on the border of the English town of Dedham, a proximity that reflected Eliot's—and Indian sachem Tahattawan's—belief that "if the *Indians* dwelt far from the English, that they would not so much care to pray, nor would they be so ready to hear the Word of God, but they would be all one *Indians* still."[12] Eliot believed that teaching the Indians the gospel would be useless without also bringing them to "civility," or Puritan ways of work, schooling, and living.[13] Within a few years of Natick's founding, a total of seven praying towns had been established in Massachusetts Bay Colony: Nashobah, Wamesit, Punkapaug, Hassanamesit, Natick, Okonokhamesitt, and Mugunkaquog.[14] By 1674, seven more had been formed among the Nipmucks in central Massachusetts, and by 1675, 2500, or 20 percent of New England's Indians, had "yield[ed] obedience to the gospel." For these Indians, as for the English, stringent qualifications for acceptance into the church applied: only Indians who showed long-term commitment to gospel living were counted as converts. And as with the English, their progression from baptism to full communion was a long, halting, often incomplete process.[15]

Christian Indians in these praying towns built social, economic, and legal relationships with the English. Several of the towns had schools for instruction in reading and writing, and Harvard College established a short-lived Indian school. Christian Indians sold their manufactures and produce at English markets, and English patrons helped them establish native-run court systems supervised by colonial magistrates, parallel to the county court system among the English.[16] Residents of the praying towns had already submitted to Massachusetts's authority. Their coming under an organized English-style government within the praying towns must have increased the English colonists' sense of security, trusting that these Indians, at least, were no danger to them. The English connection distanced the praying town Indians from non-Christian Indians, whose contacts with the English were more sporadic and remote, and it created a sense of familiarity and an increasing ease of communication between English and Indian believers. But the growth of Indian plantations side-by-side with English "outtowns" was also a source of conflict.[17]

The history of Natick offers a good illustration of the conflicts English expansion introduced and the clash between local and colony authority that undermined peaceful relations with neighboring Indians. Natick was founded in 1651 after John Eliot petitioned the town of Dedham for a grant of 2000 acres of land within its township. Unfortunately, the Indians' chief planting fields and many of the homes of Natick's sixty families were

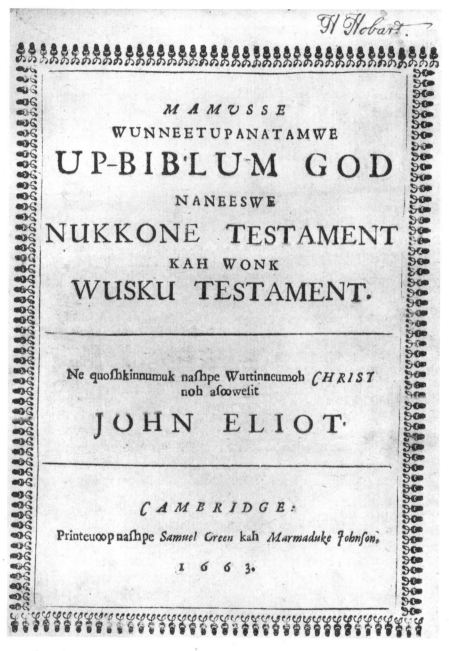

H Hobart

MAMUSSE
WUNNEETUPANATAMWE
UP-BIBLUM GOD
NANEESWE
NUKKONE TESTAMENT
KAH WONK
WUSKU TESTAMENT.

Ne quoſhkinnumuk naſhpe Wuttinneumoh *CHRIST*
noh aſoowesit

JOHN ELIOT·

CAMBRIDGE:
Printeuꝏp naſhpe *Samuel Green* kah *Marmaduke Johnſon.*
1 6 6 3.

Figure 8. Title page of John Eliot's 1663 translation of the Bible into the
Massachusett language. Courtesy of the Annenberg Rare Book and Manuscript
Library, Van Pelt-Dietrich Library Center, University of Pennsylvania.

outside the 2000-acre grant, and on the south side of the Charles River, an area that Dedham citizens wanted for grazing their horses and cattle. The bounds of the Indian plantation were offically laid out in October 1652. By the next spring, the first lawsuit between English and Indian townspeople over land "which the Indians do challenge" within Dedham's bounds reached the colony magistrates. Conflict played out in court and on the ground for the next two decades.[18] The General Court recommended expanding the boundaries of Natick's grant, and a committee of "Christian friends & Neighbors" urged Dedham to "yield up those Lands" to the Indians out of "gracious Gospel principles of self Denial, Love, peace, & desire to further Christ's work among the Indians," but the conflict continued, reaching the General Court again in 1662.

The Court decided in favor of the Indians, insisting that their "native right" in the lands they occupied be respected, but local English ignored the ruling. In 1669, John Eliot petitioned the General Court on behalf of the "poor Indians at Natick." He complained that, in spite of the Court's decision, "some of Dedham do invade our line; upon one side, they forbid the Indians to plant, take away their rails which they have prepared to fence their grounds, and on another side have taken away their lands and sold them to others, to the trouble and wonderment of the Indians."[19] The Court again appointed a committee to look into boundary disputes, but claims and counterclaims persisted.

The same process of English expansion butting up against the presumably valued work of evangelizing the Indians, and local wishes superseding those of colony leaders can be seen in another Indian praying town, Okonokhamesitt, which Eliot had lamented in 1662 as "in effect overthrown." This Indian plantation had been established in 1658, just two years after the founding of the English town of Marlborough and well before land distribution among the English was settled.[20] Marlborough was an offshoot of Sudbury, one of the original frontier towns. Long-standing disputes among residents of that town, chiefly along generational lines, had finally led the younger group to petition for a new plantation, where they could allot their land individually, rather than according to the communal pattern favored by those remaining in Sudbury. Not surprisingly, even after breaking away from their parent town, this more individualistic group found it difficult to agree on many things, including the establishment of a church and selection of a minister.[21] In the Marlborough pattern of settlement, English houses sprang up "very scatteringly" over the whole grant of land, each man keeping his dwelling and farming lands together.[22] As a result, Okonokhamesitt found itself planted literally in the midst of the English, its meeting house abutting English land. One of the most valuable parcels in the Indian tract was a 150-acre apple orchard. Daniel Gookin, appointed by colony leaders as a superintendent to the Indians, complained that "it brings little or no profit to them, nor is ever like to do; because the Englishmen's cattle, &c. devour all in it, because it lies open and unfenced."[23] By 1673 the Indians had abandoned the plot. While not entirely "overthrown," the Indian mission was embattled and dwindling: "The Indians here do not much rejoice under the English men's shadow; who do so overtop them in their number of people, stocks of cattle, &c. that the Indians do not greatly flourish, or delight in their station at present."[24] In both Dedham and Marlborough, individual and local aspirations undercut the colony's communal commitment to sharing the gospel with the Indians, even to the extent of resisting colony laws and legal decisions favoring the Indians.

Both these conflicts were fueled by English desires for land, which were themselves fueled largely by concerns for posterity. Each new plantation established in Massachusetts quickly divided its lands, divvying up house lots, wood lots, and marshland grass lots among the settlers in the town. While most men received generous allotments of land, few had enough to supply all the needs of their children or their children's children. As the second generation began their own families, the colony experienced a population boom, untempered by the high mortality of old England and Virginia to the south. Between 1650 and 1670, the New England population more than doubled.[25] The only solution to the demand was to expand settlement, an inherently precarious move, both because it put pressure on the Indian population of the area and because it threatened the colony's ability to maintain orderly communal towns.

Conflicts over land were compounded by simultaneous political changes, which further narrowed the range of options available to Indians desiring autonomy. Before the arrival of the royal commissioners, whose troops effortlessly deposed the Dutch, Indians had easy access to a rival international power when they were dissatisfied with the English. The 1653 war threat, in which the Narragansetts were implicated, gives clear evidence that both the Dutch and their neighbor Indians saw each other as potential allies against the English.[26] Similarly, Plymouth officials received word in 1667 of Wampanoag sachem Philip's "readiness to comply with French or Dutch against the English, and so not only to recover their lands sold to the English, but enrich themselves with their goods." Philip strenuously denied the charge, but Plymouth leaders found it plausible enough that they organized a costly expedition to investigate.[27] When Dutch New Netherland became English New York, however, the option of an Indian-Dutch alliance vanished.

The early 1660s saw a change in inter-Indian alliances as well. The decline in the fur trade and wampum production and distribution undermined one of the primary interactions between New England Indians and the Mohawks, and many southern New England Indians shifted their loyalties from that Iroquois nation to fellow Algonquians from the northeast, such as the Wabanakis, Sokokis, and Montagnais. These Algonquians were

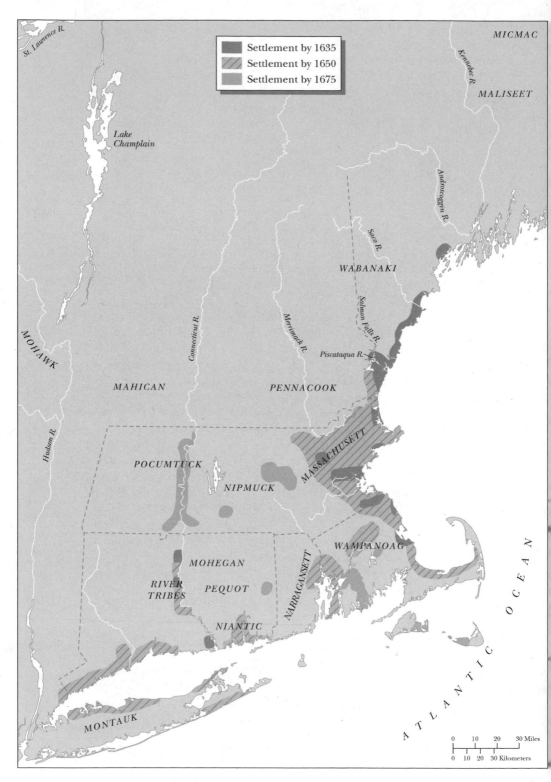

Map 2. The expansion of English settlement, 1620–1675.

Legend:
- Settlement by 1635
- Settlement by 1650
- Settlement by 1675

MICMAC

MALISEET

St. Lawrence R.

Kennebec R.

Androscoggin R.

Lake Champlain

Saco R.

WABANAKI

Salmon Falls R.

Merrimack R.

Connecticut R.

Piscataqua R.

MOHAWK

MAHICAN

PENNACOOK

Hudson R.

MASSACHUSETT

POCUMTUCK

NIPMUCK

WAMPANOAG

MOHEGAN

NARRAGANSETT

RIVER TRIBES

PEQUOT

NIANTIC

MONTAUK

ATLANTIC OCEAN

0   10   20   30 Miles
0   10   20   30 Kilometers

allies of the French and implacable enemies of the Mohawks and other Iroquois peoples. When the Pocumtucks and Massachusetts turned their loyalty to their Algonquian kin, the Mohawks began devastating raids against them, ambushing isolated fishing or hunting parties, looting, wounding, scalping them, and sometimes taking captives.[28] Daniel Gookin reported that the Indians' terror of the Mohawks was so great that many refused to enter the woods to search for roots and nuts or to visit their usual fishing, hunting, and planting places. Instead, the Indians barricaded themselves in forts, "by which means they were brought to such straits and poverty, that had it not been for relief they had from the English, in compensation for labor, doubtless many of them had suffered famine."[29] Despite peace agreements between the Iroquois and English in 1664 and the Iroquois and French in 1665, the Mohawks continued their attacks, and the ostensible peace made the Massachusetts government reluctant to counterattack on behalf of its Indian subjects.[30]

Although Massachusetts did not go to war on behalf of the Christian Indians under its protection, the magistrates wrote to the Mohawk sachems to complain of the raids and to remind them of their agreement of friendship with the Massachusetts Bay Colony and its subject Indians. In the letter, the magistrates urged the Mohawk sachems to consider English dress and hair styles unmistakable signs that the Indians they encountered were English "friends" and under English protection. As an example, the magistrates described the murder of a young Indian servant at Northampton. The magistrates declared that not only had the Mohawks been seen in the area, but also "not long after this time the Mohawks showed a lock of hair at Albany, which was short hair as this youth's was.[31]

In 1669 the Massachusett Indians, against the advice of the English, decided to strike back against the Mohawks, joining fellow Algonquians from the northeast in a disastrous attack on a Mohawk village. With ample advance warning of the expedition, the Mohawks put up fierce resistance. By the end of the fight, Massachusett sachem Chickatabut and more than fifty warriors lay dead. This was a crippling loss for the Massachusett Indians, who had already been reduced from 24,000 to a mere 750 people by epidemic disease.[32] Continuous, devastating warfare had a profound impact on the Indians surrounding Massachusetts Bay Colony, driving them from their traditional subsistence practices into closer dependence on the English. The labor-poor English saw this as a "good effect" of the inter-Indian hostilities, "namely, to turn them from idleness; for now necessity forced them to labor with the English in hoeing, reaping, picking hops, cutting wood, making hay, and making stone fences, and like necessary employments, whereby they got victuals and clothes."[33] The numbers of Indians living within or on the edge of English settlements and adopting English dress and hair styles must have been substantial, as evidenced by the magistrates' use of those outward signs as proof of subjection to the

English. Warning the Mohawks against attacking Indians who were subjects of the English, the magistrates requested "that none of your people kill, rob or spoil any Indian that lives within a day's journey of Boston who are generally clothed in English apparel & their hair Cut after the manner of the English."[34] Indian laborers flooded into English settlements from all over New England. Massachusetts's subject Indians in the nearby Christian Indian settlements were an obvious source of labor, but the more distant Narragansetts also sent many laborers, and some came from as far away as Maine.[35]

While the influx of Indian labor may have met the immediate needs of both Indians and English, it reflected the narrowing options that were making wage labor and land sales the chief means of Indian subsistence. Once Indians had sold their land it was nearly impossible for them to return to former ways of living. Wage labor created its own set of problems. The Indian labor pool among the English increased rapidly in the 1660s and 1670s, placing a great strain on an important aspect of authority among the Puritan colonists, the imperative to maintain orderly family government.[36] James Carr, accused of stealing linens from a Boston housewife, testified to this threat to order in 1668. Appearing before the justices, Carr reported his wanderings: born in Scotland, he had lived eight years in Virginia, as well as in New York and Barbados. Arriving in Boston with no money, he had "got his victuals among [the] Indian[s]."[37] The Indian labor force collected on the fringes of English towns offered an attractive place of refuge for strangers and wandering young men "away from family government," an alarming development for a colony devoting increased energy to ensuring that all such men were safely ensconced in homes under the watchful eye of a godly father. By providing a haven for would-be criminals, the Indians on the outskirts of English settlement made the English increasingly suspicious of them.[38]

Deprived of rival alliances by the English conquest of the Dutch and their great distance from the French, and in enmity with the Mohawks, New England Indians in the decade following the royal commissioners' visit found themselves alone with the English, with no outside powers to play off for advantage. This may explain the continuing appeal of royal authority to many Indians. Given the narrowing of the political field, the Indians' only recourse against the English, short of armed resistance, was to go over their heads to the king. The Narragansetts, Wampanoags, and Mohegans had all used this strategy in 1664–65, and the Narragansetts in particular clung to the hope that royal authority offered to make them equal to the English, and hence able to accept or reject their demands. Ninigret revealed the Narragansetts' persistent attachment to this line of authority in his words before the Rhode Island Council in 1669. He affirmed that he had maintained loyalty ever since himself heard the words by the Commissioners, spoken as from King Charles his mouth, and hath since laid it up in his heart that the King did look upon himself and Sucquansh [Pessacus] and their Indians as his subjects, together with the English; and said he understood that the English of this Colony were to help them, if any should be too mighty for them, and they to do the like to the English if any should invade or make war upon the Colony.

Ninigret's words clearly describe an alliance rather than a subjection. To further point out his equal standing with the English, Ninigret made another explicit comparison. The Pequots, he pointed out, "paid tribute to the English, being overcome of them." Likewise, he had conquered the Montauk Indians, who now paid tribute to him, "even as the Pequits did the like."[39] The Narragansetts were a nation, like the English, able to conquer and exact tribute. They owed allegiance to the king as his subjects, but only friendship to his other subjects, the English colonists. In July of the same year, Samuel Maverick wrote to his former companion on the royal commission, Richard Nicolls, reporting on Massachusetts's most recent demand for back tribute from the Narragansett sachems: "they paid them not, telling them they would pay King Charles and none else."[40] While the English of Massachusetts and the other United Colonies did their best to ignore these protests, other English encouraged such appeals to the king. Samuel Gorton was instrumental in both Narragansett submissions to the king, and he and his son maintained ties with them as well as the Wampanoags in succeeding years.[41] Their support of the Indians' efforts to alert the king to Massachusetts's oppressions added strength to their own petitions against Massachusetts.

As Indians struggled with the new realities of political life, they chafed under increasingly close contact with the English. English complained that Indians in their communities stole blankets, clothing, and other goods and threatened them when they passed them on the road. Indians complained that English mowed the grass on their land and that English livestock broke into and devoured Indian cornfields.[42] Both clung to their own interpretations of who held authority in the area, the English insisting that Indians continue to report to United Colonies commissioners or colonial governments, and many of the Indians holding to the model of friendship and alliance laid out in the earliest English-Indian treaties or to the royal commissioners' decrees, under which they answered only to the king.

Not surprisingly, such contrary views led to conflict. On September 5, 1668, the Massachusetts magistrates, on behalf of the "proprietors of Lands & farms in the Narragansit country," sent a letter of complaint to the Narragansett sachems: "Several indians belonging to you or some of you" had "offered wrongs unto their people as Burning their hay killing sundry horses and in special about one month since forced some of their people from their labors in mowing grass upon their own land, and assaulted others in the high way as they rode about their occasions by throwing many stones at them . . . using many threatening speeches unto their persons." These disturbances took place in the "King's Province," or Narragansett country, the area simultaneously claimed by Massachusetts and Connecticut investors, Narragansett Indians, and the Rhode Island government acting in the stead of the royal commissioners. The Indians' campaign of harassment against the English who persisted in farming there shows their clear insistence on the commissioners' judgment that the land was theirs. For their part, the Massachusetts magistrates ignored the commissioners' judgment, which had been suspended pending the king's decision, and insisted that the Indians adhere to their original treaties with the local English. The English protest that Indians had driven Englishmen "from their labors in mowing grass *upon their own land*" betrays no hint of awareness that the Indians were asserting their own right to the land. Indian harassment of the English was, the magistrates declared, "not only contrary to humanity but to the covenants made with us," under which the Narragansett sachems had agreed to take all disputes to the Massachusetts magistrates or, later, to the commissioners of the United Colonies.[43] The continuing power struggle between English and Indian is clearly evident in this exchange.

As complaints of abuses went back and forth between Indians and English, Indians pinned much of the blame for the trouble on the younger generation. While youth were a convenient scapegoat for those wanting to avoid responsibility for abuses, the charges against them were probably true. As with the English in the Natick-Dedham dispute, the Indians were not always able to enforce the obedience of those under their authority. Narragansett sachem Mixam gave evidence of this difficulty when he described his warriors' use of his boat in a raid he had not approved: "my men were a sort of proud Childish men and took her away."[44] Pocumtuck sachems admitted to similar problems, telling the English magistrates, "our men that are young and foolish may have done some particular wrong to the English; this should not break the league betwixt us and the English seeing we do not countenance our men for so doing." Strikingly, in the same communication the sachems pointed out that some English, too, had wronged them, "though we know they are not countenanced by the Governors for so doing."[45] The Pocumtuck sachems, like the magistrates in the praying town disputes, did not countenance disobedience, but could not prevent it, and they did not think such misdeeds should undo the friendship each party desired. By making explicit comparison with the English, the Pocumtucks were, as they had done before, asserting their equal standing, their belief that expectations for Indian and English people should be the same.

For the English, too, the years following the royal commissioners' visit were uncertain. The General Court had entrusted the colony's fortunes to God, appealing over the head of the king himself for support in its resistance to the crown. Royalists within the colony were appalled at their leaders' brazen disobedience to the king's demand for agents. Thomas Bredon sneered that the General Court's substitution of a shipment of pine masts for the demanded agents was "Sacrifice, not Obedience."[46] Samuel Maverick noted with disgust how "exceedingly they [the magistrates] boast of the gracious letters they have received from His Majesty and of his kind acceptance of the Masts they sent him, as also of the provision they sent to the Fleet at Barbados."[47] Absence of any kind of royal censure in the king's letters to the colony must have reassured the magistrates that their continued holding to their course would succeed, and they appointed a day of Thanksgiving on November 24, 1670, for God's "continuing our peace & liberties" in the face of great threats.[48] Witness to the belief of colony leaders that they could return to their old course is their persistent use of the term "commonwealth," which the royal commissioners had ordered them to stop using in 1665. John Davenport used the term unblushingly in his 1669 sermon, declaring that "This special Form of Civil Government of Commonweales, by men orderly chosen, the Scripture ascribes unto God."[49] Laws and proclamations made after 1665 used the term as well.[50] The General Court also failed to alter laws the commissioners had requested be changed, and in 1668 its members violated the king's explicit order that the royal government established in Maine be continued until he directed otherwise, again demonstrating their belief that their own authority, not the king's, was final.[51]

Massachusetts justified this action, like its previous takeover of Maine government, by petitions received from settlers sympathetic to its government. In addition, the magistrates claimed that Maine fell within their patent, a point they declared themselves willing to argue before the king. In the meantime, they sent a committee of Major General Leverett, Edward Tyng, Captain Richard Waldron, and Captain Robert Pike to reassert their claim. The Massachusetts agents arrived in York, Maine, in July 1668. They found former Massachusetts marshal Nathaniel Masterson in prison, where he had been thrown for opposing the royal commissioners in 1665. Hauling him out, they appointed him clerk and marshal of the new Massachusetts government. The agents then announced that court was in session, entered the meeting house, and began reorganizing their long-dormant government. Outside the building, Henry Jocelyn and other officials of the royal government appointed by Carr, Cartwright, and Maverick held their own court, pointedly calling attention to "his Majesty's commands." The two courts battled for the attention and loyalty of the townspeople until dinnertime, when the Massachusetts men adjourned to find something to eat. When they returned, they found that the royal justices of the peace had stolen a move on them, taking possession of the meeting house: "the house [was] full and the gentlemen [of the former royal government had] taken up our seats." From those bastions of authority, Jocelyn and his fellow royal officers declared "that the Massachusets were traitors, rebels, and disobedient to his Majesty, the reward whereof, within one year, they said, should be retributed."[52]

Resistance to yet another change in government was not surprising. Authority had shifted hands four times in five years—from Massachusetts to Gorges's commissioners, back to Massachusetts, to the royal government, and to Massachusetts again. Henry Jocelyn, William Phillips, Robert Jordan, and most of York lined up against Brian Pendleton, Nathaniel Masterson, and others appointed to office by Massachusetts. Phillips was particularly outspoken in his objection to the renewed imposition of Massachusetts's authority, charging his fellow townsmen to "take heed how you act and under what Authority you Act" and warning that "those who were for the Bay government their necks might stretch for it." Aware that authority was precisely the issue at stake, Pendleton, chosen as an associate in the new government, took care to preface his warrants and declarations with the phrase "required in his Majesty's name & under the Authority of the Massachusetts." Nevertheless, Phillips's repeated warnings to the people, as well as his efforts to rip down every notice commanding attendance at elections for Massachusetts officers, had the intended effect. One witness claimed that half the townsmen failed to attend the election and that those who did show up thought "it not meet to choose one neither did choose any. Some of them I think did answer they could not meddle till the difference about the government was reconciled." Discouraged, Pendleton wrote the Massachusetts General Court that, in consequence of Phillips's speeches, only seven "adhere[d] unto me" at the election. The rest refused to cast their votes or fortunes with either side and "depart[ed] silently away."[53] Pendleton feared the consequences for other towns yet to vote. Despite the residents' understandable aversion to choosing between the competing powers, the Massachusetts officials appointed new officers (including the chameleon-like Henry Jocelyn and Edward Rishworth) and got the courts running again.[54] Richard Nicolls reported his astonishment that Massachusetts would resume its government in Maine, especially after the king's letter of April 1666 directing otherwise, but Massachusetts leaders resolutely hung on.[55]

They did so in the face of widespread chaos and open resistance. Nathaniel Phillips reported that "the Province is certainly in a very confusion, every one obeying whom they list for the accomplishing of their own ends."[56] William Phillips, who had raised such vociferous objections to Massachusetts's takeover, soon found himself hauled before the Massachusetts General Court and imprisoned. He was released only after posting a 500-pound bond that he would not "oppose the Authority of the Massachusetts, but Rest quiet."[57] Despite such substantial fines from the Massachusetts government and local court proceedings against resisters, protests continued, as they had and would for decades.[58] In July 1669, the court noted that John Bonithon had "carried himself Contemptuously to the Associate Court at Saco as appears by his paper" and ordered him to appear and yield obedience to the new government. Bonithon failed to appear until a year later, when the court, with the same careful phrasing Pendleton had employed, ordered him to answer for "his Contempt of his Majesty's Authority settled in this Colony." In spoken words as well as his guilty "paper," Bonithon had gravely offended Massachusetts's authority, saying "the bay men are Rogues & Rebels against his Majesty, & saying that Rogue Major Leverett he hoped he will be hanged, & if he wanted a hangman he would be a hangman for them." The county court ordered Bonithon to appear at the next Court of Assistants in Boston and in the meantime to keep "his Majesty's peace & submit him self unto his Majesty's Government here established." Only after considerable prodding was Bonithon persuaded to take the oath of fidelity to Massachusetts.[59] Bonithon was joined in his resistance to the reimposed order of the Bay Colony by the long-disgruntled Robert Jordan and a string of others in succeeding years.[60] Towns, too, resisted the new order, as they had in the previous decade. The county court scolded Kittery for choosing Nicholas Shapleigh, James Heard, and Richard Nason—Quakers all—as town commissioners, "Contrary to law."[61]

The resistance of these individuals was fueled by hopes that royal officials would again intercede for their friends and servants in Maine. In July 1669 Daniel Dill was presented at court for spreading the rumor that "there was Twenty sail of Ships coming out of England & prince Robert [Rupert] to settle government in this Country as he said he heard."[62] While Dill's story was groundless, the hopes it represented were not, and they were kept alive by a constant stream of letters crisscrossing the Atlantic from English and New English foes of the Massachusetts government. Bonithon testified as much when he finally appeared before the Massachusetts Court of Assistants in September 1671. He confessed he was very sorry for his abusive carriage toward the court and for breaking the oath of fidelity he had sworn the previous summer. In explanation, he claimed he had been "blinded by a letter from Mr Gorge[s]."[63] Discontents such as Samuel Maverick continued to send their complaints to sympathetic ears in Whitehall. In his letter to Nicolls, who was back in his position as groom to the bedchamber of the king, Maverick enclosed a letter from Samuel Gorton and mentioned the continued "groans" of the "loyal party" "under the burden of the Massachusetts government . . . as by frequent letters from all parts I am informed." They were "in a far worse condition than we found them" during the commissioners' visit four years earlier. "That I should live to see His Majesty's loyal subjects and my ancient friends enslaved, as now they are," he exclaimed, and he begged Nicolls to include him "though unworthy" in any designs made to reduce Massachusetts to obedience.[64]

Not only in Maine, but in Massachusetts itself many opposed the colony's stance toward the crown. Although Massachusetts officials insisted that its inhabitants were united in support of their actions, Maverick claimed that the "loyal party" supporting the king represented eighty percent of the Bay Colony's inhabitants.[65] Without existing petitions or other means of counting this "party," it is difficult to judge the accuracy of Maverick's claim other than by counting those who publicly declared their loyalty to the Massachusetts government. Approximately 1300 men from at least fourteen towns in the colony signed petitions in 1664 and 1665 expressing support for the Bay Colony government and urging resistance to any royal intervention. One of these petitions, bearing 106 signatures, was signed wholly by nonfreemen. Given the colony's 1665 population of 25,000, those signing petitions probably comprised over a quarter of the adult male population.[66] It is as unlikely that the remaining three quarters favored a change in government as it would be that everyone who failed to become a member of a congregational church in full communion was an Anglican, Baptist, or Quaker. But neither is it likely that all of them represented the extremely conservative position the General Court felt forced to adopt under the acute threat of the royal commissioners' visit. At such a time of crisis, both the commissioners and the General Court exaggerated the extent and nature of their respective positions. Maverick's claims echoed the royal commissioners' charge that the magistrates were a faction, a minority directing the government in opposition to the wishes of most inhabitants of the colony. The magistrates, of course, denied such claims, continuing to insist on the unity and contentment of the governed with their governors.[67] In reality, many of the colonists' political positions fell between these two extremes. Three, rather than two, parties is a better approximation of the political situation in the Bay Colony in this period. There were those firmly opposed to any kind of change (the "commonwealth party"), those who favored accommodation to the king within bounds (the "moderates"), and those who publicly proclaimed their preference for royal government (the "royalists").[68] Those who signed the 1666 petition in support of sending agents to the king represented the moderate position, but Maverick claimed them as royalists and protested the reprisals they suffered for speaking out against the General Court's intransigence.[69] As late as 1676, royal agent Edward Randolph did the same, noting the "severe check received by those who signed a petition in 1666 asserting the King's jurisdiction" and enclosing a copy for the king's perusal.[70]

In actuality, any reprisals the petitioners suffered were very short-lived. Edmund Batter was back serving in the General Court within a few years, Thomas Brattle was a member of the expedition to reassert Massachusetts government in Maine, and Thomas Savage and several others served as officers in King Philip's War in 1675. Their prominence in the colony, both before and after the 1666 petition, indicates that their opinions did not marginalize them or disqualify them for the regard of their fellow citizens or further participation in colony affairs. Under threat of losing everything precious to them, however, many of those who otherwise favored a flexible approach to royal demands may have joined the commonwealth party in proclaiming their ardent desire that the colony's charter freedoms be continued. But they believed the best way to accomplish such an end was not resistance but thoughtful accommodation. The fact that they insisted that preservation of the liberties granted in the charter "was the Sole Reason why they have petitioned" is in itself evidence that resistance to the General Court did not equate with a desire for royal government, as Maverick and Edward Randolph asserted.[71]

The commissioners' division of church members and nonmembers into loyal and disaffected camps was, likewise, inaccurate and reflected the gulf in religious practice between old and New England. In New England, all were expected to attend church, but only those who had undergone a saving experience, confirming their election by God, became members in full communion. In old England, *all* who attended church were members. Thus by counting all not formally accepted into church membership as "disaffected," Maverick was greatly simplifying the situation. Many, if not most, of the nonmembers occupying pews would count themselves as Puritans and were waiting for a spiritual confirmation that they should go on to full communion. Many never received that experience but continued to attend church faithfully and could hardly have been called disaffected.[72]

Encouraged by such characterizations of the colony as Samuel Maverick's stream of letters supplied and by continued prodding from Mason and Gorges, the Council for Foreign Plantations began again to consider taking action against New England. In response to Gorges's report that Massachusetts had seized the government of Maine in 1668, the Council made a formal recommendation to the king in 1671 that he again send commissioners to New England to settle boundary disputes.[73] On August 12, 1671, the Council reminded the king of its recommendation and belief that, "for the well grounding of the King's future proceedings," sending commissioners was necessary. In a notable recognition of the shortcomings of the 1664–65 commission, the Council added that "due regard [should be] had to their qualifications of ability and integrity to send faithful and judicious advices and yet with temper, not too much contrary to the present humor of the people."[74] Three months passed with no action, and when Lord Arlington hinted to the king that he should proceed, Charles responded that November was no time to send ships to the colonies and deferred the matter once again. Men such as Gorges and Samuel Gorton of Rhode Island continued to appear before the Council, pressing it to action, but more urgent business, including another Dutch war, averted the king's attention and further postponed a new commission. Massachusetts leaders eagerly watched for news of any action that concerned them in England and continued to give thanks for the preservation of their liberties. But in spite of England's failure to act against Massachusetts and the colony's determination to continue on as if the commissioners had never come, they had come, and in coming had ignited a fire that continued to burn among English as well as Indians.

The political uncertainty of this period—over whether the king would intervene to punish Massachusetts and whether Massachusetts could maintain its authority over Maine, the Indians, and even some of its own citizens—was matched by a religious crisis arising out of growing doubt that the New England way would continue into the next generation. The visit of the royal commissioners coincided with the coming of age of the second generation of colonists in Massachusetts Bay, children at the first migration in the 1630s or born since. The colony's anxiety over the spiritual welfare of this booming young population increased with their advancement into maturity. The transition from the first to second generation was marked by a series of deaths of prominent leaders—ministers and magistrates—in the colony during the 1660s. As these men died, their colleagues gave pointed reminders to the colonists remaining behind of their need to fill the large shoes of their predecessors, and how far from doing so they were. Preaching the funeral sermon of Reverend John Wilson, Richard Mather lamented the vacuum of leadership, asking, "Your Fathers where are they?"[75] And some took the spate of deaths as evidence that God was preparing to punish the colony: "When Kings call home their ambassadors, it is a sign they will declare war," preached Increase Mather.[76]

The laws passed during this period offer additional evidence of the colony's concerns with carrying the holy commonwealth into the next generation. In 1668 the General Court issued a decree on family government to every town in the colony, instructing the town constables to send in the names of any young persons living outside of family government so that they could be placed under the supervision of "such as will look more strictly to them." The order continued,

The neglect whereof, as by sad experience from Court to Court abundantly appears, doth occasion much sin and prophaneness to increase among us, to the dishonor of God, and the ensnaring of many children and servants, by the dissolute lives and practices of such as do live from under family Government, and is a great discouragement to those family Governors who conscientiously endeavor to bring up their youth in all Christian nurture as the Laws of God and this Common Wealth doth require.[77]

If family government were firmly in place, orderly government of the "great family" would surely follow and the colony's authority would be preserved. Ironically, John Bonithon's sons Thomas and John, Jr., were charged under the new family government laws for "living In a disorderly family *in the house of their father* Mr. John Bonighton a Condemner of this authority." Though they lived with a parent, his own disorderliness placed his sons in violation of the spirit of the law. At the same session, the young Bonithons were also presented for failing to appear at military training according to law and for absence from public worship, evidence that the court's judgment was warranted.[78] Troubled with reports of youth gathering in other people's homes to drink and carouse in the evenings and reports of disrespectful behavior during church services, the Court also passed laws banning gatherings without the knowledge or permission of masters or parents and requiring supervision of youth in the churches.[79]

Colony leaders used their authority to uphold religious practice, believing that God-fearing colonists would in turn uphold their authority. Believing that law needed the bastion of godly instruction to succeed, the magistrates issued a declaration "To the Elders and Ministers of every Town within the Jurisdiction of the Massachusets" in March 1668, urging them to expand their religious instruction beyond worship services. They noted that in ancient Israel the Levites were sent out to spread the "good knowledge of the Lord throughout all the Cities of Judah," and they urged the elders and ministers to do likewise, instructing "all the people (especially the Youth)," publicly and privately. They should inquire into how well the people were learning doctrine and religious behavior and see if the youth were learning to read, a necessity among a godly people. Doing all this would, they declared, discourage evil and bring about "more Love and Unity amongst the people, and more Reverence and Esteem of the Ministry."[80] Other laws targeting reform, particularly of the youth, were passed in October 1668 and in May 1670.[81]

The fact that laws were passed but youthful disobedience continued to occupy the proclamations of fast days throughout the next decade shows that ideal and actuality were not meeting, to the great chagrin of the first generation. The king's restoration to the throne had brought to an end hopes for a divinely mandated form of government in old England. The sole responsibility for creating such a community now rested on Massachusetts, and its rising generation showed less inclination than their forbears to shoulder that burden. One response to this dilemma in the religious community was what came to be called the halfway covenant, which extended the right of baptism to the grandchildren of the first generation, even if their parents had not advanced beyond baptism to full communion. Supporters of that approach considered it necessary to ensure a future generation of Saints, and to extend the saving experiences of church worship to people who would otherwise be cut off from them. To opponents, however, the halfway covenant signified not insurance that the New England Way could continue but an admission of its failure. The split response to

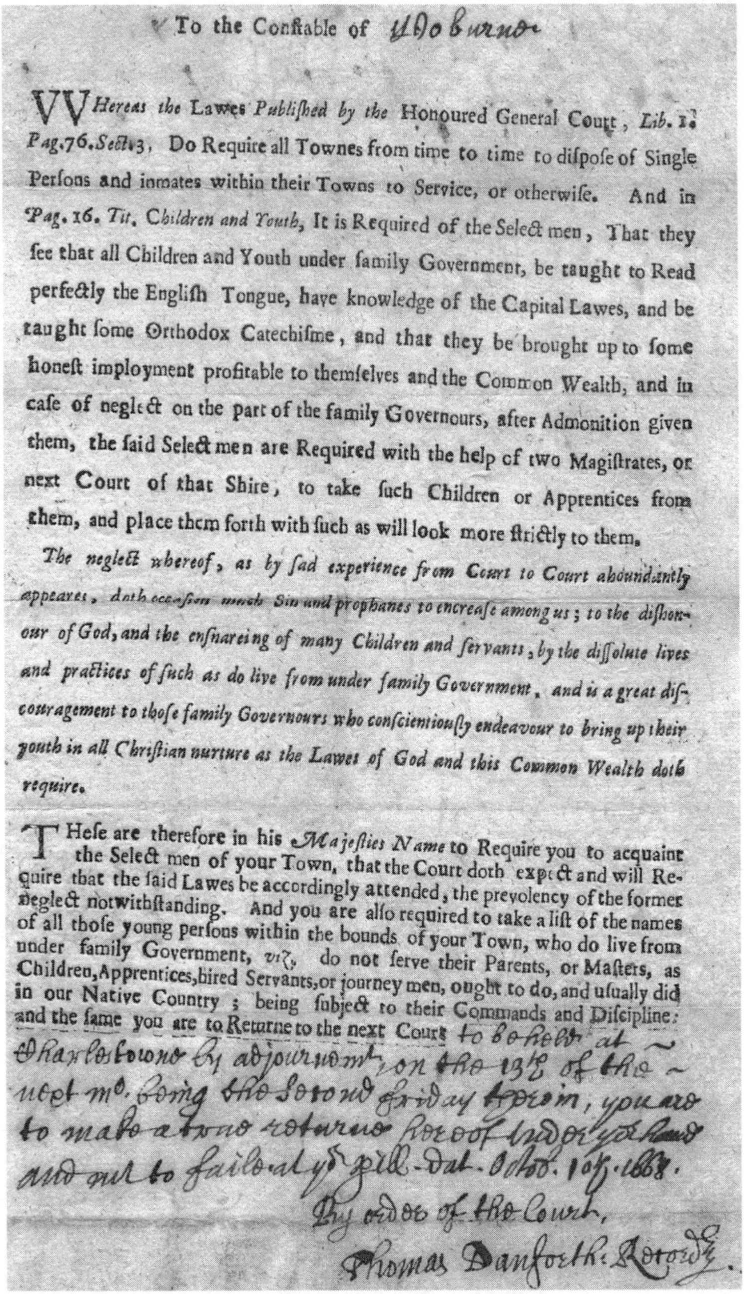

To the Conſtable of *Woburne*

VVHereas the Lawes Publiſhed by the Honoured General Court, Lib. 1. Pag. 76. Sect. 3, Do Require all Townes from time to time to diſpoſe of Single Perſons and inmates within their Towns to Service, or otherwiſe. And in Pag. 16. Tit. *Children and Youth*, It is Required of the Select men, That they ſee that all Children and Youth under family Government, be taught to Read perfectly the Engliſh Tongue, have knowledge of the Capital Lawes, and be taught ſome Orthodox Catechiſme, and that they be brought up to ſome honeſt imployment profitable to themſelves and the Common Wealth, and in caſe of neglect on the part of the family Governours, after Admonition given them, the ſaid Select men are Required with the help of two Magiſtrates, or next Court of that Shire, to take ſuch Children or Apprentices from them, and place them forth with ſuch as will look more ſtrictly to them.

The neglect whereof, as by ſad experience from Court to Court abundantly appeares, doth occaſion much Sin and prophanes to encreaſe among us; to the diſhonour of God, and the enſnareing of many Children and ſervants, by the diſſolute lives and practices of ſuch as do live from under family Government, and is a great diſcouragement to thoſe family Governours who conſcientiouſly endeavour to bring up their youth in all Chriſtian nurture as the Lawes of God and this Common Wealth doth require.

THeſe are therefore in his *Majeſties Name* to Require you to acquaint the Select men of your Town, that the Court doth expect and will Require that the ſaid Lawes be accordingly attended, the prevolency of the former neglect notwithſtanding. And you are alſo required to take a liſt of the names of all thoſe young perſons within the bounds of your Town, who do live from under family Government, viz, do not ſerve their Parents, or Maſters, as Children, Apprentices, hired Servants, or journey men, ought to do, and uſually did in our Native Country; being ſubject to their Commands and Diſcipline: and the ſame you are to Returne to the next Court *to be held at Charlestowne by adjournmt on the 13th of the next mo. being the ſecond friday therein, you are to make a true returne hereof under yr hand and not to faile at yr perill. Dat. Octob. 10th 1668.*

By order of the Court,

Thomas Danforth. Record.

Figure 9. Laws concerning family government issued by the Massachusetts General Court in 1668. Middlesex County Court, Folio Collection, 1668, folio 49, group 4, Judicial Archives, Boston. Courtesy of the Massachusetts Archives.

the innovation reflected the growing divisions, not just between Puritans and outsiders, but within the religious community itself.

Given the intertwining of religious and political life in Massachusetts, church disputes frequently became civil crises, creating or reflecting divisions in colony leadership. One of the most wrenching of those divisions took place in 1669 in Boston's First Church. In his 1669 letter to Richard Nicolls, Samuel Maverick reported that minister John Davenport had "made such a rent in the Church of Boston as will never be reconciled."[82] Called from New Haven to lead the First Church, he insisted that his congregation join him in rejecting the halfway covenant. Half refused and broke off to form the Third Church of Boston. A committee apointed by the House of Deputies laid the blame for the resulting dissention squarely at the feet of the colony's ministers, who had agreed to the division.[83] In response, the ministers addressed a letter to the General Court protesting the charges of "innovation," declension "from the primitive foundation work," invasion of the rights of churches, and subversion of gospel order laid on them by the committee, which had charged that such actions were the root of "God's controversies with the land." The ministers asked to be allowed to defend themselves publicly from such charges or to call a synod to discuss the issues raised.[84]

Affront over the deputies' charges against them was one reason why the ministers who supported reform mounted a successful campaign to elect deputies who agreed with them in the May 1671 elections.[85] Under its new management, the General Court rejected the findings of the previous House of Deputies, though it was careful to add the caution that in general the "acts of this honored Court, being the supreme authority, are not liable to question by any." This caveat reflects Court members' sense that the widespread criticism arising out of the church crisis threatened colony leaders' and ministers' authority. Certainly, the turnover in the ranks of the deputies gave clear evidence that this was the case. The previous House of Deputies had acted in an "hour of temptation," and the new General Court declared that its findings were "not to be improved against the reverend elders . . . or to be made public." Neither did the Court know of any "just cause of those scandalizing reflections contained in the said papers indefinitely against magistrates, elders, & churches." They judged them "unduly calumniated and misrepresented" and were certain that they, like the members of the General Court, were committed to the congregational way and established practice of the churches "in their present & most athletic constitutions."[86] Clearly, at this crisis the voice of the colony rejected extreme positions, supporting a more moderate approach to both religion and politics.

Divisions threatening to colony leaders' authority also appeared in their response to continuing religious dissent in Massachusetts. During the May 1665 confrontation with the royal commissioners, Thomas Gould organized the first Baptist church in Boston, clearly borrowing the commissioners' authority for his action. Once the commissioners had left town, the magistrates summoned Gould and his followers to answer for what they had done, which they considered an affront not only to the churches but "also the peace of the government."[87] In 1668 the General Court appointed ministers to reason with the dissenters, to no avail.[88] Fines and imprisonments were as ineffective for the Baptists as for the Quakers, some languishing in prison for over a year without yielding an inch. They continued to turn their backs on baptism or to attend the Baptist meeting on Noddle's Island in Massachusetts Bay. And the dissension grew. In 1671 eight Woburn Congregationalists in full communion were charged with rejecting the sacraments and refusing counsel by joining the Baptists. The county court directed Charlestown, Cambridge, Watertown, Reading, and Billerica to send elders to the Woburn church to hear the dissenters' grievances and to "endeavor healing."[89] The fact that the Woburn Baptists were respected and long-standing members of the colony, as opposed to Quakers on a suicide mission from Barbados or Rhode Island, must have made their dissension even more troubling.

Quakers and Baptists threatened the colony's authority because of their explicit attacks on its political and religious leaders and because the questions they raised exposed divisions in the community. Knowing that many community members were sympathetic, if not to Quaker doctrine, at least to their persons, the magistrates had forbidden people from going to speak with imprisoned Friends and had ordered substantial guards on execution days.[90] When the magistrates banished Thomas Gould and several other recalcitrant Baptists from the colony in 1668, sixty-four men, many of them prominent, petitioned the Court to pardon the dissenters. The petitioners denied any sympathy with the convicted Baptists' beliefs or actions but claimed that "the men are reputed godly, and civil, and peaceable in their conversations." Moreover, manifesting a liberal attitude toward religious belief shared by a growing number of people within and outside the colony, they asserted that "the things wherein they differ [are] circumstantial and disputable among learned & sober and pious men" and they should not be forced to suffer "for conscience sake."[91] Like the signers of the 1666 petition in support of sending agents to the king, these men argued for greater accommodation as a way to ward off negative attention from outside the colony, pointing out that the Baptists' suffering troubled many of "God's people at home and abroad." To distinguish themselves from those whom the magistrates considered a threat to order, the petitioners concluded their plea with the wish that "your Authority may be long continued as a blessing to this common wealth."[92]

Even couched in this submissive language, such expressions were threatening to many of the colony's leaders. As with the 1666 petition, the Court called the most prominent signers to answer for "many reproachful expressions against the Court and their proceedings" and received a humble apology.[93] The Court did not execute its banishment order, however. Thomas Gould, William Turner, John Farnham, and their adherents continued worshiping in their church on Noddle's Island and were not prevented from constructing a church within Boston itself in 1674. Colony leaders cast a blind eye on these proceedings and gradually accepted the presence of Baptists among them. In a notable evidence of the Baptists' growing respectability, William Turner served as a captain in King Philip's War in 1676.

Accommodation of dissenting religious groups in the colony progressed in fits and starts. Laws against them did not change and in fact were tightened under the crisis of war in 1675. But enforcement lagged noticeably. In addition to the noted leniency toward Baptist practice following 1668, the General Court lacks any record of prosecution of Quakers from 1662 to 1675. Still, there were many in the colony who argued for a return to the religious purity of the founding days. In June 1671, as Thomas Gould, William Turner, and John Farnham were languishing in prison, the freemen of Cambridge petitioned the General Court to be even more severe against the Baptists. They argued that leniency toward dissidents gave them political power, rather than confining it to those "by the vote & suffrage of the freemen of this colony chosen as their Rulers & governors."[94] Even among members of the General Court, the Baptist question proved divisive. In 1665 the deputies had refused their consent for the magistrates' first recommendation of banishment for Thomas Gould and his followers. In 1670 a Court-appointed committee recommended the deletion of the phrase "or shall purposely depart the congregation at the administration of that ordinance" from a law against religious dissension. This change clearly accommodated Baptist practice, and the magistrates refused to consent to it.[95] The issue of tolerance or punishment of religious dissension continued to divide the colony throughout the decade following the royal commissioners' visit, a disunity troubling to many. Recognizing the threat such divisions posed, the Cambridge freemen petitioning in 1671 invoked the biblical maxim that a house divided against itself cannot stand. The late contentions among the colony's churches had left them in a "bleeding & languishing state & condition," and they prayed that the honored Court would find a way to heal their division.[96]

It cannot be coincidental that, in the midst of this upheaval over how far religious differences could be allowed, the General Court met to consider amendments to its book of laws. Notably, the Court made a particular effort to ensure that all future reprintings of the Book of Laws be prefaced with the seal of the Massachusetts Bay Colony and a statement that the charter required all laws to be obeyed. This was in direct contradiction, or perhaps direct response, to the royal commissioners' stipulation that the Book of Laws' title page acknowledge the king as the "fountain" of all Massachusetts's liberties.[97] Now, undoubtedly aware of renewed proceedings against them in London and painfully conscious of divisions within the colony itself, the magistrates underlined their own authority, republishing the colony laws and giving the colony's charter—not the king—as the source of their power. By doing so, they assumed battle stance, a position from which they would retreat again and again.

In the midst of these trials—Indian resistance to English authority, the renewal of attacks on the colony in England, religious disputes at home, and anxiety over whether the colony's second generation would continue in their parents' footsteps—a renewed challenge came from the Indians, who were undergoing their own struggles with shifting alliances, transition to a new economy, generational tensions, and English expansion. Under the pressures of an increasingly constricted political landscape, many Indians felt more acutely the English pressure for them to fit into their hierarchical ladder. The English expected surrounding Indians both to obey colonial authorities and to ensure the obedience of their followers. Those Indians who had accepted the English interpretation of subject status— chiefly the Christian Indians in Massachusetts—understood these expectations and tried, though not always successfully, to fulfill them. Those Indians who continued to resist English assumptions of superior authority—including the Narragansetts and Wampanoags—found such expectations an affront to their own authority. Plymouth's attempt to hold Philip, the sachem of the Wampanoags, accountable for his subjects' wrongdoings in 1671 was such an offense, an assertion of English authority that he strenuously resisted. It almost brought on a war.

In March 1671 the Plymouth magistrates demanded that Philip and other Indians appear to answer a colonist's complaint against one of Philip's subjects.[98] Philip refused. Such a rejection of an English court order was threatening to Plymouth's authority, but the manner of the refusal caused instant alarm. Hugh Cole, sent to summon Philip to the court, returned with the tale that the Indians were armed and repairing weapons, clearly in preparation for war. At Cole's approach, twenty or thirty Indians had rushed at him with staves in their hands. Only after seeing how few Englishmen accompanied Cole did the Indians place their weapons on the ground. Cole demanded why they behaved so, and they explained that they were expecting Englishmen to come to carry them to Plymouth, but "they were not willing to go." Cole next went to Mount Hope and saw many of the same Indians there with Philip's men, "and they were generally employed in making of bows and arrows and half pikes, and fixing up of guns." A general gathering was taking place, with "Indians of several places repair[ing] toward Mt. Hope." News of the situation spread rapidly, accompanied, as many times before, by rumors of an Indian plot to exterminate the English. On March 24 Josiah Winslow wrote to Plymouth governor

Thomas Prince with the news that two hundred Indians had gathered with the intent to kidnap the governor and Winslow and ransom them for a large "fine" and favorable terms in making peace, a plan thwarted by the Englishmen's too-early rising.[99]

Reports flew about the colony of Philip's engaging other Indians in his uprising, particularly the Narragansetts. One Indian claimed that, notwithstanding their "fair words" before the governor, Philip and the "squaw sachem" of the Narragansetts were proceeding with their "plot gainst the English within 10 days after & had offered or given the baskets of peage to the nargansett to help them."[100] Preparations for war were apparently afoot among the Narragansetts as well as the Wampanoags; English families were fleeing the King's Province for safer shelter, bringing with them reports that the Narragansetts there, "together with their warlike preparations threaten to kill the men first & then flay the women alive & one of them that had heretofore lived wth the English asked some of the English why they came from their own country & wished them to be gone else they would slay them as they do cattle."[101] Given such reports, Plymouth colonists warned Governor Prince against personally attending the treaty conference arranged in Taunton on April 12, 1671, to reduce Philip to submission.[102]

When the conference was held, at which Prince was nonetheless present, the Plymouth representatives ordered Philip to deliver all his guns to the colony. He agreed, undoubtedly under some duress, and they released him. As promised, Philip handed over some firearms, and Plymouth declared the surrendered guns forfeit and directed their distribution among the towns and military companies of the colony.[103] Reports soon came in that at least sixty guns had been seen at Mount Hope the day after the Taunton conference and that the Indians continued gathering and preparing for war.[104] At that news, Plymouth leaders rushed to prepare for war themselves, calling a military council and sending out word for towns to be in readiness for attack. At the same time, the magistrates called on all sachems of Indian villages within the colony to submit themselves to Plymouth and affirm their loyalty to English government. In early July, Indians from Mashpee, Satuitt, Wakoiett, Wakatasso, Caukohchise, Ashemuit, Saconess, Mannomett, Agawam, Sepecan, Weweante, and adjoining places made their submissions.[105] Plymouth officials sent to Awashonks of Saconnet, who had not yet submitted, to come in and deliver her guns. Expecting resistance, the colony simultaneously planned an expedition against her under General Josiah Winslow and appointed a day of humiliation to pray for its success. Before the appointed day, Awashonks submitted and promised to send in her guns.

As Plymouth made aggressive attempts to ward off conflict, Indians at Mount Hope continued war preparations, and Indians from surrounding sachemships continued to flood in to Philip's seat.[106] In September 1671, the Plymouth Council sent James Brown and James Walker to Mount Hope to confer with Philip. They arrived in the midst of a dance, and most of the Indians, including Philip, were drunk. When Brown attempted to speak with the sachem anyway, Philip knocked Brown's hat from his head, an "incivility" that was laid to Philip's charge later. It is striking that Philip aimed at the hat. Quakers were frequently upbraided in New England courts for refusing to remove their hats, evidence that they did not honor authority.[107] Brown certainly would have removed his hat to stand before the governor and council, but he did not remove it before the Indian sachem. So, as the magistrates did for the Quakers in court, Philip removed it for him. Philip expected to be treated with honor, as befit his station, but even English messengers refused, or did not think, to give it. Like the Rhode Island authorities, who considered fine coats "unfitting and improper" gifts for Indian sachems, English messengers did not think Philip, or any Indian, deserved deference. When Philip insisted on it, striking off the sign of disrespect, the English accused *him* of incivility and insubordination; he was beneath the English and must behave accordingly. Returning the next day with Rhode Island's Roger Williams as interpreter, Brown requested yet again that Philip come to confer with the Plymouth Council, something Philip had refused to do since the Treaty of Taunton. Philip excused himself, saying that he had another engagement. He had been invited to Boston by John Eliot and was expected there the following Tuesday.[108]

This invitation had been delivered by Anthony and William, Christian Indians from Natick, as a last-ditch effort to prevent Plymouth from going to war against the Wampanoags. John Eliot believed such an outcome would badly prejudice their hopeful progress in introducing the Gospel among Philip's people.[109] "Though they yet pray not to God, yet we hope they will; and we do mourn and pray for them, and desire greatly that they may not be destroyed." William and Anthony had brought with them a letter, penned on August 1 by Eliot in behalf of the entire church at Natick, laying out what divine counsel from the scriptures directed in such a case. First, Eliot stated that Deuteronomy 20, verses 10–11, showed that God required Plymouth to offer peace "before they war upon you; so it is your duty to offer, accept, and desire peace; and we pray you for God's sake, and for your soul's sake, obey this word of God." Second, he noted that 1 Corinthians 6, verses 1–6, gave God's command that when differences arose, they should be put to arbitration, "and therefore we do exhort you to obey this word of God; and whatever differences are betwixt you and Plymouth, refer them all to the judgment of the rulers of the Massachusetts; and whatever they judge, do you obey; lay down your lives and all you have at their feet." If the Wampanoags accepted this advice, the Natick men were to go next to the governor at Plymouth and inform him that

Philip's people "yield willing obedience to both those texts of scripture. . . . the instituted way of making and establishing of peace."[110]

Significantly, Anthony and William's instructions echo the many Indian submissions Plymouth had demanded in this time of crisis. Like the Indians who had submitted, Philip's Wampanoags should "yield willing obedience" and "lay down [their] lives" and all their possessions (or at least their guns). But the source of authority here was scripture—God's law, not Plymouth's. By implication, Plymouth was to yield its own authority, which it was exercising in raising troops and preparing for war, to a higher law, one which preached peace. The presence of the letter among the papers of Plymouth's deputy governor Josiah Winslow shows that William and Anthony indeed carried out the second half of their instructions. But Plymouth leaders were offended at their mission and turned their blame not on Eliot or the Christian Indians, but on Philip, crying against his carrying stories to their friends and brethren of Massachusetts and creating a rift between them.

Philip arrived in Boston on Tuesday, probably stopping on the way at the Christian Indian village of Punkapoag, as the letter directed.[111] In Boston, Philip laid out his grievances against Plymouth. The magistrates listened, then tried to determine the root of Plymouth's complaints against the sachem. The exchange between them has not been preserved, but Edward Rawson's letter to Governor Prince of Plymouth suggests that the nature of Philip's subject status was a principal topic: "Gentlemen," Rawson wrote to Plymouth, "we do not understand how far [Philip] hath subjected himself to you but the treatment you have given him & proceedings towards him do not render him such a subject as that if there be not a present answering to a summons there should presently be a proceeding to hostility." Philip would have explained that Plymouth was angry at him for refusing their summons, and based on Rawson's letter, he must have protested to the Massachusetts magistrates that he was not bound to come at Plymouth's call or treat with them any further.[112] This response would have been consistent with the treaty of 1621, in which Plymouth and the Wampanoags affirmed their friendship. While the later treaties acknowledged subjection to the king, none of them mentioned subjection to the colony of Plymouth. It is striking that at least at this point Massachusetts leaders questioned the extent of Plymouth's authority over the Wampanoag sachem.

Plymouth leaders were quick to make their own understanding of Philip's status clear to both Massachusetts and Philip. In their eyes, Philip was not merely a friend, but a subject under their authority. Plymouth would later charge Philip with "endeavoring to insinuate himself into the magistrates, and to misrepresent matters unto them," leading them to believe that his subjection to Plymouth was no more than in a way of "neighborly and friendly correspondency."[113] The phrase raises echoes of Pessacus's and Canonicus's letter to Massachusetts twenty-five years earlier in which they denied the colony's jurisdiction over them, claiming that both they and the English were now "subjects . . . unto the same king." Like Philip, these sachems stressed the "former love" (or "friendly correspondency") between them and the English and their hopes that it would increase. They insisted that royal arbitration was the only way disputes between them could be settled in the future: they must both "repair, unto that honorable, & just government."[114] Again echoing the substance of the Narragansetts' letter, Philip, too, denied his subjection to the local English, declaring, "The Governor [of Plymouth] was but a Subject, and . . . he would not Treat except his Brother King Charles of England were there."[115] He saw himself as an equal, not an inferior, to Plymouth's English magistrates and, as his reference to Charles II as a "Brother" suggests, even to the king.

After their meeting with Philip, the Massachusetts magistrates warned Plymouth against proceeding to armed conflict, which they did not believe could be admitted under the United Colonies Articles of Confederation, adding: "the sword once drawn & dipped in blood may make him as independent upon you as you are upon him." Independence seems precisely the way Philip viewed his relation to Plymouth, but certainly not how Plymouth viewed the same relationship.

Consider Philip's history, which must have been playing through his mind as he laid out his case before the Massachusetts magistrates. He had come to power in 1663 on the death of his brother Alexander (Wamsutta), who had similarly refused a summons from Plymouth. An armed expedition compelled Alexander's obedience, but the sachem died on his return trip of shame, disease, or poisoning, with many Indians favoring the last version of events.[116] Philip's own summons could not help but raise the memory of a time when Plymouth used its authority to humiliate and then destroy a Wampanoag sachem. When the royal commissioners had visited New England in 1664, they had met with several Indian nations. They had accepted the submission of the Narragansetts, who continued to recall the event and their direct relation to the king in the succeeding decade. They had visited Philip as well, confirming his lands to him. It would be surprising if they did not then explain to Philip, as they did to the Narragansetts, that their power to confirm land lay in their role as representatives of the king. The land was Charles II's, ceded by him to his subject, Philip Pokonoket. By his scribe John Sassamon, Philip had also written a Montauk sachem on Long Island, urging him not to yield obedience to the Niantics, but to wait for the royal commissioners to settle affairs, thus demonstrating that he accepted their final authority in judging disputes and directly flouting the United Colonies' repeated insistence that they should mediate in all such affairs. Like Pessacus, Philip seems to have seen his relation to the king as direct, not mediated through an English colony. The only way to settle disputes between the Indians and Massachusetts, Pessacus had argued, was to take them directly to the king. Philip's resistance to Plymouth's assertion of authority over him calls this exchange to mind. Why should Philip, a king like Charles, have to obey Plymouth? Plymouth's governor was a subject like himself, not a monarch.

Philip failed to appear before the Plymouth magistrates on September 13, 1671, and, in spite of Rawson's expressed reservations, the Massachusetts magistrates agreed to send men to meet with Plymouth and Philip on September 29. Governor John Winthrop, Jr., of Connecticut also accompanied Major General Leverett, Thomas Danforth, Captain William Davis, and several others of Massachusetts. The meeting was a disaster for Philip. Plymouth had evidently convinced Massachusetts and the other members of the United Colonies that Philip was in fact in subjection to Plymouth, as the rebukes they addressed to the sachem make clear. The assembled English pressed him to admit that he had violated the Treaty of Taunton by holding back arms and that he had abused Plymouth's authority in several other instances. They laid four other charges on him as well, including carrying himself insolently toward the colony by refusing to come to court when called, harboring Indians who were not his own men and were Plymouth's "professed enemies," taking the dispute to Massachusetts instead of the Plymouth court and thereby creating differences between the colonies, and behaving uncivilly toward several in the colony, particularly Indian messengers Hugh Cole and James Brown. After listening to Philip's defense, the representatives of Massachusetts and Connecticut expressed themselves satisfied with Plymouth's proof of the charges and urged Philip to acknowledge his wrong. "There is a great difference between what he asserted to the government in the Bay and what he could now make out concerning his pretended wrongs," they said. He must mend his ways and make reconciliation or "expect to smart for it."[117]

The English drew up a submission, which Philip and five other sachems signed on September 29, 1671. That document signaled a dramatic change in Philip's status in relation to Plymouth. While as in earlier agreements, the sachem acknowledged himself a subject to the king, he also—for the first time—acknowledged himself subject to "the government of New Plymouth, and to their laws." Thus Philip agreed in writing to what Plymouth had been assuming in practice for years. It is notable that of the dozens of Indian submissions flooding into the colony since April, only Philip's mentions any authority above that of the government of Plymouth. It is possible that Philip's own insistence that he was subject to King Charles, something he proclaimed at his visit to Boston the same month, pushed Plymouth to include the king in his submission at the same time that they demanded that he acknowledge the colony's authority. But Plymouth's reading of that line of authority would prevail: Philip was subject to the king, but only through the mediation of the colony and its laws. The agreement went on to stipulate that Philip pay damages of 100 pounds, repair to the governor (not to the king) for any differences between himself and the English, neither sell land nor make war without the governor's permission, and send the colony a form of tribute: five wolves' heads to the governor yearly.[118] If the English view of Philip's subject status was not clear to him before, it was certainly clear now. By October, the last of Plymouth Colony's Indians had delivered up their arms and submitted to the colony's author-ity. The threat of war was past, at least for a while. Philip's demotion from his own sense of equality, as a "brother" to King Charles, to a subject at the beck and call of Plymouth colony must have brought him shame. Indeed, the bitterness evident in the grievances Philip would express to Rhode Islander John Easton four years later clearly stems from the events of this tumultuous year. As long as his and other Indians' expectations were dashed, discontent would continue to fester. In this time of tension and uncertainty, it is no wonder the English continued to pray for unity, and Indians continued to prepare for war.

Chapter 4

Allies Fall Away

Rumors that the Wampanoags were plotting against the English had hung in the air of Plymouth Colony for months, but so had tales of Indian uprisings in past years, and they had come to nothing. June 1675 would prove a deadly exception. Christian Indian John Sassamon had been found dead beneath the ice of Assawompsett Pond on January 29, shortly after warning Plymouth authorities that Philip, sachem of the Wampanoags, was preparing for war. Sassamon's death had hung like a pall over the colony since that time. Three of Philip's men were accused of the crime, tried, found guilty, and executed by the English government at Plymouth on June 9. With that execution, the Indians of the colony traded their rumblings of discontent for action and began swift and open preparations for war.[1] Events propelling the actual outbreak of hostilities fell in rapid succession in the final days of the month.

June 11. Longtime Indian messenger John Brown, who lived in Swansea on the border of Philip's seat at Mount Hope, had written of his misgivings over the Indians' hostile preparations to Plymouth Governor Josiah Winslow earlier. Now he wrote in near panic: The Indians

have been and are in arms to this day as appears by the witness of English of Credit. Yea this day there is above 60 double armed men and they stand upon their guard. One reason say they is because they hear you intend to send for phillip but they have sent their wives to Narroganset all or some and an Indian told one Thiday that he saw 20 men came to phillip from Coweset side and they flock to him from Narroganset Coweeset pocasset Showomet Assowomset. . . . They gave us an Alarm by 2 guns & 1 in the morning before day and the continued warning of the drum. And the above said Indian told me that he heard that the passages between Tanton & us were guarded by Indians and that the younger sort were much set Against the English and this day one Indian left both work and wages saying he was sent for to fight with the English within 2 days. The truth is they are in a posture of war.[2]

June 19. Governor Winslow wrote Philip, asking that he and his people lay down their arms, and requested his presence in court. Philip's reply came in a letter from Samuel Gorton, Jr., writing for the sachem. Philip was ready to lay down arms and "send his people about their usual . . . employments." However, Philip insisted that reports of hostile intentions were false. Then, in clear reference to the indignities he had suffered in the crisis of 1671, the sachem requested that Winslow would "excuse and acquit them from any payment of damages, or Surrendering their arms, they not apprehending themselves blame worthy, in these late rumors." He was not presently free to attend court and hoped the English would accept his assurances, adding a grim warning that "great danger will befall them, in case they there appear with harsh threats to the Sachim."[3]

June 21. Governor Winslow wrote Massachusetts governor John Leverett, reporting the Indians' preparations for war. Since receiving John Brown's news and reports from others in Plymouth, Winslow had sent messengers to the Saconnets and Pocassets nearby, seeking confirmation of their subjection to Plymouth. Like Philip, these sachems had denied hostile intentions, but their warriors continued to parade their arms to the dismay of nearby English.[4] Fearing that Indians outside Plymouth's jurisdiction would join with Philip, Winslow asked Leverett to "secure us from trouble from those Indians that appertain to your Colony or are under your protection as we suppose the Narrigansets and Nipmouks are."[5] Leverett promised his help and immediately ordered messengers to determine whether or not the Nipmucks and Narragansetts acknowledged and would hold to their subjection to English authority. At the same time, he directed messengers to mediate with Philip, as they had in the crisis of 1671.[6]

June 24. Making their way to Swansea, on the borders of Philip's seat, Leverett's agents Captain Thomas Savage, James Oliver, and Thomas Brattle came upon two Plymouth men dead in the road, their heads nowhere to be seen.[7] Beyond, in Swansea, seven more English and one Indian youth were dead. War had begun. By its end it would sweep up all the Indian and English peoples of New England, killing thousands and displacing thousands more.

That war began when it did was directly linked to the contest of authority that had been raging among the various peoples living in or concerned with New England since the founding of New Plymouth. The immediate cause of the war, Plymouth's execution of three of Philip's men, was merely the last in a series of English affronts to Philip's authority that made him consider armed uprising preferable to continued humiliation and loss. Authority would also be the key issue in the expansion of the war beyond the local contest between the Wampanoags and Plymouth. Initial reports suggested most Indians wanted to keep their distance from the fighting. However, as the English of Massachusetts rushed to confirm the subjection of neighboring Indians, they made it clear that they viewed them not as their friends and allies but as untrustworthy subordinates. This disregard for Indian honor, friendship, and authority pushed many formerly peaceable Indians to join Philip in the war in order to defend their sovereignty.

The violence at Swansea was probably triggered by the English response to several days of Indian looting in the town.[8] There is no evidence that the killing followed any prescribed schedule. It may even have been a horrible accident, a premature leap from threatening mischief to bloodshed. But events before and after make it clear that a war *was* planned, if not at that time, then soon. The reasons why Philip seems to have decided on armed resistance to the English were a combination of worsening living conditions for Indians and English trespasses on Indian sovereignty. English abuses and humiliations had become more galling after Plymouth forced Philip to acknowledge subjection in 1671, and Plymouth's interference in the events surrounding Sassamon's murder underlined that fact.

Philip made it clear that affronts to his authority were his chief complaint when he met with a delegation from Rhode Island in the days preceding the violence at Swansea. Philip refused to meet with Plymouth leaders, but agreed to confer with John Easton and other men from Providence. To them, Philip poured out his grievances about English infringements on Indian rights and authority. First Philip addressed English undermining of Indian livelihood. The English had taken Indian land through written contracts that went beyond verbal agreements, finding or appointing pliable sachems to treat with, getting Indians drunk, and then finagling them out of their property.[9] English livestock, too, frequently trampled Indian crops: "The English Cattle and horses still increased that when they removed 30 miles from where English had anything to do, they Could not keep their corn from being spoiled, they never being used to fence."[10]

These complaints were hardly new. Philip had brought them before Plymouth and Rhode Island authorities many times, and English authorities, if not individual colonists, had tried to prevent abuses. Increase Mather insisted that Plymouth's governors had been "as careful to prevent injuries to [Philip] as unto any others; yea, they kept his Land not *from* him but *for* him."[11] Nevertheless, Indians had continued to lose land. Since 1673, Philip's own land at Mount Hope had been hemmed in by English land purchased from the sachem Totomomocke by Swansea colonists.[12] Attempts by Indians to prevent fellow Indians from selling land had met little success in the English courts that Indians increasingly resorted to, and the English would not recognize the validity of Indian justice in cases that involved the English.[13] Self-serving individuals among both English and Indians undermined the efforts of both English and Indian leaders to preserve Indian rights and maintain harmony between the two peoples. Even Philip admitted that the abuses went both ways: The "English were so eager to sell the indians liquors that most of the indians spent all in drunkenness and then ravened upon the sober indians and they did believe often did hurt the English Cattle, and their kings Could not prevent it."[14]

More serious were English infringements on Indian governance. Undoubtedly referring to the recent execution of three of his men, Philip complained that Plymouth had no business meddling in crimes between

Figure 10. Philip, sachem of the Wampanoags, as imagined by Paul Revere for the 1772 edition of Benjamin Church's *Entertaining History of King Philip's War*. Courtesy of the American Antiquarian Society.

Indians: "in what was only between their indians and not in townships that we had purchased, they would not have us prosecute." Philip and the Indians with him denied ordering the murder of Sassamon; Indians would not, they protested, fake an accidental death. However, in what sounded suspiciously close to an admission of guilt, the Wampanoag delegation proclaimed that Sassamon deserved to die. The man had tried to cheat Philip out of land by writing Philip's will in his own favor but reading it otherwise, "and . . . if Philop had done it [the murder], it was their Law so to execute whom their kings judged deserved it, that he had no Cause to hide it."[15] Either way, the incident involved only Indians. Philip had demonstrated in 1671 that he rejected local English authority over Indian matters, that only his "brother" King Charles was his equal, not his fellow English subjects. English interference in the present case "Exasperated" Philip, who claimed "that the English Authority have Nothing to do to Hang any of his Indians for killing another."[16]

Sassamon's status as a Christian Indian rankled Philip also, as yet another example of how English influence had undermined Indian authority. The royal commissioners had reported to the king that Massachusetts secured the conversion and submission of local Indians "by teaching them not to obey their heathen Sachems, and by appointing rulers amongst them."[17] Philip complained that "Christian Indians were, in every thing more mischievous, only dissemblers, and then the English made them not subject to their kings, and by their lying to wrong their kings," as he claimed Sassamon had done.[18] The Christian Indians had withdrawn their subjection to Indian rulers, placing themselves directly under English rule. Thus, while Philip's people were subject to him and he to King Charles II (through Plymouth Colony, the English would insist), the Christian Indians were subject to no Indian, but only to the English colony.[19] Philip's anger at the Christian Indians was probably also connected to his experience heeding John Eliot's 1671 advice that he present his grievances to Massachusetts; the consequence had been a humiliating diminishment of Philip's strength and authority.[20] Philip would soon feel the affront to his authority again. In August, Philip's subjects at Nantucket, most of whom were converts to Christianity, publicly disowned their subjection to Philip, disarmed themselves, and declared their subjection to King Charles.[21] In doing so, they disobeyed Philip's call to arms and appealed to England's king for the traditional right of protection given to his subjects.

Philip summarized these grievances by making a striking comparison between the Indians' status when the English first arrived in Plymouth and their present condition: "When the English first Came their king's father was as a great man and the English as a little Child. He Constrained other indians from wronging the English and gave them Corn and showed them how to plant and was free to do them any good and had let them have a 100 times more land, than now the king had for his own people."[22] Philip's people had lost not just land, but status: Once a "great man" compared to the "little Child" who had come so unprepared to the American shores, the Wampanoag sachem now found their positions sadly reversed.

Although Easton and his companions in the Rhode Island delegation openly sympathized with Philip and his people over Plymouth and Massachusetts usurping Indian land and power, they urged Philip to reconcile with Plymouth, not to settle the dispute "as dogs decided their quarrels." The Wampanoag rulers agreed war was "the worst way" but asked how else their grievances could be redressed. "Arbitration," replied the Rhode Island delegation. Philip immediately balked. Arbitration was what the Plymouth, Massachusetts, and Connecticut mediators had given him in 1671 at Taunton, where

all English agreed against them, and so by arbitration they had had much wrong, many miles square of land so taken from them for English would have English Arbitrators, and once they were persuaded to give in their arms, that thereby Jealousy might be removed and the English having their arms would not deliver them as they had promised, until they consented to pay a 100 [pounds], and now they had not so much land or money, that they were as good be killed as leave all their livelihood.[23]

In response to these justifiable fears, Easton's delegation suggested not a Massachusetts or Connecticut mediator, but someone outside of the dispute: Governor Edmund Andros of New York. For their part, the Wampanoags could choose a disinterested "indian king." This suggestion gave Philip pause: "They said they had not heard of that way and said we honestly spoke." Easton's and Philip's delegations parted on good terms, but within days hopes for an amicable settling of Philip's dispute with Plymouth would be dashed.

No reports placed Philip near Swansea when the gunfire began. He may have been home, mulling over the suggestion of arbitration, which, by Easton's report, he had received favorably. Violence has a momentum of its own, however. The Massachusetts delegation sent to treat with Philip abandoned their plan when they saw the decapitated English in their path. There was no question in their minds that war had begun. But what kind of war did they imagine it to be? Certainly not the devastating race war popularized from the nineteenth century to the present. Rather, it was a local dispute that had to be kept from spreading. Even under the high tension of war, it took weeks before the first tentative speculations emerged that what began at Swansea might end in a "general" Indian uprising.[24]

Surrounding Indians, even more than the English, saw the violence at Swansea as a small affair that did not involve them. One Nipmuck sachem, after hearing details of the hostilities from a Massachusetts messenger, dismissed it as "the war between king philep and pelimoth."[25] By August those same Nipmucks would be active allies of Philip, and the Massachusetts messengers sent on a neighborly mission of inquiry on Plymouth's behalf would be fully engaged in fighting the Indian uprising, not only in Plymouth, but within their own borders. As Massachusetts attempted to confirm Indian submission to its authority, the gulf between English and Indian interpretations of subject status yawned wide. The clash between the two peoples' perceptions led to immediate misunderstanding, suspicion and, too soon, expansion and acceleration of the war.

For the English of Massachusetts, joining forces with Plymouth was a swift decision, but not an easy one. While Massachusetts magistrates would later go to great lengths to justify the war to inhabitants of the colony and those observing the crisis from across the Atlantic, that defense would mask a deeply ambivalent attitude about entering the war at all.[26] Edward Rawson, secretary of the Massachusetts Council, wrote that when Plymouth first called for assistance, "there was not wanting objections against our then sending them relief, the justice of the war being by some then much questioned, & to each one of us unknown . . . and were we not under a considerable temptation to lie still & free ourselves (if honestly we might) from that trouble, charge, & loss that did accrue[?]"[27] Even self-defense did not, at the time, seem a justifiable reason for joining with Plymouth in the war. Massachusetts itself claimed that initially the Indians in arms offered no violence to the Bay Colony: "the enemy then declaring, [that] they had no quarrel with the massachusets, & [when] some of our people providentially fell into [their] hands after they had taken arms, upon examination, [that] they were of this colony, they let [them] freely pass & repass."[28] Why should Massachusetts colonists attack Indians who apparently had no intention to push the war across the border into the Bay Colony?

Both jurisdiction and uncertainty about the justice of the war argued against Massachusetts entering it. The colony had, however, had previous experience of the consequences of refusing aid to fellow members of the United Colonies during the Dutch-Indian war scare of 1653. This refusal nearly destroyed the union, raising questions of when and why members could refuse aid that had taken decades to answer.[29] As recently as 1668, the colonies were still debating whether to revive the United Colonies, and its meetings had not taken place regularly since 1664.[30] The consequences of this breach were serious enough that the Massachusetts Council would later tell Connecticut that any who broke the league would be in transgression of God's law. If it was a violation of God's law to refuse assistance to a member of the United Colonies—to break covenant with friends—then not only ties of alliance but divine authority required that Massachusetts help fight Plymouth's Indian enemies. Council members considered themselves "bound by coven[an]t, all the above said objections & considerations not withstanding to send in speedily for [their] relief & succor." When the call came from Plymouth, Massachusetts set aside all scruples of jurisdiction and "who was the noxious & piccant party" and answered it.[31] Connecticut was nearly as prompt as Massachusetts to lend assistance, and even Rhode Island provided transportation, medical assistance, food for soldiers, and translators for negotiations.[32]

While divine authority and the obligations of a covenant relationship demanded that the English assist each other against Philip, subjection to English authority demanded that surrounding Indians refrain from joining his cause and come to the assistance of the English if they were attacked. Within days of the outbreak of war, English messengers rushed to confirm the allegiance of surrounding Indians, both those who had freely submitted to English authority and those, like the Narragansetts, whose past treaties with the English implied they had submitted to English authority. Nine dead Englishmen at Swansea gave proof that Philip had broken his subjection to Plymouth. It was critical that other Indians be kept from joining his ranks. It was for this reason that Governor Winslow had sent messengers to neighboring sachems in the past weeks and had asked Massachusetts Governor Leverett to do the same for Indians he believed were in subjection to his colony, the Nipmucks, Narragansetts, and Pocumtucks. If Governor Leverett could confirm their subjection, they might be prevented from joining the fight against Plymouth.

On June 24, Massachusetts messengers visited eight Nipmuck towns, where thirteen Indian sachems and rulers put their hands to confirmations of their continuing submission to the Massachusetts government and their promise not to join or assist Philip.[33] On the same day Narragansett and Niantic sachems Canonicus, Quiapen, Ninigret, and Canonchet also pledged continuing fidelity to Massachusetts. Pocumtuck Indians near the Massachusetts towns on the Connecticut River pledged their continuing fidelity within days of the Swansea attacks as well.[34] If Philip had ambitious plans for the war, they did not seem to be shared by surrounding Indian leaders, who saw the war as a local dispute and hoped to avoid entanglement. Some younger Indians may have slipped away from their sachems' rule to join Philip, but for the most part Indians in authority were reluctant to break ties to the English, and their authority held initially.

The process of reconfirming submissions revealed that at least some of the Indians had taken a striking view of the implications of their subject status. Denying any interest in joining with Philip, Nipmuck sachem Thomas Wihtasuksacupin declared, "they do account themselves as English men and therefore they will not fight against themselves."[35] By virtue of their submissions to English authority, these Indians claimed English identity.[36]

The idea that political choice, rather than ethnicity, should determine identity and loyalty was one Philip challenged immediately as he worked to gain support for the war. Philip apparently used fear to recruit allies, spreading the word "that the English had a Design to cut off all the Indians round about them, and that if they did not Join together, they should lose their Lives and Lands."[37] Proof that his words had the desired effect is evident in the reply of Indians near Swansea and Rehoboth to the English who reproved them for carrying guns: "they were only on their own Defence, for they understood that the English intended to Cut them off."[38] When Philip spread the word that the English, regardless of covenants of mutual protection, intended to "cut off" all Indians, he encouraged the Indians to join the battle along ethnic lines, not political ones. English unity in supporting Plymouth may have inadvertently bolstered Philip's efforts to separate Indian and English interests. Not only did the English colonies join ranks quickly, but they broadcast their unity in a way that may have been threatening to the Indians. It may, in fact, have hastened the war.

That all New England's English colonies should have joined forces with each other so promptly does not surprise us, with our present-day focus on Indian/English antipathy. It did, however, surprise the Indians of seventeenth-century New England. When messengers from Massachusetts, accompanied by Rhode Island interpreter Roger Williams, went to Narragansett in late June to assure themselves of the sachems' loyalty, the Narragansetts demanded to know why the two colonies had joined with Plymouth and "left not Phillip and Plymmouth to fight it out." The English delegation replied "that all the Colonies were Subject to one K[ing] Charles and it was his pleasure and our Duty and Engagement for one English man to stand to the Death by Each other in all parts of the World."[39] John Easton's Rhode Island delegation had made a similar claim in their meeting with Philip the previous week, warning that "when in war against English blood was spilled that engaged all Englishmen for we were to be all under one king."[40] Having demonstrated that English identity, rather than politics, would direct their loyalties during the war, Rhode Islanders reaped the consequences. They became enemies in the eyes of the Narragansetts, who burned Providence in March 1676. When Roger Williams demanded of Indians outside the town why they had burned his home, which "hath Lodged kindly Some Thousands of You these Ten Years," they responded that the Rhode Islanders "were their Enemies Joined with Masathusets, and Plimouths, Entertaining, Assisting, [and] Guideing of them."[41] Though noncombatants, the Rhode Islanders suffered far more severely from the war than Connecticut, which supplied troops throughout the hostilities.

English claims of unity based on shared English identity and subject status must have come as something of a shock to both Philip and the Narragansetts, who had witnessed deep and wrenching divisions between the New England colonies for years. Divisions had been particularly evident since the visit of the royal commissioners a decade earlier, which had sparked heated disputes over the ownership of lands in and around Rhode Island. Given this history of contention, Rhode Island's assistance to the other English must have surprised the Indians. Long shunned by the other colonies as a haven for religious dissidents and rabble-rousers, Rhode Island had not even been permitted to join in the United Colonies. A surprising rumor repeated by Nipmuck Hassanamesitt Indians underscores the Indians' belief in the bitterness between Rhode Island and the other English colonies. The Indians claimed that the English of Rhode Island "did encourage the nariganset [to fight] with the english of Plimoth and . . . that they would supply them with ammunition this [indian knew]."[42] No other evidence supports this claim, and it may have been a conscious attempt to discourage the English and undermine alliances during the war. The fact that the Nipmucks said it, however, shows that they thought it believable. Given the colonies' past history of delay, conflict, and failure to cooperate, all observed by surrounding Indians, the rumor that Rhode Island was assisting the Indians in the war may have seemed more plausible than united action by the English colonies. Philip and surrounding sachems would not have been foolhardy to assume that disagreements would forestall military cooperation and to base their actions on that assumption.

Beyond surprise at the sudden spirit of cooperation between the previously antagonistic colonies, the Indians must have been struck by the irony that the English claimed their union was based on mutual subjection to the king, a status the Indians themselves shared. Philip had explicitly renewed the Wampanoags' subjection to the king in 1671, as had the Narragansetts at various times in the previous decades. Were not they, too, subjects of the king? If being subjects of the king were not enough to make people English, then Englishness must be linked to ethnicity. And if that were true, the Indians were not and never could be English, and Philip's threats that the English meant to "cut off all the Indians" were frightening. indeed.[43] Both the English rush to ally with other English and their suspicions and mistreatment of allied Indians would soon strengthen Philip's efforts to separate the interests of English and Indians.

It is unclear how far Philip's appeals to other Indians to join the uprising spread before the outbreak of hostilities. Many of the rulers of Nipmuck towns interviewed by Massachusetts messengers on June 24 and 25 denied any knowledge of the war. On the other hand, a man and woman from the nearby Pocumtuck Indians claimed that Philip had tried "to engage them in the War" earlier in the spring, using the traditional means of sending a gift of wampum.[44] Within weeks of the first bloodshed, Philip stepped up his efforts to draw still-uncommitted sachems into the war. Canonicus, the old sachem of the Narragansetts, freely admitted to English messengers from Connecticut that Philip had sent him two English heads.[45] By admitting the gift had been sent but denying any engagement to Philip, Canonicus was trying to avoid the incriminating implications of the exchange. Philip may, in fact, have hoped the English would learn of the gift and challenge—or attack—the Narragansetts, driving them into his camp.[46] Canonicus later sent Rhode Island's Richard Smith seven enemy heads to profess his loyalty to the English.[47] The Massachusetts Council wrote Springfield's leading resident John Pynchon that Philip had sent two English heads to the nearby Quabaug and Wabquasset Indians as well, "but they declined then to accept them having Immediately before Engaged under their hands to our English Messengers to be faithful to us."[48]

While gifts of blood and money were speeding across the region, rumors flew as well. Ninigret, a longtime enemy of Mohegan sachem Uncas, urged the English not to trust Uncas's promises of fidelity and assistance. Instead of accepting twenty of Uncas's men, Ninigret urged, the English should take forty of his, for reasons, he intoned ominously, that he would explain later.[49] John Pynchon reported the dubious news that Ninigret had sent twenty English scalps to his bitter enemies, the Mohegans, and Plymouth's Nathaniel Thomas warned Governor Winslow against trusting Uncas, having heard the "credible report" that the Mohegan sachem had sent twenty men to aid Philip with the promise "that if he sent him six English heads, all the Indians in the country were engaged against the English."[50]

These rumors reflect growing English fears of a pan-Indian uprising as much as reality.[51] It is hard to tell which of these accounts accurately reflect Philip's activities and which are the sachems' efforts either to deny their engagement to Philip or to cast suspicion on traditional enemies. Regardless of which is nearer the truth, all the sachems the English were able to speak with confirmed their submission to English authority. If, as the English soon came to fear, Philip hoped to recruit all Indians against all English, he failed initially. Young men might flock to him from surrounding sachemships, but their leaders and a significant number—perhaps most—of their followers held back.

Despite English efforts to confirm their authority over surrounding Indians, the borders of Plymouth did not long contain either Philip or the war he planned. Within a month, the local fight "between king philep and pelimoth" had jumped its bounds and escalated into a war that spanned New England, engulfing Indian and English peoples from Rhode Island to Maine. Before the end of July, Philip and his people slipped the noose English troops had cast around him in Pocasset and marched to the Nipmuck country. There combined forces of Nipmucks, Wampanoags, and, by early September, Pocumtucks launched devastating attacks against English towns in western Massachusetts, assaulting and burning Brookfield, Deerfield, and Springfield and raiding other towns with such frequency that the English who did not abandon their homes altogether were reduced to barricading themselves in fortified garrison houses, leaving the rest of their towns to ruin. Given the sachems' professions of loyalty, how do we explain this sudden defection to Philip's cause?

Philip's effective persuasion undoubtedly played a part in bringing surrounding Indians over to his side. But his claims of English intent to destroy all Indians required confirmation to be convincing, and the English provided that in abundance. In nearly every case, the defection of subject Indians to Philip was precipitated by English actions. The English behaved toward their allies and subject peoples with suspicion and hostility that betrayed the basic conflict between English and Indian understandings of subject status. As long as the Indians and English were at peace, conflicting understandings of subjection could coexist, though not without some chafing and resentment, as Massachusetts learned in the aftermath of the royal commissioners' visit to the Narragansetts. Maintaining ties continued to be preferable to breaking them. Once war erupted, however, English toleration for differing interpretations of subject status and for the Indians who held them vanished, and they began to see all Indians who resisted English definitions of authority as enemies.

On July 14, three weeks after the Nipmucks had peacefully confirmed their submission to the Massachusetts government, Massachusetts agent Ephraim Curtis met a frighteningly different reception from them. Curtis was escorting Mohegan sachem Uncas, who had been in Boston to offer his military assistance to Massachusetts, back to his home in Connecticut.[52] On the way, the company stopped at several Christian Indian villages, in one of which they heard a report that the Nipmuck Matoonas, once constable in the praying town of Pakachoog, was abroad in the woods with fifty of Philip's men. Traveling on, the company spotted a fresh Indian trail and followed it to a river, where they were hailed by Indians on the other side. The company consulted on whether to speak with the Indians. At Curtis's urging, they crossed over and were instantly surrounded by a throng of young Nipmuck men, "many Indians with their guns presented at us ready cocked and primed." The English, on horseback, pushed through the crowd, calling for the sachems. At this, more Indians crowded in, waving their guns at the English messengers and shouting "with such noise that the Air rang." Curtis urged them to lay down their guns. They demanded the same of him, adding that the English should dismount as well. Curtis refused, and the "uproar" continued, with the young warriors declaring, "they would neither believe me nor my master without he would send them two or three bushels of powder." Finally, the sachems arrived and, with the assistance of Curtis's Natick Indian guides, who were "very industrious all this time to still the tumult & to persuade the Indians," restored calm.[53]

Soon afterward, Curtis met with five sachems of the Nipmucks ("four too many to govern so small a People," William Hubbard huffed).[54] In conference with the Indian leaders, Curtis asked "the reason of their rude behavior toward us."[55] The sachems' reply revealed that Philip's propaganda had traveled fast and far. They said they had heard that the English had killed a Nipmuck man near Merrimack River "and that they had an Intent to destroy them all."[56] One week later Curtis returned to treat with the Nipmucks at more length and asked his question again: "why they were so Abusive to us the Last time. They said that black James the Constable of Chabonagonkamug had told them that the English would kill them all without any exception because they were not praying Indians."[57] Ironically, Black James's statement, perhaps intended to bolster his own status or even to coerce conversion, inadvertently confirmed Philip's claims that the English intended to cut off all the Indians. And the death of the Nipmuck man near Merrimack, whether by accident or because he was among the enemy, seemed like proof of his words. Whether the English intended to destroy all non-Christian Indians matters less than what the Nipmucks believed about English intent. They would not adhere to English subjection if it meant sacrificing their lives.[58] Even as Curtis treated with the Nipmuck sachems, the Nipmuck Matoonas was leading the attack on Mendon in Massachusetts, the first assault on an English town outside of Plymouth.

Not only English words but English actions bolstered Philip's claims, making it clear that the English saw Indian and English allies as unequal. The English effort to make a treaty with the Narragansetts is a case in point. Massachusetts and Connecticut officers descended on Narragansett territory in early July 1675 to secure sachems' promises of nonassistance to Philip and aid to the English. They were joined by a company of armed men to enforce compliance, if necessary. The chief sachems had already given assurances of their fidelity in June, but continued reports of Narragansetts among Philip's forces, Narragansetts robbing English houses nearby, and hostile Indians fleeing to the Narragansetts for refuge prompted a second expedition to secure a signed treaty. Once they had arrived in Narragansett territory, the English agents encountered a frustrating lack of cooperation. They repeatedly tried but failed to obtain meetings with the chief sachems and finally accepted the signed assurances of several lesser sachems to the treaty of July 15, 1675.[59] The treaty required that the Narragansetts turn over any hostile Indians who had sought refuge with them, provide active assistance against Philip's forces, and satisfy the English for any thefts or damages committed by Narragansetts.[60]

One of the demands the Narragansetts and other Indian peoples considered a violation of their view of subject status was that they give hostages for their fidelity. Connecticut authorities, who consistently urged a more moderate approach to Indian allies, urged the Massachusetts officers treating with the Narragansetts in July 1675 to abandon their plan to demand hostages. Governor Winthrop declared that he had "never heard of such a thing required of neutrals." He reminded the officers of the Narragansetts' long-standing amity with the English, their invaluable assistance in the Pequot War, and the fact that they were "the greatest body of all the heathen near us" and that "it were very good & necessary to have that friendship continued." It would be far better to get voluntary "engagements for continued friendship freely given than that the potentest of all our neighboring heathen should be made open, professed enemies because we may have suspicion of them or cannot be so confident or certain of their continued fidelity."[61] Massachusetts officials disregarded this advice. While the Narragansetts resented the demand for hostages, they complied, prodded by the English army encamped nearby. By July 17, twenty-one Narragansett hostages had arrived in Boston.[62] In early September, Massachusetts officials urged Pennacook sachem Wannalancet to give his son as a hostage as well, in spite of the fact that the Pennacooks had given no cause for suspicion.[63] The English also demanded hostages from the Pocumtucks around Springfield, although they had confirmed their submission early on and had in fact assisted English military forces in the area.[64] Implicit in the English demand for hostages was the belief that Indians were not, in fact, "neutrals" but were potential enemies who could not be trusted. Objecting to this assumption, the Narragansett sachems protested that they "will give not hostages, but say that they have been friends to the English."[65] As friends and allies, they expected trust and equal treatment. Agreeing to give hostages would be acknowledging that they were of a lower status, less trustworthy than Massachusetts's English allies, none of whom had been asked to give hostages for their fidelity.

For many English, the events of early August provided justification for their distrust of Indian allies. On August 2, Ephraim Curtis and Captains Thomas Hutchinson and Thomas Wheeler led a party of men to yet another meeting Curtis had arranged the previous day with the Nipmuck sachems at Quabaug. When the Indians failed to appear at the appointed rendezvous, the English decided to press on to the Indian village. On their way they crossed a narrow passage between a steep incline and tangled swamp. There a group of Quabaug Indians fired upon the English from ambush, killing eight and mortally wounding Hutchinson.[66] Curtis, guided by two Christian Indians, managed to escape and reach Brookfield with news of the attack. On hearing the report, more than eighty frightened townspeople crushed into a single garrison house, where they were forced to remain for two days while Indians burned the rest of the town, taunted the besieged English, and repeatedly tried to set the garrison itself on fire. When a large English force at last arrived on August 4, the Indians withdrew.

News of these attacks pushed the English in neighboring towns into a panic. Many abandoned their own homes for ones considered stronger. John Pynchon reported, "At this very night three families are come into my house more than were before, all our people being in fear of a sudden surprisal at home."[67] The English also seized the arms of the neighboring Pocumtucks. Suspicious that a young Indian man sheltered in Springfield had been involved in the recent attacks, town residents called for his death. Instead, Pynchon sent the man to Major Willard for security. At that, the townspeople turned their anger on Pynchon, who felt the "Lashes of men's tongues" so acutely that he begged the Massachusetts Council to release him from his military command.[68] "I wonder at such a spirit in people," Pynchon wrote, "for our most faithful Indians tell me they cannot think but that [the Indian man] was coming in from his hunting wigwam to the English out of dislike of the enemy, he having a father, mother, wife, and children at Northampton."[69]

English suspicions of the Pocumtucks were fueled by the reports of their Mohegan Indian allies, who "told the English plainly, that no good would be done, while any of that Company went along with them in Pursuit of the Enemy; for as was said, they would always give some Shout when they came near the Enemy, as if they should thereby wish them to look to themselves."[70] Others reported that local Indians had been reluctant to fight when out with English troops, "alleging they must not fight against their mothers and brothers and cousins (for *Quabaog* Indians are related unto them)."[71] Even Pynchon repeated the tale that "when [their Pocumtuck allies] went out with the English, while the enemy killed them in the front they would in the rear."[72] Whether these rumors were true or false, they served Mohegan interests, bolstering their status as the most trustworthy and favored Indian ally to the English. The English reaction to the reports tipped an already precarious situation over the edge to disaster. Needing the Pocumtucks' assistance in an expedition against hostile Indians, the English returned the arms they had seized from them, but a fresh flood of accusations followed the mission. The English again demanded surrender of Indian guns. The Pocumtucks first delayed, then fled with their arms, "whereby," William Hubbard averred, "they plainly discovered that they had secretly plotted to join with Philip's Party."[73] English forces under Captains Thomas Lathrop and Richard Beers immediately pursued the fleeing Indians. At a swamp between Hatfield and Deerfield the Indians turned and fought, killing nine English before the pursuers themselves turned back. The Indians then fled north. By war's end, they had settled in New York, from whence they would join future wars against the English of their homeland.[74]

The immediate outcry over the English bungling of this affair belies Hubbard's judgment that the Pocumtucks' flight was premeditated. John Allyn of Connecticut wrote Governor Winthrop that they were "much afflicted by the present war unhappily broke forth up the river, by the Imprudent demands of Captain Lathrop . . . for their guns, which else might possibly have been prevented."[75] Connecticut minister James Fitch wrote with similar disapproval: "After these Indians had been improved against the Common enemy the English demanded their Guns, & this was the occasion of the sad event specified."[76] Even Hubbard admitted, "Some think the English failed in Point of Prudence, not managing that Business so warily as they might, which if they had done, their Defection had been prevented."[77] Clearly, some English recognized that seizing guns from allies was foolish. It was an overt demonstration that the English considered themselves superior to the Indians, free to treat them as untrustworthy children. Indeed, the only English who had been similarly disarmed were those considered an immediate threat to government authority, such as the followers of Anne Hutchinson in the 1630s. By disarming Indians, the English proved they saw them as similarly threatening and unworthy of trust.[78] Such a demonstration of distrust could be answered in only two ways. One, the Indians could stay and risk the English turning their guns on them, or, two, they could flee and be counted traitors. But flight could as easily be self-preservation as treason. Given the harsh and uncompromising treatment of the English, it is not surprising that many Indians chose the second alternative.

Within weeks of the Pocumtucks' flight, Indians, probably including exiled Pocumtucks, made a series of devastating attacks on the English. On September 1, Indians raided Deerfield, burning many buildings and killing one man. Soon afterward, Indians attacked and killed eight Englishmen in the woods near Squakeag. Pushed to desperation by the recent attacks, the English began abandoning towns, first Squakeag, then Deerfield. Troops and carts sent to help carry off supplies became easy targets for Indian attack. Leading such a group toward Squakeag on September 3, Captain Beers and his thirty-six men marched directly into an Indian ambush. Fewer than half escaped with their lives. Two weeks later Captain Lathrop's mission to evacuate Deerfield met a similar fate, but on a grander scale. More than sixty men perished with their commander at the place afterwards known as "Bloody Brook." Scarcely a week went by from September to November without a new report of another Indian attack, ambush, or burning a Connecticut River town. In only one attack, on Hatfield on October 19, were the English able to successfully prevent the Indians from inflicting high casualties and burning the town. In the wake of the defection of their Indian allies, English towns and troops fell one after another, with little standing between them and extinction but well-studded garrison doors.

If Indian alliances with the English had been preserved, it is likely that few if any of the attacks of fall 1675 would have occurred and that any that did would have been quickly repelled. Wampanoag involvement in attacks from August to November was minimal, Philip and many of his men having moved to New York for the winter.[79] Nipmuck and Pocumtuck defection dramatically increased Philip's fighting power. The consequences of this defection make it hard not to condemn the English for their leaps to judgment. The eagerness of many in Springfield to condemn and execute their Indian visitor on little more evidence than his appearance shocks us, as does their revolving door approach to their Indian allies. Setting these rash actions in context may help us understand them, however. In early August, news had just come of the treacherous attack on Hutchinson and Wheeler's mission of peace, and of the assault on Brookfield, all carried out by Nipmucks from Quabaug, near relatives of the neighboring Pocumtucks. Mohegans fighting with the English claimed that on learning of these attacks the Pocumtucks gave eleven shouts of joy, one for each slain English colonist. Would the English hearing such news stop to question the motives of the messenger, or respond only to the fear even then raising the hair on the backs of their necks? Seizing the guns of their Indian allies must have seemed a prudent course to many English, few of whom considered the impact such an action would have on those allies. War is not a time when people feel the leisure to wait and see. English despair at their inability to respond to Indian attacks with any kind of success, grief over their devastating losses, and anxiety over when the Indians would strike next undoubtedly account for their reluctance to trust the Pocumtucks as allies and for the growing antipathy many English manifested toward all Indians, including their former neighbors.

While this context makes English action understandable, it does not follow that it was also inevitable. English refusal to trust the Indians arose from both the severe stress of war and the clash between Indian and English conceptions of authority. The English saw the Indians as subjects—subordinates—and could not allow them to act independently, as the Indians did when they chose to withdraw rather than meekly accept the seizure of their guns. Indians, believing themselves friends and allies, hence equals to the English, were alarmed at being treated like inferiors. Their flight from Springfield demonstrated their refusal to accept such a position. Under the stress of war, neither could tolerate the other's expectations. But such an outcome was not inevitable. Unlike the river towns of Massachusetts, Connecticut towns went virtually unscathed during the war. Connecticut officers arrived in Springfield the day after the Pocumtucks' flight and roundly denounced the Massachusetts colonists' actions. In spite of similar rumors of the treachery of Connecticut's Mohegan allies, the English of that colony refrained from seizing Mohegan guns or openly questioning their fidelity, and the Mohegans remained faithful throughout the war.[80] Connecticut's reluctance to enforce subjection on their Indian allies, likely influenced by their relative security from attack, helped preserve the alliance, while in Massachusetts the clash of expectations caused the breakdown of the Indian-English alliance and the prolongation and expansion of the war. Evidence suggests that the Pocumtucks were by no means united in their desire to join Philip and that they would have remained faithful to the English had not English distrust and domineering forced them to flee. Christian Indian James Quannapohit reported that the Pocumtuck sachem Sancumucha, plunged into the war in the aftermath of the attack on Springfield, was "ready to kill Philip, . . . [who] had brought all this trouble on them."[81]

The disastrous autumn of 1675 was a direct consequence of English attitudes and behavior toward both Philip and their Indian allies. English insistence on subordination and interference in Indian governance, combined with the growing strains on Indian/English relations arising from English expansion, had convinced Philip that war was his only remaining alternative to preserve Wampanoag sovereignty. English abuse of authority also drove formerly faithful Indians into combat. In their desperation to keep them from joining Philip, the English wielded their authority harshly, emphasizing the English view that Indians were inferior to them—subjects, not friends or allies. Seizing arms and demanding hostages from allies sent the same message: The Indians were not equal to the English, and they could not be trusted. The English rush to confirm the fidelity of neighboring Indians implied that they thought political choice, not ethnicity, would determine allegiance, but their distrust of their Indian allies demonstrated otherwise. Their failure to treat Indian allies equally and trust them as they did their English allies forced the Indians into war, confirming Philip's prophecy "that the English had a Design to cut off all the Indians round about them, and that if they did not Join together, they should lose their Lives and Lands."[82]

Chapter 5

The "Narragansett War"

Fall 1675 was a doleful season for the colonists of New England. The Pocumtucks' and Nipmucks' flight had been followed by a series of devastating attacks on outlying English towns—Deerfield, Squakeag, Northampton, Stony Brook, Springfield, and Hatfield, several of them more than once—and there was clear evidence both Pocumtucks and Nipmucks had taken part. The defection of these Indians heightened English anxiety about the faithfulness of the Indians remaining in friendship with them. The Narragansetts, in particular, were a source of grave apprehension, not only because they were the largest and most powerful group of Indians in the region but because of their long history of resisting English authority and insisting on a direct relationship to the king—their right as fellow subjects. Since the Pequot War the relationship between English authorities and Narragansett leaders had been a continual failure of expectations on both sides. That enduring conflict made the English less likely to trust Narragansett professions of fidelity during the war. The situation was further complicated by a simultaneous crisis of authority within the Narragansett community, with young and old pulling in opposite directions on whether to join Philip. Obligations of kinship, which crossed tribal lines, created a further conflict with authority because they clashed with English demands that the Narragansetts turn over all hostile refugees. Under threat of war, the Narragansetts' persistent refusal to recognize English authority as final and to place English demands ahead of their own needs and obligations convinced the English that the Narragansetts were a perilous threat that must be crushed. And the Narragansetts' insistence on their independence from local English authority—their direct relationship to the king—had spread, nourishing Philip's and the Wampanoags' actions as well as their own.

The English showed their long-standing distrust of the stubbornly independent Narragansetts by persistent, open suspicion of them. On October 20, Rhode Island colonist Mary Pray wrote to Captain James Oliver of Massachusetts to pour out her "grief for our friends and countrymen." More than sorrow, Mary felt anger at the continued onslaughts that in her mind were the result of trusting the Indians too much, particularly the Narragansetts. They were "false treacherous imps," Mary raged. "This false peace hath undone this country; these rogues are undoubtedly they that maintain the war westward against the English."[1] Mary Pray was one of many in the embattled regions of New England who believed the Narragansetts could not be trusted. Their abiding resistance to English assumptions of superiority had brought them into repeated conflict with the United Colonies commissioners and colony authorities. Their petitions to the king had helped bring on the royal commissioners' visit, which had deeply shaken confidence in the stability of Massachusetts government, and in the last few months they had done little to satisfy English leaders that the peace they signed in July 1675 was genuine. Rhode Island trader Richard Smith wrote, "we are in jealousy whether the naragansets will . . . prove Loyal to the English" and noted ominously, "A great body of people of them ashore [gathered] together, may do much mischief."[2] The Massachusetts Council also expressed its misgivings, writing to John Pynchon, who lived on the besieged frontier, "there is no great confidence to be put in the Narragansets so that the Lord hath his rods hanging round about us & we know not how soon he will use them upon us."[3] Wait Winthrop, who attended the July treaty with the Indians, wrote, "If we do not speedily engage the narogansets to the English they will be tempted to fall in with Philip."[4] For their part, the chief sachems of the Narragansetts revealed their disquiet over submitting to Massachusetts by refusing to show up for the treaty signing.[5] The Narragansetts' obvious reluctance to sign the treaty must have redoubled English fears.

The English gave greater heed to their suspicions than to their disastrous experience attempting to enforce the submission of their Indian neighbors in central Massachusetts. Even while the effects of Pocumtuck and Nipmuck defection were spreading like wildfire through the outlying towns, Massachusetts agents were exerting the same kinds of pressures on the Narragansetts that had driven the Pocumtucks to flight. Rumors that the Narragansetts harbored many of Philip's supporters troubled the English for months, as did claims that Narragansett warriors had joined in some attacks upon the English.[6] Both reports, if true, were evidence of flagrant violation of the Narragansett treaty of the previous summer, and the United Colonies demanded a reconfirmation of the treaty in September 1675.[7] This conference was attended by a Narragansett sachem, Canonchet (Nananawatenu), the nephew of Canonicus and son of the murdered sachem Miantonomi. Corman, Ninigret's aged counselor, accompanied Canonchet to Boston, where both learned firsthand the depth of English antipathy towards Indians. Promised safe conduct by United Colonies officials, the men arrived in Boston in the evening and apparently attracted a crowd of onlookers. Colonist Sarah Pickering, who was working in her shop, "had her eye fixed upon an old Indian that was passing by, one of them that were sent by the narrowgansit sachems to speak with the commissioners

Figure 11. The only known contemporary portrait of a seventeenth-century New England Indian. Oil on canvas by Charles Osgood, 1837–1838, from an original by an unknown artist, 1681. This portrait has usually been identified as of Ninigret II, but is now thought to be of an Indian named David who once saved the life of John Winthrop, Jr. Courtesy of the Massachusetts Historical Society.

of the colonies." As she watched, Englishman William Smith approached Corman, "& laying his hand upon him threw him with violence to the ground, so [that] his back & head came first to the ground, his heels flying up."[8] With such a harsh welcome, it is no wonder that the treaty was not signed until October 18.[9] The terms of the treaty were the same as those agreed to by lesser sachems in July 1675. They included the turnover of any hostile Indians in refuge with the Narragansetts, active assistance against Philip, and satisfaction for any Indian thefts or abuses.[10] The English gave the Narragansetts the deadline of October 28 for delivering hostile Indians.[11] These terms, which required the Narragansett sachems to ensure complete obedience of all their people, old and young, and to place loyalty to the English above kinship ties, were a recipe for disaster. Generational conflicts within Narragansett society made compliance difficult. Obligations to kin made compliance nearly impossible.

Reports of generational conflict among the Narragansetts must have heightened English fears that their tenuous alliance truly was a "false peace." Long after the July treaty was wrested from reluctant Narragansett representatives, reports filtered in to the English that Narragansetts had been engaged with Philip for months. According to these reports, large numbers of Narragansett warriors had attended the war dances Philip held in late spring of 1675. English observers reported that "for diverse weeks (if not months)" before the war began, "Canoes passed to and again (day and night between Phillip and the Nahigonsiks)."[12] Although Narragansett chief sachem Canonicus did not approve of their going, neither could he prevent it. He admitted openly that he "could not Rule the Youth and Common people, nor persuade others Chief amongst them Except his brother Miantunomu's Son Nananautunu [Canonchet]."[13] After war erupted, Canonicus repeatedly tried to demonstrate his loyalty to the English. Each time he met with an English messenger, Canonicus swore his fidelity, and he delivered enemy scalps to local Englishmen such as Richard Smith. Smith reported, "I believe that Conanicos of him self & some others inclines to peace rather than war: but have many unruly men, which cares not what become of them."[14]

Among all the Indians drawn into the war, there was clear evidence of divisions between the generations, with the younger lobbying to join forces with Philip and the older resisting. Significantly, there is also evidence that the younger Indians, particularly young sachems, saw themselves as a discrete group, with their own interests. Before the outbreak of war, in one of a seemingly endless string of offenses and counteroffenses between the Mohegans and Narragansetts, Canonchet, the son of Miantonomi, accused Uncas's son Tatuphosuit of a murder. Demanding that the English give him justice, Canonchet warned, "If there should partiality be showed to him . . . then all We Young Sachems shall have a Temptation laid before us to kill and murder etc. in the hope of the like Impunity."[15] Most striking is

Canonchet's reference to himself as part of a group: "We Young Sachems."
Englishmen, whether from hearing Canonchet and others use the phrase
or because they also recognized a distinct group, referred to "young
sachems" as well.[16]

Generational conflict was not unique to the Narragansetts. The Pocumtucks and Nipmucks, now fled to Philip, had been rent by generational
conflict over the war. Similar conflict among the Narragansetts could not
help but fill the English with suspicion and alarm. The Nipmucks who cir-
cled Ephraim Curtis, intimidating him with their guns and "uproar," were
the young men, "[who] were very Surly and Insolent, the elder ones showing some Inclination to maintain the wonted Peace."[17] Indeed, only after
the sachems arrived had Curtis been able to safely dismount and speak to
them. Young and old Pocumtucks, too, disagreed on whether to hold to
the English, in spite of their open distrust, or to flee. Even after reporting
the apparently treacherous actions of the Hadley and Springfield Indians,
William Hubbard admitted, "But the Sachems and the elder Ones of them,
seemed loath at first to engage against the English."[18] When English troops
entered the Indian fort deserted by the fleeing Pocumtucks, they found the
body of the sachem Sopus: "the chief man of those . . . Indians being
against their motions they slew him before they left their Fort."[19] There was
more than one way to overrule authority. Conflict continued even after the
Nipmucks and Pocumtucks had abandoned their English alliance. Job Kattenanit and James Quannapohit, who went as spies among the Nipmucks
in January 1675, reported that "the cheif men & old men . . . were inclinable to have peace again with the English, but the young men (who are
their principal soldiers) say we will have no peace."[20]

Philip's Wampanoags, too, had shown clear signs of the same kind of
conflict between older sachems and "giddy inconsiderate young men"
before the war had begun.[21] Plymouth agent John Brown reported to Governor Winslow that "the younger sort were much set Against the English."
Peter Nunnuit, husband of the Saconnet sachem Awashonks, noted the
same generational division. He reported to Captain Benjamin Church that
Philip had "entertained the young men from all parts of the country. . . .
He observed to him further that the young men were very eager to begin
the war and would fain have killed [Plymouth's messenger] Mr. Brown, but
Philip prevented it." When Church went to speak with Awashonks, he
"found but few of her people with her. She said they were all gone, against
her will, to the dance, and she much feared there would be a war."[22] The
same story played out among the Indians in Maine, where war erupted
within months of the Plymouth hostilities and lasted until 1678. Sent to
negotiate with sachems of the area in February 1677, Richard Waldron
reported the older Indians' claim that "none of them had any Hand in the
War, but only some of their young Men, whom they could not Rule."[23]

Both Indians and English recognized generational divisions among the

Indians, with Increase Mather lamenting that "this miserable War, hath been raised and fomented by proud and vain young men."[24] But that did not prevent the English from insisting that all Indians comply with the requirements they laid out for the sachems to prove their fidelity. If a few renegade warriors joined in a raid against the English, the English considered their sachem's treaty promises broken. This is one of the chief ironies of the war. Philip admitted openly that Indians did, in fact, "hurt the English Cattle" but denied responsibility: "Their Kings could not prevent it." English destruction of Indian land, crops, and livestock had likewise continued. English authorities could not prevent all wrongs and admitted as much. Both English and Indian leaders protested that these offenses were done by ungovernable young men, people beyond the reach of English or Indian authority. But while both sides sought to excuse behavior they could not control, they also refused to accept the excuses of their enemies. If abuses occurred, they must signify the intent of all English—all Indians.

Another barrier to the Narragansetts' total compliance with English expectations was the existence of conflicting obligations of kinship. Choosing between claims of kinship and political allegiance was not easy. New England Indians were certainly aware that their family ties with hostile Indians inspired English suspicion. When the Narragansetts declared to the English agents on June 24, 1675, that they had already sent away Wampanoags who had married into the Narragansetts, they were admitting as much.[25] But their actions throughout the war indicate that the claims of family and of the English were irreconcilable. John Easton acknowledged that the Narragansetts had indeed sheltered some refugees from the war, "but according to their barbarous rules they accounted so was no wrong or they could not help it."[26] When friends and relatives such as Weetamoo and her Pocasset people turned to the Narragansetts for refuge, they would not turn them away: "At least 100 men, women and children of wettamore the pocasett sachem squaw and her with them" had come in to the Narragansetts, Richard Smith reported in early August, adding, "she is kind to [Canonicus]: & he desires all favor for her that can be."[27] His desiring "favor" for someone the English considered an active accomplice of Philip was, of course, in direct conflict with the articles of the treaty signed by the Narragansett sachems, though not by Canonicus, on July 15, 1675. No Indians in hostility with the English were to be sheltered; all captives were to be turned over immediately to the English. But Canonicus and the other chief sachems had not actually signed that treaty. Their efforts to appease the English throughout the summer and autumn of 1675 demonstrate their desire to remain at peace, but they resisted the full extent of subjection the English demanded. They would not betray the obligations of kin.

The Indians rightly feared what would become of their relatives once they were in English hands. Those Wampanoags who surrendered to Plymouth in August 1675 were granted "mercy," that is, they were not executed. Instead, they were sold out of the country.[28] This treatment infuriated the Indians and discouraged them from surrendering. Narragansett sachem Canonchet cried, "if they yielded to the English they should be dead men or slaves, & so work for the English."[29] To their sachems' pleas for peace, Nipmuck warriors protested, "why shall we have peace to be made slaves, & either be killed or sent away to sea to Barbadoes &c. Let us live as long as we can & die like men, & not live to be enslaved."[30] Given the proven consequences of placing English demands ahead of family loyalty, it is not surprising that the Narragansetts tried to steer a course between them, agreeing to terms but delaying compliance.

The Narragansetts' desperate effort both to maintain ties with the English and protect their friends and family members is evident in an incident in late August 1675. A group of Nipmuck Wabaquassucks, still maintaining their subjection to the English even after the defection of many of their neighbors, sent a messenger to the Connecticut and Mohegan troops to tell them they had captured 100 women and children and 16 warriors "of Philip's Company." They asked the English forces to come the next morning to take the captives into custody. This clearly was meant as a demonstration of loyalty. But when the English forces arrived, they found the captives gone and the camp in disarray. The Wabaquassucks reported that in the night some Narragansetts "had Come & violently taken away not only all those Philip's Company, but several of the Wabaquassucks Indians with them." In the struggle, the Wabaquassucks had killed six of the sixteen Wampanoag male captives and displayed their lopped-off scalps and hands to prove it. A Wabaquassuck man escaping from the Narragansetts later relayed the news "that the Narragansetts had killed the remainder of the sixteen of Phillip's men with one Nipmuck Indian & marched away with the women & children."[31] This action seems to have been a desperate attempt to satisfy contrary demands. The Narragansetts killed Philip's warriors, in accordance with English demands for military assistance, but, rather than let the English take the women and children and sell them into slavery, they spirited them away.

This was only one of numerous rumors and witnessed accounts of the Narragansetts serving as a refuge for people who had been swept up in Philip's enterprise, willingly or not. Connecticut authorities such as William Leete and Governor John Winthrop acknowledged that family obligations among the Indians conflicted with the demands of English authority and argued for moderation in the English response.[32] Once Indians learned of the fate of those who surrendered to Plymouth, they turned to neutral Indians for refuge, not to the English. Many sought shelter with Ninigret, hoping he could obtain mercy for them and ensure that "such as are taken by them [captives], & those that so have surrendered themselves to mercy" did not meet the same fate, "especially sundry of them being of their blood relations & affinity, whom to surrender for slaughter or foreign captivity, doth run hard against the grain of nature." Insistence that all captives in Indian hands be delivered to the English would only further inflame the country, Connecticut's William Leete argued.[33] Leaving them under Narragansett or Pequot guard, on the other hand, and spreading the word that any Indians who assisted the English in the war could expect good pay and the right to redeem those captives at war's end, could be a great incentive to draw away forces from Philip.[34]

Unfortunately, proposals to exercise moderation never moved from paper to policy in Massachusetts or among the United Colonies commissioners. Narragansett failure to adhere to the terms of their initial, forced treaty met a swift, uncompromising response. On October 28, 1675, the deadline for Narragansett delivery of captives arrived, but the captives did not. The United Colonies commissioners met on November 2 to decide on a course of action. Connecticut's Governor Winthrop again urged moderation, and the absence of a commissioner from Connecticut delayed the decision until November 12. On that date, the combined commissioners ordered each colony to send the required number of soldiers for a thousand-man expedition to force the Narragansetts into compliance.[35] This was essentially a declaration of war. To the Narragansetts, delay was the only course when faced with the alternatives of outright war or delivering kin to "slaughter or foreign captivity." To the English, however, the delay was indisputable evidence that the Narragansetts were in league with Philip. In a letter to Richard Smith, messenger to the Narragansetts, Massachusetts magistrate Daniel Gookin complained bitterly of the Narragansetts' many excuses and their failure to deliver up Indian captives as they had promised. "We judge they do but juggle with us," Gookin wrote, "And that the womponoages & the narragansetts also are abroad (though they pretend a hunting) yet in conjunction with some of Phillips' company."[36] Despite Gookin's distrust, there is little evidence even as late as December that the Narragansetts were actively engaging with Philip, other than some renegade youngsters, and there is strong evidence that the Nipmucks and Wampanoags did not consider the Narragansetts their own allies. When James Quannapohit was examined by the Massachusetts Council on his return from spying on the enemy Indians, Thomas Danforth asked pointedly, "whether he could learn whether the Narragansetts had aided & assisted Philip & his company in the summer against the English." Quannapohit replied, "he understood by those indians [the Nipmucks, Quabaugs, Pakachoogs, etc.] that they had not, but looked on [the Narragansetts] as friends to the English all along till now & their enemies."[37] Unfortunately, largely because of the inflexibility of English demands, the long, anxious détente collapsed and the Narragansetts paid a heavy price.

On December 19, 1675, the combined forces of the United Colonies went to war against the Narragansetts. The English army numbered more than one thousand men drawn from the three members of the United Colonies: Plymouth, Massachusetts, and Connecticut. They had been preparing for the attack for nearly two months. Gathering for the final stage of their march at Richard Smith's garrison in Wickford, Rhode Island, the English secured an Indian guide and followed him to a vast, ingeniously constructed Narragansett fort within the Great Swamp near present-day South Kingston. As they marched, darkness fell, and with it the first dust of a storm that would drop nearly three feet of fresh snow before the night was over.[38] After a brief search, the advancing English found a weak point in the fort, a small gap in the palisadoes. As English soldiers pushed their way into the opening, Indians shot them down. Nevertheless, more and more poured in, eventually forcing the Indian defenders to fall back. Through the growing storm, English and Indians fired on each other, advancing and retreating as the wind whipped blinding snow into their faces and chilled their aching limbs. Finally, against the objections of Captain Benjamin Church, some English officers lobbied to burn the numerous wigwams within the fort.[39] The chief officers agreed and set the wigwams afire. Those trapped inside died in the flames, which also consumed the Indians' carefully gathered food stores. The remaining Indians abandoned the fort, and the English did not follow them. At least twenty English had died in their attempt to enter the fort, and more than two hundred were wounded. Nearly fifty more would die of wounds or exposure in the cold, hungry retreat from the battle.[40] The death toll among the Indians was far worse. Two to three hundred warriors perished in the battle, and at least as many old men, women, and children died in the shooting and conflagration within the fort. Those who survived the attack retreated into the Nipmuck country, where the local Indians had long since committed to fight with Philip, and where the Narragansetts, too, now joined the cause. If ghosts haunt the site of so much anguish, they are those of both Indians and English who perished in the fire and snow. Three hundred years after the Great Swamp Fight a Narragansett woman visited the site and reported seeing "a vision of the face of an old man with white hair and a beard looking frightening and staring at me with ice in his hair."[41]

The Narragansett-English friendship collapsed because of conflicts over authority between the English and Narragansetts and within each society. Under the stress of war, neither Indians nor English could tolerate challenges to their interpretation of their own status in relation to the other. Faced with English demands, the Narragansetts could either bear the humiliation of submission or fight. As a Rhode Island official put it, the United Colonies had "forced [the Narragansetts] to war or to such submission as it seems they could not subject themselves to."[42]

Given the reluctance of many if not most of the Narragansetts to enter the war and Rhode Island's blaming of the United Colonies for "forcing" those Indians into combat, it is a striking irony that one of the names that contemporaries attached to the wider conflict was the "Narragansett War." Conquerors generally get to name wars, and the names they choose often reflect their judgment of who was at fault.[43] By the eighteenth century, fault was clearly pinned on Philip, hence the name by which we know the war today: King Philip's War, or Metacom's War. That is not, however, what contemporaries called it.[44] For them, it was almost always some version of the "Indian War," or, significantly, the "Narragansett War." Joshua Scottow, who served as a captain in the war, referred to it exclusively as the "Narragansett War" in his 1694 history of the Bay Colony, failing to mention either Philip or the Wampanoags at all.[45] Boston merchant Richard Wharton, too, used "the Narragansetts" to represent the enemy, complaining in February 1676 that if the English had provided the supplies so desperately needed, "the Narragansets had been utterly subdued."[46] Even the order in which Plymouth messenger John Brown listed those he believed were joining with Philip reflects the position the Narragansetts occupied in English fears. Of six Indian tribes he claimed were "flock[ing]" to Philip, the "Narrogansets" appeared first.[47] Some contemporary Indians, too, stressed the Narragansett role in the war above that of the Wampanoags. Writing to Massachusetts governor Leverett, Maine Indian sachems Deogenes and Madoasquarbet complained that the English had seized their guns and taken hostages "because there was war at naragans."[48] In spite of the fact that the Narragansetts spent the first six months of the war as neutrals, the English viewed them from the start as enemies. They had never behaved towards the English as obedient subjects, and the English could not trust them.

The Narragansett view of their status was entirely different from the English view. In their eyes, by joining Philip they were resisting fellow subjects, not their sovereign.[49] Thus there is bitter irony in the fact that the English charged the Narragansetts and Wampanoags with treason for engaging in the war. In August 1676, Rhode Island officials tried a number of Indians for that offense. The court declared that the Indians had "rebelliously adhered to Indians of another Colony called Plymoth, namely, Philip chief Sachem of the Indians in that said Colony" who had murdered "many of his said majesty's good Subjects . . . against the Peace of our sovereign Lord the King." For these acts, Rhode Island condemned the convicted traitors as "Rebel[s] in the Face of the Court" and executed them.[50] The irony of Rhode Island officials charging Indians with treason for attacking "his said majesty's good Subjects" seems to have been lost on the English. For over thirty years, through such men as John Easton and Samuel Gorton, Rhode Islanders had encouraged Indian sachems to view themselves as equal subjects of the king with the same status as the highest-ranking English officials. Nevertheless, when Indians attacked, the English of every New England colony, including Rhode Island, immediately invoked the English view of authority, with English governments directly above the Indians, to charge their former subjects with treason. Despite the fact that Rhode Island had assisted the Narragansetts in submitting themselves directly to the king on several occasions, colony officials revealed in their treason trials that they had done so not to raise the Indians to equality with themselves but to bolster their own quest for authority against Massachusetts. English leaders also charged Philip, the sachem of the Wampanoags, with treason. In the narrative of the war that the Plymouth commissioners for the United Colonies drew up, they recalled Philip's uprising of 1671 and his engagements afterwards: "he then not only renewed his ancient covenant of friendship with them; but made himself and his people absolute subjects to our sovereign Lord King Charles the second; and to that his Colony of New Plymouth."[51] Because Philip was an "absolute subject" of both king and colony, his war against the English was, the commissioners believed, clearly treason.

Like the Narragansetts, Philip was charged with treason because he insisted on a direct relationship to the king and rejected English claims of superiority over him. While his views were consistent with the 1621 agreement that his father, Massasoit, had made with the English, it is likely they were also influenced by his observation of and interactions with the Narragansetts. Philip was rumored to have counseled with the Narragansetts on at least two previous occasions when the English feared an Indian uprising, and he clearly adopted the Narragansett pattern of appeal to the king. That pattern is evident in Philip's actions during the war, when he used royal authority as a refuge, as suggested by his flight to New York in the winter of 1676. Why did Philip choose New York for his winter harbor? Consider the following circumstances: before the fighting began, Philip met with messengers from Rhode Island and, by their report, favorably received the suggestion that he turn to an outside mediator, someone unlikely to side with Plymouth, as Massachusetts and Connecticut had done in 1671. That mediator was Governor Andros of New York. Easton's delegation had encouraged Philip to see royal authority as separate from, even opposed to Plymouth's and Massachusetts's authority, by telling him that the Indians "having submitted to our king to protect them others dared not otherwise to molest them." Rhode Island had stayed out of the fracas of 1671, earning Philip's praise.[52] Perhaps because of that and because of the royal commissioners' seal of approval on Rhode Island, Philip saw the colony as a more likely source of justice than the United Colonies. His willingness to meet with Rhode Islanders, at the same time he had refused to meet with Plymouth, supports this possibility.[53] Perhaps Andros, a royally appointed governor, also appeared to be someone from whom Philip could receive assistance, or at least not be attacked while he gathered his strength.

Andros's status as a royal governor probably also encouraged Philip to see New York as a place of refuge. The royal commissioners had encouraged both the Wampanoags and the Narragansetts to make their submissions directly to the king, or to them in his stead. With the commissioners gone, Andros was the best approximation: a royal governor. One poignant incident in November 1675 suggests that seeing the king as a refuge had spread well beyond the Narragansett and Wampanoag sachems. In that month a group of captive Indians was brought before the Massachusetts General Court to be examined before being sold out of the country. Among them was a Wampanoag woman who made the special request that she be sent to "King Charles his country."[54]

The strife between New York and the other English colonies would also have encouraged Philip to see Andros as a potential ally. It would be surprising if the astute Philip were not aware of New York's border disputes with Connecticut. The latest flare-up in that dispute would have gone a long way toward convincing him New York would be a safe haven. On June 28, 1675, days after war began in Plymouth, Governor Andros sent a fleet of four ships manned with soldiers to the mouth of the Connecticut River. There the ships raised the flag of the duke of York and remained in siege outside Saybrook for several days. The English of Connecticut knew what Andros wanted: in behalf of the duke of York, whose patent overlapped Connecticut's, Andros had previously demanded surrender of all lands between the Connecticut and Hudson rivers, reiterating the demand as recently as June 1675. Such surrender would mean the virtual extinguishment of Connecticut, whose major towns, including Hartford, lay on the western shores of the river. Connecticut refused to allow Andros to land, in spite of his protestation that he had come to offer help in the "troubles with the Indians."[55] Scorning this claim, Samuel Symonds of Massachusetts wrote to Connecticut's Governor Winthrop, "If a man pretends friendship, & to help against the Indians, you will consider how his actions suit with his words, and act accordingly."[56] If Philip or other Indians knew of this standoff, it could only have strengthened their sense, nurtured by the royal commissioners, that the colonies of New England were in royal disfavor and could look for no help from the king or his royal governor. Connecticut's English believed that the Indians knew about this intercolonial struggle and that it encouraged their hostilities. In a proclamation to English colonists, the Connecticut Council complained that Andros's actions "tend[ed] to the encouraging of the heathen to proceed in the effusion of Christian blood, which may be very like to be the consequences of his actions, and which we shall unavoidably lay at his door."[57]

If Philip hoped, by fleeing to the royal colony of New York, to take advantage of a political situation in which Massachusetts was in disrepute and New York was unlikely to offer it aid, he was not far wrong. Andros held a royalist disdain for his independent neighbors that may have been evident to the Indians. This attitude is reflected in an exchange between Andros and Sir John Werden, secretary to the duke of York. Werden wrote urging Andros to prevent gunpowder sales to any of the Indians at war with New England, adding snidely, "though their neighbour Christians deserve small courtesy, yet still their being Christians makes it charity not to furnish their enemies with opportunity to hurt them."[58] Royalist distaste for the United Colonies did not go so far as to support the Indians against them. Andros sent gunpowder to assist in defense—but to Rhode Island, not to any member of the United Colonies. Later, in response to Massachusetts governor Leverett's request and repeated pestering from Connecticut, Andros agreed to ask local Mohawks to refrain from aiding Philip in the war.[59] Nevertheless, Philip remained safely in Andros's colony for months. Both of the chief chroniclers of King Philip's War claimed that hundreds of Indians in hostility with the United Colonies had sought refuge in New York. Hubbard recorded an Indian captive's testimony that over 250 warriors, plus women and children, had fled to Albany and were sheltered there by Mahican Indians.[60] John Pynchon of Springfield, who was in a better position to know the Indians' movements than Hubbard, claimed that "The body of them is drawn off toward Albany, where they are harbored under Andros, his government. . . . We shall be in danger to be continually disturbed if he do harbor our enemies in his government."[61] Indians captured by the English testified that the Mohawks, traditional enemies of many of the New England Indians, had wanted to attack the Pocumtucks who fled Springfield "but the Governor of New-York secured them."[62] During much of the winter of 1675–76, New York was a haven to Philip, a place where "having submitted to our king to protect them others dared not otherwise to molest them." Although Andros had banned sales of powder, that had not kept the Indians from getting ample supplies.[63] Captured Indians testified that powder came from Albany, chiefly from Dutch merchants who ignored bans on sales to hostile Indians.[64] With or without Andros's compliance, Indians got what they needed: bullets, powder, security, a situation that must have been encouraging to Philip.

Reports of New York's material assistance to Philip's Indians were widespread enough that Massachusetts leaders sent a letter to Governor Andros protesting the sales, decried the practice in their published declaration preceding the Narragansett campaign, and preached against such abuses in sermons and accounts of the war.[65] "Men that worship Mammon, notwithstanding all prohibitions to the contrary, will expose their own and other men's lives unto danger, if they may but gain a little of this world's good," wrote Increase Mather.[66] Massachusetts's protest of the sales to Indians, though never directly accusing Andros, further undermined the colony's relationship with him. Andros sent indignant complaints to England to add to a pile of objections against Massachusetts from the Dutch United

Provinces, Mason, Gorges, and English merchants suffering from Massa-chusetts's trade violations.[67]

Undoubtedly, Andros's indignation was fueled by his knowledge that the Mohawks, with his encouragement, had delivered Philip a stunning blow in the spring of 1676, killing many of his warriors and scattering the rest.[68] Afterward, Philip and many of his followers fled back to Mount Hope in disarray. One wonders whether the Indian weakness apparent to many observers in the wake of this attack was rooted in disillusionment. Philip had been explicitly encouraged by John Easton to seek Andros's help, and his long stay in New York without any harassment must have confirmed the wisdom of taking his people there. The Mohawks' attack, encouraged by Andros, proved that English claims that Indians were equal subjects of the king did not extend far enough to cover armed resistance to the English. Politics was one thing, but in a fight, the English would stand together.

Not all Indians broke their ties with the English to join Philip and the Nar-ragansetts. For many, a troubled relationship with either the Wampanoags or the Narragansetts weighed heavier in their decision to join or resist Philip than any English offenses they may have suffered during the war. The Mohegans, who had offered their assistance to Massachusetts on July 9, 1675, remained faithful allies to the English throughout the war, as did the Pequots. Ninigret's Niantics likewise held to the English, occasionally supplying warriors, and the Christian Indians, as a whole, maintained their submission to English authority.[69] Rumors of disloyalty, which had so disas-trously unraveled English alliances with the Nipmucks, Pocumtucks, and Narragansetts, existed for the Mohegans, Pequots, and Niantics as well. No Indians were free from English suspicion during the war. Governor Wins-low, hearing of Uncas's offers of assistance, expressed his fears that the Mohegans would join Philip, and Englishman Joshua Tefft, who reportedly assisted the Narragansetts in the Great Swamp Fight, claimed that both Mohegans and Niantics purposefully fired above the heads of the Narra-gansetts during battle.[70] Connecticut's Major FitzJohn Winthrop advised wariness in dealing with Indian allies: "tis good to suspect them a little, although no great reasons appear for it." He advised meeting with neutral sachems on "open ground to prevent that treachery & surprise which they use in dark & mountainous places."[71] Abundant reports from English and Indians claimed that Indians in and around Connecticut were perfidious.[72] Nevertheless, the English continued to call on the assistance of Mohegan, Pequot, and Niantic soldiers, and those Indians continued giving good ser-vice throughout the war.

That the Mohegans, Pequots, and Niantics did not end up in flight to the enemy as did the Pocumtucks owes much to their political circumstances. Previous relations between Indians and English in the area and conflicts between the area's Indian groups made maintaining submission to English authority the best and perhaps the only choice for these Indians. The Pequots had been in subjection to the English since the Pequot War. Reduced in population and power since their defeat, they relied on the English for protection from their overbearing Mohegan supervisors as well as their enemies. For their part, the Mohegans had been bitter enemies of the Narragansetts for years, making alliance between the two peoples nearly impossible. In addition, the Mohegan sachem Uncas had consistently enjoyed English favoritism over his Narragansett enemies, placing him in a position of power among Indians in the region. By cultivating his position as chief ally of the English, Uncas ensured that he would retain that position after the war. William Hubbard suggested as much when he noted that Uncas's "own Advantage . . . hath led him to be thus true to them who have upheld him."[73]

Though bitter opponents of the Mohegans, the Niantics had their own reasons to resist Philip. Since the execution of Miantonomi, Niantic sachem Ninigret had been the Narragansetts' chief negotiator with the English, deferred to by Canonicus and the other Narragansett sachems. A strong leader, Ninigret seemed more able than his fellow sachems to persuade his warriors to obedience during the war. And Ninigret made it very clear that he would not assist Philip, who had murdered eleven of his men the previous spring.[74] But even if Philip had not so earned his enmity, the astute leader was quick to point out that loyalty to his fellow English subjects prohibited his assisting Philip: "he cannot forget the kindness that he received from King Charles, and the commissioners when they were in these parts. . . . he saith it again & again that King Charles and his commissioners have so engaged his heart, so that if the English can find that if he prove false to them he shall desire no favor from them."[75] Ninigret had used royal authority before in order to resist Massachusetts's demands for tribute, stating clearly that, as a subject of the English king, he was equal to the English magistrates and would pay tribute to no one but the king himself. Now Ninigret called on his subject status to prove his loyalty. While Ninigret wielded his royal subject status to both resist and support the English, both uses served the same end: bolstering his own authority in relation to the English colonies.

Further removed from the fighting than his Narragansett kin, Ninigret served as a refuge for many fleeing the conflict. On at least one occasion, however, he bowed to expedience and turned nine Wampanoag refugees over to the English.[76] But, as Philip had with Plymouth, Ninigret resisted English demands that he turn over his weapons as a proof of his fidelity. Ninigret insisted that he needed arms to defend himself against the neighboring Mohegans, who had killed one of his men recently. Wisely, Connecticut messenger Tobias Sanders did not insist on the surrender.[77] Allowing Ninigret to preserve his interpretation of his status in relation to the king, however contrary to Massachusetts's and Plymouth's views of that status, may have helped keep him and his Niantic people in the English camp.

Unlike the Mohegans, Pequots, and Niantics, whose homelands always remained on the outskirts of the war, Christian Indians were in the heart of the most intense conflict. When barns and houses began burning around them, the English turned their suspicions on the Indians in praying villages close at hand. But for most Christian Indians, Philip was not a viable refuge from the taunts and violence of the English. As Philip complained often and loudly, the Christian Indians had rejected their sachems' authority when they joined English-supervised praying towns. And Christian Indian interference in Philip's plans—from the "arbitration" they spearheaded, which so disastrously diminished Philip in 1671, to John Sassamon's betrayal and the testimony against Philip's men by William Ahaton and others—had confirmed Philip's antipathy for his praying kin. So ardent was his hatred that he hired several followers to find and execute Christian Indians James Speen, Andrew Pitimee, Captain Hunter, Thomas Quannapohit, and Peter Ephraim. Knowing such a fate awaited them among the enemy, who taunted them as "the English's brothers," Christian Indians cannot be faulted for choosing to remain among the English.[78] As English suspicions and hostility toward Indians grew, however, many Christian Indians would come to regret their choice, and some would flee to Philip.

By January 1676, largely as a result of their own mishandling of alliances, the English had lost the best weapon they had for fighting Philip on his own ground—their Indian allies.[79] Their own suspicions and their hostility to Indian interpretations of subject status had driven thousands of once-friendly Indians into Philip's camp. First the Nipmucks, then the Pocumtucks, and finally the Narragansetts had fled in fear of their lives and turned enemies. Many of these Indians had clearly preferred peace, but war was apparently a preferable alternative to a humiliating subjection. The "Narragansetts, Cowessits, Wompanoags, Nipmucks, and Qunticoogs" who spoke with Roger Williams after burning Providence confessed they were in "a Strange Way," but that the English had forced them to it.[80] Desperate English efforts to secure the assistance of other Indians, such as the Pennacooks, also failed.[81] Seeing how the English behaved toward neighboring Indian groups, Wannalancet's people fled, maintaining an uneasy neutrality as far from the hostilities as they could get without starving. It was a situation far worse than the English could have contemplated in the first days of war, when the majority of Indians in New England had openly declared their determination to hold to the English. The English did well to look to themselves as the cause of New England's catastrophe, to lament what might have been: "we have greatly incensed [God] to stir up . . . the Heathen in this Wilderness to be as Thorns in our Sides, who have formerly been and might still be, a Wall unto us therein."[82]

Chapter 6

A Perilous Middle Ground

August 7, 1676. Three women and three children followed a guide, John Stoolemester, through the woods toward Concord to pick berries. All were Christian Indians. They had left their camp on Cambridge Neck with the permission of Daniel Gookin, superintendent of the Indians, in whose care they had been since May, when the General Court released the Indians from exile on Deer Island. Reaching Hurtleberry Hill, the women and children began their work, pushing aside brambles to pluck the ripe berries beneath. Stoolemester watched briefly, then wandered off, gun in hand. There was a thudding, a snap of branches; a group of English soldiers on horseback emerged from a wood. They saw Stoolemester and ordered him to halt. One soldier seized Stoolemester's gun; others urged their fellows to kill the Indian. Hoping to save himself, Stoolemester tumbled out his story: he had just been released from English military service and had not yet turned in his weapon. He was there only to pick berries with a group close by. The soldiers hesitated; the man's English was good. Someone decided: they would let him go. Stoolemester lost no time leaving. The English had changed their minds before.

The soldiers rode on toward Hurtleberry Hill and soon caught sight of the women and children. They called to them, spoke briefly, exchanged bread and cheese for fruit then moved off. Four of the soldiers hung back as the rest of the group rode away. Together they retraced their route, found the women and children, chased them to the north end of the hill, and murdered them. Leaving the bodies where they fell—after first stealing their coats—the men rode home.

When Stoolemester reached his camp, he told of his rough treatment at the hands of the English soldiers. The story flew among the Indians, soon reaching Andrew Pittimee, the husband of one and brother of two of the murdered women. Alarmed, Pittimee went to Daniel Gookin in Cambridge, told him his fears for his wife and sisters, who had not yet returned, and requested two Englishmen to help him find them. After two days of frantic searching, Pittimee, fifteen or sixteen other Indians, and the two Englishmen found the bodies of their kin, "some shot through, others their brains beat out with hatchets."[1]

Pittimee and Thomas Speen, husband of another of the murdered women, quickly brought charges against the Englishmen—Daniel Hoar, Daniel Goble and Stephen Goble from Concord, and Nathaniel Wilder from Lancaster.[2] On August 11, four days after the murders, the men were confined to prison in Boston, and on September 4 they were brought to trial before the Court of Assistants.[3] The four men acknowledged that they had committed the murders. Fellow soldiers must have noted their departure from the patrol, and these soldiers were undoubtedly among the witnesses. (Only men who had met the Indians picking berries could have answered the Court's questions during the trial.)[4] While admitting to the deed, the defendants pleaded innocent on the grounds that the killings were legally warranted.[5] Daniel Hoar's father, a lawyer, later complained to the Court that "as I humbly conceive [Daniel] had not broken any law."[6] The General Court had, indeed, decreed that any Indians found more than a mile from the center of their villages or, later, from the islands where they were exiled during the war, could be legally killed. The Court's questioning reflects this decree. Examiners asked if any of the witnesses knew the names of the women and children, "to whom they belonged," and whether Indian Superintendent Gookin's permission was mentioned. Answers would establish whether the women were Christian Indians and had official license to leave their camp. Though the women and children had received the required permission, all but one witness pleaded ignorance of that fact: they did not "hear any such thing said that Major Gookin gave [the women and children] leave to . . . go for berries."[7]

These arguments did not persuade the judge or jury, which sentenced all four men to death.[8] Their conviction enraged many colonists, including William Marsh, who swore that "there was no fear of those being hanged for there were three or four hundred men that would guard them from the gallows." According to Marsh, not only did hundreds oppose the execution, but their planned resistance was known to the prisoners: "There was enough would stand to what he had said who . . . had been at prison too and spoke with those men."[9] The colonists' determination was not surprising, coming after over a year of terror, when English property and life were in constant jeopardy on the frontier and hardly safe within the largest towns. Why, they must have thought, should English soldiers suffer for simply doing their job—killing Indians? What *was* surprising was that these four Englishmen were tried, convicted, and sentenced to death by a jury of Englishmen—the only time during King Philip's War that anyone was punished for committing violence against an Indian.[10]

The women and children killed at Hurtleberry Hill were Christian Indians, members of a group in a precarious position during the war, when their ethnicity and political allegiance made them suspect to both English and Indians.[11] As acknowledged subjects of Massachusetts colonial government, these Indians had the right to buy and sell land and other property, to receive equal treatment under law, to carry firearms, and to move freely about the colony, just as their English neighbors did.[12] These rights and freedoms were frequently invoked by supporters of the Christian Indians and by colonial magistrates throughout the war. But the besieged English populace became increasingly hostile toward all Indians, Christian included, and resisted the Bay Colony's extension of legal protections and freedoms to them. As fighting escalated, the Christian Indians lost not only the trust of the English but also land and freedoms. Some lost their lives. Because of marked resistance to its effort to protect Christian Indians, the Massachusetts government was sometimes helpless to uphold Indian rights during King Philip's War, and that impotence undermined its authority with its other subjects.[13] The contest of authority in Indian and English New England—dramatically accelerated by the violence of war—appears clearly in this struggle within the Puritan community between friends of the Christian Indians and foes.

The Christian Indians' 1644 submission to the Massachusetts Bay Colony gave them the status of subjects to the English, a relationship colony leaders defined as distinct from and inferior to alliance.[14] While Indians acknowledged and, seemingly, accepted this subordination, it placed them in an awkward position in relation to the Indian sachems who also demanded their subjection. Philip, the sachem of the Wampanoags, complained to Rhode Island's John Easton in June 1675 that the Christian Indians were "not subject to their kings."[15] Indeed, John Eliot had worked to set up the kingdom of God among converted Indians, appointing leaders over groups of tens, fifties, and hundreds following the biblical model. In doing so, he hoped "Christ shall reign both in Church and Commonwealth, both in Civil and Spiritual matters." Some Christian converts assumed that this new Christian government and their political connection to the English dissolved their ties with their sachems, a situation causing enough disgruntlement among surrounding sachems that John Eliot taught his converts that they should still pay them tribute, "render[ing] unto Ceasar what is Ceasar's."[16]

Within the Christian Indian community, English religious beliefs and responsibilities introduced new sources of authority that also destabilized old allegiances. Following one of Eliot's sermons, one man asked, "'Suppose there should be one wise Indian that teacheth good things to other Indians, whether should not he be as a father or brother unto such Indians he so teacheth in the ways of God?" In other words, should an Indian religious leader be a political leader, too? Should he be a "father" rather than a "brother" to the Indians "he so teacheth in the ways of God?"[17] Waban, who became a religious and political leader in the praying town of Natick, is a noted example of this assumed connection between religious and political power. Though "no sachem," Waban's conversion and teaching among other Indians raised him to new stature and authority.[18] Such shifts in authority and their new beliefs and connections to the English drove a wedge between the Christian Indians and their unconverted kin and friends, leaving them vulnerable to attack when King Philip's War began.

From the very start of King Philip's war, Gookin had urged that Massachusetts put the Christian Indians, whose towns and forts were so strategically situated on the colony's western border, to service against Philip's warriors. When war broke out in June 1675, the English immediately recruited Christian Indian soldiers. Major Gookin, who was a magistrate as well as Indian superintendent, requested one-third of the men of the praying towns to serve under the command of Isaac Johnson.[19] This request was consistent with the magistrates' understanding of the Christian Indians' role in the colony, based on the 1644 submission "wherein subjection and mutual protection [were] engaged."[20] The recruited Indians lived in towns close to the English, often worked among them, practiced their Puritan religion, had adopted many of their cultural practices, and had cut their ties to their former Indian sachems. Of all the surrounding Indians, they must have appeared the most trustworthy to the English. In fact, five were sent out with the first English expedition into Plymouth. By the Massachusetts Council's account, these men "acquitted [them] se[lves] with all fidelity."[21] Fifty more were sent out to join Captain Henchman's company early in July. Nevertheless, by the end of July half of these soldiers were released from duty and sent home, and the other half soon followed them.

Why were these soldiers dismissed? It was apparently because of complaints by English soldiers in their companies. Although their officers said the Indians "carried themselves well," the English soldiers charged them with offenses strikingly similar to those charged to the Pocumtucks, "saying that they were cowards and skulked behind trees in fight, and that they shot over the enemies' heads."[22] And, as with the Pocumtucks, English fears over who claimed the Indians' allegiance undermined their trust. On July 8, 1675, English officers examined several Christian Indians still stationed at Swansea over the desertion of one of their number, Old Tom. The previous day Tom had left his gun at camp and traveled to Narragansett to visit his "papoose." Although the Narragansetts were still at peace with the English and Tom had gone unarmed, he was treated as a traitor on his return. At his examination, English officers inquired to whom Tom was subject. The question is significant. Although Tom was a Christian Indian, subject to the Massachusetts colony, the officers' question suggests that they suspected his previous loyalties still held. Tom reported that he had once been subject to Shawamacut near Mohegan country and then to Josias Chickatabut, sachem of the Massachusetts. Neither was a Narragansett sachem, but the fact that Tom had family ties among Indians the English had long distrusted was a cause for alarm.

More striking is the reaction of Tom's fellow Christian Indian soldiers to his desertion. When they spotted him returning, they raised a "commotion," chased him, and, when they caught him, attacked him "as if to tear him to pieces" before English soldiers rescued the man and took him into custody. Knowing that their fidelity was under suspicion, particularly at this moment, were Tom's companions trying to out-English the English? By attacking the deserter, did they hope to prove their unwavering loyalty? Their response could very well have been, like the Pocumtucks' flight, a tactic of self-preservation. When Indian witnesses caught Tom in a contradiction, he confessed and acknowledged that he "deserved death" but preferred to "die quiet," which Captain Johnson believed meant "that he might not be delivered unto the hands of the Indians," who must prove their own loyalty through their fierce justice to traitors.[23]

Tom was not the only Christian Indian to come under suspicion. On July 19, Natick Indians appealed to the Massachusetts Council for the release of "Sam: who is in prison upon suspicion of a false report he did make touching the slaughter of so many of phillip's men." By either miscounting or exaggerating to please his English officers, Sam had given a "false" report and found himself in jail, suspected, somehow, of being in league with Philip. The Natick petitioners begged that Sam's mistake would not be "accounted a capital offense."[24] Clearly, the English were taking few chances. Christian Indians were, after all, Indians, and blood could prove stronger than bond.

The Christian Indian soldiers dismissed in July 1675 were the last who would serve with English troops until April 1676, nine months later. (Gookin would point to smoldering, deserted towns and hundreds of English dead as proof of the colony's foolishness in dismissing those who best knew how to fight Philip.)[25] The release of the Indian soldiers was the first in a series of contractions of Christian Indians' freedom that continued throughout the war. In July 1675, the General Court repealed a law allowing sales to "any Indian or Indians, not in hostility with us, [of] powder, shot, lead, guns, hand guns, rapier blades, swords, &c."[26] Although Christian Indians had submitted to English law and shown their loyalty by giving warning of Philip's plans to attack, the colonists were unwilling to trust them with weapons or in warfare against other Indians.[27]

By taking away the Christian Indians' right to bear arms, the Court broke its commitment to "mutual protection," a covenant that required not only that the Indians be "governed and protected" by the English but that they give warning of impending attack and aid in the "maintenance"—or defense—of the colony.[28] The next loss of freedom came in August 1675. After the destruction of Hadley and Springfield, public outcry against Indians became so great that "the Governor and Council, against their own reason and inclination" ordered that all Christian Indians be confined to five praying towns.[29] The Indians were allowed to go no more than a mile from the center of each village on "peril of being taken as our enemies." If Indians found outside of these limits were killed by the English, "the

Council do hereby declare that they shall account themselves wholly innocent, and [the Indians'] blood . . . will be upon their own heads."[30] Popular
clamor had pushed the magistrates to act "against their own reason and
inclination." It was a pattern that would appear again and again.

In October the Massachusetts Council met to consider complaints and
petitions from anxious English settlers "for removing the praying Indians
from their plantations," which were uncomfortably close to English homes
and farms. An extended "paper" submitted in the Indians' favor reminded
the Council of the 1644 covenant of mutual protection and of the fact that
"in judgment of charity, several of them are believers."[31] This intervention
delayed action, but after the burning of an English barn in Natick and a
haystack near Wamesit—events angrily blamed on Christian Indians—the
Council ordered the Natick Indians removed to Deer Island.[32] There they
were to remain, with the warning that "it shall be lawful for the English to
destroy those that they shall find straggling off from the said places of their
confinement, unless taken off by order from authority, and under an
English guard."[33] Job Kattenanit, a Christian Indian scout caught while venturing from the island with a certificate of safe passage, was consigned to
jail by the governor "to satisfy the clamors of the people."[34] Thereafter
Deer Islanders became more cautious. When Joseph Rowlandson of Lancaster tried to recruit a scout from the island to help ransom his family
from Indian captivity, he found no takers.[35]

The magistrates found themselves having to mediate between two
camps—English settlers certain that the Christian Indians were enemies
and those like Gookin and Eliot who insisted on Indians' loyalty and
resisted attempts to revoke their rights to bear arms and move freely about
the colony. The magistrates attempted to satisfy both sides; they expressed
regret while simultaneously breaking the covenant of mutual protection,
and they ducked when colonists abused Christian Indians and ignored the
Council's orders concerning them. For instance, the Hassenamesit and
Nashobah Indians, who had voluntarily moved into garrisons within nearby
English towns, were seized and taken to Boston by Samuel Mosely, a non-
commissioned captain acting on his own. Mosely was popular with the
soldiers, as well as with the colony at large, and, "although members of
the Council were very indignant at his insolent conduct, he was not even
reprimanded."[36] When Mosely hounded the neutral Pennacooks and
burned their homes and food stores, the General Court meekly sent messengers to apologize to their sachem Wannalancet, and Mosely again
escaped reproof.[37] English soldiers under explicit government instructions
to safeguard the fields and homes of exiled Christian Indians burned and
looted them instead, with impunity.[38] While the Council disapproved of
such harassment, its inaction sent a contrary signal to people such as
Mosely, who took "great delight in that exercise."[39]

As the fighting grew more fierce, the English reluctantly called on Chris-

Figure 12. Medallion presented at the June 20, 1676, Massachusetts Council meeting to Christian Indian soldiers serving with Massachusetts forces during King Philip's War. Courtesy of the National Museum of the American Indian, Smithsonian Institution. Photo by Carmelo Guadagno.

tian Indian scouts to guide their troops. Andrew Pittimee led six men recruited from Deer Island to serve under Major Thomas Savage in March 1676.[40] From February to April, several military commanders urged the Council to again use Christian Indians to fight in the war. Finally, on April 21, the Council consented to send Captain Samuel Hunting a group of Indian soldiers. These men fought at Sudbury, and Gookin reported that their faithful service abated much of the hatred that English soldiers had shown toward Christian Indians.[41] From this point on, Christian Indians served in the war as both soldiers and scouts. While their wives and children struggled to find food and shelter on the desolate bay islands, these men were once again given guns and the freedom to use them. Under the wary eyes of the English, they were allowed a chance to prove their loyalty.

In May 1676, after repeated petitions from Christian Indians, as well as from Gookin and others, the magistrates consented to release most of the Christian Indians living in miserable conditions on the islands. The men were to "be improved in the service of the country"—used as soldiers or guides. The women and children were placed in the custody of Major Gookin, who was directed to secure them against the enemy on Cambridge Neck.[42] From this site, on the Charles River near Watertown, Andrew Pittimee's and Thomas Speen's wives and children had set out to pick berries in the waning days of King Philip's War and never returned.

The murderers—Wilder, Hoar, and the brace of Gobles—all came from outlying towns, the areas most battered by King Philip's War. Every town on the western perimeter of Concord, including Lancaster, Groton, Marlborough, Sudbury, Framingham, and Chelmsford, had suffered raids, attacks, or burnings, and three had been abandoned.[43] Wilder came from Lancaster, but after Indians attacked that town for the second time in February 1676, he moved his wife and infant son to Sudbury, near Concord. The other three men lived in Concord, which escaped direct attack.[44] As a result, refugees from neighboring towns flooded into Concord, living reminders of the destruction that could fall without warning.

Most of the men of Concord, including the Gobles, had volunteered or been impressed for military service, leaving women, children, and old men to defend the town. These remaining townspeople had the charge of the town jail, where several captured Indian women were held. When these women escaped in June 1676, Constable John Heywood warned the governor that the escape "may produce a great deal of damage to us [that] are resident in Concord; because we are afraid they [the Indians] are acquainted with the Condition of our town, & what quantity of men we have gone out. . . . we are in daily fear . . . they will make an assault on our town."[45] Constable Heywood sent his anxious appeal in June 1676, when Indian power was waning and the war was shifting back to the region where it had begun—Plymouth Colony. Four months earlier, in late February 1676, the situation had been much more desperate: Philip was clearly winning the war. Dozens of towns had been attacked, Lancaster only two weeks before. Some of its citizens may already have been straggling into Concord.

In that month of February, Daniel Hoar was living with his parents in Concord. He was twenty-six years old and unmarried. The only son of lawyer John Hoar, he was also the only child still at home. His father's personal history provides a striking backdrop to Daniel's later actions. Nineteenth-century histories of Concord and of King Philip's War describe the elder Hoar as an eminent citizen of Concord and the region. He was the town's first lawyer and a member of a prominent and well-connected family. His father, Charles, had been a sheriff in Gloucester, England. His brother Leonard served as president of Harvard College, and his sisters Margery and Joanna married a minister and a colonel. Hoar was the "celebrated" deliverer of Mary Rowlandson, the man who "had won to himself the entire confidence of the Indians, by deserving it."[46] Historical focus on these aspects of his personal history masks a less laudatory side: John Hoar spent much of his life in bitter contention with the authorities of Massachusetts Bay. He sued neighbors—including Concord's minister Peter Bulkeley—over land disputes, and he was censured by local and general courts for failing to attend worship services, for "profane speech," and for accusing the magistrates of illegal proceedings, this last offense culminating in permanent disbarment and a sizeable fine.[47] By 1676, Hoar was well known to the magistrates, and not admired.

John Hoar's troubled history with authority would by itself have marginalized his family in Concord, but his next action cemented that position. In November 1675, the General Court, having sent the Natick Indians to Deer Island, decided to pull the Nashobah Indians into Concord, "under such care and conduct as might quiet and compose men's minds in those parts."[48] A committee composed of Major Gookin, Major Simon Willard, and John Eliot rode to Concord to inspect the Indians and find someone to supervise their care, but "there was no man in Concord appeared willing to take care of and secure those Indians, but Mr. John Hoare, whom the Council accepted and approved."[49]

As someone on the margins of society himself, Hoar may have found it easy to sympathize with the Christian Indians, who were outside both Indian and English society. He soon found his decision sorely tested. Hoar had to feed the 58 Nashobahs who pitched their wigwams on his land, and costs piled higher as he began building a "house suitable for to teach them in manufactures."[50] Like John Eliot, Hoar apparently had plans to "civilize" the Indians under his protection by teaching them English skills. Unfortunately, his undertaking came at a time when his neighbors were more than usually unsympathetic to such a project. In a letter to the General Court in January 1675, Hoar asked, "what way I shall be directed to save the Indians from the insolency of the English, being daily threatened to be shot, and one snapped at thrice at my own door by a Lankastsheir soldier."[51]

The presence of Indians soon became intolerable to the townspeople of Concord. On February 21, 1676, some residents quietly sent for Captain Samuel Mosely, a man well known for his hatred of Indians.[52] Mosely and his company of volunteers arrived on the Sabbath, while the townspeople were at worship. He entered the church, waited until the minister had finished speaking, and then addressed the congregation. Stating that he had heard that the "heathen" living in Concord were a "trouble and disquiet," he offered to remove them. Taking a few voiced encouragements as general assent, Mosely and his men marched to Hoar's house, followed by most of the congregation—"a hundred or two of the people, men, women, and children at his heels." Hoar, absent once again from public worship, was home when Mosely beat on his door. He permitted Mosely to enter and count the Nashobahs, all of whom were present. Mosely said he would provide a corporal and soldiers to guard the Nashobahs, but Hoar claimed that they were secure with him. Nevertheless, Mosely left an armed mob outside the Hoar home that night, where they amused themselves with abusive speeches to the Indians. The next morning Mosely returned and stated his intention to take the Nashobahs to Boston. Hoar insisted that Mosely produce an order from the Council for their removal. Mosely growled that his commission to "kill and destroy the enemy" was order enough. Hoar in turn protested that the Nashobahs were not enemies but friends and legally under his care. Tiring of the discussion, Mosely ordered his men to break down the door and seize the Indians. In the process, Mosely's crew made off with the Nashobahs' clothing, dishes, shoes, and other belongings, despite their captain's command to the contrary.[53] Backed by Concord's massed citizenry, Mosely carried the Nashobahs away to Boston, and from there to Deer Island.[54]

Young Daniel Hoar must have witnessed this episode. He and his family had been granted freedom "from public charges, and also from public service during [their] employ" with the Indians.[55] Freedom from impressment apparently continued throughout the war; neither Daniel's name nor his father's appears in the enrollment lists. Daniel, then, shared in the labor of building a workhouse for the Nashobahs and providing for their needs. He shared in any privations that ensued from their unreimbursed expenses. Most significantly, he became a target of public animosity against his family's Indian wards. Watching from the door as two hundred of his neighbors confronted his father, Daniel might have felt any number of strong emotions: anger at their injustice, an impulse to defend his father and the Indians he had shared a home with for three months, or, perhaps, shame and hostility toward the Indians he was forced to serve and bitterness toward the man who had caused him to be identified with the public menace. Six months later at Hurtleberry Hill, Daniel in one murderous act both embraced and rejected his father's ambiguous example.

Hostile Indians' distrust of Christian Indians because of their rejection of Indian authority intertwined with English distrust of Christian Indians, who they suspected had not fully abandoned that loyalty, leaving Christian Indians vulnerable to attack from both sides. Hostile Indians heightened English anxiety by planting rumors about the Christian Indians. Philip's captive Mary Rowlandson unwittingly passed along such a rumor when she reported that "those seven that were killed at Lancaster the summer before upon a sabbath day . . . were slain and mangled by one-eyed John and Marlborough's praying Indians" (the Okonokhamesitts).[56] One of Philip's Indians, David, had pinned the Lancaster attack on the Okonokhamesitts after he was captured by the English.[57] These Christian Indians later argued that David had accused them in revenge for their delivering his brother and son to the English, an exchange that plainly shows the tensions between the Indians on either side of the conflict.[58]

The English were quick to believe tales of Christian Indian perfidy, and firings of English barns and haystacks soon became pretexts for English violence against the praying towns. Suspicions that the Natick Indians were

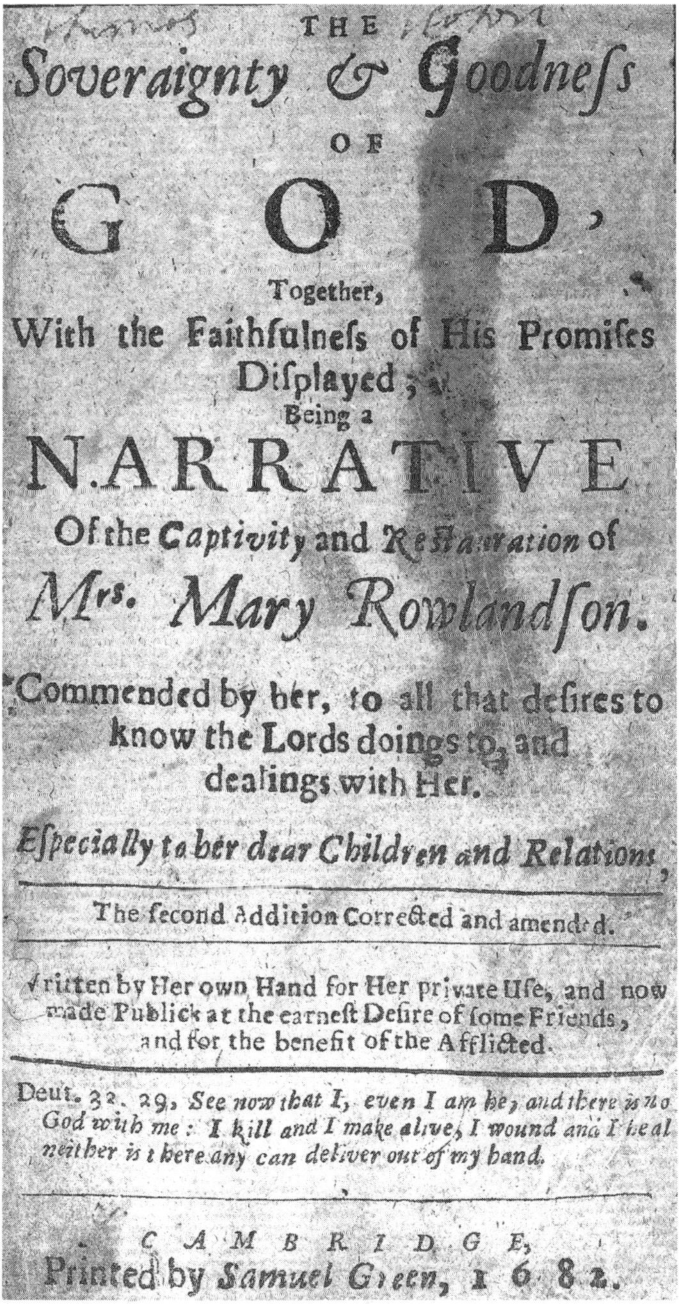

THE
Soveraignty & Goodneſs
OF
GOD,
Together,
With the Faithfulneſs of His Promiſes
Diſplayed;
Being a
NARRATIVE
Of the *Captivity* and *Reſtauration* of
Mrs. Mary Rowlandſon.

Commended by her, to all that deſires to
know the Lords doings to, and
dealings with Her.

Eſpecially to her dear Children and Relations.

The ſecond Addition Correſted and amended.

Written by Her own Hand for Her private Uſe, and now
made Publick at the earneſt Deſire of ſome Friends,
and for the benefit of the Afflicted.

Deut. 32. 29, *See now that I, even I am he, and there is no
God with me : I kill and I make alive, I wound and I heal
neither is there any can deliver out of my hand.*

CAMBRIDGE,
Printed by *Samuel Green,* 1 6 8 2.

Figure 13. Title page of Mary Rowlandson's *The Soveraignty and Goodness of God.*
Courtesy of the Trustees of the Boston Public Library/Rare Books Department.

involved in a barn burning led the General Court to confine them to Deer Island in October 1675. Two weeks earlier a haystack was burned near Wamesit, and the General Court reported that "the Waymesitt Indians are vehemently suspected to be actors & consentors to the burning."[59] A troop of forty Englishmen was sent to escort thirty-three Wamesit men to Charlestown for trial.[60] The Court found one of them guilty and ordered that he and two Indians "pretending themselves to belong to Uncas" be sold.[61] Months later at his execution in Boston, one of Philip's men, Nathaniel, confessed that he had himself fired the haystack in order "to begin a difference between the English and praying Indians living at Wamesit, that so they might either be secured by the English [sent to Deer Island] or necessitated to fly to the enemy."[62]

If Nathaniel's confession was true, his design worked very well. As the Wamesits marched home from their trial, they passed through Woburn, where some local troops were drilling. Although the English had been ordered to put down their weapons until the Wamesits had passed through, one soldier defied the order and shot and killed a young Indian man.[63] Weeks later, on November 15, 1675, a group of Chelmsford soldiers, still incensed over the destruction of the barn and haystack, went to Wamesit and called the Indians to come out of their wigwams. Two of the soldiers then fired into the group, wounding five women and children and killing one twelve-year-old boy, a grandson of Tahattawan, sachem of Concord.[64] In panic, the Wamesits fled their village, leaving even their food stores behind. The Council sent messengers to persuade them to return, but the Wamesits refused:

We cannot come home again, we go towards the French, we go where Wannalansit is . . . For when there was any harm done in Chelmsford, they laid it to us and said we did it, but we know ourselves we never did harm to the English, but we go away peaceably and quietly . . . As for the Island, we say there is no safety for us, because many English be not good, and may be they come to us and kill us, as in the other case. We are not sorry for what we leave behind, but we are sorry the English have driven us from our praying to God and from our teacher. We did begin to understand a little of praying to God.[65]

The Christian Indians had become as unwilling to trust the English as the English were to trust them.

Philip's rumor mill undermined Christian Indian faith in the English as well. In November 1675, hostile Indians captured three praying towns, Hassanamesit, Chabanakongkomun, and Magunkaquog, containing 50 men and 150 women and children.[66] Job Kattenanit and James Speen escaped and took news of the capture to Daniel Gookin, who reported that the Indians had persuaded the Christian Indians to join them, first by threatening to kill them and destroy their corn and then by declaring that "if we do not kill you, and . . . you go to the English again, they will . . . force you all to some Island as the Natick Indians are, where you will be in danger to be starved with cold and hunger, and most probably in the end be all sent out of the country for slaves."[67] As in their tales to the English of Christian Indian depredations, the attackers targeted their Christian captives' worst fears. Only weeks before, the Naticks, departing for Deer Island, had told John Eliot that they were "in fear that they should never return more to their habitations, but be transported out of the country."[68] For some Naticks, fear of enslavement was so great that, rather than risk it in exile, they followed the course of many before them and sought refuge among the Narragansetts. The Narragansetts told English messenger Richard Smith of the praying Indians' fears, and he reported them back to Daniel Gookin. Exasperated rather than sympathetic, Gookin directed Smith to find the rumormongers and bring them to Massachusetts to answer for their "flight & false reports." The Natick Indians had been taken to Deer Island for "their & our security," Gookin insisted. No harm was meant to them.[69]

Despite Gookin's protests, Indian fears of enslavement were not unreasonable. A good number of Indians taken prisoner in the war, including some Christian Indians, had already been sold as slaves.[70] Hundreds more would be sold into slavery by the end of 1676.[71] Narragansett seizures of captured Indians earlier in the war seem to have come in direct response to reports that the English would sell the captives out of the country. In the same letter in which he directed Richard Smith to apprehend tale-telling Indians, Daniel Gookin complained that Narragansetts were strongly suspected of being involved in the seizure of the Christian Indians at Hassanamesit. If this were true, might the Narragansetts have been seeking to save friends and kin from slavery, as they had done before? Might their act even have been urged by the Naticks among them who feared their friends and family would be sold?

Many English saw the departure of the Hassanamesits, Chabanakongkomuns, and Magunkaquogs as further proof that Christian Indians were in league with the enemy. While some may indeed have transferred their allegiance in the face of English suspicion and persecution, many others remained loyal to the English throughout the war. Indian scouts such as Pittimee and Speen, called from their confinement on Deer Island to serve the English, are proof of this firm, if unmerited, loyalty.

Rumors flying on both sides undermined the Christian Indians' identity as faithful members of the colony and left them with no safe haven. Philip's Indians had risen against all English, and for them that included the Christian Indians—"the English's brothers."[72] For their part, many of the English saw all Indians, including Christian ones, as enemies. Those English who championed the cause of the Christian Indians soon had identity problems of their own: John Hoar, who took on the task of providing for the Nashobahs, found an angry mob breaking down his front door.

Daniel Gookin and Thomas Danforth, magistrates who consistently defended the Christian Indians, received death threats, and Gookin was told in court that he "ought rather to be confined among his Indians, than to sit on the Bench."[73] So quickly did defending an enemy make an enemy of the defender.

What kind of people felt enough hostility for Christian Indians to defy the colony laws and leaders protecting them? Court records tell us that those brought to trial for such offences were most often men who had served or were currently serving in the English military, some in the same companies.[74] These men had particular reason to hate Indians and their champions. They had been the targets of Indians shooting from cover; they had seen their villages burnt to the ground. Many of them had lost family, friends, houses, or barns in the war. Daniel Goble's father-in-law John Brewer lost his home to Indians burning Sudbury,[75] as did Nathaniel Wilder and his family, who fled destroyed Lancaster. It is not hard to imagine how the stresses of guerrilla warfare could make men hate the enemy, anyone suspected of sympathizing with them, and anyone who looked or sounded like them. Future wars would nurture the same feelings, leading Americans to persecute German-Americans and to confine Japanese-Americans to their own Deer Islands in the desert.

But soldiers were not the only ones who demonstrated their hatred for Indians, Christian or otherwise. At least twice during the war, women were the aggressors. When Christian Indian Job Kattenanit brought his children, a woman who cared for them, and an Indian preacher and his family into the garrison at Marlborough, he explained that he had recaptured them from Philip, who had seized them in an attack on the Christian Indian town of Hassanamesit earlier. We can imagine the alarm with which the English settlers viewed these refugees. Marlborough was on the edge of English settlement, in constant peril of attack. The Christian Okonokhamesitts, who had lived among them, had confessed treason to Captain Mosely before he took them away to Boston. And now here were more "Christian" Indians coming straight from enemy territory. Who knew but that they would burn them in their beds? At nightfall a group of Marlborough residents, "especially women," confronted the Indians in their quarters and "did so threaten, and taunt at" them that both women and two of the children fled into the night, leaving a nursing baby behind.[76]

The English blurring of the distinction between Christian Indian allies and Indian enemies makes a second incident worth noting. In 1677, Indians all along the Massachusetts-Maine coast seized settlers' boats in a large-scale, coordinated effort to reignite the war. One boat belonged to several English fishermen, who managed to overpower their captors and sail back to Marblehead. A large crowd gathered on shore as they disembarked, eager for news of the uprising. Seeing two Indians with the Englishmen, they angrily demanded to know why they had not been killed. The fisher-men explained that they were taking them to the General Court in Boston for the two-pound-per-head reward.[77] At this, the women in the crowd pushed forward, "drove [the fishermen] by force" from the Indians, "and laid violent hands upon the captives. . . . Then with stones, billets of wood, and what else they might, they made an end of these Indians." Later, the Englishmen found the Indians "with their heads off and gone, and their flesh in a manner pulled from their bones."[78]

Animosity toward Indians touched both men and women, then—both those fighting in and those threatened by the war. It was also present at all levels of society. Many of Samuel Mosely's pirates and privateers were aptly described by Gookin as the "vulgar."[79] Yet Daniel and Stephen Goble, Dan-iel Hoar, and Nathaniel Wilder, who massacred the women and children at Concord, were middling people according to their own and their parents' probate records.[80] Those from higher ranks of society, such as Mary Row-landson, also expressed hostility toward Christian Indians, and contempo-rary chronicler Nathaniel Saltonstall listed men "of Note" among forty gathered in an anti-Christian-Indian lynch mob.[81] The size of this mob, and of a later mob of forty thwarted by the Council in a plot to kill the Deer Islanders, suggests that anti-Indian animosity had spread to a significant portion of the English population.[82]

While neither gender nor class were barriers to anti-Indian violence, it does seem to have had a generational slant. The four Concord murderers were young men ranging in age from about twenty to thirty-five. All four were born in New England, as was the notorious Samuel Mosely.[83] The few who championed the Christian Indians, on the other hand, seem to have been elite members of the first generation, notably magistrates Thomas Danforth and Daniel Gookin, minister John Eliot, military leaders Thomas Savage, Samuel Hunting, and Daniel Henchman, and the lawyer John Hoar.[84]

Between the first and second generations in New England lay a sea of conflict. The older colonists feared that their children, born and raised in New England, would grow as wild as their environment. Cotton Mather would raise the specter of "creolean degeneracy," and ministers and mag-istrates rained harangues on youth from pulpit and court bench.[85] None of these young New Englanders had chosen to be part of the city on a hill, but they were held up as evidence of its decline. Sermons told them that their parents had been heroic people who sacrificed all to found a godly com-monwealth: they, on the other hand, were corrupt, faithless, a grief to their forebears. Even the blame for King Philip's War was laid at their feet. Increase Mather declared that God had no need to send war as a prod to repentance "until the Body of the first Generation was removed, and another Generation risen up which hath not so pursued, as ought to have been, the blessed design of their Fathers, in following the Lord into this

Wilderness."[86] When the magistrates passed a series of laws in November 1675 to reform the sins that had caused God to send the Indians upon them, they specifically targeted youth, appending "especially amongst the younger sort" to nearly every declaration, just as they had in the years following the royal commissioners' visit.[87]

Coming of age in the second half of the seventeenth century held other burdens as well. Children of the first settlers faced a world of sharply limited horizons. While most sons did not set their sights beyond their fathers' positions, moving to Massachusetts could alter even those expectations. Children of the well-educated leaders of the colony chafed under their narrow opportunities for schooling. Joseph Eliot, the son of minister John Eliot, begged an acquaintance visiting in London to send him some recent treatises, "out of a pity to a famished man."[88] As early as 1655, John Winthrop's son John Winthrop, Jr., was told by an English acquaintance that "where you are is too scanty a stage for you to remain too long."[89] And, despite his eminence in New England society, Richard Mather's son Increase recorded in his diary his longing to go to England, where "I might have opportunity to follow my studies and increase learning."[90] Daniel Hoar's father John was a well-educated man who worked as a lawyer in Massachusetts. In England, Daniel might have followed in his footsteps; he was, after all, an only son. Like most of his generation in the English colonies, however, Daniel grew up to hew logs and scrabble a living from the ground. His petition to the General Court for relief from his murder sentence contains the phrase "Your poor Petitioner hath lived as a servant unto his father all his days and hath gathered nothing for him self save his clothes."[91] The contrast with his father must have been galling.

In a colony where farming was the occupation of virtually everyone, the rising generation faced more limited prospects as well.[92] Even the first generation had quickly outstripped the farming and grazing capacity of the lands immediately around Boston. Their children had to accept smaller land parcels or move farther out. And the farther out they moved, the more they were exposed to attack by Indians—the same Indians, to their mind, that the Council was trying to protect.

Tensions between young and old exist in every age, but they must have been intensified by the radically different experiences of those born in England who chose to start again and those born in New England, with its dramatically contracted educational, cultural, and occupational range. The young of Massachusetts Bay formed their ways of viewing the world within an American, not a European, framework. The principles that motivated their parents to try to maintain a godly, equitable government may have been less compelling for many of the second generation, who bore the brunt of pre-war tensions and wartime destruction. It is not surprising that under these conditions some rejected the constraints placed on them by their elders and lashed out against any Indians they could find, including

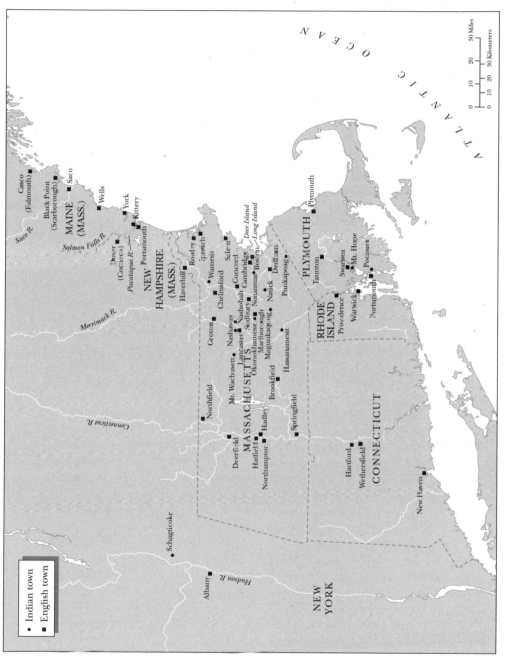

Map 3. Indian and English settlements during King Philip's War.

those under government protection. The limits of the magistrates' ability to hold these people in check is evident in the Christian Indian cases that came before the court during the war.

Throughout the war, the magistrates of the Bay Colony fought an uphill battle against popular opinion to protect Christian Indians' rights. But was their diligence, like Gookin's, a result of faith in Christian Indian loyalty or simply a reflection of commitment to English law? The trial of the Okonokhamesitts is a good place to begin answering this question. Okonokhamesitt was one of the fourteen praying towns in Massachusetts Bay until the General Court reduced the number to five. Unlike the others, it was set within an English town—Marlborough. Forty Okonokhamesitts had built themselves a fort there, and the government had furnished them with arms and ammunition for their defense. The first Indian attack on Lancaster was on August 22, 1675. When Indian rumor pinned the blame on the Okonokhamesitts, the English commander of the garrison at Marlborough confiscated the Indians' guns and ammunition, an "act entirely without the sanction of the Court," and the townspeople sent for Captain Mosely, who was patrolling nearby.[93] Mosely marched fifteen of the Indians to Boston for trial, where most were found innocent. Two, Joseph Spoonhaut and David ("Phillips man," who had accused the rest), were found guilty and sold out of the country. One, "Litle John Indian," was "proved to be a murderer of the English in the war [and] was Condemned to be hanged & was executed accordingly."[94]

The Court records are brief and straightforward, leaving the impression that the trial was also, but the recollections of some of those who observed the trial belie this impression. Nathaniel Saltonstall reported that the Okonokhamesitts were "at several Times tried for their Lives, and condemned to die." Not one trial, then, but several. And not verdicts of innocence, but guilt. How did the Okonokhamesitts escape death? Saltonstall tells us, with clear disdain, that Daniel Gookin made the difference. He was "daily troubling [the Court] with his Impertinences and multitudinous Speeches," actions for which "the Commonality were so enraged against Mr. Elliot, and Captain Guggins [Gookin] especially, that Captain Guggins said on the Bench, that he was afraid to go along the Streets; the Answer was made, you may thank yourself."[95] The magistrates, too, appear to have been annoyed at Gookin's persistence, but not enough to ignore his and Eliot's pleadings. They did retry the Okonokhamesitts and found almost all innocent.

The English colonists were quick to show their displeasure. On the night following the last trial, "about forty Men (some of Note)" gathered at Captain James Oliver's house. Apparently thinking Oliver would sympathize with their intent to carry out vigilante justice, they urged him to lead them in breaking into the prison to hang the condemned Indian held there. Instead of joining them, Oliver took his cane to the two or three men closest to him "and cudgelled them stoutly, and so for that Time dismissed the Company."[96] He then hurried to his neighbor, Edward Tyng, a magistrate, and together they reported the night's doings to the governor. The Court met the next day and issued an order for "the Execution of that one (notorious above the rest) Indian, and accordingly he was led by a Rope about his Neck to the Gallows."[97]

It is unclear from the record whether the original convictions of the Okonokhamesitts reflected the opinion of the jury alone or of the magistrates as well, but the record does indicate Court disapproval of Gookin's ardent defense of the Christian Indians. Regardless of their personal feelings about Christian Indians, however, the magistrates were committed to equal protection under law for all God's children. Their irritation at Gookin did not stop them from retrying the Okonokhamesitts when presented with sufficient reason for doing so. Just as clearly, the principal concern for the magistrates was not to champion the Indians but to uphold the law. Even with staunch defenders Gookin and Eliot present, the magistrates could scarcely resist the popular tide against the Christian Indians, and they did appease the populace by speeding up the hanging of one Indian man. The hanging was on the magistrates' terms, however. A disorderly lynching could not be allowed; an orderly execution could.

Several other General Court actions also illustrate their commitment to uphold the law, which protected both English and Indian. On two occasions, confronted with demands to restrict Christian Indian freedoms, the Court consulted past legal proceedings for guidance. In the first, the Court acknowledged the 1644 agreement with Christian Indians for mutual protection and subjection. The second occurred in February 1676, when the Court met to deal with petitions concerning the Christian Indians on Deer Island: "Some would have them all destroyed; others, sent out of the country; but some there were of more moderation, alleging that those Indians and their ancestors had a covenant with the English about thirty years since, wherein mutual protection and subjection was agreed." The Court searched the record for the agreement, which included the Indians' expressed desire to be taught the Puritan religion. The review "abate[d] the clamors of many men against these Indians," and the magistrates left them alone for the time.[98]

The magistrates' searching of the legal records demonstrates their desire to follow legal precedent, which had extended full protection to Christian Indians. Popular opinion, however, repeatedly hampered their ability to enforce the law. Two cases of violence against Indians came before the Court between the Okonokhamesitt and Concord trials. The first was the trial of a soldier named Knight, who had shot the Wamesit man returning from Charlestown. Knight was tried for the offense, "but was acquitted by the jury, much contrary to the mind of the bench . . . The jury was sent out again and again by the judges, who were much unsatisfied with the jury's proceedings; but yet the jury did not see cause to alter their mind, and so the fellow was cleared."[99]

The following month two men, George Robbins and John Largin, were tried in the Court of Assistants for killing and wounding Christian Indians at Wamesit, an event that was probably triggered by popular displeasure at the Court's failure to convict the Wamesits of barn burning.[100] Again, the men were cleared by the jury, "to the great grief and trouble generally of magistracy and ministry and other wise and godly men."[101] The magistrates, unable to sway the jury, bound the men over to the next county court in April to be tried for a lesser offense, "their wounding of the Indians under the Court's protection."[102]

In both cases, the will of the magistrates and the will of the jurymen were directly at odds. Sending the jury out again and again, an action that bordered on browbeating, failed completely. The witnesses, too, refused to cooperate. They were, in Gookin's evocative words, "mealy-mouthed" in their testimony about what seemed to be quite clear: raising a gun and shooting in defiance of orders.[103] It is also significant that the Englishmen in the Wamesit case, displeased with the magistrates' decision about the barn burning, took the law into their own hands. Indeed, their reaction is similar to that of the Marblehead women who complained that, "if the Indians had been carried to Boston, that would have been the end of it, and they would have been set at liberty."[104] To prevent what seemed a miscarriage of justice to them, they killed the Indians themselves.

The magistrates were clearly troubled by the actions of the juries in these cases, but this does not mean they were, like Daniel Gookin, champions of the Christian Indians. Their initial willingness to speedily condemn the Okonokhamesitts argues against that conclusion, as does their irritation at Gookin and their overlooking of Moseley's misconduct throughout the war. Rather, their distress was caused by their inability to maintain obedience to law and by the overt challenge to their authority.

Not only did the populace flout laws and resist magistrates, but they showed active hostility toward leaders who were most supportive of the Christian Indians. John Eliot and Thomas Danforth came under public criticism and on one occasion may have suffered an attempt on their lives. Daniel Gookin endured all that and more. In nearly every incident of violence against the Christian Indians, Gookin played an energetic role in seeking justice. His reward was to become "a Byword both among Men and Boys," and some began to question his loyalty.[105] In November, when Job Kattenanit was put in prison despite carrying Gookin's written authorization for his journey, rumors circulated that Gookin had sent the Indian man out to "give intelligence to the enemy."[106] In February 1676, copies of an anonymous notice began appearing around Boston: "Reader thou art desired not to suppress this paper, but to promote its design, which is to certify (those traitors to their King and Country) Guggins and Danford, that some generous spirits have vowed their destruction, as Christians we warn them to prepare for death, for though they will deservedly die; yet we wish the health of their souls."[107]

On March 7, Richard Scott of Charlestown was brought to court for reviling Gookin. Scott had served under Mosely in December 1675, as well as under four other commanders during the course of the war, once fighting in the same unit as Daniel Goble.[108] At the Court of Assistants, Elizabeth Belcher testified that on February 28 Scott said in her presence that Gookin was an "Irish Dog, [that] was never faithful to his country, the son of a whore, a Bitch, a Rogue, god confound him, & god rot his soul, saying if I could meet him alone, I would Pistol him, I wish my knife . . . were in his heart." Scott also claimed that he and several others had planned violence against Gookin, but "some English Dog discovered it."[109] Found guilty for having "vilely reproached" Gookin, Scott was sentenced to pay him one hundred pounds, and another fifty to the country.[110] This fine, equivalent to an average householder's entire estate, suggests the magistrates' desperate need to put down the lawlessness that Indian hatred had aroused and restore order and peace. Scott went to prison on March 11, bound over to further trial for his "scandalous expressions."[111]

Threats such as those Richard Scott uttered were very nearly realized on May 7, 1676. On that day, Gookin, Eliot, Thomas Danforth, William Stoughton, Captain Daniel Henchman, and Eliot's two cousins set out in a small boat to inspect the Indians exiled on Long Island in Massachusetts Bay. A larger vessel approached them, traveling a parallel course. Suddenly, it "turn[ed] hard upon [them]." Recalling the incident, Eliot added, "whether willfully or by negligence, god, he knoweth." The smaller boat was hit, submerging the stern and plunging the five older men into the icy water. Before the craft could sink, the rigging snagged on the larger boat and held fast. Eliot's cousins clambered up the tangle of crafts, then helped the half-drowned men aboard. Later all made a safe return to the mainland. Said Eliot, "Some thanked God, and some wished we had been drowned." This and other incidents left Eliot deeply discouraged. Although he had faithfully recorded his ministry to the Indians in a series of letters to England, Eliot found the war years too painful to commit to paper: "the history [of the war] I cannot, I may not relate, the prophane Indians prove a sharp rod to the English, & the English prove a very sharp rod to the praying Indians."[112] Although a few of the magistrates thought that Gookin and his fellows had brought their problems on themselves, their investigation and prosecution of both this case and that of Richard Scott demonstrate that they would not ignore outright threats to their authority. The people, however, had their own card to play. On May 3 the yearly election of the magistrates took place, and for the only year in his thirty-four years on the Massachusetts Council, Gookin was voted out of office.[113]

Figure 14. John Eliot (1604–1690). Oil portrait, artist unknown. Courtesy of the Henry E. Huntington Library and Art Gallery, San Marino, California.

On Thursday, September 26, 1676, Daniel Goble, lying "upon bed clothes," was carted to a square in Boston where a rough gallows had been erected. His month in prison had weakened him or exposed him to some pestilence that prevented him from standing.[114] His nephew Stephen had been hanged the previous Thursday, but Daniel was not alone at the gallows. Three Indians also awaited execution, all guilty of "imbru[ing] their hands in English blood": One-ey'd John, Maliompe the sagamore of Quapaug, and Old Jethro.[115] The last was the father of Peter Jethro, a Christian Indian whose loyalty to the English proved stronger than blood. He turned the old man in himself, an act Increase Mather found so shocking that he dubbed Peter "that abominable Indian."[116] Across a gulf of over three hundred years, we wonder if this joint execution was a demonstration of equal justice or simple expediency. One by one the offenders were led to the noose and fell to their deaths. No one rose to protest the execution of the lone Englishman on the gallows: William Marsh, who had sworn to prevent the hangings, had been safely in prison for over a week.[117]

Two weeks later Nathaniel Wilder and Daniel Hoar presented a petition to the General Court. In it, the men humbly "acknowledg[ed] the justice" of the Court in sentencing them to death but begged for mercy. Wilder and Hoar's petition is a study in submissiveness They wrote as "deplorable petitioners" and insisted that, unlike many other men, they "were known to be industrious in [their] own callings, and not given to the now reigning sin of murmuring against our Rulers and disturbing the peace of the Lord's people." They asserted that they had not themselves committed the murders, but, "being left of God [were] now drawn in by the chief Actor to see and conceal that wickedness." They acknowledged the "wildness of [their] natures in following the multitude in many of the sins of the time" and had found "sufficient reason to abhor [them]selves." Finally, they gave themselves up to the mercy of God and those "whom God hath placed over this Israel, that we may improve them in witnessing against the evils of our days, and preserving the order we are placed under (to be prized & prayed for of all good men)." Having wished fervently for the preservation of that order that had brought them to their present impasse, they came "with ropes about [their] necks in hope of Mercy" and signed themselves "The miserable and condemned."[118] One wonders if Daniel's lawyer father John Hoar, who had experience with offending authority—and seeking to placate it—had a hand in penning this petition.

The General Court pardoned Wilder and Hoar on October 11, 1676, on condition that each pay a fine of ten pounds, half toward costs of court and half to Andrew Pittimee and Swagon (probably Thomas Speen).[119] The hanging of two Englishmen for these murders was not enough to satisfy the demand for justice of those men whose wives, sisters, and children had died at Hurtleberry Hill. Minister Edmund Browne of Sudbury recorded two frightening disturbances in the colony just months after the Goble executions. In the first, Swagon aimed his gun at a colonist, "saying that he must kill an English man," and was only prevented from carrying out his threat by his companion, Maugust, who pushed the muzzle of his gun aside. In the second, Andrew Pittimee's brother snatched the bridle of an English colonist's horse and declared that he, too, needed to kill an Englishman.

He also failed, driven off by a truncheon-wielding colonist coming upon the scene. Both incidents apparently took place within or close to English towns, suggesting that the Indians' grief and desire for revenge had pushed them beyond any concern for the consequences of their actions.[120]

Why did Wilder and Hoar escape hanging? Their petition, combined with other evidence from the trial, offers some clues. The two men claimed that a "chief Actor" had done the deed; they themselves had merely observed and promised to keep silent. Indeed, court records do seem to set Wilder apart. A note appended to his sentence declares: "[The jury] find a special verdict. If being present & seeing the fact done & consenting it be murder then we find him guilty according to Indictment if not not guilty."[121] The wording of Daniel Goble's sentence, on the other hand, and his failure to seek a pardon hint at court recognition of his role as "chief Actor." Otherwise nearly identical to the other sentences, it contains an additional closing phrase, "the Lord be merciful to thy soul." While the jury recognized that Wilder's and, by association on the petition, Hoar's involvement was not as damning as Daniel Goble's, that did not stop them from delivering a death sentence. To gain time, the men resorted to petition. The magistrates and deputies, unlike the jury, were swayed by the men's pleas of innocence, and probably also by their self-abasement, and freed them.

While these clues hint at reasons for Wilder's and Hoar's reprieve, a more interesting question is why, after repeated failures to bring English killers of Indians to justice throughout the war, did Stephen and Daniel Goble hang? One answer may be simple timing. Men acquitted for earlier murders of Christian Indians had the support of a populace and jury still under direct threat of Indian attack. Worse, until after the winter of 1676 it was quite clear that Philip had the upper hand. In contrast, when the Gobles, Hoar, and Wilder killed six Christian Indians in August, the fighting had shifted to Plymouth Colony, leaving most Bay Colony towns unmolested. In addition, since their service in the Sudbury fight and other battles beginning in April, Christian Indians had been in constant use, as both soldiers and scouts. Gookin and others testified that their faithful service had done much to abate hostility among English settlers.[122] The brutal murder of defenseless Christian women and children may have finally stung the conscience of a people no longer in immediate danger.

For Indians such as Swagon and Pittimee, this justice was too little, too late. Although the courts were finally able to secure a conviction for violence against Indians, the fear and suspicion of Indians remaining in the colony would persist long after the fighting ended, threatening both their personal safety and their livelihood. Wartime hardships sped the Indians' diminishment within English society, a process fueled not only by population loss from the war, but by the heightened antipathy of the English, many of whom were convinced that all Indians were enemies undeserving of trust.[123] Under threat of Indian attack, English opposed to the extension of legal protections to Christian Indians flouted the laws that should have protected these subjects of the Bay Colony. Caught between the English and the hostile Indians, the Christian Indians suffered deeply from the civil unrest that accompanied the conflict. Violence against Christian Indians had a further effect, undermining the authority of colony leaders who proved impotent to restrain English violence at their own doorsteps. Such resistance would grow as the war continued, weakening the colony for its larger struggle to preserve its authority within the English Atlantic world.

Chapter 7

Massachusetts's Authority Undermined

A disheartened Daniel Gookin reported the results of the latest Middlesex County impressment order to the Massachusetts magistrates on February 5, 1676: "It is humbly tendered & presented to Consider of the defects: almost the half of so small a number failing." Ten county towns had been sent orders to impress a total of twenty men. Eight of those impressed failed to appear. The worst offenders were the outlying towns of Concord, Sudbury, and Woburn, each of whom had sent returns for two men, none of whom showed up for service. "It was so the last press," Gookin lamented, "& nothing done." In consequence, "the country service is disappointed & Authority slighted: & the obedience to your orders discouraged."[1]

Resistance to impressment was only one manifestation of widespread resistance to colony authority that wracked Massachusetts throughout King Philip's War. War created competing demands on residents of the Bay Colony. The calls of family, conscience, and self-preservation battled with the demands of the authorities waging war, forcing people to make choices that put them at odds with their leaders. Ironically, while the English had insisted that their Indian allies manifest their loyalty through total compliance with English demands, they were unable to maintain obedience among their own people. English colonists ignored government orders or acted outside them when they disagreed with colony magistrates. Resistance made the magistrates reluctant to exercise their authority, and this undermined their ability to govern during the war or to bring it to a swift and successful close.

One of the most urgent demands the English faced in the war was the same one that faced them in peace: manpower. Finding a sufficient supply of men for soldiering and scouting duty was hampered by nearly constant resistance to impressment. Impressments began immediately after fighting began and soon became familiar enough to become the stuff of practical jokes. In January 1676, Thomas Moore complained to the Council against Nathaniel Fox. A thoroughly besotted Fox had pounded repeatedly on Moore's neighbor's door the previous Wednesday demanding tobacco. When Moore tried to stop him, Fox turned on Moore, swore at him, then, "with scurrilous words said that I impress you In his majesty's name clap-

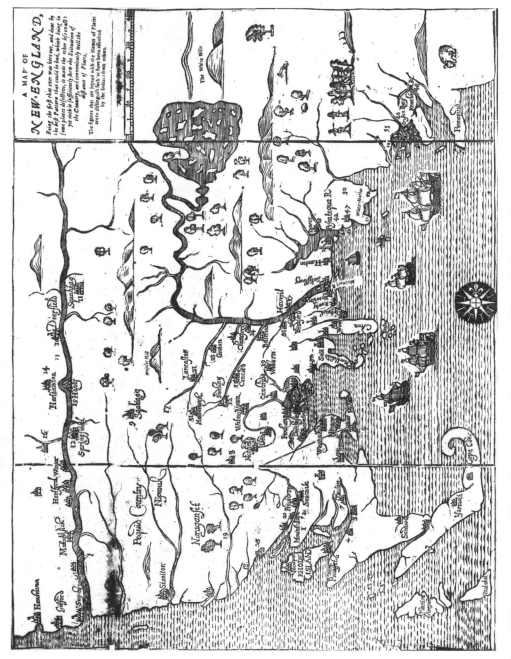

Figure 15. John Foster's map of Massachusetts, engraved to accompany William Hubbard's 1677 account of King Philip's War, and depicting both Indian and English settlements at the time of the conflict. Courtesy of the American Antiquarian Society.

ping me by the shoulder said with an oath that . . . if I would not he would not go."[2]

Fox's familiarity with both the form and urgency of impressment argues that he had had personal experience with a constable demanding his service, as had hundreds of men in Massachusetts Bay Colony. Each town committee of militia was sent an order for the number of men it was to impress. On receiving the order, it directed the town constable to round up the required number of men and give them a time to appear, sometimes within half an hour. After the men had arrived, the constable made out a return for the Massachusetts Council, listing who had appeared and the state of their arms, ammunition, and supplies. Impressment orders exempted none but the "unfit" from service, though magistrates, deputies, and ministers, when they did serve, did so by appointment or voluntarily. Both poor and rich men appear in the military records for the colony, church members and nonmembers, residents of the colony and passers-by. Many did not want to serve, and resistance to and resentment of the burden of service nourished divisions already present in the colony.

Many suspected that the colony was unequal in its impressments, that some families bore great burdens while others were unfairly spared. Sudbury minister Edmund Browne, writing on behalf of a widowed neighbor whose servant had been impressed "almost in every impressing unless he then were out in service," begged for his release. "The poor fellow hath nothing to fight for," Browne argued, while some families had several "able persons . . . of which not any one hath been impressed." He then added ominously, "I hear . . . it may stir up evil blood or Spirits if impresses continue."[3] Edward Randolph, who arrived to renew the royal investigation into Massachusetts's charter abuses in the summer of 1676, had heard similar complaints from his sources in the colony. He reported that more than 600 English, including twelve captains, had died in the war, "most of them brave and stout persons and of loyal principles, whilst the church members had liberty to stay at home and not hazard their persons in the wilderness."[4]

While this claim is vastly exaggerated, typical of Randolph's vitriolic reports about Massachusetts, at least one form of privilege—wealth—did play a role in men's ability to avoid combat service. Men of means, a status signalled by the title "Mr.," could legally hire someone else in their place, as "Mr Broune of Salem" did when he arranged for Zachary Curtis to serve.[5] Virtually all hired substitutes appear in impressments for Boston and Salem, centers of commerce and homes of a number of wealthy merchants. Of eleven men impressed in Boston on December 1, three obtained substitutes.[6] Within days, two more impressments in Boston yielded twelve and ten men each. One in the first group was a substitute for another man; two in the second were hired in the places of Mr. James Lord and Mr. William Harrison.[7] But not all who hired substitutes were wealthy. In a petition to the Council, William Griffith explained that he had hired a substitute because his "great family" was completely dependent on his labor. By January 1676 that substitute, Samuel Johnson, had been garrisoned at Black Point, Maine, for over three months, and Griffiths could no longer support him: "To pay Six or Seven pounds out of his Labor besides the maintenance of his family, (in this time when trading is so dead) will be Exceeding difficult," Griffiths pleaded, and he asked that Johnson be released from service. The Council granted his petition.[8]

Just as not all who hired substitutes were wealthy, the wealthy were not entirely protected. The "Mr Eliakim Hutchinson" listed on an impressment return in December 1675 hired no substitute, whether because he was willing to serve or was short of funds.[9] Running short of funds was certainly a possibility, particularly because hiring a substitute did not prevent a man from being impressed again. On May 1, 1676, Abraham Briggs sent the Council a petition from prison, asking to be released and dismissed from his impressment. Being "much occupied" with business for friends in England, he had hired a substitute when he was first impressed, only to be impressed shortly afterward. Before he had time to appeal his case he had been seized by an officer in the Boston militia and thrown into jail.[10]

It is hard to say whether poorer men were unfairly targeted, as some alleged. What is clear is that there was a significant undercurrent of resentment in the colony, enough to make the Council cautious about granting release from service. In March 1676, Lieutenant John Wayman of Woburn petitioned the Council for the release of his son. For reason, Wayman gave his own past service at Mount Hope and Narragansett, where he was wounded and where his oldest son was killed. In addition, he had had a servant in the country's service at Hadley all winter. The Council granted the request, but at the same time reminded the committee of militia of "complaint made by some against the committees of militia in several towns" and urged them to take care to "carry it impartially in the execution of warrants for Impressing soldiers."[11] Wayman was an officer and a man with servants. He could, as the Council warned, easily be charged with receiving favoritism. But he was also a man who had given service personally, who was supporting a servant in the field, and who had, most significantly, already lost one son. Such arguments carried weight with the Council.

Whether because men thought impressment unfairly targeted them, or for other reasons, such as the need for their presence in their own towns or families, resistance to impressment became a problem immediately after the outbreak of war and grew epidemically. Setting a pattern that would be followed by hundreds, rank and file, was Captain Richard, who "shamefully refused the employment" of commanding the June 24, 1675, expedition to Mount Hope to investigate Plymouth's report of an uprising.[12] By the following February, some towns would report that nearly 50 percent of impressed men likewise refused to appear for service.[13]

Resistance to impressment occurred in Plymouth as well as Massachusetts, though there is no evidence that it began earlier than the grueling aftermath of the Great Swamp Fight in January 1676. The Plymouth General Court's order for recruiting men in preparation for December's Narragansett campaign suggests, on the contrary, that the colony had enjoyed a high degree of voluntarism.[14] Connecticut's Council of War noted some minor resistance to fortifying garrisons but neither mentioned nor issued orders against resistance to impressment.[15] Why the difference between Connecticut and the other two New England colonies, particularly Massachusetts? Men resisting service rarely spelled out their reasons, but it is likely that Connecticut's relative freedom from assault throughout the war decreased potential soldiers' fears for their families and homes. It is also possible that Connecticut's relative political stability played a role. Unlike Plymouth, which never obtained a legal charter, and Massachusetts, which had faced the threat of having its charter revoked almost since the colony's inception, Connecticut had obtained a charter from the king in 1663 and had avoided any affront to the royal commissioners in 1664–65. This firm political footing may have bolstered the colony's authority among its citizens, who could not, like discontents in Massachusetts, hope a "change in government" would save them from the consequences of their disobedience.[16]

Preparations for the Narragansett expedition, which required over 1,000 men, give clear evidence of the rampant resistance to Massachusetts's war effort. The returns coming in showed a woeful lack of cooperation and preparation. The constable of Charlestown reported that he had impressed the required 21 men, but 6 failed to appear as ordered, "who do absent themselves, skulking from place to place, avoiding this Immediate press, which the Militia humbl[y] request the Honored Council by their Authority to address, if they see cause."[17] Constables from Roxbury, Boston, Ipswich, Salem, and Cambridge Village also reported no-shows, whom they had searched for but could not find.[18] In response to these difficulties, the Council issued an order on November 18, 1675, allowing courts to impose fines, punishment, or imprisonment at their discretion. Any men withholding arms or service from the colony were to be accounted enemies.[19] Such measures were necessary because, despite General Court orders requiring military companies to be ready to march at a moment's notice, there had been "a great neglect herein." By December 28, as the Council issued orders for another expedition, it found it necessary to include a second order against avoiding impressment because of "several Inhabitants in the several Towns to Avoid the Impress in their Towns & discharge their Duty sculking from one Town to Another thereby disappointing the service of the Country."[20]

Regulations notwithstanding, an increasing number of men failed to report for service after being impressed. In addition to the men failing to appear for service in Middlesex county, reports of delinquent soldiers flooded in from Suffolk and Essex counties, and on May 3, 1676, the General Court responded with yet another order against resisting impressment.[21] This time the Court ordered a fine of four pounds for foot soldiers and six pounds for troopers who failed to appear when impressed for service. If that neglect was accompanied "with refractoriness, reflection or contempt upon authority" the prescribed penalty was death "or some other grievous punishment."[22]

The Court's coda on contempt of authority was clearly directed at such men as Samuel Leach, who both refused to obey the constable's order impressing him for service and rejected the alternative—providing material support for the wife of a man impressed in his place. Calling the constable issuing the order a "wopper-jawed rogue," Leach declared "that he would take no notice of the warrant for it was more than the Selectmen or the Major General or the Governor himself or the King could do and said he would get some copies of their warrant, to set up in other towns to publish what fools they were."[23] Leach, who was seen "recling" and had to be set upon his horse to ride home, was undoubtedly drunk during this public repudiation of every level of authority, from the constable to the king. Nevertheless, the town's inability or unwillingness to enforce his service undermined its own and the colony's credibility. Despite threats to punish such outbursts with death or something "grievous," and despite numerous court appearances of impress evaders and deserters, there is no evidence that anything but fines was used to punish those who resisted Massachusetts's efforts to wage war. The colony had great need for money and had quite enough corpses, but empty threats did nothing to bolster colonial authority.

An important aspect of all this resistance to impressment is that it did not come just from isolated individuals who took to their heels (or hid their horses) when the country's service beckoned. A significant amount of the resistance came from colony "fathers." Town officers refused to send their militias, parents resisted the impressments of their sons, and masters withheld their servants from military duty. Normally, a servant's master would be expected to fit him out for war, supplying the clothing, arms, and ammunition required as well as losing the time the master had paid for. Many masters could not spare the arms and ammunition because of their own need, or their arms had already been impressed for someone else. Some, stung once by the loss of their valuable labor, simply washed their hands of continuing responsibility. Corporal Jonathan Remington of Middlesex County wrote in his return that one servant, John Salter, "saith his master will give him his time & so will take no care to fit him out: How he will be provided I know not."[24] In February the Council heard testimony from John Walley over a Mr. Cornish's refusal to allow his servant to be impressed.[25] The "Mr." before Cornish's name suggests that he was a man of means and status, who may have been able to spare his servant more readily than other men. He apparently did not think so. Neither did Mr. John White, Senior, of Muddy River, who, despite having been spared service to a greater degree than any man in the town, refused to allow his servant Michaell Ramsford to serve when impressed. White went to the governor to secure Ramsford's release from the impress but could not get it. Nevertheless, he insisted, "my man shall not come." Ramsford himself, "to prevent any damage to his own person," gathered arms and ammunition and set off for the prescribed meeting place, "but was met by his master who took him home along with him."[26] These men seemed to hold their own authority as heads of the family—"fathers" to their servants—above that of town and colonial fathers. Judging by their actions, they believed the hierarchical ladder stopped with them.

Parents, too, resisted the impressment of their sons. Major General Daniel Denison's return of impressed men listed three "very lusty young men" impressed for service who "by the artifice of their parents absconded for the present though their parents have been required to bring them forth or be ready themselves to march."[27] All but one of Lynn's contingent of men for the same expedition failed to appear. When called to account for this, the Lynn committee of militia revealed that each missing soldier had a father intervening in his behalf. Joseph Browne's father Thomas gave the excuse that "his son thought the Constable was in Jest." Nathaniel Newhall's father John reported his son was "not fit to Travel." This was news to the militia committee, particularly since Nathaniel reported himself "willing to go." Nathaniell Engeles's father Robert also claimed his son was unfit, volunteered to go in his place, then failed to appear. Thomas Brewer's father Crispus appeared and pleaded his son's insufficiency, once again news the militia committee had "never heard of before." All four were fined the required four pounds for nonappearance.[28] With family fathers denying or getting around the demands of colony fathers, it is no wonder that Gookin lamented the slighting of authority and feared its consequences.

Not just persons, but whole towns resisted the impressment, out of desperation in the embattled backcountry and exhaustion elsewhere.[29] As early as September 1675, Woburn's militia committee petitioned the Council for no more impressments, arguing that all its men were needed to defend the town.[30] Concord sent a similar petition along with its impressment return in December. Reminding the Council that a company of Christian Indians had been placed in the town who needed care and guarding, the militia committee asked "that favor may be shown us in the release of some (if it may be) of the persons above mentioned."[31] On February 26, 1676, the officers of a Boston troop petitioned the Council that no more men be impressed from among them. They had just received a warrant for ten more men and had learned that men had also been impressed from the outlying towns of Milton, Braintree, Hingham, and Weymouth. They doubted than any impressed men would appear from those towns, "who are now infested with the enemy, as sad experience demonstrates we fear their necessitous condition will enforce their non appearance, which may be offensive to Authority."[32]

These cases cover many forms of resistance: fleeing from personal service, resisting the service of sons or servants under family authority, and holding back service for the ostensible benefit of towns and neighbors. The extent and nature of the resistance indicate widespread pitting of levels of authority against each other, as well as a strong sense that individual or local needs could trump those of the colony at large. Undoubtedly, the need for male labor and defense played a large role in the widespread resistance, as it had in petitions for release from service throughout the war.[33] Particularly in the backcountry, fear of Indian attacks had limited the amount of crops that could be planted and harvested. And given the deaths of nearly ten percent of the men of the colony over the course of the fighting, labor was even more scarce than it had been previously. Four pounds may have seemed a small price to pay to keep sons and servants alive and at home.[34]

Minimal penalties may provide one explanation for widespread resistance to impressment. The government's repeated issuing of laws against resisting impressment makes it clear that it was a prime concern, but through three succeeding reiterations of the law, monetary penalties remained relatively low. Even by May 1676, penalties for resisting impressment were only 4 and 6 pounds for foot soldiers and troopers respectively. While these were not inconsequential fines, they pale in comparison to those of 50 to 150 pounds laid on men guilty of abuse of authority in the same period.[35]

There is also little evidence that the penalties for resistance to military authority for soldiers already in service were enforced. Death was the penalty for a number of offenses, including desertion. Although many cases of desertion appear in accounts and records of King Philip's War, no records mention either a sentence or enforcement of the stipulated punishment.[36] The mildest level of resistance to military authority, quarreling with a superior officer, was punishable by cashiering, or being dismissed from office. Resistance to a superior officer's correction was punishable by death.[37] In May 1676 the General Court reviewed the case of Salem's Captain George Corwin, who had given "very evil example in his demeanor & carriage to Capt. Hinchmen [Henchman], which tended to disturb & mutinize the soldiers under his command." Mindful of "clamors against the government of partial proceedings, that poorer men are punished for lesser offences, when richer men escape wth greater," the Court tried and found Corwin

guilty of contempt of authority and a poor example "tending to disorder
good discipline." Corwin's crime seems a good deal more serious than simply quarreling with his superior officer. Nevertheless, his punishment was
discharge from his command and a fine of 100 pounds. While this appears
to be an adequate assertion of the colony's authority, looking four months
ahead in the record belies that judgment. On September 6, 1676, on the
petition of the militias of Salem and Lynn, the General Court restored Corwin to office as a captain over them. Three years later, on Corwin's petition,
the Court remitted his entire fine.[38]

What can account for the colony's repeated failure to quell significant
resistance to military authority that threatened the ability to wage war? The
colony's weakened authority during the war is key. When men refused to
serve or showed contempt for officers, they were rejecting the colony's
authority over them, frequently with contemptuous speeches such as Quakers had offered to ministers and magistrates in past years. The parallel
between the two is significant. Massachusetts governor John Endicott had
argued that the colony's punishments and, more seriously, their executions
of Quakers had not been for religious but for political reasons. Quakers
had rejected the colony's authority and actively incited others to do likewise. As "open enemies to government itself . . . malignant assiduous promoters of doctrines directly tending to subvert both our churches & state,"
the Quakers were guilty of sedition, threatening the very life of the colony:
"Had they not been restrained, so far as appeared, there was too much
cause to fear that we ourselves must quickly have died, or worse."[39] Those
who resisted impressment likewise rejected—and frequently reviled—
authority and by their disobedience encouraged others to do likewise.
Their disobedience was, if less offensive than the Quakers', probably more
threatening to the colony, which desperately needed men to fight and
maintain garrisons. Yet the magistrates did very little to combat the problem. One important reason for their failure may be that, notwithstanding
the capital penalties included in their legislation, the magistrates could not
politically afford to execute any more of their citizens.

By May 1676, the arrival of a new royal agent was only one month away,
a fact that the Massachusetts magistrates, who kept close tabs on the royal
government's colonial proceedings, undoubtedly knew. Renewed discussions of Massachusetts's right to jurisdiction over New Hampshire and
Maine had been ongoing in the Committee on Plantations for over a year,
and Governor Leverett had sent a letter responding to that and other disputes in September 1675. In a letter to an English secretary of state in April
1676, the Massachusetts Council begged the royal official "to believe that
the loss & sufferings that hath befallen us hath not proceeded from want
of care in the government, or conduct & courage in the commander or
soldiers."[40] Executions would seem like proof otherwise, a point Benjamin
Batten underlined by enclosing a list of military crimes the colony consid-

ered capital in a letter sent to royal officials.[41] Martial executions could open the door to further charges that the colony's government was abusive and in violation of its charter. Both the colony's government and the town militias in charge of levying fines and forwarding cases to superior courts lacked the will to enforce the law, the towns because they understood the unique pressures of warfare in the backcountry and needed men, and the colony because it could not further tarnish its reputation with the crown.

Another reason for the magistrates' failure to prosecute resistance may have been a growing insecurity in their roles as fathers to the colony. Their stern issuing of harsh military regulations and then almost complete failure to enforce them, as in the George Corwin case, calls to mind a parent who knows he is overmatched; he threatens a disobedient child but fails to follow through with punishment. The clear ineffectiveness of such a strategy further encouraged disobedience.

On the outskirts of the colony, where war hit first and hardest, divisions among the English and resistance to colony authority were particularly strong. Resistance appeared not only in speech but in political and military action. Distance from the centers of power may have given these settlers the same illusions of impunity that had encouraged colony leaders themselves to resist royal decrees for half a century. The residents of the backcountry represented, as a whole, a different generation from those settled in Boston and surrounding towns. They were settlers who came later to New England or sons and daughters of the first colonists who lacked the land to build near their parents. When they did build in the backcountry, they often did so in ways that those still in the colony's core settlements found alarming. William Hubbard complained that the group of younger settlers who broke off from Sudbury to found Marborough placed their houses "very scatteringly" on the land, laying themselves open to Indian attack. When an Indian attack did come, the militia, sheltered in widely dispersed garrisons, could do nothing. The Indians divided into parties and burnt everything before them.[42] The new plantations were also notoriously slow to set up churches and support ministers, leading Increase Mather to compare them very unfavorably to their forbears: "the first Planters here that they might keep themselves together were satisfied with one Acre for each person, as his propriety, and after that with twenty Acres for a Family, how have Men since coveted after the earth, that many hundreds nay thousands of Acres, have been engrossed by one man, and they that profess themselves Christians have forsaken Churches, and Ordinances, and all for land and elbow-room enough in the world."[43] Such neglect, which spurred jeremiads and reformation movements, was also the source of much of the disquieting sense that God had forsaken New England, "a sad sign that we have in great part forgotten our Errand into this Wilderness."[44] Backcountry settlers' tendency to go their own way would become apparent in their resistance to the colony's wartime orders.[45]

For colony leaders, the necessity of maintaining outlying towns was self-evident. Those settlements were a bulwark to the rest of the colony. If they fell, towns closer in would fall, and finally Boston itself would be destroyed. The pattern of Indian attack, starting with towns the farthest out from Boston and then moving closer and closer in, revealed the Indians' intent to drive the English to the sea.[46] Such devastating Indian attacks, sometimes destroying entire towns, led the residents of Middleborough to abandon their homes in July 1675. Brookfield followed suit in August and Squakeag and Deerfield soon after.

In response to these disasters, the General Court issued its first order concerning the backcountry early in November 1675, directing the inhabitants of Mendon, the first Massachusetts town attacked during the war, to remain in the town. If any had already departed, they were to return. Then, expanding the order to all the towns in the backcountry, the Court stated that any inhabitants who departed the outlying towns without license from the General Court would forfeit "their interest in that place to the country for the defraying of the charge of the garrison soldiers."[47] The colony's difficulty in enforcing this order is evident in its repeated reissue, with increasing penalties for its violation.[48] In spite of the orders, a string of devastating Indian attacks on central Massachusetts towns in the spring of 1676 led to the abandonment of three more outlying towns, Lancaster, Marlborough, and Groton. While some residents remained in unburned garrisons in the towns of Springfield, Westfield, Sudbury, and Weymouth, many citizens fled to safer locales. As with the impressment regulations, however, there is no evidence that colony penalties against desertion were enforced. In fact, rather than chastise the deserters, in May 1676 the colony issued a law acknowledging the existence of those "who through the calamity of the War are forced to remove to other places" and directed them, like their hosts, to pay taxes.[49] The active role played by the younger generation in this desertion is suggested by a March 1676 petition from the town of Wrentham asking permission to remove to Dedham. Underlining the request, Samuel Fisher declared that many of the younger men in the town were planning to desert, with permission or not: "We are but: 16 men and some of them being young men do declare that they cannot stay in the town but intend speedily to be gone and leave the town for they say that they have not whereon to subsist."[50] The petition was granted.

As Fisher's plea indicates, the burdens of maintaining backcountry towns rested heavily on their residents. By Court order, the costs of maintaining garrisons and feeding and supplying the soldiers sent to assist the towns were to be borne by the towns themselves. Should the towns refuse to provide that maintenance, the colony would remove its soldiers.[51] Local resistance to that burden in Marlborough led the starving soldiers posted there to remove themselves. John Ruddock, lieutenant over the garrison at Marl-borough, wrote to the Council in early October 1675 of the town's refusal to support the country soldiers any longer. Lying directly on the path to Brookfield and the embattled towns on the Connecticut River, Marlbor-ough had been nearly cleaned out of food stores by passing troops. By October the town constable told the soldiers to go to Ruddock "for their vittles for the Town would diet them no longer [and] . . . warned them that did quarter them to quarter them no more." Soldiers desperate for food and supplies secured permission from Ruddock to go home to fetch more but then failed to return at all. Now Ruddock was afraid to release the remaining soldiers on the same errand, and their supplies were nearly gone.[52]

The colony's insistence that towns feed their garrison soldiers was a nearly insupportable demand. Very early in the war both Indians and English targeted each other's food supplies, knowing that without them, the enemy could not hold out long. Supplying and maintaining garrisons in the face of dwindling food supplies was extremely difficult. Forays out-side of garrisons to gather corn or other goods ran terrible risks, a lesson Captain Lathrop and nearly seventy men learned to their ruin when they were ambushed while hauling loaded carts between Deerfield and North-ampton.[53] But the inability to leave garrisons to plant crops carried a dou-ble penalty. No crops meant backcountry settlers could not pay the escalating and increasingly frequent demands for taxes to finance the war. Those demands must have seemed a cruel irony to those on the colony outskirts. Not only were they ordered, at peril of their property, to remain in their dangerous positions, but they had to support country soldiers with food when they did not have enough for their own families. And all these demands were being made by men safe in Boston, under little or no threat of attack, and with crops and cash ready at hand. Given their vastly unequal positions, why couldn't Boston supply the food for garrison soldiers?

While it galled the outlying towns to see their supplies eaten up by sol-diers from other towns, having their own men impressed into service out-side the town was worse. So great was the need for every last man that one town declined even to send its deputy to the meeting of the General Court. Replying to the Court's summons of all town deputies, Groton's leaders wrote, "We . . . being small in number, & daily waiting the approach of the enemy, have (not in any despising of authority) refrained from choosing one."[54] Even the speaker of the House of Deputies, Weymouth's William Torrey, wrote his regrets to the General Court that he was not able to carry out its warrant to impress a number of men from the town. The town had earlier petitioned that no more men be impressed, but not yet having received a reply, had presumed "upon your favor for the Indulgence." Its full complement of men was out already, and with twelve garrisons to sup-ply, the town lacked the provisions to send out any more soldiers.[55] As it

was, the town's settlers were "hastening to a miserable poverty if not pen-
ury."[56] Torrey couched his resistance in scrupulously polite language, as
many others did. But he was still seeking forgiveness, not permission, for
actions that were plainly contrary to order.

Indians recognized the threat to Massachusetts's authority posed by the
widespread resistance of towns and individuals and targeted it. Following
their successful assault on Sudbury on April 21, 1676, the Indians wrote a
pointed threat, instructing the English "to provide Store of good Cheer,
for they intended to dine with us upon the Election Day." In response, the
Massachusetts Council ordered an armed watch in all the towns on that
day, May 3.[57] Adding caution to defense, the Council also suggested that,
in this "extraordinary season," men send in their votes by proxy.[58] The
Indians' claim that on the day of election they would attack the very institutions the English were fighting to preserve must have further shaken
English confidence in colonial government. Given widespread English
resistance to colony orders and documented evidence of the Indians' careful observance of English weaknesses, it is likely that this incident was an
example of the Indians' adroit use of psychological warfare. Indians' observation and use of English authority patterns is evident in another incident
as well. During her captivity among the Indians, Mary Rowlandson noticed
that the Indians gathering to counsel together called their meeting the
"General Court"—the same term used by the "supreme authority" in Massachusetts. When called to meet with the Indian council, Mary sat down
with them, "as I was wont to do, as their manner is: Then they bade me
stand up, and said, *they were the General Court*."[59] Their use of this term does
not mean that the Indians had adopted an English style of government.
They had met in councils, "great men" consulting with sachems, long
before the English arrived. Rather, using the term and insisting on the
respect that accompanied it was a way of making an explicit claim that the
Indian councils were of equal weight and authority with English councils,
that they were not subordinate to the English.

As the war dragged on, disgruntled backcountry Englishmen, as well as
Indians, took aim at the colony's central authority. The war was not going
well for the English in the winter of 1676. Over and over again, Indians had
attacked the backcountry towns of Massachusetts—Lancaster, Northampton, and Medfield in February, Groton, Longmeadow, and Marlborough in
March, Sudbury in April. Increase Mather complained that the Indians,
"have advantages that we have not, knowing where to find us, but we know
not where to find them." As a result, the English could not strike back, and
by the time word of an ongoing attack reached the Council of War in Boston, the Indians had disappeared, leaving smoldering ruins behind.[60]
Understandably, many in the backcountry were alarmed at this state of
affairs, angry that the magistrates, safe in their homes in Boston, could

not—or would not—do more to protect the tax-paying citizens of the colony.

In April a group of men from Billerica and Chelmsford gathered to work at a blockhouse nearby. As the men hefted stone and boards, the talk began, grumbling over the war and the government's plodding progress against the Indians, perhaps even whispering of the renewed action against the errant colony by the crown. Those making the complaints asserted that the "dissatisfaction" with the current management of the country was not limited to themselves, but was felt by "very many persons amongst us." Sometime town clerk and surveyor Jonathan Danforth had remained silent as these complaints went on, but when the next man to speak declared that he "did verily think that the people would very shortly mutinize amongst us," Danforth broke in sharply: "In case they should so do, it would show far greater anger of god against new England, then ever yet was manifested." His words were a warning: watch your tongue. But tempers were running high now. Thomas Barret retorted that "he thought it would be the best way for us to mutinize, and then the controversy would be quickly ended, and we should all agree." This was sedition—speaking with approval of overthrowing the government—and the punishment for sedition was death. After Barret's shocking declaration, the complaints continued, but Danforth tried not to hear them: "Myself not then intending ever to say any thing about it to others, did not so mind it, as distinctly to say what it was, & who spake it." Indeed, he could not even remember who had first predicted that people would "shortly mutinize." Neither could another man present at the blockhouse, Henry Sparks, whose stubborn refusal to do any more than confirm portions of Danforth's cautious testimony earned him a brief imprisonment for contempt of authority.[61]

The reluctance of two witnesses in Barrett's trial to give full testimony in the case is evidence of the division between the center and periphery during King Philip's War. The men of Billerica, Chelmsford, Reading, and other outlying towns, including prominent citizens such as Danforth, were not willing to enforce strictures against seditious speech and evasion of impressment during the war. They could scarcely be prevailed upon even to testify. Whether or not they agreed that the government of Massachusetts Bay Colony should be overthrown and replaced by one with which all could "agree," they seemed to believe that constant attacks, fear, and shortages of food and other supplies—pressures Boston felt to a far lesser degree—mitigated such crimes.[62]

Belief that the magistrates were incompetent to wage the war was also expressed by some who did not come to the attention of the magistrates. The Billerica offenders' words echo those of Boston merchant Richard Wharton, who complained "were our great Councilors at home as expeditious and politic to supply and command as the soldiers have been diligent and courageous to fight, the Narragansets had been utterly subdued, but they are driven hungry out of their country, their army called home and frontiers left ungarrisoned, notwithstanding notice given three weeks since of the enemy's design." And like the men from Billerica, the disgruntled Wharton called for the government's overthrow: "Except God give greater wisdom to their rulers or put it into the King's heart to rule and relieve them, the colonies will soon be ruined and they reduced to the necessity of subjecting upon any terms to any that will protect them."[63] Even Sudbury minister Edmund Browne echoed such language, arguing in a letter sent to the magistrates themselves that if they did not act decisively against the Indian threat, it would "open the mouths of some to Say our Sages are Sageless."[64] Nominations for colony magistrates registered the same kinds of dissatisfaction with the rulers of the colony. John Cotton reported to his friend Thomas Walley that "At Boston the votes for nomination of magistrates, for divers old ones run very low."[65] Indeed, commonwealth party stalwart Daniel Gookin lost his office in the May 1676 elections. Moderate Joseph Dudley, who with Simon Bradstreet would lead the colony into the next century, took his place.

Backcountry hostility toward the central government manifested itself in fear as well as resistance. While there is no evidence that the colony carried through on its threat to seize abandoned lands for the payment of garrison costs, the specter of that threat hung over refugees from the backcountry, widening the rift between them and colony leaders. Displaced from their land, refugees from the outlying towns were quick to believe rumors that colony authorities were conspiring against them. On June 7, 1676, the Council ordered Henry Segar and Joseph Herndon to appear to answer for an "untrue & slanderous report raised upon the Council or some Members thereof referring to Groton, Lancaster or other towns at present in distress by the enemy." Herndon and Segar had spread word that "the council was about to sell the land at Lancaster," and that sales would be kept secret and denied by the Council if inquired into. John White, Sr., added to this "very bad news" the tale that Council member Joseph Dudley "said the country would not do well till poor men wrought for a groat a day."[66] The storyteller and two other witnesses clearly believed that the Council was plotting to transform the colony from one where most men had the independence of land ownership to one where men were dependent on wages, and shockingly low ones at that. Such an outcome would threaten the authority of fathers and citizens, who would henceforth be unable to provide for and preside over families and servants. This reaction is classic conspiracy theory, the haves plotting against the have-nots. And it carries a deeper irony. The backcountry refugees, driven from their towns by Indian attacks and starvation, feared that they would become like Indians themselves. Their land sold away from them, they would be forced to work for wages like the natives who increasingly populated English towns in the years leading up to the war.[67] A measure of what such deprivation could mean to an English person appears in a penurious woman's petition for relief, so that she would "not be forced to wander from house to house like an Indian or brute beast."[68]

Such rumors about and outright abuse of the magistrates threatened their authority. It also may have helped undermine their own confidence in that authority. The magistrates' growing insecurity in the strength and extent of their authority is evident not only in their unwillingness to impose threatened penalties or enforce military regulations but also in their reluctance to take action before obtaining evidence of public support. One example of this occurred in March 1676, following a series of devastating attacks that led to the abandonment of Lancaster and Marlborough. The Council sent a letter to the outlying towns asking their opinion on yet another war expense, this time on a vast scale. "Several considerable persons" had proposed erecting a stockade stretching from the Charles River to the Concord River as a "necessary expedient for the public welfare," and the Council sent the proposal to the outlying towns, requesting their opinion on it.[69] As the responses came in, it became clear that not only were the towns opposed to the project, they were incensed by it. Trying at first to be judicious in their response, Hugh Mason, Richard Lowden, and Jonathan Danforth listed a number of objections to the proposal, including its great expense, the large amount of time it would take, and the men it would draw off from planting crops in the backcountry. With rising exasperation, they added their doubts about "the uselessness of it when it is done, it being so easy a matter to break through it." Then, with what amounted almost to a threat, they concluded: "we might add the great discontent and murmuring of the people in general so far as we have had opportunity to discourse concerning it. That we fear the imposing of such a thing, would effect an ill consequence."[70] These pointed words are a good measure of the tension between the colonists in the backcountry and the colony government. To men who lived on the colony's outskirts and regularly traversed its distances, the proposal seemed nothing short of folly, a plan that benefited no one and could cause significant harm, to frontier residents particularly. When these responses came in, the magistrates immediately dropped the issue; the stockade remained unbuilt.[71]

The fact that the magistrates asked the opinion of the outlying towns, rather than simply imposing an order, was consistent with the colony's political principles, which required the consent of the governed. But the colony had not always asked the advice of its citizens. When colonists offered it anyway in 1661, urging the colony to acknowledge the restored king, the magistrates had responded with indignation, reminding the petitioners pointedly that they knew how to do their job. That the magistrates sought for advice in wartime—when governments frequently bypass such niceties—suggests the magistrates' increasing need for evidence of public support. In the face of widespread resistance to wartime authority, the magistrates seem to have concluded that the only way of assuring cooperation would be to first obtain consent. Both the request itself and the hasty retreat from the stockade proposal betray the magistrates' insecurity, arising from pervasive flouting of their authority.

This incident, like the increasing tendency of backcountry towns to hold back their own men, illustrates the growing divisions between those on the line of fire and those directing the war from the colony's capital. Men who could suggest such impractical, even dangerous, ideas as the proposed stockade could not be trusted to defend the interests of those on the colony's outskirts. As the war progressed, backcountry residents increasingly resisted orders from Boston and made their own decisions on how to carry on the war. Most of this increasing turn to local government centered around demands for men, an expected tug-of-war given the great need for them in all areas. Resistance was often couched in polite language, buffered by honorifics. But some carried their disobedience to more alarming extremes and made little effort to soften its impact. In April 1676 the governor and Council sent orders to the military committee of Quabaug to take the men stationed in their garrison and search the woods for enemy Nipmucks. Rather than follow the order, the officers took a vote on it. Only one was in favor of "marching forward." The remaining five opposed it, for reasons including the unfitness of the men and scarcity of provisions. Instead of a report of their mission, the officers forwarded their vote and their reasons for refusing the order to the Council.[72] The absence of any response again suggests that colony leaders were reluctant to punish such usurpations of their authority, knowing that there was little they could do about it under the circumstances.

The residents of Hadley and Northampton, towns on the Connecticut River, provide another example of the turn to local and individual management of the war. Hearing that Indians were camped nearby, men from the town organized a vigilante expedition to attack them on May 18, 1676. Arriving at the camp before dawn, they found a large group of Indians near what came to be known as Turner's Falls, sleeping after a feast of milk and English cattle they had captured the night before. At the English discharge of muskets, the Indians leapt up, crying, "Mohawks, Mohawks, as if their own native Enemies had been upon them." Clearly, the Indians apprehended more danger from their traditional opponents than from the English. In the mêlée, many Indians plunged into the falls and drowned. Others fell to English gunfire, with estimates of from 100 to 300 Indian deaths.[73] The Connecticut River colonists, described the previous October as "like Sheep ready for the Slaughter," were sheep no longer.[74] Rather than wait for orders and leadership from Boston, they seized command themselves. But self-government could be disastrous. As the English retreated from the Turner's Falls massacre, Indians attacked, and the English soldiers panicked and refused to follow their leaders' orders. In the chaos, Indians killed 40 English. Thus the morning's success "ended in a disgraceful Rout."[75]

Taking the management of the war into their own hands reflected back-country dissatisfaction, both with the way men were being impressed and used and with the course of the war, which, until the summer of 1676, was going very badly for the English. It also reflected the fact that local allegiances, rather than the authority of the colony, were motivating the back-country settlers.[76] Insistence on managing the war effort themselves, directing how—and whether—their towns should be defended, and protesting loudly at what they saw as their leaders' incompetence or chicanery all display this trend. Volunteers for military service in the war showed a similar tendency. In February 1675 the General Court noted the complaints of military officers that volunteers serving under them considered themselves independent of their command, and the Court issued immediate orders that such men obey the same martial laws as impressed soldiers.[77] Dissatisfied with how the war was being waged, all sought to seize the reins for themselves, thus securing greater protection to their own lands, families, and persons.

Some took their dissatisfaction with how Boston was directing the war to the extreme of seeking to remove themselves from the colony's authority entirely—a tactic the Narragansetts had used against the English a generation earlier. At the end of March 1676, Rev. Edward Taylor, Isaac Phelps, Thomas and Josiah Dewey, and David Ashley sent the Connecticut Council a letter in behalf of the citizens of Westfield, Massachusetts. Westfield, one of the string of embattled Connecticut River towns, had been ordered by the Massachusetts Council to abandon its most outlying garrisons and fortify the central ones. They would, of course, need men to guard those garrisons, at least thirty or forty. But when they wrote General Winslow, commander of the United Colonies forces, with the request for those men, he replied that he had no authority to send them. Learning of Westfield's failure to obtain soldiers, the Massachusetts Council advised them instead to remove to Springfield. "This they were unwilling to do," the Westfield men wrote, "especially as many of their people were dangerously ill, with the prevailing sickness, and it would be their death to remove." Apparently, their sickness would not prevent a more distant removal. They asked the Connecticut Council's assistance in transporting their estates and families to Connecticut. Their frustration with repeated Indian attacks and with the inadequate assistance the Massachusetts government had provided had driven them to the brink of abandoning not only their town, but their citizenship in the Bay Colony. The Connecticut Council was sympathetic, but not encouraging. They replied that they were "unwilling to offer any inducement to draw them off from obedience to the authority of Massachusetts, to the discouragement of other towns there."[78] There is no indication of whether Massachusetts leaders learned of this near-defection or not.

If they did, it would only have underlined the precarious status of their own authority.

Resistance to the war effort, rather than provoking colony leaders to exert their authority, seems to have had the opposite effect. Colony leaders increased their threats but did not enforce them, and their reluctance to do so may have inspired further disobedience. That disobedience in turn undermined the magistrates' confidence in their own authority. Such self-doubt could only feed the already strong tendency of the magistrates to undercut their own edicts and yield to the self-protective demands of colony subjects, whose personal, family, and town allegiances appeared to be stronger than any loyalty to the colony. If colony leaders could not find the strength to govern effectively, an alarming number of citizens seemed ready to abandon their allegiance, transferring their loyalty to "any that will protect them" or simply governing themselves.[79]

Chapter 8

A Crisis of Spirit

In May 1676, after nearly a year of warfare in New England, Lord Anglesey, one of Charles II's secretaries of state, wrote Massachusetts governor Leverett a letter containing a pointed reproof: "It is not altogether groundlessly reported, that . . . you are divided among yourselves, that you have not used ordinary providence, that you are too tenacious of what is necessary for your preservation . . . that you are poor and yet proud. This was not the spirit that carried you into that wilderness and led you on there ever since, building and planting for yourselves and God. But these calamities may come upon you to bring you to your first post, and to do your first works."[1] When Lord Anglesey charged Massachusetts with being "poor and yet proud," he was raising the specter of the colony's stubborn independence. Colony leaders had neglected the dutiful appeal for protection that subjects owed their sovereign. When he also charged them with being "divided" and implied that their sufferings were the natural consequence, he gave proof that the colony had failed to change the impression the royal commissioners had carried to London ten years earlier. That impression, conveyed by Cartwright, Carr, Nicolls, and Maverick and supported by scores of discontents before and since, was of a fractious colony in which a minority of religious nonconformists pressed their will on the majority. Leaders of the colony had ardently disputed this characterization, had disputed the existence of any meaningful disunity in Massachusetts for a decade, but here came the charge again.

In the crucible of war, the divisions within the society became exaggerated. Like Anglesey, many concluded that the "calamities" of war might have a spiritual origin, as God's punishment for divisions and spiritual complacency in the colony. If God was punishing the colony, then the divine approval that lent authority to its leaders might be slipping away. The self-doubt such speculations introduced made Massachusetts leaders vulnerable to attacks from disgruntled citizens within the colony as well as from outside enemies quick to observe weaknesses and capitalize on them. Thus, while the physical demands of war escalated, religious dissidents, Indians, and the royal government also stepped up their attacks on the colony's legitimacy and authority.

Questions over whether English engagement in the war was justifiable and thus deserving of divine assistance emerged early on in Massachusetts. In July 1676, colonist John Bishop confided to Increase Mather the misgivings of many of his friends over "this unhappy war, how it began, & whether our English were wholly innocent on that account, viz. our friends of Plimouth parts." He had been "grieved to hear" accounts that Plymouth's "dishonorable" behavior toward the Indians might have prompted the war. When such reports reached his neighbors, they had found it "very difficult, dissatisfying, & uncomfortable to conscientious parents and other Relations, to send out their children, & other dear relations unto the war, where many of them were slain, & all in danger of their lives, though that would not be the worst, but the dishonor would redound to the Name of God, if N.E. should go to war in a bad cause, or not every way justifiable in the sight of God & all the world."[2] If the war was not just, they would be committing their sons, husbands, and brothers to a dishonorable death and bringing the condemnation of God upon the colony.

Such fears go far to explain the magistrates' public insistence that the war was indeed just. In September 1675, Plymouth's commissioners for the United Colonies submitted a narrative of the beginning of the war to the combined commissioners' meeting. After reviewing it, the commissioners declared "that the said War doth appear to be both Just and Necessary, and its first Rise only a defensive War."[3] The Massachusetts Council issued a similar narrative and declaration to all the inhabitants of its colony on December 7, 1675.[4] By giving an accurate narrative of the war's outbreak, they could quiet such pangs of conscience—and perhaps assuage their own doubts as well.

The extent of English misgivings over the war is evident in Bishop's letter. In it, he mentioned a conversation with a Mr. Alden, in which Bishop expressed his concerns that no justification had "appeared in print to clear the matter." Alden had replied that, indeed, something had appeared and referred Bishop to Mather for a "full state of matters." In turn, Bishop begged Mather to send him some word that "may be satisfying to my self & all others in this important matter."[5] The justification Alden referred to may well have been the Massachusetts Council's declaration. When Mather's narrative of the war came out the following year, he further defended English involvement, claiming that even before Massachusetts joined Plymouth in the war, Indians had killed a Massachusetts colonist traveling on the road. Therefore the war was defensive and just.[6]

Both the Puritans' fear that engaging in the war was sinful and their rush to justify their actions were linked to their providential worldview. They believed God was intimately involved in their lives and that all things happened for a purpose—to warn, instruct, or punish. People with such a perspective had to find reason in the devastations visiting them, had to bring their lives back into harmony with the divine will in order to have peace restored. As residents of a holy commonwealth, they expected both greater purity of themselves and greater condemnation from God when they failed. Though the war was an onerous burden, it was also evidence of God's continued interest in the success of the holy commonwealth. Would he send such sparks to repentance if he had given them up already? In the attack on Springfield in early October 1675, John Pynchon lost his home and his mills and was left with a dangerously ill wife in a garrison crowded with dozens of frantic people. Writing to his son shortly afterward, Pynchon gave a poignant example of how a Puritan could respond to the war:

I would not have you troubled at these sad losses which I have met with; there is no reason for a child to be troubled when his father calls in that which he lent him. It was the Lord that lent it me, and he that gave it hath taken it away and blessed be the name of the Lord. He hath done very well for me and I acknowledge his goodness to me and desire to trust in him and submit to him for ever.[7]

Pynchon, like many other Puritans, drew instruction from his sufferings, a process readily apparent in letters, sermons, and government declarations throughout the war.

Fear that sin had provoked the war and would prevent English success against the Indians emerged simultaneously with the first fighting in Plymouth Colony. On June 22, 1675, the Plymouth Council issued an order for a fast day to be held on June 24, which would, ironically, turn out to be the first day of hostilities. The purpose of the fast was to "humble our souls before the Lord for all those sins whereby we have provoked our good God," and seek his favor in "subduing the heathen."[8] And what were those provoking sins? According to Plymouth minister Thomas Walley, they were materialism, a decline in former diligence to defend the truth among colonial leaders, tolerance of public false worship, and pride, particularly among the "rising generation that know not the God of their fathers but carry proudly and hearken not to the word of the Lord."[9]

Many shared Walley's opinion. In October and November 1675, the Massachusetts General Court met, consulted with religious leaders, and issued a call for reformation. They declared that, because the colony had failed to heed God's laws, God had "given commission to the barbarous heathen to rise up against us" and was "not going forth with our armies." To remedy this situation, the Court issued a list of fourteen areas requiring immediate reform. Like Walley, the Court considered tolerance of false worship a great provoking sin and strengthened laws against importing Quakers into the colony or attending the worship services of religious dissenters. They also listed irreverence, neglect of discipline in the churches, the prevalence of long hair in men and extravagant hair and clothing styles among men and women, swearing, idleness, oppression in prices, illegal trading, and other wrongs, with "especially amongst the younger sort" appended to nearly every category.[10]

The call for laws against "provoking sins" was part of a reformation movement that preceded the war but gained dramatic momentum from it. Despite the evidence of God's displeasure that Indian attacks seemed to provide, the initial response to calls for reform was split. Magistrates, notably, were resistant to many reformers' demands, including increasing penalties against and prosecution of Quakers and Baptists.[11] In December 1676, Samuel Sewall recorded an exchange that highlights the disagreements that had been evident in the colony since the restoration of the crown in 1660. Sewall lived in the home of his father-in-law, the prominent merchant John Hull. One evening several ministers came to visit Hull. One, Reverend Thomas Shepherd, spoke of the reformation then being advanced by Increase Mather. He had hopes that the movement would inspire correction, particularly of "the disorderly Meetings of Quakers and Anabaptists: thought if all did agree, i.e. Magistrates and Ministers, the former might easily be suppressed, and that then, The Magistrates would see reason to Handle the latter."[12] Wanting the magistrates to "see reason" was a call that Increase Mather, leading the reformation, made repeatedly. For nearly a decade before the war, magistrates had been content to allow Quaker and Baptist meetings as long as they did not call too much attention to themselves.[13] Even the chief reformer, Increase Mather, admitted that ignoring Quakers had a beneficial effect: "*New-England* long before the Questioning of their Charters, had come to an Entire *Toleration* of the Sectaries crept in among them, having by Experience found that their *Toleration* prov'd their *Dissipation.*"[14] In spite of the furor surrounding the banishment of two Baptist leaders in 1668, neither the banishment nor other punishments of religious dissidents were enforced. Public will was split, as was opinion among the magistrates. Some read the war's devastation as evidence of the dangerous consequences of their complacency. Many Puritans became convinced that they had allowed too much sin within the colony and that this had caused God to send the Indians—"God's sword"—to remind them of their covenants.[15] Presented with such evidence, the magistrates finally assented to reform legislation.[16]

The special focus of the reform movement was the colony's youth. As the youth constituted a large portion of the men called to military service, they became a great concern for magistrates and ministers. "Pray be careful," Josiah Winslow wrote to military leader James Cudworth on July 6, 1675, "to maintain love and good orders among your selves and towards our Allies and good orders amongst our men that god be not provoked by any accursed thing in our camp."[17] Minister Thomas Walley expressed his willingness to write spiritually uplifting letters to the men in the field and was sure he could find others to do the same: "I have many letters to write to the Army we have writers that savor of godliness and [their] letters are composable."[18] Such letters would accomplish the dual task of strengthening the morale of the army and warding off sin that might prevent God from going forth with the English forces.

CRESCENTIUS MATHERUS.
Ætatis Suæ 85. 1724.

Figure 16. Increase Mather, minister and prolific author. Courtesy of the
Massachusetts Historical Society.

Military regulations aimed at the same goal. In May 1676, Massachusetts leaders issued a list of laws to govern their soldiers, including holding daily prayer in the camps, suppression of profanity, and as much observance of the Sabbath as was possible. The list came rather late in the war and was undoubtedly prompted by scandalous reports of soldiers' conduct. Plymouth officer Nathaniel Phelps, whose men were stationed with those of Massachusetts captain Daniel Henchman, complained of "what Pitiful men [Henchman] hath under pay. That I judge one of our men to be better than 5 of his who are active to swear & quarrel & division & at little else that good is."[19] Connecticut leaders wrote in distress of the "surreptitious, uncivil, if not inhumane deportment towards the living & dead" by some of the soldiers in the Great Swamp Fight. They had tried, they wrote, to send sober men, and they hoped the Bay Colony would try to do the same, not allow an "Achan" in camp "to hide stolen stuff, or to carry worse or more uncomely than the heathen towards their fellow soldiers."[20] From Maine, Captain Joshua Scottow wrote Governor Leverett begging his prayers that "the Deluge of sin which I perceive is among our soldiers as well as Inhabitors may be stopped by reason whereof this overflowing scourge pursueth us."[21]

Such sinfulness was troubling for a number of reasons. The colony wished to present a united front to its enemies, for the practical reason that divisions weakened the colony's authority and ability to wage war and for the spiritual reason that most believed God would withhold his assistance from a people who were not united in righteousness. Hence the ungodliness of the soldiers was troubling, not only to the officers and colonial leaders but to many of the soldiers themselves. The difficulty of finding enough men to serve led Massachusetts early on to make expedient choices, including accepting and even recruiting into the army men whose behavior disqualified them for any other participation in the community. Without blinking, magistrates accepted Captain Samuel Mosely's recruiting of former pirates, several of whom exchanged death sentences for promises to serve in the army. Increase Mather reported that one man, hearing "many profane oaths among some of our Soldiers (namely those Privateers, who were also Volunteers) . . . was possessed with a strong conceit that God was against the english, whereupon he immediately ran distracted."[22]

God was against the English. That much seemed obvious to the colonists through most of the first year of King Philip's War. Over and over again, Indians descended on outlying settlements with no warning, reducing many towns to ashes and forcing inhabitants all along the colony's outskirts to crowd into garrison houses, leaving their crops and homes to the Indians. While English towns fell or were abandoned, English troops were, for the most part, idle. Increase Mather complained that the Indians "have advantages that we have not, knowing where to find us, but we know not where to find them, who nevertheless are always at home, and have in a manner nothing but their lives and souls (which they think not of) to lose."[23] Idleness was compounded by indecision. The members of the United Colonies, individually prone to prolonged debate before taking action, were even slower to make military decisions together, so much so that "some Indians that were friends to the English derided (in a Jesting way) the Englishes sparing delay."[24] Hostile Indians, too, noted English tardiness: Mary Rowlandson declared, "*I cannot but remember how the Indians derided the slowness, and dullness of the* English Army, *in its setting out.* For after the desolations at *Lancaster* and *Medfield*, as I went along with them, they asked me when I thought the *English* Army would come after them? I told them I could not tell: It may be they will come in *May*, said they. Thus did they scoff at us, as if the *English* would be a quarter of a year getting ready."[25]

While Indian attacks fell swiftly, the English pondered policy and lamented their inability to wage war in a "civilized" way: "It is the Manner of the Heathen that are now in Hostility with us, contrary to the Practice of all Civil Nations, to Execute their bloody Insolencies by Stealth, and Sculking in small Parties, declining all open Decision of their Controversy, either by Treaty or by the Sword."[26] Such tactics were clearly effective; between August 1675 and March 1676, Indians attacked over twenty English towns. They burned large portions of many of them, forcing residents to pack into the buildings still left standing. Damage was so severe at Brookfield, Deerfield, Squakeag, Lancaster, Groton, and Marlborough that the English abandoned those towns, fleeing to garrisons and houses in settlements nearby. English successes during this period were few, leading the discouraged colonists to ask themselves and each other repeatedly, "What are we doing to provoke God's wrath?"

While the providentially minded colonists sought to discover and repent of the specific provocations of their sufferings, there was no lack of people happy to tell them why God no longer supported the Massachusetts Bay Colony. Quakers, particularly, made hay of the Puritans' distress. Thomas Walley reported that "A Quaker told me [the cause of the war] was for my saying in my sermon they were blasphemers and Idolaters and for the persecution they have had from us."[27] To the Quakers, and to many observing New England from across the Atlantic, the Quaker executions of a decade earlier were the most grievous blot on the Massachusetts record. Why would not divine justice reward "blood for blood & cruelty for cruelty"?[28] Quakers stepped up their public protests during the war, probably in response to both the recent reinvigoration of laws against them and renewed royal attention to charter abuses.[29] Samuel Sewall described a female Quaker's protest visit to a public worship service at Boston's Third Church, saying that she entered during the sermon clad "in a Canvas Frock, her hair dishevelled and loose like a Periwig, her face as black as ink, led by two other Quakers, and two other followed." Such displays had been relatively common twenty years earlier, but the magistrates' increasing laxity toward Quaker worship had led to a dramatic dwindling in their occurrence. Many of those at worship with Sewall in the Third Church might never have seen a Quaker in active protest. Said Sewall, "It occasioned the greatest and most amazing uproar that I ever saw."[30] The Third Church members' sensitivity to being viewed as religious rebels themselves undoubtedly heightened their response, just as it may have prompted Quaker targeting of that particular congregation. Quakers also sent written condemnations of the war and "scurrilous verses" to Massachusetts magistrates, disturbed church meetings and sessions of General Court, and marched through Boston's streets calling the city's residents to repentance.[31]

A heightened Quaker presence in the public arena during the war was troubling to the magistrates and ministers for several reasons. As their October and November reform legislation illustrates, they read the scourge of war exactly contrary to the Quakers: their tolerance for heresy, not their punishment of it, was provoking to God. Therefore, seeing more Quaker protests, or hearing of more illegal Quaker meetings was evidence of communal unrighteousness. As long as such demonstrations continued, it would be clear to God "that we were not yet fit for Deliverance, nor could Health be restored unto us except a great deal more Blood be first taken from us."[32] Protests were also alarming because they reminded colony leaders of the increasing division in Massachusetts over how far religious dissidence should be tolerated. The magistrates' initial resistance to the reform movement is evidence of this split, as is Sewall's recording of Reverend Shepherd's wish that the magistrates would "Handle" Quaker dissidence. The colony's drift toward greater tolerance was brought up short by the war, with its seeming proof of God's displeasure. War led to a retreat—albeit temporary—from the process of accommodation among colony leaders. This is not surprising: threatened polities tend to retreat to conservative positions. But neither is it surprising that reinvigoration of religious dissent laws led to a renewal of Quaker protests that served both to remind Puritans of their failure to reform the colony and to invite the attention of the king. It also may have led to increasing resistance to government policies among its citizens, a possibility suggested by the Massachusetts Council's 1677 order to fine constables who neglected the new orders to search homes on the Sabbath for evidence of Quaker meetings.[33]

As this decree indicates, the heightened Quaker presence during the war was not merely a religious issue. As with so many other aspects of life in seventeenth-century Massachusetts, religion entwined with politics. Quaker refusal to give due respect and obedience to magistrates, ministers, and other superiors was an insidious influence, an "infection." Seeing Quakers offer disrespect and disobedience to colony leaders could encourage "The minds of the simpler, or such as are less affected to the order & government in church and commonwealth" to similarly abuse authority.[34] Under the stresses of war, the colony could not afford to have potential soldiers influenced to defy the colony's authority. On principle, Quakers refused to bear arms, a stand that earned some of them a painful run through the gauntlet of Boston's military company.[35] Significantly, Quakers were only "some" of those thus punished. Their presence among the group of those resisting impressment must have seemed strong evidence to the Massachusetts magistrates that their dangerous opinions were spreading.

For those English who did serve in the army, Quaker refusal to do likewise was galling, adding to the divisions besetting the region. Conflicting reports of Quaker treatment of United Colonies troops illustrates this division. Rhode Islander John Easton, a Quaker, reported that following the Great Swamp Fight, Quakers offered refreshment to the Boston troops, "but [Boston] troopers Said [by] their Captain they despised it and so left the [food]." Massachusetts resident Nathaniel Saltonstall gave a different account. He reported that some 150 Rhode Islanders hosted and fed the Boston troops, "only some churlish Quakers were not free to entertain them until compelled by the Governor. Of so inhumane, peevish and untoward a Disposition are these Nabals, as not to Vouchsafe Civility to those that had ventured their Lives, and received dangerous Wounds in their Defense."[36]

Certainly, Quakers did their best to spread their message of peace during the war. A Quaker meeting in Rhode Island issued a proclamation condemning the colonies for raising arms: "Are not fightings, killing, blood shed, murder with carnal weapons, rendering evil for evil?" they asked. More pointedly, they reminded the Puritans of Christ's command to "put thy sword up into the sheath. Do good to them that hate you, pray for them that despitefully use you & persecute you."[37] Edward Perry of Plymouth sent a "testimony from . . . God against the Rulers teachers & people of the land" to the leaders of all the colonies participating in the war. He condemned them for their sins, which had provoked the war, "above all blood, blood, even the blood of my children & servants." Then, raising divine authority above the political authority of the colonies' leaders, he wrote: "the Lord wills & Requires that those that are in authority & place of Goverment in Plimouth & boston Colonies do cause this whole testimony to be printed at your printing place: That so this testimony may be publicly testified throughout the English plantations in newengland that all may hear & fear & Return."[38] Not surprisingly, no one accepted Perry's line of command, and the warning remained in manuscript.

One of the most damning Quaker reports was penned by Edward Wharton and printed in London in 1675. Wharton evoked the memory of the Quaker executions, writing to a Friend in London that he and two others had spent the night building a memorial over the graves of martyred Friends. Wharton's sense that the war opened the door for Quaker demonstrations to have greater impact in the colony and abroad is clear in his statement, "the Lord having put it into my heart, that now was a fit and seasonable time, it being a day of great Calamity and distress upon most part of New-England." When news of their memorial spread in the morning, "many hundreds, of Town and Country, flock'd about it, Reading, taking, and giving Copies of the Inscription which was Engraven upon the Front end of the Work: And much people were seriously affected, saying, one to another, that the destroying of those good people, is that which hath brought the Displeasure and judgment of the Lord upon this Country." The inscription read: "Although our Bodies here / in silent Earth do lie, / Yet are our Righteous Souls at Rest, / our Blood for Vengeance cry."

Vengeance was presently being visited on New England, Wharton insisted, though he had not heard of "much hurt" coming to Friends. In fact, he reported that "some of the Indians did say to some Englishmen, That they did not think the Quakers would come out against them." If Quakers were escaping harm, might not they, rather than the Puritans, be in the right? Furthermore, the destruction visiting the colony was in clear fulfillment of a Quaker prophecy that declared "great Calamities" would come upon New Englanders because of their persecution of the Quakers: "their Young Men should fall by the Sword, and Worms shall cover them; and the Cup which they had filled to others, should be filled double to themselves."[39] Such reflections threatened the authority of the magistrates, who had ordered the Quaker executions. News reached them during the session of General Court of both the nature of the inscription and the "divers people" from "divers towns" who flocked to see it, and the magistrates immediately "sent some to pull it in pieces."[40] But the words had gained a life of their own, appearing not only in Wharton's narrative, published for eager readers in London, but also paraphrased in other letters sent across the Atlantic.

Benjamin Batten was one of a number of New England merchants who wrote frequent letters to and spent considerable time in London. A familiar sight at the Exchange on the "New England Walk," eight of these merchants, including Batten, were called to testify before the king about Massachusetts's trade abuses in April 1676.[41] Batten sent a version of the Quaker tomb inscription to a royal official in London that same year, along with a copy of the Massachusetts laws and ordinances of war passed on October 26, 1675. Many of the military offenses listed, including sedition, selling arms or ammunition, and desertion, were punishable by death. By sending this list and the tomb inscription together, Batten made the link between Quaker executions and potential martial executions explicit. By including both, he was urging the royal government to be on the alert for more bloodshed—more violation of English law—by the overzealous colonial rulers.[42] This evidence of Massachusetts's offenses would be added to the complaints piling up in England, where renewed investigation of the colony was well under way.

While refusal to serve in the army, clamorous public demonstrations, and verbal and written commands to repent disturbed many in the colony and undermined efforts to maintain order and respect for authority, they had even more far-reaching effects. Quakers penned at least six accounts of the war, most of them claiming the war was a direct consequence of Quaker persecutions. At least three of these accounts were published in London during or following the war, and at least one other may have been sent to a royal official in the colonies, New York's Governor Andros.[43] In both London and New York, there was a ready audience for such attacks on the magistrates as this verse by George Joy:

Repeal those wicked and pernicious Laws,
That Innocents be not destroyed without a Cause
And grant such Rulers as may be devout
For Christ and Saints, and turn the other out

At a time when Massachusetts's civil as well as physical existence was hanging in the balance, these attacks added weight to those urging revocation of the charter.

Massachusetts Bay Colony leaders needed the stability of both widespread acceptance of their political authority and God's sanction of that authority in order to inspire the united support of colony citizens. Both were challenged during wartime from within and without. Not only Quakers challenged the colony's authority, but other residents as well. The colony was growing and changing. A continual influx of merchants and fishermen, particularly in the coastal towns and trade centers, was making the region increasingly diverse in religious belief and ethnic origin. The continued dominance of Puritans in government was becoming more irksome to those who did not qualify for the privileges of freemen, which, despite reforms promised the previous decade, were still overwhelmingly held by church members. Particularly in the colony's northeastern towns such as Salem, Newbury, and Rowley, with their greater amount of trade and fishing, the Puritan system of government became a butt for the jokes of some inhabitants. Because of the religious basis of civil law, challenges to government struck at the heart of English fears that God had departed from their colony, leaving them to division and ruin.

The case of sailor Isaac Woodbury, called to court in December 1675 for his refusal to take the oath of a constable after being elected to that position, illustrates the widespread flouting of the law limiting the vote to freemen. Witnesses related that Woodbury's election to the unenviable position of constable was engineered by non-freemen, "out of a design they had against [him]." Several men with packets of votes made out in favor of

Woodbury had stood outside the place of voting and urged other free-men—who were, apparently, willing enough—to take them in.[44] This case is striking for several reasons, one of which is Woodbury's dismay at being chosen by his neighbors. As a sailor, he could not serve as constable without putting his livelihood at risk. And he was not alone in balking at public service. So widespread was resistance to accepting the office of constable that the General Court allowed Salem to raise the fine for refusing to serve to ten pounds in May 1676.[45] Similarly striking is this case's evidence of how lightly freemen took the responsibility to vote wisely, an obligation preached ardently by ministers such as William Hubbard and John Daven-port.[46]

Another incident in Salem, a 1676 church dispute, also showed that some non-freemen were trying to seize the authority denied them under colony laws. Town residents were at odds over which of the two men shar-ing the pulpit, Charles Nicholet and John Higginson, should be minister. To end the standoff, the town held a vote and selected Nicholet. However, immediate protests over the result revealed that those voting were not just the church members, or even the freemen, but a "promiscuous vote of the town," most of whom "were not expressly qualified so to vote by law." The Puritans believed that such a vote was not only irregular, but manifested a "dangerous tendency"; with such disorderly voting, the laws and practices that preserved the distinctiveness of the holy commonwealth could be undermined. Both the defying of Massachusetts laws and the quarreling in the church displayed a disunity unbefitting Christians. Coming at a time when the colony's leaders had just issued laws against the sins that had pro-voked God to send martial rebukes, such discord was "dangerous" in a very literal sense. Noting Satan's gain in it, the General Court's committee urged the town to hold a day of humiliation and return to the joint preach-ing of Mr. Nicholet and Mr. Higginson.[47] Ministers mediating a dispute in the nearby town of Rowley similarly rebuked the townspeople for breaking into discord when the colony was at war: "We cannot but have a deep sense of the evil of your divisions in such a time of Jacob's Troubles."[48]

Widespread insecurity about the "procuring Causes" of the war made the attacks of Quakers and non-church members particularly stinging. Not surprisingly, Indians were also tuned into the religious and political vulner-abilities of the English and exploited them during the war. Attacking on the Sabbath, targeting churchgoers, or tearing a Bible in pieces and leaving it for English troops to discover all struck at what the English had shown to be most precious to them.[49] And, whether the Indians planned them that way or not, such attacks were devastating psychological warfare. Stuffing a Bible into the exposed entrails of an Englishman who thought the book would protect him was proof otherwise.[50] Could God be fighting for the English and allow such desecrations? One chronicler of the war noted the daunting fact that Indians seemed to attack on the very days the English set aside to fast and pray for relief.[51]

By focusing their attacks on English religion, some Indians seem to have been expressing their antipathy to one form of subjection to the English—acceptance of their beliefs and lifestyle. Philip had earlier declared to John Easton that "they had a great fear to have any of their indians should be Called or forced to be Christian indians. They said that such were in every thing more mischievous, only dissemblers, and then the English made them not subject to their kings, and by their lying to wrong their kings."[52] Attacks on religion could have served as warning that the Indians would no longer yield themselves, or allow their people to yield, so completely.

Indian words as well as actions struck at English fears that they had lost divine backing. During their attack on Brookfield in August 1675, Indians scoffed, "Now see how your God delivers you or will deliver you" and mocked the English desperately praying within the besieged garrison, "saying come and pray and sing psalms, and in contempt made an hideous noise somewhat resembling singing."[53] In Groton, Indians burned the church, then went to the garrison where the town's minister, Samuel Willard, was housed and crowed, "*What will you do for a house to pray in now we have burnt your Meeting-house?*"[54] Indians attacking Saco, in southern Maine, mocked the impotency of the English colonists' prayers with, "Where *is* your O God?"[55] The frequency of attacks on religion and sacred spaces led even such redoubtable men as Increase Mather to question not just whether God had departed from the English, but whether he was actually aiding the Indians: "God seemed to withdraw from the English, and take part with the enemy."[56] This was a far cry from the confidence some English felt at the start of the war, enough for Plymouth Governor Josiah Winslow to declare "our god will get himself a glorious name, by the overthrow of his blasphemous enemies."[57] As the war progressed, many in New England grew convinced that God's "enemies" were English. It is no surprise that Indians—among whom were captured or deserting Christian Indians, former servants, and those who, like the Springfield Indians, had lived in close contact with the English—were familiar with these fears.

It is hard to evade the conclusion that Indians targeted Puritan anxiety over the spiritual causes of the war. Not only did they focus on Puritan religion in their tauntings and on Puritan churches and sacred days in their attacks, but they made claims that seemed to be direct answers to the speculations of Mather and others. William Harris of Rhode Island reported news of the "Enemy triumphing & boasting that god was departed from the English, & was with them."[58] Indians who burned Providence told Roger Williams afterward that "God was [with] them and Had forsaken [the English] for they had so prospered in Killing and Burning us far beyond What we did against them."[59] In Maine, English captive Francis Card reported that the sachem Squando "doth inform [the Indians] that

God doth speak to him, and doth tell him that God hath left *our Nation* to them to *destroy.*"[60] Indian claims that God was against the English constitute evidence of the Indians' careful observation of the English. They understood and used what preoccupied their opponents most.

While Indians' pointed use of religion to undermine English confidence suggests purposeful psychological warfare, we should not consider it mere rhetoric. For many Indians, claims of divine backing may have been not just taunts but also expressions of belief. Indians appealed to their own deities for guidance during the war, practicing spiritual divination. While a captive, Mary Rowlandson witnessed such a ritual, a combination of singing, acting, and inducing a trance through which her captors asked their spirit beings whether and when they should attack the English and if they would triumph.[61] Some Indians also continued to hold to their newfound Christian god, even after abandoning their political allegiance to the English, voluntarily or by force. Many Christian Indians had been treated most un-Christianly by their English neighbors, and, given the powerful argument of Indian success, these Indians might well believe the Christian God had taken their part.

Fears over whether God had withdrawn support from the English bolstered attacks on the Massachusetts government by Indians and Quakers, encouraged political divisions within the colony, and undoubtedly contributed to the rampant resistance to authority plaguing Massachusetts. Because the colony's religious and political life were so closely linked, those who attacked its spiritual standing before God frequently dredged up its political failings as well. Massachusetts's precarious standing before the crown seemed to be a secret to no one. Religious dissidents, unwilling subjects in Maine and New Hampshire, and royalist agitators within the colony knew and berated the colony for its past wrongs. Emboldened by pending royal action against the colony and by colony leaders' timidity in prosecuting resistance, many English colonists withheld support and openly resisted the colony's authority, knowing that in a time of clear weakness little would be done.

Knowledge of the perilous state of Massachusetts extended far beyond its borders. As the Indians and Rhode Islanders had done, many correspondents to England used the war's devastation as a tool to bolster their own standing with the crown. While few items of colonial or even domestic news made it into the only official English newspaper of the time, the *London Gazette,* one letter describing the war, from Benjamin Batten to Thomas Allin, comptroller of the Royal Navy, was paraphrased in the *Gazette* in February 1676. Other letters and books were soon published in London: nineteen accounts in all, totaling over 15,000 volumes on both sides of the Atlantic.[62] Nonpublished accounts reached England as well. Virginia's royal governor William Berkeley provided Whitehall with frequent updates of the travails of his northern neighbor, punctuating his news with observations that the Indian devastations were the colony's just deserts. In addition to sending two letters to Thomas Ludwell, secretary of state of the Council of Virginia, Berkeley sent letters discussing the Indian war to English secretaries of state Henry Coventry and Sir Joseph Williamson and one to the king and Council. In all these letters, he stressed New England's badly weakened condition, claiming that "many of them must be forc'd to desert the place which divers already had done But that they have made several laws to the contrary."[63] Massachusetts's troubles were made worse by the stop the war had put to its trade. Berkeley claimed that trade in beaver was completely halted, as well as half of the fishing trade. If the war continued, he wrote, New England would be "the poorest miserablest People of all the Plantations of the English in America." But Berkeley's sympathy for Massachusetts had limits: "Indeed . . . I should Pity them had they deserved it of the King or his Blessed father."[64] But they did not deserve it. Writing to Secretary Coventry on April 1, 1676, just months before Nathaniel Bacon's Rebellion would cripple his own power in Virginia, Berkeley charged:

let all men fear and tremble at the justice of God on the King's and his most Blessed father's Enemies and learn from them that God can make or find every where Instruments enough to destroy the King's Enemies. I say this because the New England men might as soon and as well have expected to have been invaded by the Persian or Mogul as from their Indians and yet what cannot God do when he is provoked by Rebellion and undoubtedly the New England men were as guilty of the late Blessed King's murder by their Council's Emissaries and wishes as any that most apparently acted in it.[65]

Virginia, which was seeking to preserve and perfect its own charter, had a vested interest in highlighting its own obedience in contrast to Massachusetts's defiance. Trying to obtain more colonial control over taxation, Virginia's agents had been rebuffed with "the objection from the example of New-England." In response, the colony's agents argued that "no disobedience of that plantation ought to cause apprehension of the same in Virginia, whose people steer a quite contrary course from them, for they endeavored as much as they could to sever themselves from the crown; whereas the chief desire of the petitioners is to be assured of the perpetual immediate dependence thereon." Further, they argued that Massachusetts embraced a republican form of government, while Virginia's government imitated monarchy. Massachusetts colonists insisted on electing their own governor; Virginians begged the king to choose their governor for them. In a final slap, the agents proclaimed, "The New-Englanders imagine great felicity in their form of government, civil and ecclesiastical, under which they are trained up to disobedience to the crown and church of England."[66] Such reports could only have bolstered the determination of many in England to act against Massachusetts, to strike the rebels while they were on their knees.

While Berkeley sent frequent reports of Massachusetts's troubles to the king, the colony itself remained silent. Writing to Massachusetts governor Leverett in May 1676, Lord Anglesey chided him for failing to send official word of the state of the war or to request aid, "as if you were independent of our master's crown, needed not his protection, or had deserved ill of him, as some have not been wanting to suggest and urge testimony thereof." The colony's long silence was particularly offensive because news of the war was so plentiful from other sources, such as Berkeley. "We have successive and frequent tidings (like Job's messengers) of the great devastations and spoils that are made by fire and sword upon those plantations," Anglesey wrote.[67] The king could, he continued, "send ships or men to help you, or furnish you with ammunition, as the case requires, or, by a general collection, open the bowels and purses of his people here towards you . . . if you are not wanting to yourselves and failing in that dutiful application which subjects ought to make to their sovereigns in such case."[68] Anglesey's reproof echoes that of John Easton, who was also critical of Massachusetts leaving the king out of the war. Easton, a Quaker and a citizen of Rhode Island, was outraged that the United Colonies had proceeded to war against the Narragansetts without first obtaining the king's approval. In his narrative of the war, Easton charged, "we know no English should begin a war and not first tender for the king to be umpire."[69]

Why had Massachusetts delayed seeking royal aid for so long? Many feared that outside assistance, even from the neighboring royal colony of New York, would prove more harmful to the colony than Indian depredations. Even without his ill-timed aggression toward Connecticut, Andros's position as a royal governor made him suspect to Massachusetts. Royal agents had seriously threatened the colony's authority ten years earlier. What was to stop Andros from asserting royal control once his troops arrived to "assist" against the Indians? Evidence that New Englanders feared such royal interference appears in several letters. Massachusetts colonist Samuel Nowell wrote: "As for ourselves in New England, we are fearing a General Governor should be sent."[70] If such a political change occurred during the war, the new governor would no doubt come with troops who could as easily enforce a change in government as defend the English from their enemies. John Cotton gave voice to such a fear, writing to Thomas Walley, "The rumor of soldiers out of O.E. [Old England] is yet uncertain."[71] Massachusetts had always kept close tabs on the English government's continuing debates over the colony's status.[72] They were well aware that John Mason's heir was again pressing the Committee on Plantations and Privy Council to send another group of royal commissioners or, better yet, a royal governor to New England. Even Massachusetts leaders' failure to send official accounts of the war may reflect their reluctance to add fuel to the ongoing proceedings against them. They knew that royal officials would be displeased to hear that the United Colonies commissioners, so discountenanced by the royal commissioners, were managing the war.

Nevertheless, on April 5, 1676, after a month in which Indians attacked and burned the towns of Groton, Marlborough, Rehoboth, Simsbury, Warwick, Wickford, and Providence, killed eleven at Clark's garrison in Plymouth, and massacred Plymouth's Captain Peirce and forty-two men, the Massachusetts Council finally sent the royal government an account of the war and did, in fact, request assistance. They were very particular about the type of assistance they needed, however—not manpower, but money: "We are unwilling and ashamed, but necessitated to make known the truth unto your honor that for the carrying on of this war & bringing of it to a good and hopeful conclusion, we want money ammunition & arms for the Country is become poor & brought very low."[73] While Massachusetts's belated request for aid was wending its way across the Atlantic, royal officials were busy preparing their own list of requests—or demands—for the colony. On March 10, 1676, the king ordered Edward Randolph to go as his agent to Massachusetts to deliver the complaints of Mason and Gorges.[74] Perhaps these preparations occupied all the time the king and Council had allotted for New England. There is no evidence that aid—financial or material— was sent through any royal channels.[75] Regardless of Lord Anglesey's professions, not only did the king offer no assistance before or after Massachusetts's plea for help but he began plans to launch his own attack on the hapless colony.

The vanguard of royal intervention appeared in the person of Edward Randolph. Through royal belt-tightening, plans for up to five commissioners empowered to act for the king had shrunk to this one relatively impotent messenger, who arrived in Massachusetts in June 1676.[76] The issues Randolph raised as agent were essentially the same raised in 1664: the legitimate extent of Massachusetts boundaries, its obedience to English law, and its treatment of the Indians.[77] Randolph was sent with a long list of questions for Massachusetts, ranging from the colony's violations of English law to the provoking causes of the war. He was also directed to demand that Massachusetts send messengers to England authorized to act for the colony within six months.[78]

Immediately after his arrival, Randolph presented himself before the magistrates. The meeting did not go well. Randolph read the king's letter outlining Mason's and Gorges' complaints and demanded that the colony send messengers to answer the charges. Suspecting that Randolph might not be a fully authorized messenger from the king, the magistrates pressed him to reveal whether he had any royal business other than Mason's complaints. When it became clear that he did not, they dismissed him as "Mr. Mason's agent."[79] That action, their way "of discountenancing all affairs that come to them from the King," enfuriated Randolph. Primed for conflict, Randolph recorded every hint of disrespect for him and, by implication, his royal master. Only three of the assembled magistrates "uncovered" their heads in respect as he read them the king's letter, he complained to Charles II, and he huffed to Secretary of State Coventry that they "yet glory in their affronting Sir Robert Carr and other of the King's commissioners."[80] His authority slighted, Randolph adopted an imperious tone with the magistrates, demanding that they immediately convene the General Court to vote on whether to send the messengers. In response, the magistrates declared that Randolph had "exceeded his errand, and in a menacing way [advised him] not to be found slighting or imposing on their authority."[81]

A bristling insistence on their own authority was expected behavior from the magistrates, but they soon had added reason for their antagonism. In July, Randolph traveled to New Hampshire, passing through "several of the most considerable towns" and publishing the contents of Mason's complaint. The "whole country" complained of Massachusetts's "oppression and usurpation," Randolph reported, and they had "been for a long time earnestly expecting to be delivered from the government of the Massachusets Bay." While he was in New Hampshire, several "principal inhabitants" of Maine visited Randolph, begging relief from their long oppression by Massachusetts and urging him to "represent their condition to your Majesty."[82]

Not surprisingly, when Randolph returned to Boston and again sought the General Court's answer to the king's letter and Mason's petition, Governor Leverett charged him with a design to "make a mutiny and disturbance in the country and to withdraw the people from their obedience to the magistracy of that colony and the authority thereof."[83] Randolph's hobnobbing with discontents in Portsmouth had rekindled complaints against Massachusetts's usurping government, and like-thinking residents of Boston were probably also crowing that the colony's day was hastening to an end. So suspicious of Randolph's intentions were the magistrates that they refused to allow him to see the contents of their reply to the king, in spite of the fact that he would be their courier to the crown.[84]

Firsthand experience with the implacable magistrates soon convinced Randolph that nothing short of force would serve to bring Massachusetts into compliance with English law. Writing to an English secretary of state in July, Randolph urged him to send three frigates and three ketches to blockade all of Boston's shipping, "for the least stop on their trade, together with the present disturbance from the Indians, would turn them all on their magistrates and force them to an humble and ready submission." A blockade was well and good, but war was even better. Why not also get the ships to "perform other acts of hostility against these revolters"? Being under attack from both the Indians on the frontier and a royal fleet offshore "would bring them to the King's terms, and do more in one week than all the orders of King and Council in seven years."[85] Massachusetts had never been in such a vulnerable position, and might never be again. Now was clearly the time to bring the colony to heel.[86]

Such cold-blooded plotting makes it clear why Randolph was considered the "evil genius behind the downfall of the Puritan commonwealth in Massachusetts."[87] But we should not consider either Randolph or Mason a perfect mirror of the royal government's attitude toward the colony. When Mason had urged the Committee on Plantations to send a royal governor in January 1676, it had demurred. Besides the great expense that would involve, its members reasoned that doing so would look like "awarding execution on those people before they were heard."[88] Clearly, whipping Massachusetts into line was more important to people who had a personal stake in New England, such as Mason and Gorges, or who had a career to make there, such as Edward Randolph, than to the royal government at large. For that government, Massachusetts was a very small, not very lucrative item in a calendar stuffed with more pressing and profitable business. Hence the most characteristic aspect of the half-century-long tug-of-war over the Massachusetts charter was delay, created not only by the slowly grinding wheels of royal bureaucracy, but by the vast distance between Old and New England.[89] Responses to specific royal queries or commands generally took six months, and if Massachusetts's response was not obedience but argument, as it almost always was, a simple exchange could take years. Under such circumstances, it is not surprising that once the royal commissioners had left the scene Massachusetts returned to its former ways. Nor is it surprising that men such as Randolph felt compelled to resort to force. Given Massachusetts's history of obduracy and the inherent delays of distance, royal action was the exception, and it had to be driven by someone with a sense of mission. To the magistrates' dismay, that person was present in Edward Randolph.

Although Randolph's visit was short, it was long enough to build enormous antipathy on both sides. Following his return to England, Randolph wrote lengthy answers to the list of queries sent with him, casting barbs at Massachusetts leaders at every opportunity. Like the commissioners a decade earlier, Randolph repeatedly emphasized divisions in the colony and, also like them, gave a highly exaggerated report of the proportion of colonists favorable to the establishment of royal government. By his report, the inhabitants were "generally" well affected to the king and his government and "very desirous of submitting to a general governor to be established by his Majesty." Most of the magistrates, on the other hand, were of "different principles." They and "some few others of the same faction, keep the country in subjection and slavery, backed with the authority of a pretended charter."[90] Not only were these leaders, who "direct and manage all affairs as they please," far in the minority, but their adherents—church members all—were an "inconsiderable" proportion of the inhabitants, no more than one-sixth. And they were the dross of the country. Randolph sneered that at Harvard College's annual commencement, the speeches (in English, not Latin) were attended by "throngs of illiterate elders and church members."[91] The governor and magistrates were, he claimed, "most of them inconsiderable mechanics packed by the prevailing party of factious ministry who have a fellow-feeling both in the command and profit." The ministry were "generally inclined to sedition, being proud, ignorant, and imperious."[92] The more numerous—and better affected—inhabitants were only prevented from protesting their condition by fear of such reprisals as those who signed the 1666 petition in favor of sending agents to London received. To emphasize his point, Randolph appended a copy of that petition to his report, but he failed to also append any evidence of either past or continuing reprisals against those who signed it.[93]

In response to royal queries about the cause of the war, Randolph repeated charges that Captain Wynborne, who had visited New England in 1673, had made before the Committee for Trade and Plantations in December 1676. Wynborne had described the practice of forcing Indians to labor ten days on Castle Island as a penalty for drunkenness and then getting them drunk on the ninth day to get their labor for another ten. This "barbarous usage made not only those poor sufferers, but the other Indians, to vow revenge," Wynborne claimed. Randolph echoed his words: the enforced labor "did highly incense the Indians."[94] Randolph also noted wrongs Philip had suffered before the war, as well as the Massachusetts Council's list of provoking sins, but he concluded by laying the blame for the extent of Indian depredations on the dealings of Massachusetts (not Plymouth) with the Indians: "whatever be the cause, the English have contributed much to their misfortunes" by training the Indians in the use and repair of firearms, admitting them to their musters, and gathering the Indians in praying towns with trained bands and officers. The Christian Indians, Randolph declared, again without offering substantiation, "have been the most barbarous and cruel enemies to the English of any others."[95]

While Randolph and Mason kept up the pressure on the royal government to act against the wayward colony, Massachusetts leaders debated how to respond to the king's demand for agents. The magistrates summoned a council of elders to advise them, and that group declared that only good could come from honoring the colony's "political fathers."[96] A decade earlier the magistrates had responded far differently to the king's demand that they send agents to answer to him. Then they had asked no one's advice in making their decision, and when colonists submitted their opinions anyway, the Court had issued a stern reproof. Clearly, just as they had with the stockade proposal, the colony's leaders felt the need for evidence that others in the colony supported their course of action before they would move. In response to the elders' suggestion, the magistrates appointed William Stoughton and Peter Bulkeley as agents and began gathering depositions and commissioning maps for them to use to address the boundary disputes. At the same time, Daniel Gookin, superintendent of the Indians, arranged to have two Indian boys accompany the agents to England. Wynborne's and Mason's charges of the ill usage Indians had received in Massachusetts and the spur it had given to war needed to be refuted. The boys, healthy and well-dressed, would be living testimonies of the care the colony gave its Indian subjects.[97]

The colony did its best to present a united front, in contrast to persistent charges of disunity from Randolph, the royal commissioners, and their allies in New and Old England. Both positions were exaggerated. While Randolph's claims that a tiny minority oppressed the rest of the colony were inaccurate, the colony in fact was divided. The split between moderates and the commonwealth party was still present, and while some continued to call for accommodation to the king's demands, others insisted on holding to practices known to be offensive to the king, even if it cost them their charter. In December 1676, just as the Massachusetts agents were preparing to depart, Samuel Sewall recorded that the Rev. Thomas Shepherd had spoken in favor of suppressing "the disorderly Meetings of Quakers and Anabaptists," adding, "As to what it might injure the country in respect of England, trust God with it."[98]

Well into the most devastating war ever to strike New England, the Massachusetts government found not only its physical but its civil existence assailed from all sides, greatly compounding the sense many felt that God had withdrawn his approval and assistance from the colony. Religious dissidents attacked the Massachusetts government, as did Indians and political enemies. The war was truly on two fronts, as the Massachusetts Council publicly acknowledged: "we having greatly incensed [God] to stir up many Adversaries against us, not only abroad, but also at our own Doors."[99]

Divisions plagued the Indians as well as their English enemies, dispiriting them and undermining their efforts in the war. Unlike the English, whose hierarchical systems of governance were generally similar to each other, the Indians' styles of government varied. Philip's Wampanoags, like many coastal Indian peoples, followed a model in which hierarchy was dominant.[100] The Narragansetts followed a similar pattern, which may explain both their ability to remain out of the war until the Great Swamp Fight and Niantic sachem Ninigret's success in keeping his people out of the war altogether. Among the Nipmucks, whom William Hubbard derided for having "four too many [sachems] to govern so small a People," government by consensus was more dominant, and many young Nipmucks deserted their more cautious sachems to join Philip's cause.[101] These contrasting approaches to authority were complicated by the ties each people had to the English, connections that many sachems among them wished to preserve. Contradictory sources of authority soon came to undermine Philip's efforts. The decision to join Philip or remain loyal to the English had been

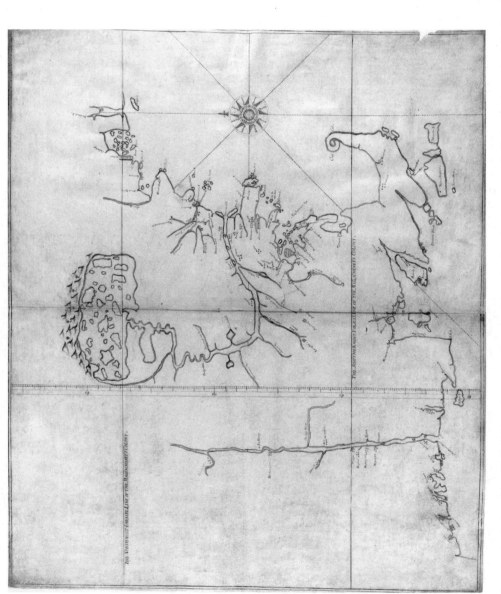

Figure 17. This map, depicting the official Massachusetts colony position that its charter granted all the land south of the headwaters of the Merrimack River, was sent to England with colony agents William Stoughton and Peter Bulkeley to assist them in defending the claim to Maine and New Hampshire. Courtesy of the John Carter Brown Library, Brown University.

wrenching for many Indian groups. For some, the choice had been forced on them by English suspicion and hostility, and even after months ostensibly engaged in the war, their resistance to Philip continued. English observers reported that Indians surrendering to colonial governments "[cried] out against King Philip, and other ill Counselors, as the Causes of their Misfortunes."[102] Such evidence that many Indians failed to support Philip increased divisions, making Indians who were still fighting the English suspicious of each other. Following the Great Swamp Fight, Narragansett Indians sent an English head to an Indian council gathered in central Massachusetts as a demonstration of their new commitment to the Indian war. Instead of welcoming the messengers, Indians attending the council shot at them and said "they had been friends to the English, and that head was nothing."[103]

As among the English, the physical pressures of war aggravated existing divisions. Indians had had the upper hand through most of the first year of the war, but by spring of 1676 the tide was turning. Both sides recognized that food supplies could be a more significant factor than gunpowder in protracted warfare. All through the fighting, both English and Indians sought to destroy or take for themselves their enemies' stands of corn and livestock. Looting and destruction made grain scarce among both peoples, but particularly among the constantly moving Indians. Driven from food stores and unable to plant fields, many Indians began to fall prey to hunger and disease, which weakened both body and spirit. Mary Rowlandson testified to the impact of food shortages on the Narragansetts. She and her captors were starving much of the time. At one point her master's maid took a three-week journey to Narragansett country to gather corn from storage, only to return with a paltry peck and a half. Clearly, English raids had plundered many of the Indian food stores. Without corn, the Indians were reduced to eating bones, tree bark, and, when they could get them, plundered provisions from the English.[104]

The winter had been unusually severe. And even when it was warm enough to begin planting, such an undertaking was perilous. Any large gathering of people to fish, plant, or repair weapons ran the risk of surprise and massacre, such as befell the Indians camped at Turner's Falls. At the start of the war, Uncas and other Indian sachems had given Connecticut colony leaders explicit instructions on which tactics would discourage their Indian opponents so that "the enemies' hearts will be weakened or damped."[105] Clearly, nine months later sickness and starvation had done the English armies' work for them, leaving the Indians "to their own Divisions, Taking away their Spirits," and "Cutting off their Principal men, *Sachems* and others."[106] Diminishing numbers and divisions among those remaining significantly hampered Philip's ability to press the war forward.

As early as January 1676, immediately following the Great Swamp Fight, recognition of the desperate situation of Philip's allies made some sachems doubt the wisdom of joining the fight. When Pomham told fellow Narragansett sachem Canonchet that they only had powder enough for a single charge for each of 400 guns, Canonchet declared, "had he known they were not better furnished, he would have been elsewhere this winter."[107] At that point, of course, Canonchet's only choices were to fight or die. His participation in the swamp fight had marked him as "a man of death" among the English. Known for his courage and leadership ability, Canonchet became one of the principal leaders of the war. Despite his reservations about shortages of food and powder, Canonchet led the Indians in a string of devastating attacks on outlying English towns from February through early April, his vigorous pursuit of the war appearing in striking contrast to Philip's absence during most of the winter and spring. In April 1676, however, Canonchet was captured by a force of Connecticut soldiers and allied Mohegan Indians and executed at Stonington.

Canonchet's death was a critical turning point in the war, seriously undermining Indian morale and leadership. It was also a significant event for the English, who knew his death would strike a blow to Indian hopes. But what the English writing of the event seemed to find most compelling was the manner of Canonchet's death, the sachem's regal bearing in his last moments. The author of "News from New England" described Canonchet's capture and the English attempt to interrogate him. To this attempt, and to "many other interrogatories he made no other reply, but that 'he was born a Prince, and if Princes came to speak with him, he would answer them, But none of those present being Princes, he thought himself obliged in honor to hold his Tongue.'" Nathaniel Saltonstall added that Canonchet refused to "hold Discourse with such Persons, below his Birth and Quality." When informed he was to be executed, Canonchet asked that it be done by the Mohegan sachem and English ally Uncas, "acknowledging him his fellow Prince." The incredulous tone of both accounts suggests that the writers found Canonchet's pretensions to royalty ludicrous. The English rejected the idea that Indians could be their superiors in status or that they were worthy of deference. Indians who demanded such respect earned the epithet "insolent" and the scorn of the English. William Hubbard demonstrated this attitude when he proclaimed that Canonchet was "heir of all his Father's Pride and Insolency."[108] For Canonchet, just as clearly, yielding to common English soldiers' questioning would be ludicrous. To the last, he refused to acknowledge their equality with him. For their part, the English refused to recognize Canonchet's authority, drawing and quartering him after his execution in the manner of a traitor, a person who defies his superior.

One chronicler of the war argued that the Indians' devastating attack on Sudbury on April 21, 1676, came in revenge for Canonchet's death. Indeed, it exacted a heavy toll on the English. But the Sudbury fight was the last significant victory for the Indians, the "Rage of an Expiring

Enemy," as one English observer put it.[109] Stripped of their finest leader and suffering the effects of a long, lean winter, the heart seemed to go out of Philip's allies. An Indian woman taken captive by the English reported that after the Turner's Falls massacre only Philip and one other sachem kept the war going. All the others "would gladly yield to any terms of Peace with the English."[110] One sachem of this mind was the Nipmuck leader Sagamore Sam, who welcomed English messengers treating for peace in the spring of 1676. He reflected the divisions splitting the Indians. The sagamore reported that Philip and Quinnapin had sent him orders to kill the English messengers, but he would not: "I said if any kill them, I'll kill them."[111] By June so many Indians had lost the will to fight that alliances broke down: "they from that Time began to separate one from another, and every Nation of them to shift for themselves."[112] Benjamin Church reported conversing with Indians who said "they were weary of fighting, and that they had fought so long by *Philip's* Instigation, but they could not tell for what End, and therefore were resolved they would fight no longer." Unwilling to continue under Philip's leadership, these Indians asked Church to go to Plymouth's governor for them and declare their willingness to submit to English authority once again.[113] The Indians' dwindling spirit was readily apparent in battle; they seemed to give up almost without a fight. On June 28, 1676, English and allied Indians captured 28 of the enemy, "and this without the Slaughter or hurt of the *Indians* our Friends."[114]

The fact that Indian alliances began splintering soon after Canonchet's death is significant; it illustrates the impact of generational divisions on the Indian war effort. A young man himself, Canonchet was also the leader "to whom the young fighting men did adhere."[115] But even the able and respected Canonchet could not ensure the obedience of all his followers. During the winter of 1676, when the Indians experienced victory after victory in the English backcountry, Canonchet made a bold and shrewd proposal. Rather than fight every group of English soldiers "sent out hither and thither, which they could easily espy, and by scouts discern and avoid," he suggested that the Indians stage simultaneous attacks on twenty different English "out plantations." Each group of twenty fighting men under an Indian captain would

make their assaults; and burn and kill and destroy all they could, forcing those few left into their Garrison Houses, out of which they might easily afterwards weary and take them; the news whereof coming from so many places at once, to them in the Bay, would appall and amaze them, as not knowing what parties, with safety to send out to so many places at once to help them, but be forced to leave them to our wills, and losing thereby their wonted supplies of victuals, will be forced to seek peace with us upon any terms.[116]

This proposal showed Canonchet to be a perceptive observer of the besieged English. The English had responded with despair to even two or three attacks within a week. Twenty simultaneous assaults would, undoubt-edly, do much more than "appall and amaze" them. Canonchet's advice was "liked by the olden Indians." The younger warriors, however, rejected it: "the young men and strength of their soldiery, they liked not this coun-sel, but they will fight the English forces wherever they see or hear of them, and question not to overcome them; and the English armies being destroyed, then all the towns are their own, with the more ease; and this later self conceited counsel carrieth and the other is rejected."[117] Thus, even under a strong leader, internal divisions kept the Indians from pursu-ing a strategy likely to have been highly effective.

After Canonchet's death, divisions grew. Older sachems, most of them reluctant to fight, would not step into the breach created by the powerful leader's death. Many sachems had already died. The death toll among Indi-ans during the war, compounded by disease and starvation, ran very high, triple the English toll, which did not exceed 1,000.[118] Just as privations of war had undermined the Massachusetts war effort, starvation, sickness, and loss of leadership weakened Indian alliances. The vacuum of leadership made sustaining a united effort nearly impossible. By June 1676 it was clear, at least in southern New England, that the English had won. For the Indi-ans, choices were few: they could continue fighting, which Philip and a few stalwarts such as Totoson did for several more months; they could abandon their homelands and seek refuge in a new area, which many did, settling in Schagticoke on the invitation of New York's Governor Andros; or they could resubmit to the Massachusetts or Plymouth governments, hoping for mercy.[119]

Starting in late June 1676, both Massachusetts and Plymouth issued proc-lamations granting mercy to Indians who surrendered to English authority. Almost immediately, Indians began flooding in. Their deplorable condi-tion bore mute witness to why surrender was preferable to remaining in the field. English witnesses reported the Indians "almost starved," and some of the Indians admitted that in recent battles "their Arms shook and trem-bled so, that they could not so readily discharge their Guns as they would have done."[120] It is unclear whether those who chose to surrender knew that "mercy" meant only that their lives would be spared, and then only if they had not participated in any "murders," acts that the English thought went beyond the pale of civilized warfare.[121] Even if they kept their lives, they could be sold out of the country, and many were. Some of those who surrendered, including some Nipmuck sachems, agreed to help the English fight the remaining enemy and to convince other Indians to sub-mit to English authority. Thus active undermining of Philip's authority by former allies began in earnest.[122]

Even those who did not submit to the English showed little interest in continuing the war. An Indian captive reported to Samuel Hunting that most of the Indians who had been in hostility with the English had fled to the north, some to Pennacook, others to Fort Albany in New York. A few remained near their cornfields in the Wachuset area, but they had convened a general meeting and "agreed not to fight the english any longer which he saith is the reason they have killed no english lately." Increase Mather's son and fellow minister Cotton Mather attributed the Indians' abandonment of the war effort to their belief that their spirit beings no longer supported them. These beings ("*daemons*," Mather called them) "who visibly exhibited themselves among them at their *powwowing* or conjuring, signified still unto them, that they could now *do no more for them*," leaving them "dispirited . . . like men under a *fascination*."[123] Samuel Hunting also reported that in contrast to the Indians' earlier claims that the English God had abandoned the English for the Indians, they now said "that god's hand is against them the sickness destroying many of them many more being very feeble and unable for service."[124] Such statements may have influenced the English, too, to believe that God now favored their cause. Increase Mather reported that English successes in the early summer of 1676 corresponded with a burst of renewals in church covenants, particularly in Plymouth Colony, where the colony leaders encouraged it. Mather believed this harmony of divine and civil authority was pleasing to God, and the course of the war seemed to confirm it.[125]

The summer of 1676 was the nadir of Indian fortunes. Former allies of Philip, the Nipmuck sachem Sagamore Sam, Saconnet sachem Awashonks, and others had broken with him and begun actively assisting the English. Many sachems and warriors were dead; others had surrendered or scattered to places of refuge. Confidence was at a low point, and Philip was left nearly alone to carry on the fight. Having spent much of the winter in New York with many of his followers, Philip found his safe haven violently disrupted by a Mohawk attack in the spring, initiated by royal governor Edmund Andros.[126] Returning to Mount Hope by late July 1676, Philip was pursued by Plymouth's Captain Benjamin Church and his force of surrendered Indians. Church's soldiers captured or accepted the surrenders of dozens of Indians as they made their way through the sachem's territory, using Indian tactics of ambush and stealth against their very tutors. Finally, on August 12, 1676, one of Church's Indian soldiers shot and killed Philip. Many English, who had pinned their antipathy and fears on "that monster that hath Caused us so much mischief," must have hoped the conflict was at an end now that its leader was dead.[127] But the war was only half over. Fighting continued in Maine, where the same problems of disunity would undermine the efforts of both Indians and English to bring the war to an end.

The loss of heart evident among Indian and English participants in King Philip's War arose from the striking divisions within both societies. Contrary views of the justice or practicability of the war made some colonists hold back from supporting their leaders' edicts, and disobedience undermined leaders' ability to wage war effectively. As the war stalled, questions about divine displeasure with the colony and renewed threats to its charter from England kept confidence spiraling downwards. Divisions also troubled the Indians. As among the English, some Indians questioned the wisdom and justice of the war, and the lack of unity prompted suspicion among the ranks. Generational divisions and the deaths of several important Indian leaders combined with the severe stresses of winter fighting to dishearten and further divide the Indians from each other, leading to the surrender of hundreds of former combatants. But the surge in confidence Massachusetts and its allies drew from this turn of fortune was only temporary. The fighting dragged on in Maine, and Massachusetts's efforts to wage war in a place where dissatisfaction with the Bay Colony's authority had festered for decades met dramatic resistance. The insults of war would heighten these colonists' protests against Massachusetts's intrusion and help bring looming threats of royal intervention to realization.

Chapter 9

Massachusetts Fights Alone

Since Indian John Wompas had returned from England early in the summer of 1677, he had troubled his English neighbors with an unrelenting stream of threats, boasts, and drunken tirades. Appearing before magistrate Daniel Gookin on October 8, 1677, Hannah and Daniel Meade presented their complaints about Wompas. He had approached Daniel sometime in the previous summer and had made a point of telling him of his recent return from England, where he had gone to petition the king about a land dispute. Meade, like many others in Massachusetts, was anxious for news of England, particularly since the colony's agents, Peter Bulkeley and William Stoughton, were there seeking reconfirmation of the Massachusetts charter. He urged Wompas to tell "whether he had seen the country messengers there." Wompas replied, "he had seen them, & spake with them & that the king sent for them to come to him upon the Sabbath day & that they refused to go at that time because it was against their judgment, & contrary to their religion." If there had been any doubt in the king's mind about where he stood on Massachusetts's hierarchical ladder, Stoughton and Bulkeley had removed it. God outranked King Charles II. With clear relish, Wompas went on to describe the agents' visit to the king the following day, where Stoughton got upon his knees and begged for the patent's renewal, and the king's perturbed answer: "that his grand father had [given] them their patent but they had forfeited it and acted contrary to it." Wompas seconded the king's opinion, speaking "many words in a disdainful way of the English: both of the Authority of the country & of the people, saying that they had acted . . . weakly in managing the war with the indians: & that they & the English had nothing to do to send men to the eastward it being out of this jurisdiction."

In September, Wompas visited the Meades' house again. Daniel was away from home, but Hannah was there with her friend Goody Man. Wompas brought Christian Indian Andrew Pittimee with him, called for beer, helped himself to tobacco, and then launched into a "disparaging . . . contemptuous" tirade against English management of the Indian war: "And said he further what had the english to do to send out soldiers to the eastward or to the southward; they should have stayed at home they had nothing to do there."[1] Fresh from a visit to the king and bearing his royal letter,

Wompas had clearly been imbibing more heady stuff than beer. Massachusetts, he argued, had no right to carry the war into Maine or Rhode Island, "both out of [Massachusetts] jurisdiction." Furthermore, in the weeks leading up to his trial, Wompas tweaked his English neighbors on their shaky standing before the king: "He boasted of his Being the king's subject & when the english to whom he spake replied that they were his majesty's subjects as well as he, wompas answered he questioned that . . . as if they were not legal subjects to his majesty."[2] "New England hath lost the day," he intoned to Hannah Meade, and "it is known in old england."[3]

Maine was, as Wompas pointedly noted, "out of [Massachusetts] jurisdiction."[4] This fact hampered Massachusetts's war efforts significantly. Many Maine residents resented the Bay Colony's continued presence in the region and resisted the authority of its military as well as civil officers; demands for men and taxes to support the war merely aggravated these tensions. Distance compounded the expenses of transporting and feeding soldiers, and Massachusetts's United Colonies allies, doubtful of the colony's right to Maine, hesitated to provide support badly needed by the exhausted colony in the ending stages of the war. For those who resisted Massachusetts governance—Indian and English—appealing to royal authority during the war became an attractive recourse, as well as a growing threat to Massachusetts's political stability.

War ravaged the coastal towns of Maine and New Hampshire twice as long as it raged in southern New England.[5] Indians attacked the Maine town of Falmouth in September 1675, just months after the outbreak of war in Plymouth, and peace was not finally settled until April 1678. The extra year and a half of hostilities drew men and supplies north from war-weary Massachusetts to defend a land many of them, including William Hubbard, deemed not worth saving: "the whole [of Maine] being scarce worth half those Men's Lives that have been lost these two last Years."[6] Hubbard's dismissive evaluation reflects the ongoing tensions between Massachusetts and Maine, unresolved conflicts that dramatically affected the course of war in that region.

Much contemporary writing on the war displays a similarly contemptuous attitude toward Massachusetts's neighbors to the northeast, arising from the long-standing cultural and political conflict between the two regions. Maine's "scattering" pattern of settlement, which Hubbard attributed to overlapping patent claims ("every considerable Parcel of land being by Patent granted to several particular Persons"), hindered establishing towns. This made wartime defense very difficult.[7] In the minds of many from Massachusetts, it also reflected Maine's obstinate resistance to any kind of communal order and spiritual life. Hubbard complained that "these Scattering Plantations in our Borders" were "desirous to shake off all Yoke of Government, both sacred and civil, and so transforming themselves as much as well they could into the Manners of the Indians they lived amongst."[8] Increase Mather held up the Wakely family, one of the first English casualties of the war in Maine, as a prime example of the consequences of such a mode of living. Thomas Wakely, the family patriarch, was "esteemed a godly Man." Like many others, however, Wakely's move to Maine separated him from regular worship and fellowship with the godly, prompting some twinges of conscience: "He would sometimes say with tears, that he believed God was angry with him, because although he came into New-England for the Gospel's sake, yet he had left another place in this Country, where there was a Church of Christ, which he once was in Communion with, and had lived many years in a Plantation where was no *Church, nor Instituted Worship.*"[9] Distant neighbors provided no refuge for Wakely when Indians attacked, burning his home, killing him, his wife, their pregnant daughter, and two children, and carrying three others away as captives.[10]

The same observers who disapproved of Maine's flouting of the communal model saw the Indian attacks on Maine's English, who had thrown off both civil and religious government, as just. Having chosen to live like Indians, Maine's settlers were "most deservedly . . . left to be put under the Yoke and Power of the Indians themselves," Hubbard declared.[11] This phrase suggests that Indian success against Maine's English was divine justice, but Massachusetts writers claimed it was retributive justice as well, arguing that Indian attacks came in response to the repeated provocations of Maine settlers loath to follow civil or godly law.[12] Several historians have claimed that the English who chronicled King Philip's War refused to acknowledge any provoking causes for the Indians' uprising, justifying the English role as purely defensive.[13] While that is an exaggeration for the war in southern New England, it applies not at all to the war to the northeast, where both contemporary and modern historians acknowledged English provocations that would have upset even the most amicable relations between people.

It is not surprising that disapproving ministers from Massachusetts derided Maine residents for abusing the Indians, but some Maine residents themselves admitted fault. Writing to Governor Leverett on September 22, 1675, Maine trader Thomas Gardiner claimed that the Indian uprising was caused "by our own Actings." In explanation, he described the response of his neighbors when news of war to the south reached them in July: "Sir upon the first News of the wars with the Indians at Plimouth divers persons from Kenibek & Shepscott got together making them selves officers & went up Kenibeke River & demanded the Indians' Arms."[14] How these self-appointed officials represented their authority is unclear, but the Indians reluctantly surrendered their weapons and gave hostages for peaceful behavior. Not satisfied with this show of submission, or believing there were yet more arms hidden away, Lieutenant Silvanus Davis sent a messenger to again demand the Indians' guns. This time, the Indians refused, in spite of the agent's threat that if they did not surrender their arms, the English would kill them all.[15] (Describing this incident, William Hubbard proclaimed, "*He that sendeth a Message by the Hand of a Fool* saith Solomon, *cutteth off the Feet and drinketh Damage.*")[16]

The English seizure of guns had severe consequences for the Indians, driving many to starvation and open hostility. Over the years, New England Indians had become increasingly reliant on English guns to obtain both food and the furs vital to their trade. This was particularly the case in Maine, where harsh weather and a shortened growing season discouraged agriculture. When the English seized Indian guns, they put the Indians in a vulnerable position that quickly grew insupportable. "Indians in these parts did never Appear dissatisfied until their Arms were Taken Away," Gardiner reported.[17] Penobscot sachem Madockawando confirmed Gardiner's claim, saying "that if the English were their Friends as they pretended, they would not suffer them to die, For want" of powder.[18] The winter of 1675–76 was unusually bitter; deprived of powder and guns, many Indians suffered terribly, some resorting to eating hides taken in earlier hunts, "which they soaked in water till they became soft and eatable."[19] In a letter to Governor Leverett, Indians Deogenes and Madoasquarbet complained that "because there was war at naragans you come here when we were quiet & took away our guns & made prisoners of our chief sagamore & that winter for want of our guns there was several starved."[20] Under such straits, the Indians faced a stark choice: "die, or leave their Country, and go all over to the *French*."[21] Gardiner had warned of such consequences, saying "I doubt of such Actions whether they may not be forced to go to the french for Relief or fight Against us having nothing for their support Almost in these parts but their guns."[22]

English trade practices, too, provoked Indian hostilities. Richard Waldron, one of the highest ranking officers appointed by Massachusetts to carry on the war in Maine and New Hampshire, was also a leading Indian trader in the area with a reputation for unfair dealing. Historian Samuel Drake claimed that "It is a tradition to this day all over that part of the country, that Major Waldron took great advantage of [the Indians] in trade."[23] The first home attacked in Maine was that of trader Thomas Purchase, also known for his sharp dealings with Indians. One Androscoggin claimed he had paid Purchase one hundred pounds for liquor and gotten nothing but "Water drawn out of Mr. Purchase his Well."[24] Hubbard claimed that the Indians involved in the autumn attacks on the Purchase and Wakely homes were the men who had been taken as hostages in July; they had quickly escaped the English, "trusting more to the Celerity of their own Feet than to the Civility of their *English* Friends."[25] The English attempt to ensure peace in Maine had clearly backfired. Seizing guns and hostages had an enduring impact on Indian-English relations in Maine. As with the Narragansetts, English demands demonstrated their belief that the Indians were untrustworthy inferiors, not "friends." This demonstration seriously undermined Indian trust in the English, who had so clearly demonstrated their lack of trust in them.

Massachusetts's ability to fight the war in Maine was greatly hampered by its colonists' war weariness and the resistance of local residents to its efforts. Continual fighting in Maine and New Hampshire required both more men and more money, but a year and half of war in the south had exhausted and depleted militias, coffers were long empty, and few taxes could be wrung from the devastated locals to make up the deficit. Not only was the colony hard pressed for soldiers to go to the northeast to fight, but the inhabitants of that region were themselves reluctant soldiers. With few local forces to help them, the southern soldiers sent to defend Maine and New Hampshire made little headway against the Wabanaki Indians. So pitiful was the Massachusetts effort that some in Maine, already disposed to bitterness against the Bay Colony, thought the neglect was purposeful, revenge for Maine's past attempts to overthrow Massachusetts jurisdiction. Writing in 1676 to the king by way of royal agent Edward Randolph, some complained they had been "suffered to be ruined by the Indians for having formerly expressed their duty to your Majesty when your Majesty's commissioners were in that country."[26] Such charges cut two ways. Not only were they evidence of continuing resistance to Massachusetts's authority, but they were also proof that the war itself had been added to the list of the colony's misdeeds clamoring for redress from the king.

Maintaining obedience to law and order was a serious wartime problem for the English in Massachusetts; in Maine the problem reached epic proportions. In neither their provocations of Indians nor their resistance to carrying on the war were Maine residents behaving differently from many colonists in Massachusetts. But Maine's distance from the centers of authority made it more difficult for Massachusetts to enforce obedience there, and the colony's attempts to assert authority not only were less successful, but reopened divisions formed in past conflicts between Massachusetts and Maine. One of the first sites of conflict was the defense of the frontier. Massachusetts had resolved to maintain the defensive line of English settlements; Maine settlers were determined to flee the destruction. A large number of Maine residents made a rapid exodus from their homes as soon as reports of Indian attacks reached them. Gardiner reported in September 1675 that everyone in the Kennebec region had deserted houses, crops, and cattle and sought refuge on Monhegan and Damariscove Islands, the result of which "will be A famine."[27] Farther south, settlers left for Salem and other strongholds near the Piscataqua River or gathered with neighbors in garrison houses.[28] Desperately trying to maintain a toehold in the region, Massachusetts-appointed officers in Maine wrote the General Court in June 1677 that "very many of the Inhabitants of the County of yorkeshire and of the county of dover and portsmouth . . . have left their habitations & garrisons and are gone into other parts of the country." They begged the magistrates to order the deserters to return and also requested assistance in enforcing orders against the remaining settlers departing "without licence from authority."[29]

For those who did not join the exodus from Maine, the garrison living required under Indian attack revived long-standing grudges between supporters of current and previous government regimes. Richard Waldron wrote to Governor Leverett that most residents of the Casco Bay region had collected in the garrison house of Major Brian Pendleton; some, however, insisted on going to Major William Phillips's house instead. Phillips and Pendleton had been ardent opponents during the 1668 Massachusetts takeover of Maine government. Phillips had finally yielded to Massachusetts, and in 1676 both he and Pendleton held military commissions from the colony, but old wounds still festered. When it became necessary for the English to gather in garrisons, the old lines were redrawn. John Bonithon, a passionate opponent of Massachusetts rule, refused to house himself under Pendleton's roof, traveling to Phillips's garrison instead. Only after a sleepless night of constant bombardment from Indian guns and a near escape from having the house burned around them did the residents of Phillips's garrison join Pendleton at Winter Harbor.[30]

In Maine, where the devastation of war was most severe, the financial burdens of war were also heavier and resistance to wartime expenses more determined. Joshua Scottow, captain of the garrison at Black Point, petitioned the General Court for reimbursement of more than 150 pounds he had spent to maintain the garrison. The Court consented to the request but ordered that the accounts be remitted to the York County Court in Maine for payment. Such a course was as good as a guarantee that the expenses would never be reimbursed. York County could only pay what it gathered in taxes, and few in Maine could or would pay. Adding insult to injury, the Court appended to its reply the order that all residents of the garrison "take Care for Supply & Maintenance of that garrison at their own Charge."[31]

The danger of Indian attack persisted in Maine well beyond the end of danger in Massachusetts. Many Maine residents, in exile from their homes, lacked any income from farming, fishing, or other businesses. Those remaining were often prevented from gathering harvests or planting new crops by the same dangers their neighbors had fled. Given these pressures, as well as Maine's abiding resentment of Massachusetts's interference, it is not surprising that Massachusetts officers had little success collecting taxes north of the Piscataqua River. When Kittery town leaders received notice that the May 1676 General Court had issued a new round of taxes, they sent a letter complaining of the excessive burden. Five months later, when the Court inquired why no rates had been sent in, town officer Nathaniel

Fryer replied that the town was too long and the notice too short to let the selectmen know their duty.[32] "Scattered" living had its advantages.

Maine residents showed a persistent commitment to self-preservation by resisting—or ignoring—demands for taxes. They showed the same spirit by placing personal and family welfare above wartime trade and military regulations. A group of Maine fathers applied to Captain William Hathorne, a prominent resident of Salem stationed in Wells, for permission to leave the garrison to gather provisions from their homes. Hathorne refused their request; they went anyway, protesting that their families would starve otherwise.[33] James Andrews of Casco Bay refused the demand of the Falmouth military committee for a barrel of powder, contending that he had only one, "which I had purchased for the defence of my own family and the rest of my neighbors that were come into my house for security." Imprisoned in George Munjoy's house until he would agree to give up the barrel, Andrews sent his complaints to the Massachusetts Council, which ordered that twenty pounds of the powder be returned to him.[34] Concerns for their family welfare—or personal profit—may have motivated traders such as Thomas Gardiner, a Mr. Oliver, and John Earthy, who continued to deal with Indian and French clients in spite of orders to the contrary.[35] Hubbard undoubtedly had such men in mind when he decried persons to the "Southward and Eastward, that never were, nor would be, subject to the Laws of our Jurisdiction . . . Such as make the Advantage they have in their Hand the Rule for their Consciences to act by."[36]

With many of the men, women, and children flown to safer quarters, those remaining soon sent desperate requests for Massachusetts soldiers, or "country soldiers," to man garrisons.[37] But country soldiers required food, which had to be supplied by local residents, who had little enough for their own families.[38] Some towns refused to accept soldiers at all, in spite of need.[39] Others accepted, boarded, and fed them but resented the imposition for both the burden it imposed and the incarnate symbol of Massachusetts interference. Their resentment could only have been increased when it became clear that many of the soldiers sent from Massachusetts had no interest in defending Maine. Black Point garrison captain Joshua Scottow reported that of the fifty soldiers he had requested from Massachusetts, only thirty-eight had arrived and "divers of them insufficient for service" and "mutinous" to boot. Like Massachusetts officials in the south, Scottow felt his personal authority insufficient to control the disobedience of his soldiers, complaining "some [were] so mutinous that we cannot with safety inflict the punishment they deserve."[40] Some of these country soldiers and others stationed at a garrison at Falmouth deserted their posts soon after arriving and were called to answer for it before the Massachusetts Council.[41] It soon became clear that even under attack Maine was none too happy about the long arm of Massachusetts reaching in once again.

Local resentment of the burden of country soldiers was intensified when

military authority rested in the hands of stalwart supporters of Massachusetts. Joshua Scottow was a case in point. A merchant and prominent citizen
of Boston, Scottow had begun buying land around Black Point (called Scarborough by the Boston magistrates) in the 1660s.[42] In 1671 he moved to
his Maine property, into a house he had purchased from Henry Jocelyn. He
immediately fell into disputes with longtime Maine residents. One, Andrew
Alger, fought Scottow through the courts for years over the rightful possession of a fishing flake yard adjoining their properties.[43] Perhaps used to the
respect generally paid to prominent merchants in Boston, Scottow seems
to have thrown his weight around in his new neighborhood. He told Alger
that he would give him as much "hire" as he wanted if he would exclude
another man from drying his fish in the flake yard. This man was Nathan
Bedford, who drowned under suspicious circumstances in 1681. Scottow
was twice called before a court of inquest to answer charges that he was
involved in the death, but was cleared.[44] Historian James Savage scoffed at
the "strange wildness of a story" that Scottow, the eminent author of *Old
Men's Tears for their own Declensions,* had been accused of murder.[45] Whether
Scottow killed Bedford or not, the charge is clear evidence of the strong
resentment against him in the town. Despite Scottow's prominence as a
landholder, merchant, and educated man, qualities that generally accompanied office-holding in seventeenth-century New England, his neighbors
would not elect him to positions of responsibility.[46] Scottow's frustration
with this situation is suggested by his arrest in 1674 for illegally assuming
the office of commissioner for Scarborough.[47] Any power he obtained he
had to seize or have bestowed on him by the Massachusetts government, as
was the case with his position as commander of Black Point garrison.

Scottow's approach to managing his command at Black Point soon
increased the tensions already poisoning his relations with longtime Maine
residents. Locals noted that the country soldiers housed and fed in their
homes spent their working hours doing what looked like home improvement projects for Scottow. During one week, the men worked to move his
barn closer to his garrison house. They collected stones to pave his yard
and spent an entire month cutting and stripping trees for the construction
of a "Palisado" around his garrison.[48] This labor particularly irked the
locals because the Indians had been quiet for months, since winter set in.
Scottow's command over the soldiers gave him an unfair business advantage as well; they freed his hired men to continue his fishing trade: "For all
the while his fishermen were thereby capacitated to keep at sea for the
whole season; and much work was done by them which was greatly turned
to his profit."[49] His neighbors, sheltered in garrisons, lost both trade and
planting.

The locals' biggest complaint against Scottow was his failure to use his
garrison soldiers as soldiers: "for that when the Indians were facing us, killing us, and burning our houses, we Could have no helps from the Said

Scottow, notwithstanding the Soldiers were willing."[50] Local hostility appears clearly in the complaint of Richard Foxwell, commander of a garrison at nearby Blue Point. When the garrison ran short of powder, Foxwell sent a man to get some powder "belonging to the Company" from Scottow. Scottow turned him away, declaring: "if the Boston Soldiers wanted Powder, they could have it, but if the Inhabitants wanted it they must buy it. The Price was half a Crown the Pound."[51] What appeared to be favoring of Massachusetts troops over Maine residents, both engaged in the same war, could only have confirmed Foxwell's and others' belief that Scottow was not one of them.

In the minds of some Maine residents, Scottow's misuse of his position acquired the taint of murder in two incidents during the fall of 1675. In the first, which occurred shortly after the first Indian attack in the Black Point region, Joseph Oliver requested that Scottow send eight or ten men to offer protection to settlers of nearby Dunstan, where Robert Nichols and his wife had been killed. Scottow refused the request, claiming "that it would be dangerous to take away any of the men from the garrison, for if they should be killed there would be none to look after their wives and children." Andrew and Arthur Alger were at Dunstan at that time, preparing to move their belongings to safer quarters at Black Point. Strikingly, Scottow singled out his old enemy for reproof in his refusal of Oliver's request: "Andrew Alger and the rest might have come [to Black Point] as well as you and if they will not they must take what follows." The Alger brothers never reached Black Point. Indians attacked their house in October, killing Andrew and fatally wounding Arthur.[52]

The second incident occurred shortly afterward, on October 13. A company of local men under the command of Lieutenant John Winckoll were surrounded by Indians at Saco Sands, "fair within Sight of [Scottow's] garrison." Seeing that his men were "likely to have been overthrown, by the enemy," Winckoll sent two messengers to Scottow to request his help. Scottow refused it. Thomas Cousens, who fought under Winckoll, claimed that soldiers within the garrison heard the noise of the battle and offered to give the English aid, but Scottow ordered them to remain inside. The garrison at that time had forty men in it. Richard Foxwell's garrison at nearby Blue Point had only seven, five of whom he sent to assist Winckoll's party. By the time the Indians retreated, nine of Winckoll's men lay dead upon the sands, leading Cousens and a score of others to complain "if we had had relief from mr Scottow's garrison, in an ordinary way with god's blessing, we might have given the enemy a great overthrow. . . . it was generally reported at Blackpoint, that in their great distress they Could have no help, from mr Scotto garrison, he being the Commander thereof."[53]

These incidents hampered Scottow's already weak ability to command his fellow citizens. Within a year, Scottow's friend and fellow Massachusetts stalwart Richard Waldron complained that he had tried on several occasions to impress Maine residents to serve at Black Point, "and Sometimes when Soldiers were ready to march, they Said they had as willingly be hanged, as go to be under Capt Scottow, and Several ran away, and would not go."[54] Scottow's relations with neighbors were also poisoned by the rising costs of the war, particularly the expenses of the soldiers stationed at Scottow's garrison. Few Indians were seen around Black Point during the winter, and by April Scottow dismissed the country soldiers and sent them home to Massachusetts.[55] Soon afterward, he submitted a bill of his costs to the General Court, which promptly sent it back to York County to be paid. In August 1676, Nicholas Shapleigh, Edward Rishworth, and Samuel Wheelwright sent the General Court in Massachusetts their objection to bearing those costs. They complained that soldiers at Scottow's garrison were used for his own benefit, not to fight the war.[56] Townspeople echoed this objection on a petition to the Court, and Brian Pendleton and George Munjoy wrote that local Maine residents "had no hand in sending for the soldiers to Black point whereby the chief charge is brought upon us and the Country." The charge of the soldiers should, they said, be levied on the one who received advantage of them.[57]

The soldiers' charges, added to already heavy taxes, revived rankling discontent over Scottow's use of his command. In the summer of 1676 Wheelwright, Rishworth, and Shapleigh began taking depositions about Scottow's criminal failure to assist local residents in the war and his unjust demand for financial reimbursement. In August the three men carried the stack of depositions to the General Court in Boston, and by October the Court recalled Scottow from his garrison to stand trial.

But Scottow was not without some friends as well. Twenty-seven men signed a petition describing their reliance on Scottow for food, powder, and ammunition throughout the hostilities and his readiness to provide it. They also testified that Scottow was being "unjustly and as far as we can discern maliciously persecuted," particularly by Richard Foxwell, "a man noted for contention."[58] They insisted that Scottow should be reimbursed for his great expenses in their behalf. Nine of these men and two others also signed a deposition testifying to Scottow's competence as a commander. All had been present on the day the men were killed at Saco Sands.[59] Their account of the basic chronology of the day is similar to the complainants', but the Scottow they describe seems to be an entirely different man: no abrupt refusals, no puttering "upon his own occasions."[60] By their report, at first news of the attack Scottow gathered the garrison soldiers, checked their arms and supplies, and exchanged his own weapons for any that were defective. He then supplied them with powder, shot, biscuit, and drink from his own stores. Just as Foxwell and others had complained, the Scottow of this deposition determined that boats could not safely be sent to rescue the men "because of the surf of the sea, the wind blowing fresh upon the shore." Instead, in the only substantive difference between the depositions, these men attested that Scottow ordered twenty men to march over land to the besieged soldiers. When some of the company proved reluctant to go, Scottow threw his cane to the ground, threatened to give up his commission, and cried "we could not answer it to god, men, nor [our] own consciences unless we used the utmost of our endeavor to relieve those men." According to this version of events, the garrison soldiers, not their commander, were the ones who refused to fight. The garrison housed not only men but women and children, who argued that the departure of twenty men was far too many for their safety, "saying they did not do well to send out so many of their husbands and Children supposing that if they should have been cut off we had not strength Left at the Garrison sufficient to defend ourselves if assaulted."[61]

How do we explain the two Scottows, one self-serving and taciturn, the other ardently rallying the reluctant locals to do their duty? The split perception reflects the division in the community between those who supported the Massachusetts government, with its heightened wartime presence, and those who opposed it. Chief among Scottow's opponents were his neighbor Foxwell, whom Scottow had removed from command the previous October for being a "quarreling discontented person," and Shapleigh, Rishworth, and Wheelwright, all of whom had resisted Massachusetts's authority in previous political struggles.[62] The latter three had all held office in the government established by the royal commissioners in 1665 as well. Walter Gendall, who had refused to take the oath of fidelity to Massachusetts, "likewise testified to the Inhumanity of Capt. Scottow," as did at least eighteen other men.[63] A total of twenty-nine men signed the petition or testified in Scottow's behalf, only one of whom appears on the records in any act of resistance to Massachusetts's authority.[64]

While most lining up against Scottow had opposed Massachusetts before, it is striking that even men such as Pendleton and Rishworth, who had been leading officers for Massachusetts during the tumultuous previous decade, joined their neighbors in refusing to pay the cost of Scottow's soldiers in 1676.[65] Maine's desperate condition undoubtedly contributed to their resistance to the financial burden, but political winds may have turned their hearts as well. This was a moment when the wind was clearly blowing against Massachusetts. By 1676 many Maine residents were no doubt aware of the renewed application of Mason's and Gorges's heirs to have their rights to Maine and New Hampshire restored. The Massachusetts Council unwittingly spread that news—and discontent—by hiring a man to gather evidence to send to England in defense of the colony's claim to the area. That man, Edward Colcord, spent "many days" in this task, a process that undoubtedly alerted many still chafing under Massachusetts's authority that freedom might soon be at hand.[66]

A September 1676 letter from Scottow and Henry Jocelyn to Governor Leverett suggests that some in Maine took the arrival in New England of the king's agent, Edward Randolph, as a signal to renew their plea for a royal governor. Their letter includes the phrase, "because Mr. Richworth & accomplices' design being effected, as they are informed, of making this County a peculiarity, thereby have excluded them [from] the association of the united Colonies."[67] It is unclear how far Rishworth and his "accomplices" got with their "design" to remove Maine from Massachusetts jurisdiction and, hence, from the "association of the united Colonies," but after 1676 Plymouth and Connecticut did begin to resist Massachusetts's requests for aid in fighting the war in New Hampshire and Maine, viewing those counties to the northeast as "a peculiarity" not deserving of United Colonies assistance. This withdrawal of assistance would have disastrous consequences for the English war effort in Maine.

By the time Joshua Scottow left Black Point to defend himself against charges of "falsifying his trust," the war in Maine had blown up to full strength. Indians had been quiet much of the previous year, since their initial attacks in fall 1675. In August, however, they began a series of raids on the area around Black Point, striking first in Falmouth. These attacks led to a renewed English exodus from the region, with most of the new refugees settling in Salem.[68] In spite of the dangers posed by the recent Indian attacks, however, resistance to Massachusetts's military authority grew. Scottow had left Henry Jocelyn in charge of the garrison at Black Point. Jocelyn and Walter Gendall, writing to Scottow in early August for the committee of militia, complained of "the averseness of the generality of the Inhabitants to obey Military orders" and asked him to request a special order from the governor and council to "bring the Inhabitants to . . . obedience."[69] Salem's Captain William Hathorne, stationed in Wells, reported of the Black Point garrison: "the people there are in great distraction & disorder . . . they are a people ungoverned, & Attend little to the Government there established So that the most of the town will desert the place." Fearing they would do so, Hathorne reminded them of the law passed by the Massachusetts Council imposing a penalty of 20 pounds on any who deserted outlying towns. The inhabitants of Wells and surrounding towns had similar inclinations toward desertion: "the mind of this town In General is to leave the place, & though the Honored Court or Council have formerly given an Order concerning them." Major Pendleton of Winter Harbor threatened to desert the region before he would take on any more hungry country soldiers: "he had as good Remove while he had some thing, as to stay while all was spent."[70] Even as far south as Cocheco in New Hampshire, Major Waldron reported that if the army did not step up its efforts to fight the enemy "our People will quickly desert their Country."[71]

Some inhabitants of Maine soon had their chance. On October 12, a large party of Indians led by Mogg Heigon approached Black Point garrison. Captain Scottow was in Boston, where his case had been brought before the General Court. On sighting the Indians, Henry Jocelyn went out to speak with Heigon. For what must have been a very long time, they discussed the situation. By the end of the conversation, they had agreed that the English would surrender the garrison but would have until the next morning to remove as many of their belongings as they could carry. When Jocelyn returned with this news, he found the garrison empty of all but his own family and a few elderly persons. The rest had crept out the back gate and were gone. Not being there, Scottow could not collect his own belongings, which he estimated were worth about 250 pounds. He was still suing to recover damage to his reputation and estate four years later and blustering that, if he had not been forced to answer complaints at Boston, the garrison never would have been "so unworthily delivered up."[72]

The transfer of Black Point from English to Indians went without a hitch, without even a threat of violence. As the only bloodless military exchange in King Philip's War in Maine, the only instance of a surrender without a fight, it demands further examination. The explanation of events just given matches the records. But those records fail to connect this event with one that happened immediately before the surrender. Walter Gendall of Spurwink, sometime resident of Black Point garrison and one of those who had submitted a deposition against Scottow, was not among those listed at the garrison when it fell to the enemy on October 12, 1676.[73] He was present nonetheless, as a captive of Mogg Heigon. Earlier, Gendall and nine other men had sailed to Richmond Island to fetch provisions stored there. While they were loading the goods onto boats for a return trip to the mainland, Mogg Heigon and his men discovered them. The Indians attacked, and the men fought back. Badly outnumbered, their resistance was brief. James Fryer was mortally wounded in the fighting. Indians quickly subdued and captured the rest.[74]

Next came a bizarre example of vigilantism run amok. As the Indians rowed Gendall and his fellow captives away from Richmond Island, Gendall overheard Mogg Heigon discussing a plan to capture Black Point. Never one to let another man steal the action, Gendall interrupted, offering "the Indians to lead them on to this design, in such manner as they should not lose one man: & further added that he was as willing other men should be taken as himself."[75] A short time later Mogg Heigon met with Jocelyn outside the garrison. Gendall, who was seen going "along with medorkowando towards Blackpoint in a canoe," may have been at this meeting, in which Heigon offered Jocelyn exceptionally generous terms of surrender.[76] Why, other than because he had a reputation for kindness, would Heigon have offered such terms?[77] He must have come to believe that it was in his interest, saving his own men from the dangers of any armed resistance the garrison might put up. He would gain the fort, which Gendall surely reminded him was the strongest point on the Maine coast, and the English would leave. He would not gain captives, but he had more than ten already, and perhaps too few boats to transport more or men to guard them. By convincing Heigon of the benefits of this plan, Gendall gained as well. He and the other residents could do what they had been itching to do for months: desert. "It is verily believed by us all," testified witnesses in Gendall's later trial for treason, "that the said Gendall was of Counsel to the Indians for the taking of this garrison; he knowing the weakness of those to desert."[78] Whatever he may have said to Heigon, Gendall's actions suggest that he believed the reluctant soldiers at Black Point stood little chance of withstanding a large Indian assault. But while the parleying went on, the residents, knowing nothing of the terms they would receive, did what Maine residents had become notorious for doing throughout the fighting; they followed their own inclination and took to their heels.

The abandonment of Black Point unleashed whatever weak hold on order was keeping the other Maine towns from deserting. Hearing guns firing at Black Point two days after the surrender, three boys took a canoe from Winter Harbor to investigate. They returned in a panic, claiming that there were 500 Indians and 300 French near Black Point and another 100 Indians at Richard Foxwell's house at Blue Point "& that if you love their lives be gone as soon as you can for they say they will be with you to morrow morning or at night at farthest." At this report, the soldiers stationed at Pendleton's garrison ran for their boats and began hurling their belongings aboard, "as mad to make away as ever I saw any men." Pendleton put the women of his family in a boat, then told the men that if they would remain in the garrison with him, he would "never leave them so long as I could live: but they would not hear of it." All boarded the boats and sailed south to Piscataqua.[79]

Few of those who abandoned their homes had been able to take all their goods with them. Those who crept out the back of Black Point garrison had only the clothes on their backs. Livestock and crops were particularly difficult to transport and were usually left behind. These abandoned goods became the focus of looting sprees by remaining Maine residents as well as Massachusetts soldiers sent to defend the region, and those actions further increased the antipathy between the embattled region and the central government in Boston. One of the first caught looting was Walter Gendall, Mogg Heigon's captive. In response to Joshua Scottow's petition, the Council had allowed two boats of soldiers slated for service in Maine to detour to Black Point to help him gather any of his goods still remaining. Stopping at the Piscataqua settlements, Captain Thomas Moore and Sergeant Bartholomew Tipping recruited refugees from Winter Harbor to go along with them to Black Point, promising them that they could collect their own goods after the expedition. On arrival at Black Point, the men immediately spied Indians—including Mogg Heigon—in a canoe. Drawing closer to land, they saw others "skulking from rock to rock."[80] But these men were not Indians: they were Englishmen Walter Gendall and William Lucas. On interrogation, Lucas admitted that he had, on Gendall's urging, "acted so like indians the better to impede our landing & that the said W Gendall for his so doing & for helping him to convey away provisions was to give the said Lucas one year's bread & meat for his family." Believing Gendall was stealing other men's goods, Tipping confiscated them, an action Gendall protested loudly. Gendall accused Tipping of taking "Corn of his own which in his return from Kennebecke he had fetched from his own barn" and which he needed for his family, who had taken refuge in Piscataqua. Tipping and his men, Gendall reported, took not only food, but many other goods, claiming "all was theirs."[81]

Tipping's report convinced the Massachusetts Council to call Gendall to Boston to stand trial for treason. In September 1677, he was convicted, sentenced to run the gauntlet of the Boston militia, deprived of all his property, and banished from the colony. While this punishment was certainly severe, it paled in comparison to that of Joshua Tefft of Rhode Island. For crimes similar to Gendall's but with far less abundant incriminating evidence, Tefft was executed and his head fixed on a post in the time-honored punishment for traitors.[82] Why was Gendall spared? It may have been because he was from Maine. In 1677, Massachusetts's pretensions to jurisdiction over Maine were very much in doubt, both within and outside of the colony. Even the most hard-line of Massachusetts officials must have recognized that the colony's hopes for its charter would be completely dashed if the king learned that they had executed a Maine resident for breaking his oath of fidelity to Massachusetts. The colony's hesitance to carry its pretensions to jurisdiction over Maine to their logical conclusion gave Gendall time to escape from prison and return to Casco Bay, where within a decade his ambition and natural gifts of persuasion propelled him to high office.[83]

The Massachusetts officers who captured Gendall soon found their reputations blackened in all the towns where Maine residents had taken refuge. Tipping had likely told Gendall just what kind of punishment he deserved when he found him masquerading as an Indian, loaded with other men's belongings. Gendall's revenge was to spread the news among the Maine refugees that Tipping was defrauding them of their property.[84] Other reports soon came in to Piscataqua that Massachusetts officers and solders were seizing goods all along the coast and claiming them as "free plunder."[85] Captain Moore had given Pendleton his promise to recover his oxen and other goods when he sailed to Winter Harbor. Instead, he slaughtered the oxen and plundered the goods Pendleton had been unable to fit on his boat earlier. "I may say with good Jeremy pity me, pity me, oh my friend," wrote Pendleton to the Massachusetts governor and Council in 1676, "God hath emptied me from vessel to vessel."[86] In addition, Pendleton complained, instead of taking the Winter Harbor men to their homes to secure their goods as he had promised, Tipping impressed them and their boat into his service. Gendall and others also trumped Tipping's authority by complaining of these abuses to Major General Daniel Denison, who wrote Tipping an outraged letter, reminding him pointedly that "he mistook his errand if he thought they were sent only to serve themselves, for certainly it was to secure the place & assist any inhabitants in the recovery of their own &c." The letter and its reprimand soon became common knowledge to residents from Piscataqua to Black Point. Its bearer, Walter Gendall, "instead of delivering him [the letter,] published [it] to the people." Hearing that the country soldiers were not securing but stealing their goods, the refugees in Piscataqua rose in what Denison called "a mutiny."[87]

The soldiers from Massachusetts not only had done little or nothing to preserve the Maine towns but had actively looted them when they were abandoned. The men under Tipping's command were scarcely fit to be called soldiers. Mogg Heigon reported they were "all drunk." Indian John Wompas called them "green horns." Early in 1677 soldiers serving in Maine plundered all the iron in the deserted settlements near the Kennebec River, "so much as things Ripped off The Doors of Houses," leaving the residents who returned to guard what property was left with no tools to make repairs or anything with which to forge new tools. Maine settlers must have felt the irony that they, derided as lawless and disorderly, were being plundered by soldiers from Massachusetts behaving like criminals.[88] Such behavior did nothing to lessen the antipathy that was fueling complaints to the king and bolstering Mason's and Gorges's renewed efforts to wrest the region back from usurping Massachusetts.

Like the contending English of Massachusetts and Maine, the Wabanaki Indians were divided among themselves. Some sachems were in favor of maintaining war. Others preferred peace, but claimed with striking frequency that they were unable to rule their young men who thought differently. Pennacook sachem Wannalancet testified to this difficulty when he asked the English at Cocheco not to sell liquor to the Indians, "professing that that was a principal cause of the mischiefs that had been done, and that they were not able to keep their men in subjection, when once they were become mad with drink."[89] Even though sachems such as Wannalancet informed the English of Indian divisions and the English had had ample experience with the same problem among the Narragansetts, Pocumtucks, and other Indians to the south, the English continued to hold sachems accountable for their people's compliance with peace treaties and terms of subjection. The chasm between their expectations and Indian ability to meet them goes far to explain several unsuccessful attempts to settle peace in the northeastern theater of the war.[90]

The Indians first sued for peace in January 1676.[91] The winter was unusually severe, and the Indians, many of whom had turned in their weapons on English demand, were scarcely able to maintain life, let alone warfare.[92] Peace remained all through the spring, and when summer came, Pennacook sachem Wannalancet and a large number of Indians, including some refugees from the war to the south, submitted to the English to demonstrate Indian commitment to peace. Wannalancet, Squando, and six other Indian sachems signed a peace treaty with the English on July 3, 1676. At the same time, the Massachusetts government issued a declaration of mercy toward any Indians who would come in and submit themselves to English authority, "except [those] known to be notorious in their mischief against us." Many of those who did come in, either with Wannalancet or after hearing of the declaration, were given explicit assurances that they would receive neither punishment nor enslavement if they would bring other Indians into submission. Among those submitting were Christian Indians James Printer and Nehemiah, who had cast their lot with Philip rather than risk English hospitality on Deer Island.[93] Over the course of the summer hundreds more came in, both south in Plymouth and Boston and at Cocheco. But the peace in Maine did not last.

On August 11, 1676, a group of Indians led by the Christian Indian Simon, who had recently escaped from prison in Cocheco, attacked Anthony Brackett's garrison house in Falmouth, capturing or killing thirty-four men, women, and children. This new outbreak of violence owed much to new provocations from the English, who ironically had been unable to control their own people. In his September letter Gardiner acknowledged the propensity of some Maine English to abuse the Indians, claiming that the Indians "fly for fear from Any boats or English they see & good Reason for they well Know it may Cost them their Lives if the wild fishermen meet with them."[94] An incident in the summer of 1676 demonstrates the unfortunate truth of this judgment. Two English fishermen had come across the wife and son of Squando, the sagamore of the Saco Indians, as they were canoeing on the river. Perhaps to test contemporary theories that Indians could swim naturally from birth, the men seized the child from his mother and threw him into the river. He promptly sank to the bottom. After several failed attempts to reach him, his frantic mother succeeded in rescuing the boy, but he died within a few days. Soon after, the once peaceable Squando swore to cut off all the English, holding out against reconciliation even when other sachems urged it.[95] Maine fishermen from Monhegan Island further demonstrated the reckless self-government and hostility toward Indians that was poisoning English/Indian relations when they offered a five-pound reward to anyone who would bring in a dead Indian.[96]

Another English offense with serious consequences came at the hands of William Waldron and Henry Lawton, coastal traders who saw the war as a chance for quick profit. As early as fall 1675, many Indians captured in combat were sold into slavery outside the colonies. Using this as a pretext for their action, Waldron and Lawton sailed to Maine and seized seventeen Indians, including Maine sagamore Waron and his wife. None of these Indians had been involved in warfare with the English, but all were sold into slavery in the Azores. The Massachusetts Court of Assistants imprisoned Waldron, Lawton, and John Houghton for "man-stealing," but at their later trial Waldron and Houghton were found innocent. Nevertheless, the Court ordered that the proceeds from the sales at Fyall be used to recover the Indians. Lack of punishment and the excessive amount of time between the crime and the trial could not have given Maine Indians confidence in English justice.[97] The offense continued to grate, some Indians claiming that it was "one of the principal Grounds of their present Quarrel."[98]

Ironically, throughout the war the English held expectations for Indian compliance with authority at a level that they were never able or willing to achieve themselves. The English repeatedly dismissed Indian complaints of English wrongs as either trifling or outside their control. To Penobscot sachem Madockawando's complaints of English violence, English agents replied that "the Persons who had so done, were not within the Limits of their Government, and therefore though they could not *call them to account* for *so acting*, yet they did *utterly disallow* thereof."[99] The death of Squando's child provides a clear example of this double standard. Writing to those still negotiating for peace in July 1677, the governor and Council directed them to say "If Squando or any for him appear you may acquaint him that the Governor was wholly Ignorant of any Injury offered to him or his child at Saco." Further, they should "endeavor to Satisfy those Indians that the Governor & Council are Ignorant of those many Injuries by them Complained of, which had they been made & proved to them; they would have endeavored to have had satisfaction made them; and that the persons that have done the injuries were disorderly persons that lived out of our Jurisdiction."[100] Similarly, Hubbard dismissed continued Indian complaints over the kidnapping by Waldron and Lawton, arguing that the offenders were never "countenanced amongst us" and that the Indians themselves were at fault for failing to make "any orderly Complaint" to proper authorities.[101]

Nowhere in all the records of King Philip's War did the English accept a similar excuse for misbehavior from the Indians. Over and over again, the Indians attributed attacks to disorderly young men or other sachems—those beyond their authority. But the English acted as if the lines of authority among the Indian groups involved in the war were both clearer and stronger than the authority the English had been able to maintain among their own people. In reality, neither side could ensure strict obedience of its own, and both took the offenses of renegades and ungovernable young men as evidence of the intent of the whole people. Hubbard and other English who expected the Indians to maintain total obedience or answer for the offenses of every warrior were clearly guilty of hypocrisy. Some Indians fell into the same trap. Squando used the offenses of a few "wild fishermen" as a pretext for his attacks on all English, and the English felt his revenge acutely. After Squando's men burned Brian Pendleton's house, Pendleton wrote in anguish to the Massachusetts Council, "Indians who I never dealt with once in all my life nor never wronged in anything but did hope Squando would become a Christian & did what I could to further it: yet they fired all my houses for dwelling."[102]

The conflict between expectations and reality significantly hampered efforts at peace and undermined both peoples' faith in treaty promises, just as it had with the Narragansetts before the Great Swamp Fight. Both Indian and English capacity to trust had been stretched perilously thin by the continuous violence of the war. New Hampshire minister Joshua Moodey testified to this when he complained that "though as yet [the Indians'] actions are not contradictory to their words so far as we know, there is no trusting of them, they often mean worst when they speak best."[103] When even "fair" words might mask murderous intent, the violence of Simon and other Indians who escaped from Cocheco and attacked Falmouth raised English suspicions about the peaceful intent of the hundreds remaining. Simon had lived among the English. He had, in fact, spent enough time with them to learn to read and write. He put these skills to use in Falmouth. The night before the attack, Simon arrived at Anthony Brackett's garrison, presented an English pass that he had skillfully forged, and asked for shelter for the night. Brackett accepted the token of trust and admitted him. After the English had gone to sleep, Simon opened the doors for his companions to attack the garrison, killing many and taking Anthony and Elizabeth Brackett and several of their children as captives.[104] If one Indian could prove a villain, why not all?

In the tense aftermath of the Falmouth attack, five prominent Maine refugees at Cocheco displayed the further erosion of their trust in the Indians by writing to the Massachusetts General Court, begging it to reconsider the fidelity of the Indians in the town. Since the peace treaty of the previous summer, Indians had been flooding into Cocheco, some on their own, and others enticed in by Christian Indian scouts such as Peter Jethro. Their proximity alarmed many of the English. It also incited their envy. The Indians, "by the care of . . . Some of their English friends," were clothed, fed, and sheltered; they were, in fact, better provided for than many of the English refugees. And while they were "fed & nourished in our bosoms" these "Chocheco friends . . . so called" had unlimited freedom to "Egress & Regress from place to place, beyond all Control, none knowing whither nor what they go about." The writers strongly suspected that many of these Indians had been involved in the recent assaults on Casco Bay and Kennebec River and feared Cocheco would be next. Despite their professions of loyalty and submission to English authority, the Cocheco Indians were "very bold & surly, full of contumacy & scorn against the English." Could they really be trusted to scout and bring in enemies, or were they "Acting quite Contrary" in order to "defeat all our Enterprises, if not accomplish our total Ruins"? The Englishmen begged the Court to appoint officers to investigate thoroughly and determine "whether to Secure or destroy" the Cocheco Indians.[105]

The Court's response to this plea was immediate and decisive.[106] Major Richard Waldron, commander of the garrison at Cocheco, was traveling to Boston on September 5, 1676, when he was intercepted by a messenger bearing a letter from the General Court. He immediately turned back home. The letter contained directions for inspecting and disposing of the Cocheco Indians, over 350 of whom had come into the town by September 6, 1676. Following his instructions, Waldron informed the officers under his charge of the parts they would play in a planned subterfuge. They sent for the Indians to gather on the field in front of Waldron's garrison house, telling them that they were going to take them into service in the English army. Waldron then resorted to a notorious English trick for gaining advantage over Indians: he got them drunk.[107]

As Waldron himself described it, "I made them eat & drink & then surrounded them with the Army & calling the chief sagamores into the Center & told them what must be done." Those guilty of notorious offenses against the English would be executed or sold into slavery. Those who proved innocent "should not be damnified." At the end of the day, Waldron exulted that 100 English had taken "80 fighting Men & 20 old men, 250 women & children, 350 in all."[108] The warriors were disarmed, the guilty (judged to be most of them) separated from the innocent and sent to Boston to be sold as slaves.[109]

The outrage of the Indians—and some of the English—to this betrayal was acute. Most of those in Cocheco had only come in on the persuasion of fellow Indians, who promised forgiveness for any past assistance to the enemy in return for engaging with the English in the war. They had expected a general pardon, not a sifting of guilty and innocent, and would probably not have surrendered on such terms. Deogenes and Madoasquarbet, apparently two of the Indians who brought others into Cocheco, wrote in protest to Governor Leverett about the betrayal: "this is to let you to understand how major walldin served us. . . . we would fain know whether you did give such order to kill us for bringing your prisoners. Is that your fashion to come & make peace & then kill us"?[110] Some Indians did receive the expected pardon, and some of the 80 Indian warriors in the group were taken into the English forces. Too many others were lumped, with too little care, into groups of "guilty" Indians and shipped to Boston. Among these were some Christian Indians with fathers and brothers fighting in English forces elsewhere. Two months later the relatives and friends of Mary Nemasitt and Jacob Indian were still working out the arrangements to have them and Mary's children redeemed from the slavery they had been sold into.[111] They, at least, were successfully returned to freedom. Others were executed.

English settlers, too, argued that the events of the day would have severe consequences. Nicholas Shapleigh and Thomas Daniels, refugees in Cocheco, wrote to Massachusetts leaders that "Your pretensions of Employing them in the Country Service . . . gave us the fit opportunity of Surprisal," but they feared the results would prove disastrous. The Indians had been very willing to join the English service, and it might have done much for the "Public good" to have used them. Now, however, the English were in great fear for their lives. Those Indians sent to Boston had "divers of their relations that are abroad in these parts whom we now Expect to make Indian Spoil upon us & if the Army leave us [alone] we Judge our Selves in a More dangerous Condition than they found us in."[112]

Increased threat of a revenge attack was not the only result of the day's doings. A more significant and enduring consequence was a conclusive undermining of Indian trust in English promises. Simon's assault at Falmouth had eroded English faith in Indian fidelity. Waldron's surprise at Cocheco had the same effect on the Indians. What sway could English authority hold over Indians when the English word could not be trusted? Writing to Governor Leverett in the summer of 1677, Deogenes and Madoasquarbet claimed that both peace and a return of hostages would have come much sooner if the English had not betrayed Indian expectations at Cocheco: "Major Waldin do lie. We were not minded to kill no body. Major Waldin did wrong to give cloth & powder but he gave us drink & when we were drunk killed us. If it had not a been for this fault you had your prisoners long ago. . . . Major Waldin have been the cause of killing all that have been killed this summer."[113] Even thirty years later, the incident remained fresh in the minds of many Indians in the northeast. Some who participated in the 1704 attack on Deerfield explicitly justified that assault as revenge for the betrayal at Cocheco in 1676.[114]

It cannot have been coincidence that Indian attacks in the northeast escalated immediately after the Cocheco surprise, just as Shapleigh and Daniels feared would happen. And these attacks were no longer led by ungovernable young warriors such as Simon but by sachems who had previously assented to peace treaties. With this shattering of faith in English promises, Gardiner's warning that English action would force Indians to turn to the French was realized: Indians began to look to Canada for support and, more importantly, supplies.[115] The report of three hundred Frenchmen by the English fleeing Black Point was one of several accounts of Frenchmen among the Indians and of French powder and arms supplying them. While Englishman Francis Card was held captive among the Wabanaki Indians in 1677, he reported that a French messenger from Castine and four female Indian messengers from Governor Frontenac came to thank the Indians at Pemaquid for their attacks on the English and to promise them "that they would help them with 100: men and ammunition."[116] The Massachusetts magistrates accepted these reports as valid, writing to New York governor Edmund Andros that allowing the Maine inhabitants to desert their houses and towns was directly assisting not only the Indians, but the enemy French, "who are said by themselves to be [the Indians'] abettors in the depopulation there made."[117]

By November 1676, Indians had successfully driven most English settlers out of Maine. With the abandonment of Black Point and the capture of the English on Richmond Island, the war in Maine "ceased for want of victims."[118] But even with such obvious proof of their victory, the Indians continued to sue for peace. This suggests that they wanted to maintain a relationship with the English, and the obvious motivation for that was trade. Writing to Governor Leverett the week following his capture of Black Point, Mogg Heigon made a point of asking about the resumption of trade. In reply, the Massachusetts magistrates wrote, "for matter of [trade] it was obstructed upon Account of the war & [we] know not but may be free again upon Good Assurance of the Indians' fidelity."[119] On Heigon's request, the governor assured him of safe conduct to Boston to treat further for peace and sent orders to Major Richard Waldron at Cocheco to make the arrangements.

Heigon arrived at Boston in November 1676 and soon learned that the English still expected Indian sachems to answer for the behavior of all their people, renegade and submissive, and even for the behavior of Indians not under their authority.[120] The English insisted that Heigon, who signed on behalf of Madockawondo and several other Wabanaki sachems, agree to the return of every English captive and all English goods stolen, despite the involvement of Indians from several sachemships in attacks and seizure of captives and goods.[121] The English would provide for the ransom of the English hostages with goods that Heigon would deliver for them, and they gave a deadline for his return with the captives. These terms were harsh and, because they required the cooperation of sachems Heigon had no authority to command, almost impossible to meet. Heigon pointed this out, protesting that the sachems might not believe him when he brought the English message or he might be captured himself.

Heigon's apprehensions were justified. An English boat carried him to the Maine coast and waited for him to return with English captives. The appointed time for his return came and went and, though the boat stayed several days past the deadline, Heigon failed to appear. He may have been unable to find or persuade the other sachems, or the harsh terms may have turned Heigon himself away from peace. When Englishman Francis Card returned from captivity in January 1677, he reported that Mogg Heigon's friendly overtures had changed to hostility. Heigon had come to Card's Indian captors and derided the "kind entertainment" he had received at Boston, boasting that he "hath found the way to burn boston." Together with the other sachems, Mogg proclaimed his intent to "take vessels and so to go to all the fishing islands and so to drive all the country before them."[122] Their hopes of peace dashed by their own mistrust and inflexibility, the Council immediately ordered an expedition to attack Indians in Maine, under the command of none other than the man who had earned the Indians' lasting enmity: Major Richard Waldron.[123]

Waldron was not the magistrates' first choice for the job. They had first asked Plymouth to send Captain Benjamin Church, the man responsible for concluding the war in the south. Church's family obligations, as well as Plymouth's growing reluctance to assist Massachusetts in Maine, made the smaller colony decline the request.[124] If the Council had seriously intended the expedition to seek peace, the choice of Waldron to lead it was a disastrous mistake. He was commissioned to recover captured English and their boats, hunt and destroy the enemy, or, if the Indians made honest overtures of peace, to negotiate with them.[125] A mediator less likely to secure the confidence of the Indians in peace negotiations could scarcely be imagined, nor one less likely to engage the loyalty of the Indian forces serving under him. Here his contrast with Benjamin Church is stark. As the Council's request acknowledged, Church was the only commander the Indians would "cheerfully serve."[126] In comparison, Waldron's standing among his Indian soldiers, who included relatives of those same Indians whom he had "surprised" five months earlier, was dangerously weak.[127] "Major Gookin hints that the Indians' Aversion to coming hither [to serve in the army at Cocheco] is not with out Some Reasons of weight," Waldron wrote to the Massachusetts Council, "without telling me what they are." It comes as no surprise that a man who needed to be told the reasons for the Indians' "Aversion" to serving under his command found his Indian troops "high & Ungovernable."[128]

Waldron's forces were swelled by men under Captains Hunting, Frost, and Lieutenant Fiske. Once all had assembled at Black Point, Waldron led them on a search for Indians among the offshore islands and north to the Kennebec River. On their second day of searching, they sighted an Indian canoe and tracks. As they prepared to follow the trail, five Indian canoes landed on an island nearby and signaled their readiness to parley. Waldron sent the company's guide, John Pain, to speak with them. The Indians sent their messenger, Simon, in return. In his own diary of the expedition, Waldron recounted his conversation with Simon, of whom he demanded "Why did you break your Covenant with me?" Simon replied that one Blind Will had "stirred us up to the War here" and asked in turn why the English had come.[129] Waldron's hawkish reply was: "We came to fetch off the Captives and make War as we see good." Simon reported that the English captives were in good health and would be returned by morning and that the Indians "intended Peace." They would have sued for it at Boston earlier, but Mogg Heigon had told them the English would be coming to treat for peace in person. Waldron then dismissed Simon and sent for Squando.

The sachem sent the reply that he would meet Waldron halfway between the two islands, alone in a birch canoe. "[I] would not venture in your Leaky Canoe," Waldron snorted, "and . . . if he had no more to say, the Treaty was ended." Despite this rebuff, Squando promised to bring in the captives by the next day. He did not, and a week later the captives were still not delivered.

Over the next week the English and Indians skirmished once, and the English followed assorted leads to the captives' whereabouts. On February 26, 1677, the English arrived at Thomas Gardiner's fort at Penobscot, spied Indians there, and came ashore. Mattahondo, a sagamore, greeted them, declaring "he was glad to see English Men there, and that he desired Peace." Pointedly, he requested that Maine resident Captain Sylvanus Davis be the one to parley with him, rather than Waldron. Davis went ashore to discuss details of ransoming the captives; Waldron soon joined them. Alert for treachery, he judged the Indians' "Words Smoother than Oil, yet were there drawn Swords in their Hearts."

The delivery of captives was set for the next morning, upon payment of a ransom in goods. Waldron had also demanded that the Indians agree to join the English to fight against the Androscoggins. They refused, pleading business elsewhere, and this refusal convinced Waldron "not to enter into any League of Peace with them." Instead, invoking his earlier tactics at Cocheco, he proposed "to fight them, or surprise them after they had dispatched the Business about the Captives." The next morning Waldron arrived at the appointed place of exchange loaded with goods. Because he planned treachery himself, he expected it from the Indians and soon found it. Spying the tip of a lance hidden beneath a pile of wood, Waldron seized it, raised it above his head, and berated the Indians for their "Falsehood and Treachery, for hiding Weapons just by, wherewith to destroy them as soon as they had delivered the Goods." Waldron's account betrays no sense of the irony of this situation, only outrage. Waving his cap over his head, he signaled his men ashore, and a chaotic battle ensued. By its end, five escaping Indians had drowned in their capsized canoe, and the sachem Mattahondo, whom even Waldron acknowledged "seemed sincere about the Peace," lay dead among several others. Those not killed or fled were captured, including Madockawando's sister. One Indian, Megunaway, suspected of fighting at Turner's Falls, was summarily executed. The day set to settle peace had ended in bloodshed. Waldron sent a captured Indian woman north to arrange for further parleys, but before the date set for her return the expedition was recalled to Boston.[130] Waldron's expedition had been seriously hampered by his personal reputation, which undermined his authority over both the Indians serving under him and the Indians with whom he treated for peace. What began as peace negotiations ended, more than once, in battles, largely because of Waldron's belligerence and suspicion. Knowing of his involvement in the betrayal at Cocheco, the Indians did not trust him either, and his treacherous behavior with Mattahondo's people showed that such distrust was justified.

Massachusetts's next military foray into Maine came four months later at Black Point. After the English surrendered the stronghold in October 1676, the Indians abandoned it. Remaining English took it up again, and in May 1677, Indians attacked once more, raining gunfire on Black Point for three days before withdrawing. Learning of this attack and conscious how few of the Indians' assaults had been returned, the Massachusetts Council decided to raise a large expedition to rendezvous at Black Point on June 26, 1677. On June 1, the Council sent requests to Plymouth and Connecticut to supply their proportion of 200 Indians and 100 English for the expedition.[131] Both colonies refused and sent letters outlining why they could not assist Massachusetts.

Massachusetts Captain Benjamin Swett and Lieutenant Richardson arrived at Black Point on June 28, with 200 Indian soldiers but only forty English and these "young, raw, and unexperienced."[132] Within hours, a large body of enemy Indians appeared on an open plain near the fort—an unusual practice for the Indians, who made it a policy not to come against an army in force. The move should have immediately raised English suspicion. Instead, a group of soldiers under Swett's command, joined by some local inhabitants, marched against the Indians. The Indians immediately retreated, and the English pursued. For well over a mile the English followed the fleeing enemy, until they found themselves in a situation ominously similar to the one Captains Edward Hutchinson and Thomas Wheeler and their companions had faced two years earlier: caught between a swamp and heavy brush and exposed on the downward slope of a hill. Once the English were in place, an Indian ambush descended, throwing the Massachusetts troops into a panic. Trying to maintain some semblance of order, Swett called for a retreat towards the palisaded garrison at Black Point. Few followed his command, choosing to "shift for themselves." Before the retreating company could reach the garrison, Swett, Richardson, and most of the officers were killed; Swett's body was cut in pieces at the garrison gates. More than sixty English and Christian Indians were left dead or wounded along the path of retreat. A few injured men dragged themselves and others back from the swamp under cover of night to relate the full extent of the disaster to the garrison inhabitants.[133] Indians followed this attack with a concerted effort all along the coast, seizing over twenty English boats and crew. The attacks evoked Mogg Heigon's boast to Francis Card the previous January that he had found a way to "burn Boston" by capturing English ships and using them to attack the town. The fact that fires did rage in Boston in the same period may have raised the specter of Mogg's threat in the minds of many there.[134]

To Massachusetts, the cause of the destruction of the Black Point expedition and the escalation of the war was clear: the failure of Plymouth and

Connecticut to honor their obligations of mutual assistance under the United Colonies Articles of Confederation. In the month following the disaster, the Massachusetts Council sent two stinging letters of rebuke to its sister colonies, decrying their violation of the articles and complaining that "the sad event of that neglect [was] the loss of & Captivity of about one hundred men."[135] Plymouth's refusal particularly stung because that colony's pleadings had drawn Massachusetts into the war in 1675. Reminding Plymouth of that fact, the Massachusetts Council complained that if Massachusetts had refused aid when Plymouth called, "is it not too too apparent how deplorable their condition had been, long before this day, and would not you your selves have been the first in condemning us for our breach of covenant"?[136] Both Plymouth and Connecticut gave several reasons for their refusal, including insufficient notice, disproportionate demand for troops, no clear need for such a large force, and reluctance of their troops to join unless they were under the sole command of their own colony's officers.[137]

Deeming these objections too insignificant to address, Massachusetts responded only to the final excuse both colonies gave, the same issue John Wompas held over the heads of his English neighbors: Massachusetts jurisdiction over New Hampshire and Maine was disputed by the king. "What ever quiet possession you have of late had in some of those eastern parts," Connecticut wrote, "yet we have heard that you took it by power, & not with out gainsay or opposition of some inhabiting." Plymouth's response was even more pointed: They could "not own that by the Confederation we are . . . engaged to Assist therein; it being very questionable whether those places be within lines of confederation; That matter now lying before the King and Council to determine." In their eyes, as the panicky Maine residents had warned, the region to the northeast had become a "peculiarity." In addition, Plymouth charged, the war there could not withstand the examination of justice, they "being also Jealous that by . . . Rude people (through your not exerting or their not owning your government and Subjection to your good laws), those Indians have been greatly abused and provoked to take arms."[138]

Plymouth's and Connecticut's refusal to assist Massachusetts rested primarily on the king's renewed investigation of Massachusetts's charter abuses. Edward Randolph, who arrived in 1676, had not confined his visit to Massachusetts and its disputed possessions. He had visited Plymouth governor Josiah Winslow as well. Randolph reported that Winslow disapproved of Massachusetts's aggression and declared that the country would not be at peace until it was settled directly under the king's government, to which Plymouth and Connecticut would readily submit.[139] Both colonies knew that Massachusetts agents were in England defending the colony against charges of overstepping its authority. Joining with Massachusetts in the discountenanced league of the United Colonies could put their own charters at risk and expose them to the same charges of independence and disloyalty that Massachusetts was presently facing.

Massachusetts's shaky claim on Maine led its United Colonies allies to pull back from the continuing warfare there, and New York's royal governor Edmund Andros took advantage of the conflict to highlight Massachusetts's political vulnerability and fulfill the territorial aspirations of his patron, the duke of York. Andros kept himself well informed on the progress of the war and on Massachusetts's diminishing political fortunes. And although he offered his assistance at several points during the war, it is not surprising that the Massachusetts magistrates often responded with hostile suspicion. Andros was, after all, the same man who had tried to "help" Connecticut in the early days of the war by sailing up the river to Hartford and attempting to seize disputed land for the duke of York.[140] In the magistrates' view, Andros had done too little to prevent the sale of powder and guns to New England's Indian enemies.[141] Most recently, in the wake of the disastrous Indian attacks all along the Maine coast in the autumn of 1676, Andros had sent a royal sloop to Boston and the Piscataqua River settlements, offering "free passage" to New York for any driven from Maine. The addition of these settlers would add to the population and strength of the colony of New York. The Massachusetts General Court had been highly offended at the offer, which they accounted as abetting those who had "in a very dishonorable manner forsaken those places that might with meet care have been kept out of the enemy's hands." Leaving the lands a "prey not only to the Indians, but also to the French who are said by them to be their Abettors in the depopulation there made" was, the Court insisted, not in his majesty's interest.[142]

In spite of these affronts and their longstanding resistance to offers of assistance from the king's royal governor, in May 1677 Massachusetts was in such desperate straits that the magistrates requested Andros's help in engaging the Mohawks to fight against the Kennebec Indians.[143] Andros agreed to try and also offered to help mediate a peace between them and Massachusetts, but his efforts appeared to be more helpful to himself than to the beleaguered colony.[144] As the Massachusetts forces were being decimated at Black Point, officers from New York were busy constructing and provisioning a fort at Pemaquid and seating themselves there "in right of the duke of York." Once his officers were settled, Andros issued orders restricting any Indians or English other than New Yorkers in those lands and stipulating that henceforth all who fished on the Maine coasts had to pay customs to the duke of York. Massachusetts leaders saw this as a direct violation of their rights under their charter, which stipulated that all English subjects be allowed unrestricted fishing on all English coasts, as well as use of adjoining lands to salt and dry their fish. The Massachusetts General Court protested that by making his restriction, Andros denied "a liberty which our kings have always reserved in the charters for these terri-

Sir Edmund Andros, Knt.

Figure 18. Edmund Andros, 1637–1714, royal governor of New York, 1674–1681, governor of the Dominion of New England, 1686–1689. Courtesy of the American Antiquarian Society.

tories."[145] Andros seemed to apply his restrictions over all of Maine, not just the lands above Casco Bay, where the Massachusetts claim to territory ended. In October 1677, the General Court sent Andros a letter protesting his restrictions and his threats to enforce them with "his highness sloop." The amicable relations they hoped to maintain with all English subjects, him particularly, would "be best preserved and continued if we do all walk within our own lines."[146] Andros must have snorted at that. He well knew that the Massachusetts agents were defending themselves in England at that moment because of charges that they had reached far beyond their "own lines." And in doing so, they had unseated a government established by the king's own agents. Who better to reassert the king's right than the only royally appointed officer in the region, Edmund Andros?

Within days of the Black Point disaster, Andros's officers began negotiating with Indians for the release of English hostages and for a settled peace. "Being informed who were there settled," the Indians offered to submit to the New York agents. However, they made a notable exception to their offer: their submission was "not to include the Massachusetts." This phrase gives clear evidence that in the wake of the war Maine's Indians had abandoned any desire for continued alliance with Massachusetts, choosing to shift their allegiance to another, hopefully more trustworthy, power. The phrase is also striking for the context in which it was written. It was part of a self-serving description "concerning the Indians" that Andros submitted in person to the Committee for Trade and Plantations in the spring of 1678, as the Committee was considering a whole series of complaints against Massachusetts.[147] Andros also gave this committee an account of the "violent proceedings of the Magistrates of Boston during the late Indian War, and their neglect of the matters he moved them in for a more timely suppressing the Indians, and for receiving the assistance he was ready to give them, both in sending them a considerable force from his own Government, and by drawing the Mohawks his neighboring Indians, to join against those in enmity" with them.[148] Not surprisingly, Andros did not relate to the committee any of the reasons the United Colonies or Massachusetts had for being suspicious of his offers of help, nor did he mention Massachusetts's tardy petition for his assistance. His presentation of events must have confirmed the royal government's belief that Massachusetts was "upon the very brink of renouncing any dependence on the Crown" as well as that their dangerously independent government was abusing the Indians, thus bringing the devastations of war upon themselves.[149]

In spite of the Indians' request to exclude Massachusetts from the terms of peace, Andros's agents insisted on full submission to both English governments, which the Indians acquiesced to within a month.[150] But Massachusetts leaders were dissatisfied with the terms obtained. They wrote to New York's agents insisting that the stipulations of their previous, quickly broken treaty with Mogg Heigon be met, including the return of every captive and stolen vessel. The New York agents, Anthony Brockholtz, Mathias Nicolls, and Ceasar Knapton, felt hobbled by Massachusetts's inflexible terms and protested. Somehow the Massachusetts stipulations had been broadcast publicly "(to Indians as well as others) [and] It was like to spoil all we had done, & make a new breach, Some of the looser Indians threatening to rescue the [Indian] Captives by force." Even after the Indians returned English captives, the English continued to hold six Indian captives in prison, once again violating the Indians' trust. Fortunately for the peace, Madockawando arrived and agreed to all terms, "almost contrary to our Expectation."[151] Again, by demanding that every boat and all tackle and cargo captured in the July uprising be returned, the English from Massachusetts were assuming that Indian authority was stronger and more inclusive than English authority had ever been. Sporadic Indian attacks continued for several months, but on Indian application a peace treaty was signed the following April 1678, and a wary calm settled on the region.

With the signing of this peace treaty, King Philip's War was finally over. During the three years that it had raged, Massachusetts was laid open to charges of abuse of the Indians, continued defiance of English laws, and disobedience to the king's commands concerning Maine. When the Indians sought to shift their former alliances with Massachusetts to New York's royal governor or the French, that seemed to be evidence in itself that charges that Massachusetts had mistreated the Indians were true. Massachusetts's handling of the war, criticized so pointedly by John Wompas and decried by dozens of Maine refugees, had added fuel to an already raging fire. Even Massachusetts stalwart Joshua Scottow wrote in complaint that through the colony's neglect Maine residents had been "put upon to make application for Relief unto a foreign power [New York], which how Honorable it will be to this Government, or how consistent with their Oath of fidelity may be questioned."[152] Like the Indians, many of the English in Maine had concluded that royal authority such as that vested in New York's governor was a more sure source of protection and stability than distant Massachusetts. That conclusion would become increasingly widespread in coming years.

The conclusion of the war in its southern theater of Massachusetts, Plymouth, Connecticut and Rhode Island was a shattering defeat for the Indians, who were scattered, sold into slavery, or decisively marginalized as wage laborers and outsiders. The outcome of the conflict in Maine was equally shattering, but for the English, not the Indians. Most English towns in Maine had been abandoned during the war. Those few that were resettled were deserted again during the succeeding wars with the Indians, which began within a decade and raged into the next century, fulfilling John Wompas's 1677 threat that "the english should feel the Indians ere long."[153] Where Indians had been forced to make reparations for damages in previous conflicts, either by direct payments or forced sale of combatants, the English paid in Maine. Signing on to the treaty of April 12, 1678, the English agreed to give tribute—the traditional token of subjection—of a peck of corn per family to local sachems every year thereafter.[154] Maine, where English authority was contested more hotly than in any other region of New England, found itself in fulfillment of Hubbard's words, "left to be put under the Yoke and Power of the Indians themselves."[155] Massachusetts, too, emerged from the war in the northeast chastened and weak. As a result of overreaching its authority, the colony had been left to fight the war alone. Not only Indians but fellow colonies had pulled away from association with Massachusetts, leaving it isolated and vulnerable to royal intervention, a danger that would only increase in coming years.

Chapter 10

Surrendering Authority

"Last night had a very unusual Dream," Samuel Sewall wrote in his diary on January 2, 1686. In the dream, Jesus Christ came to live in Boston, choosing as his residence the home Sewall shared with his father-in-law, John Hull. Sewall marveled at "the goodness and Wisdom of Christ in coming hither and spending some part of His short Life here." His reflections held no small measure of pride as well: "How much more Boston had to say than Rome boasting of Peter's being there!" Sewall exclaimed. Christ's choosing to dwell in Boston was a fulfillment of his dearest hopes and those of many other Puritans in Massachusetts Bay Colony. They had tried to make it a true Christian Commonwealth, a place built on and governed by Christ's law. His coming—walking Boston's streets, living among its people—must mean that their offering, their "City on a Hill," was acceptable to him. A sweet dream, indeed, but Sewall awoke to a heartbreakingly different reality.

That very month news arrived on a ship in Boston Harbor that *The Rose* frigate was ready to sail from England and that Edward Randolph, appointed the deputy governor of the new royal colony of Massachusetts, was on board. The newly appointed governor was already present in the colony—Joseph Dudley, a political moderate and longtime associate of the despised Randolph. Rumors flew about the colony in the succeeding weeks and months. One reported that not Dudley, but one Vincent would be governor (a story "which Mr. Dudley laughs at"). A ship from Madeira brought news the governor would be Colonel Percy Kirk, a report contradicted within two weeks by news on yet another ship. All rumors were laid to rest on May 14, 1686, two days after the general election, in which Dudley was voted out of his office as magistrate. *The Rose* sailed into Boston harbor, Randolph on board, and once ashore he lost no time in displaying the royal documents that established his own and Governor Joseph Dudley's authority and—more tellingly—confirmed the crown's judgment against the Massachusetts Bay Charter.

The transition from the old charter government to royal government was swift and uncompromising. Old and new rulers assembled together in the townhouse on May 17, arrayed on opposite sides of the room. When Governor Dudley displayed the exemplification of the charter's condemnation,

Figure 19. *Judge Samuel Sewall*, 1729, oil on canvas, by John Smibert. Sewall (1652–1730) was a magistrate, merchant, and judge. Courtesy of the Museum of Fine Arts, Boston, bequest of William L. Barnard (by exchange), and Emily L. Ainsley Fund; photo 2003.

former deputy governor Thomas Danforth suggested the Court might give its "Answer" later. Dudley curtly informed him that that would not be necessary: "They could not acknowledge them as [a court], and could no way capitulate with them." In a move plainly intended to mark the transition, Randolph's Anglican minister performed a wedding at Samuel Shrimpton's house on May 18, using the Book of Common Prayer banned under the old charter government.

On Friday, May 21, 1686, the magistrates and deputies met at former Governor Bradstreet's house to confer about the new government's request for keys to the fortifications in Boston Harbor. It was a somber meeting. Samuel Nowell "thanked God for our hithertos of mercy 56 years . . . [and] for what we might expect from sundry of those now set over us." Sewall, a longtime magistrate, suggested singing a hymn—the seventeenth and eighteenth verses of the third chapter of Habbakuk:

Although the fig tree shall not blossom, neither shall fruit be in the vines; the labor of the olive shall fail, and the fields shall yield no meat; the flock shall be cut off from the fold, and there shall be no herd in the stalls:
    Yet I will rejoice in the Lord, I will joy in the God of my salvation.

Choking with tears, the marshal general, Daniel Gookin, announced the meeting adjourned until the following October—still clinging to hope in a government that was all too clearly ended. Sewall noted, "Many Tears Shed in Prayer and at parting."[1]

Samuel Sewall described the turnover of Massachusetts government as a time of profound loss, when the charter was wrenched from the colony and replaced with a hostile, outside power. While he depicted the events of May 1686 as a turning point, in reality the charter government had been lost well before then. Under constant attack from royal government, battling resistance to its administration and challenges to its territorial reach within and outside the colony, Massachusetts had little authority left by the time the turnover took place. These attacks, combined with the threat of renewed war with the Indians and changes in the social and religious attitudes of the society, helped destabilize the government, rendering its leaders helpless to either rule or defend the colony. Political turmoil in New England mirrored that in old England, where a series of political upheavals—the Popish Plot, the exclusion crisis, and wars with Dutch, Spanish, and French—undermined authority and stability there and lent hope to those who resisted royal intervention in the colonies. All this disorder created a vacuum of authority in New England, a situation that the competing groups in the region—English colonial governments, Indian nations, the English and French crowns, and opposing religious and political groups—sought to turn to their own benefit, at the continued cost of stability and safety. More than ten years of such upheaval did much to ready the English population of Massachusetts to accept the royal government embodied in the Massachusetts charter of 1691. The new royal government was widely hailed by Massachusetts residents—a change Sewall and many of his fellow thinkers could scarcely have imagined on that sorrowful day in 1686.

To understand what would lead a people so long resistant to any infringement on their authority to accept, even welcome, royal government, we need to return to the aftermath of King Philip's War.[2] Under attack by Indians on one side and by the king, in the guise of Edward Randolph, on the other, Massachusetts colony leaders were torn over how to respond to the crown's challenge in a way most likely to preserve their liberties. After much debate, the General Court had voted to send the agents demanded by the king and appointed William Stoughton and Rev. Peter Bulkeley to fill the office. They departed in December 1676. In the colony they left behind, anxious residents gathered in prayer meetings, the "Chief design (it seems) in Meeting to pray for Mr. Stoughton."[3]

Their wait for news of the success or failure of the mission was punctuated by several disturbing incidents striking at Massachusetts's authority and raising fears about continuing divisions in the colony. In January 1677, an anonymous person tossed a letter into Governor Leverett's house and fled. The letter spelled out the messenger's threat to burn certain houses on January 23. Nothing occurred on that day, but by the following October several fires had raged through Boston. On October 10, in direct response to these seditious actions, the General Court issued an order requiring everyone in the colony, strangers included, to take the oath of fidelity to the government of Massachusetts Bay. In addition, in order to identify who had and had not taken the oath, the Court ordered that a list of all inhabitants be taken.[4] While this measure was intended to bolster the colony's authority and discourage the threatening actions against it, it coincided with political events in England in a way that once again made Massachusetts appear an enemy to royal authority. The colony's insistence on oaths to its government came at a time when England was taking similar measures, ordering all inhabitants to take the oath of supremacy in response to a rumored attempt to dethrone Charles II in favor of his Catholic brother James—the "Popish Plot." Alert opponents of the Massachusetts government were quick to point out that colony leaders had ordered an oath not to the king but to the colony. In response, Charles called for colony leaders to administer the proper oath immediately. They acquiesced, but the incident did only harm to their ongoing battle to preserve the charter.[5]

Faced with these threats to their authority from both within and outside the colony, Massachusetts leaders took steps to increase the security and stability of the region. Indians remained a grave concern despite the fact that their numbers had decreased by 40 percent during the war, reducing them from 25 percent of New England's population in 1674 to from 8–12 percent by war's end. Nearly three thousand of the Indians who allied with Philip were killed in combat or perished from disease and hunger; another two thousand abandoned their New England homes, seeking "new habitations far remote in the wilderness." One thousand were captured and sold out of the country as slaves.[6] Nevertheless, Indians were still a noticeable presence, and chastened colonists distrusted them and feared attacks from exiled Indians.

To cement their authority over the Indians still within the colony, the General Court met in May 1677 to enact new regulations to govern the hundreds of Indians who had surrendered in the final months of the war, not to mention those who had remained in subjection to the English throughout the fighting. Suspicion of even these faithful Indians is evident in the tightened restrictions placed on their living and travel in the colony. All colony Indians, including non-Christian ones, were directed to live either in English homes or in one of the remaining Christian Indian villages—Natick, Wamesit, Hassanamesit, or Punkapoag. They were forbidden to use guns without a certificate from English authority, and they were barred from entertaining "foreign Indians" who might pose a threat to the English. Connecticut established similar policies in November 1676.[7] In all these acts, the English made it clear that the "friendship, amity, and subjection" mentioned in their earlier treaties now emphasized the final term.

While these regulations were considerably tighter than those in place preceding the war, they were not as restrictive as some in the colony wished. At the October 1677 session of the General Court, the House of Deputies approved an addition to the acts because of many complaints of Indian drunkenness and "contemptuous carriages." Under the proposed laws, Indians would have been barred from entering English towns without the permission of town committees of militia, and Indians who refused to deliver arms on demand or ran when challenged by an English person could have been counted enemies and shot at will. The magistrates refused to pass the laws, and they were dropped. But Indian freedoms continued to erode. In 1681 the Court ordered that all Indians in the colony's jurisdiction, Christian or not, settle in one of three praying towns—Natick, Wamesit, or Punkapoag—or be confined to prison.[8] During the Indian attacks of King William's War (1688–99), colony Indians were barred from entering English towns without permission from the governor and council or town military officials, and they were subjected to seizure of any arms or ammunition found on them, just as had been proposed in 1677.[9]

Diminished autonomy for subject Indians was a lasting consequence of King Philip's War. English distrust of Indian "savagery" and "incivility" had been dramatically heightened by the hostilities.[10] Some English were still willing to entertain Indians in their midst, for their labor or because of their own goodwill. For others, the war extinguished the possibility of trust between the two peoples, leading the English to insist that in the future all Indians remain separate from and subordinate to them. Sudbury minister Edmund Browne offers one vivid example of this process. Browne had preached to the Indians in Sudbury and even had Indians living in his home, but the ravages of war, felt keenly by the town to which Browne ministered, turned him against missionary work to the Indians. In 1677,

Browne wrote urging the magistrates to adopt even more restrictive measures against Indians than they did, and he argued that Indians no longer
deserved missionaries: "Great care and pains hath been taken by us to
effect [the Indians' conversion], but after many years' endeavors, their
aversion from the Gospel, their deriding yea blaspheming the blessed
name of Christ and his ways declare such unworthy of the grace of the Gospel." Mary Rowlandson offers another example of the souring of English
attitudes toward Indians. Like Browne, Rowlandson had spent years on the
outskirts of English settlement, where she and her family had regular contact with Indians, at least one living in their home for a time. And like
Browne, after the war Rowlandson condemned praying Indians with all the
rest.[11]

Under the new Indian legislation, the praying towns' primary purpose
seemed to be segregation rather than religious support. Wartime and postwar restrictions lumped Christian and non-Christian Indians together, per
haps because of English protests that they could not tell friend from foe.[12]
No longer communities where committed Christians could withdraw from
ungodly fellows, the praying towns were forced to accept all colony Indians
living outside English towns, thus keeping the countryside safe for traveling
English.[13] Through these legal changes, the rights Indians expected as subjects were trumped by the desire of the English for protection.

In addition to passing legislation to protect colonists from any Indian
threat, Massachusetts leaders acted to shore up the spiritual defenses of the
colony. The devastating war, which many interpreted as punishment for
the colony's sins, had shaken the confidence of residents in their government and godly mission. Increase Mather's call for reform during the conflict reflected that anxiety. After the war, the General Court returned to
the issue of reformation, issuing a call for the colony's ministers to gather
for a synod—only the third in the colony's history—to revise the Cambridge Platform established in 1647 and to discuss two pressing questions:
"What are the evils that have provoked the Lord to bring his judgments on
New England? What is to be done that so those evils may be reformed?"[14]
While the threat of war was past, the sense of God's judgment on New
England was still palpable. Plagues of smallpox and other diseases had
killed hundreds in recent years, and many leading ministers and magistrates had died, depriving the colony of wisdom and leadership. Finally, the
Court noted the "doubtful expectation" of the king's proceedings against
the Massachusetts charter.[15] In time-honored fashion, the Court directed
the colony to engage in a day of humiliation for the Lord's preservation of
their "liberties, civil & sacred," the safe return of their agents, and the
"blessing of Heaven" upon the synod, that it might bring "glory to his own
great name, reformation, & salvation to this his people."[16]

Like much of the political and ecclesiastical history of the Bay Colony,
the synod was less than harmonious. At its conclusion, however, the moder-

ate faction, which represented those who had long supported a more liberal approach to church membership and a desire for transatlantic unity of congregational churches, triumphed on several points. Solomon Stoddard, the champion of what became known as the halfway covenant, managed to gain enough votes to relax requirements for church membership. Rather than enduring a rigorous examination and narrative of conversion, prospective members were required only to submit a statement of faith. The synod also accepted Boston Third Church minister Samuel Willard's proposal that they adopt the same confession of faith that English Puritans had pronounced in 1658, the Savoy Declaration. By doing so, the synod publicly manifested its unity with cobelievers across the ocean. This action showed a turn from the quasi-separatism many churches had adopted in New England, a step that both paved the way for the political unity the king was increasingly demanding and indicated that the voices of moderation in Massachusetts were becoming dominant.[17]

Despite these efforts to stabilize the colony, its authority remained doubtful. News and visitors from England continued to give hope to discontented parties and undermine the authority colony leaders were so desperately working to strengthen. Edward Randolph, who returned to New England in 1679 with an appointment as a royal customs officer, was a magnet for discontent, particularly in New Hampshire and Maine, where Massachusetts's influence and authority had long been disputed. Randolph's vigorous attempts to enforce the king's navigation acts brought him into repeated conflict with Massachusetts officials,.and he recorded all affronts as examples of resistance to the crown, rather than dislike of his own irascible person.[18] Writing to Plymouth governor Josiah Winslow, Randolph complained that he was "received at Boston more like a spy, than one of his majesty's servants. They . . . have prepared a welcome for me, by a paper of scandalous verses, all persons taking liberty to abuse me in their discourses, of which I take the more notice, because it so much reflects upon my master, who will not forget it."[19] Such letters, and the strident reports on Massachusetts misgovernment that Randolph sent back to England, hampered the colony agents' efforts to defend the charter.

The agents' reports to the magistrates were not hopeful. Mason's and Gorges's heirs had repeatedly asked the king for redress of their grievances, submitting at least sixteen petitions over the course of the 1670s.[20] The agents expected these petitions to influence the king and they did. In 1679, Charles II removed New Hampshire from Massachusetts jurisdiction and established royal government there, a transition carried out by Edward Randolph.[21]

To avoid the same outcome in Maine, where, Massachusetts officials were quick to point out, they had expended thousands of pounds defending the local inhabitants' persons and property during King Philip's War, Massachusetts agents began negotiating with the heir of Ferdinando Gorges to purchase the patent he held to Maine. They finalized the purchase in March 1678. The king, who had failed to take up Gorges's repeated offers to sell the patent to him, was enraged to hear Gorges had found another buyer; he sent a letter demanding that Massachusetts sell it back to him immediately.[22] Undoubtedly hoping to thwart Massachusetts's efforts to assert its authority in the newly purchased province, Edward Randolph sent a copy of the king's demand to Maine resident Edward Rishworth, who read it publicly.[23]

Randolph's letter prepared Maine colonists to resist Massachusetts's efforts to reestablish government there in 1680. It also helped to set up a duel between competing authorities—each claiming the mandate of the king. Colonists in Maine must have lost count of the number of times the government had changed hands. Some measure of local frustration with the repeated political upheavals is revealed in the comments of Joshua Downing, jailed for refusing to sign the oath of fidelity to Massachusetts. Downing demanded that Massachusetts officers "satisfy him by what Authority they there acted, not that he refused taking the oath, but was unwilling to receive the same from every Pretender."[24] Downing was not alone in his resistance to Massachusetts's resumption of government. In 1680 nearly two hundred Maine residents complained to the king against Massachusetts, begging him to establish direct royal government over them. These petitioners included a group of fifty-six men who gathered at Nicholas Shapleigh's home in March to sign their names to a paper declaring their "dissent & nonconcurrence" in the new government. They gave as their reason the king's objection to the Massachusetts purchase of the patent, "so that by our consenting to their commands in the premises we shall endanger his Majesty's displeasure therein."[25] To sway his neighbors to resist Massachusetts's authority, Shapleigh warned "that if the People did submit to the Government directed by the Massachusetts, the Indians would speedily fall upon them & begin a new war with them, as being Rebels to his Majesty." While Shapleigh was undoubtedly using the warning of Indian attack to serve his own political ends, he also believed it to be a plausible threat—that Indians would perceive the change of government, anticipate the likelihood the king would act against the rebellious colony, and use the opportunity to strike while Massachusetts was vulnerable.[26] Indeed, rumors of Indian plans to attack the English began shortly after this period, and the repeated turnovers in government would influence Indian actions throughout the next decade.

Massachusetts's disputed authority in Maine emboldened another power to encroach on the territory there as well—New York governor Edmund Andros. He had asserted the duke of York's right to much of Maine at the end of King Philip's War. In August 1680, following Massachusetts's resumption of government in Maine, Andros ordered his officers at Pemaquid to turn the Massachusetts-appointed constable and magistrates in

Casco Bay out of their places and "also so far threatened the Inhabitants as that they are afraid to abide under his Majesty's Government & authority there settled."[27] It is significant that the Massachusetts Council describing this affront referred to its own authority as "his Majesty's Government and authority." This was precisely the point Andros and many others in Maine disputed. Who was the legitimate representative of the king?

Similar conflict over which authority should prevail reigned in New Hampshire, and the chaos there sent a vivid warning to Massachusetts leaders of what could happen were royal authority to be imposed on them. While royal government was established in New Hampshire in 1679, the colony's first royal governor, John Cutt, was too weak to stand up either for the privileges Mason demanded as owner of the province or to the increasing power pro-Massachusetts colonists such as Richard Waldron wielded as members of the New Hampshire Council.[28] After Cutt's death early in 1681, the Council appointed Waldron governor, an action that so enraged Portsmouth resident Thomas Thurton that he railed at the Council that they were "rebels against the King" and that he "hoped to see them all hanged before he was much older." The Council fined Thurton heavily and consigned him to jail for a month.[29] But the political pendulum was already swinging the other way. Before the end of the year Thurton and likeminded residents had the satisfaction of seeing Waldron replaced by the strongly royalist Edward Cranfield.[30] Cranfield, an ardent Anglican, seemed if possible to harbor more antipathy for neighboring Massachusetts than did Edward Randolph. He wrote repeatedly urging the king to send a royal frigate to force Massachusetts into compliance. He also advocated suppressing nonconformist ministers and the "pernicious and rebellious principles which flow from the College at Cambridge," an action he modeled by jailing Rev. Joshua Moodey thirteen weeks for refusing to administer the sacraments according to Anglican ritual. Cranfield also alienated locals by strictly enforcing the Navigation Acts, insisting that colonists acknowledge Mason's title to their land and pay rent, and dissolving the assembly when they refused to pass bills he recommended.[31] Cranfield's measures were so offensive to colonists that in January 1683 he found himself with an armed rebellion on his hands. He had the ringleader, Edward Gove—who he suspected had been "set on" to his rebellion by Massachusetts—arrested and sent to England in chains.[32]

Cranfield's harshness—and Gove and his followers' willingness to resist it—was likely a response to the general climate of political uncertainty, both in the colonies and in England. The spurious Popish Plot and several challenges to the right to succession of Charles's brother James revealed the political impact of religious conflicts in England and the growing resistance to the centralization of power in the crown. In response to the latest parliamentary attempt to exclude James from the succession in 1681, Charles had disbanded Parliament, and dissatisfaction with his actions divided the people and helped nurture the rebellion of such men as the duke of Monmouth, who would raise an army against the king in 1685. News of these upheavals spread quickly in the colonies, encouraging those resistant to the expansion of the crown's authority there.[33] While Cranfield knew of this political turmoil, he also knew of the ongoing investigation of Massachusetts's charter abuses. Word of the king's decision to initiate *quo warranto* proceedings against the Massachusetts charter reached New England in May 1682, undoubtedly bolstering Cranfield's resolve to act forcefully against any who resisted the king's authority.[34]

News of the *quo warranto* proceedings had a powerful impact in Massachusetts, encouraging those who resisted the colony's authority, while lending increasing desperation to other colonists' efforts to defend the commonwealth. On word of the beginning of legal action against the charter, the General Court dispatched new agents to relieve the weary Stoughton and Bulkeley.[35] These two—Joseph Dudley and John Richards—fared no better than the last set. In typical Massachusetts style, the General Court had withheld full powers to act from them, insisting that the ultimate decision power remain in its hands. Impatient at delay, the king ordered the agents to write for the necessary powers immediately.[36] The agents did write to the General Court, and when they received their reply, they showed it to the Committee for Trade and Plantations. In disgust, the committee reported to the Privy Council that the General Court continued to reserve final decision power to itself.[37] The hapless agents declared they could not take on the defense of the charter and asked the king to allow them to return home.[38] In June 1683, the king ordered the attorney general to issue the *quo warranto* against the colony, requiring it to surrender the charter. Edward Randolph was ordered to carry the order to Massachusetts, and he arrived there in October 1683.

Official notice of the *quo warranto* brought the divisions already present in Massachusetts into stark relief. Division was apparent in the response of the General Court to the king's order to surrender the charter. Governor Bradstreet and many magistrates believed that a dutiful obedience to the king was the course most likely to preserve as many of their liberties as possible. The deputies thought differently and refused to consent. Edward Randolph speculated that they did so in hopes that, as had happened several times before, political turmoil would distract the king from enforcing his commands. Whether or not that was true, another precedent did play a role in the deputies' action. Their delay in submitting to the king's command was partly occasioned by a letter sent to a member of the General Court telling of the "miserable condition" and loss of privileges in the English city of Norwich since it had surrendered its charter. The writer urged the Massachusetts leaders to continue to hold out and promised three or four thousand pounds to assist them with the legal expenses of defending their charter before the crown.[39] Thus the conflict between the crown and the Massachusetts charter mirrored and fed on the same process across the Atlantic. The deputies' refusal of consent forced Governor Bradstreet to send an apologetic letter to the king explaining the "imperfect submission" and promising to work to "prevail with the people to a better understanding."[40]

The divisions within Massachusetts governing councils and the royal disapproval evident to residents of Massachusetts and Maine dramatically undermined the colony's authority in these years. Edward Randolph reported that the majority of the colonists refused to pay a new tax the government ordered, justifying their action by the General Court's failure to deliver the charter as the king had demanded. (The king's order that no one be required to pay taxes to support the defense of the charter may also have had something to do with their refusal.) Randolph claimed there was great dissatisfaction with the General Court's action and later reported that several towns had taken the step of declaring their submission to the king independently of the Court. He also wrote that the Indians to the northeast were preparing for war, an unmistakable suggestion that the Indians recognized the vacuum of authority in the colony and meant to take advantage of it.[41] While Randolph claimed that the majority of the population disapproved of the General Court's refusal to surrender the charter, colonists continued to elect strongly pro-charter representatives to both the House of Deputies and the Council. In the May 1684 elections, colonists showed their displeasure with some of those urging surrender of the charter by throwing them out of office. William Browne and Bartholomew Gedney, both of whom had voted to surrender the charter, lost their seats as magistrates, with what Randolph called "very seditious and inconsiderable persons . . . chosen in their places."[42] In protest, magistrates William Stoughton and Peter Bulkeley left the Court, with seventy "Boston merchants and gentlemen" on horseback giving them an honor guard to their homes—palpable evidence of support on both sides of the political spectrum.

Not surprisingly, in a time of such uncertainty, there were those within the colony willing to come out openly against the Massachusetts government, believing that their opposition would soon have the backing of royal authority. Two men who resisted the colony's authority in these years were Robert and John Blood. The brothers lived on a parcel of land between Concord and Chelmsford, a location they had conveniently used to excuse their failure to pay taxes, or "rates," demanded by either town. A group of six Concord constables and deputies visited the Bloods in 1684 to demand the rates or, if need be, to seize property to pay them, but they fled when Robert Blood pulled a knife on them and declared ominously, "There was no authority in the country but he hoped there would be quickly." One year later, in June 1685, the conflict was repeated. When the constables again insisted that Blood pay his rates, he shouted, "You have no power here—your warrant did not come from King James!" Constable Samuel Hunt ordered a fellow officer to seize Robert Blood and carry him to prison. At that, Blood called to his sons for help, and they came, fists swinging. Eleazar Flagg grabbed Robert, Jr.'s neck and started to choke him. John Hayward, Jr., seized Robert, Sr.'s hair and tried to drag him out the front door. In the midst of the mêlée, a neighbor working in the yard, Thomas Read (who also refused to pay his taxes), yelled to the constables to "Keep the king's peace!" Hunt shouted back, ordering him to assist him in carrying out his duties. Instead, Read plunged into the fight on the side of the Bloods, seizing the constable's staff that Eleazar Flagg raised against one of the men. Read would later defend his act, saying that he "took the staff out of Flagg's hand that he might not break the king's peace," and that he "was constrained by [his] oath to his Majesty to defend his peace."[43]

It is apparent that the Blood family, as well as their neighbor, Thomas Read, felt justified in their resistance to colony authority. Their challenge to the constable's authority—"Your warrant did not come from King James!"—underlines their sense that Massachusetts had lost its right to govern. Only the king had that right, a fact that Read emphasized by reminding the constables of the oath of allegiance he—and they—had taken to the king. This oath gave English subjects the obligation and authority to "defend [the king's] peace." Under the traditional conception of royal authority, which offered protection in return for allegiance, "the people . . . obeyed the king not from fear, but from self-interest, because the monarch protected their rights and advanced the prosperity of the kingdom" and "all offenses were against the king's peace or against his crown and justice."[44]

Boston merchant Samuel Shrimpton, too, used the king's authority to underline Massachusetts's loss of authority. A friend of Edward Randolph, Shrimpton received news of the crown's proceedings against the colony as early as did the magistrates. Samuel Sewall noted that the ship bearing the order to the magistrates to proclaim James II, who took the throne after Charles's death in 1685, contained letters with the same instructions addressed to Shrimpton and other men perceived as sympathetic to royal authority. "Suppose this was done lest the Government should have neglected to do it," wrote Sewall.[45] Shrimpton spent much of the first half of 1686 wrangling with the Court over a case concerning his father's will. The case escalated into one over authority when Shrimpton argued that the law in question had been passed since the king had condemned the colony's charter and hence was void. He later went on to say that even the Court itself was illegitimate: "there was no Governor and Company." He repeated his arguments publicly, "in a great Crowd with contemptuous Pride and Rage." Some magistrates argued that Shrimpton should be sent to prison for his contempt of authority; others doubted their authority to give such an order. The magistrates' inability to agree only undermined their authority further, openly demonstrating their timidity and weakness. As Sewall reported, "for the Governor seemed to own before the People that the Charter was vacated in England, and insisted upon a Proclamation sent him. And the Deputy Governor said the Government must not be tumbled down till His Majesty called for it, or to that purpose: Such discourses and arguings before the people do but make us grow weaker and weaker."[46] While colony leaders tried to resist "tumbling down" until they had official, legal documentation of the charter's loss, their impotence was evident to all.

The rising acceptability of royalist sympathies, as well as the looming threat of royal action against the colony, made it increasingly problematic for colony officials to act against those who resisted their authority. Those who favored accommodation to royal government were gaining influence in the colony. One such man was Joseph Dudley, who would later serve as a royal governor. He had served as a magistrate since 1676, and in the 1685 election his likeminded friend Oliver Purchase joined him on the Council.[47] Nevertheless, the magistrates' failure to obtain the deputies' consent to the king's command suggests that pro-charter sympathies were still dominant in much of the colony. The deputies were not yet ready to surrender their authority and would require a good deal more chastening before that time would come. Blood's parting shot to the constables in 1684—"There was no authority in the country but he hoped there would be quickly"—proved prophetic. In May 1686, only weeks after Samuel Shrimpton's similar public declaration that there was no legitimate government in Massachusetts, Edward Randolph arrived once more in the colony, bearing the documents that proved the Massachusetts charter was void. He brought with him copies of similar proceedings against the Charter of London "to be dispersed by him in New England, as he shall think best for his Majesty's Service," proof that Massachusetts's political misfortunes were not unique. They were part of an empire-wide movement to centralize power in the royal government, removing it in the process from several entities, including the Bay Colony and the city of London, that had used their charter rights to resist the king.[48]

Randolph's arrival in May 1686 ushered in a new era of royal government, a process completed by the arrival, before the year was out, of Edmund Andros, appointed general governor of a consolidated government of all the colonies in the area—the Dominion of New England. Andros came with a great show of authority, accompanied by two foot-companies of soldiers to be stationed in Boston.[49] Nevertheless, his administration did not bring an end to the unsettled state of New England. Andros's previous interactions with the New England governments during his tenure as the governor of New York predisposed many colonists to view him as an enemy. His long association with the newly crowned King James II also

Figure 20. Joseph Dudley, 1647–1720, Massachusetts royal governor, 1702–1715. Courtesy of the Massachusetts Historical Society.

made him an object of suspicion. James's open practice of Catholicism alarmed many Protestants in England and in the colonies. In Massachusetts, staunch Congregationalists viewed James's representatives with marked distrust, despite the fact that most were Anglicans. In their eyes, Andros and his officers, civil and military, were part of a "papist design

Figure 21. China plate commemorating the coronation of James II. Its New English provenance suggests both the rising colonial taste for English luxury goods and a growing enthusiasm for royal government. Courtesy of the Winterthur Museum.

against the protestant Interest in New England as in other parts of the world."[50] Hence the next step was to suspect that the sympathies of these "papists" were more closely tied to their coreligionists in France and Canada than to their fellow countrymen, who they quite obviously disdained. Such suspicions would have made Andros's task of governing New England difficult under any circumstances, but his own actions compounded the problem.

The establishment of the Dominion of New England brought about many Massachusetts colonists' worst fears of the arbitrary government that would follow their loss of authority. Acting on the belief that all legal transactions under the old charter became void when it was vacated, Andros insisted that colonists take out new deeds and pay quitrents for their lands. Many colonists could not afford either the legal fees or the rent, and evidence suggests that some of Andros's officers—notably John West and John Palmer—abused their power by undervaluing titles or charging excessive fees.[51]

Under the Dominion of New England, colonists lost any real voice in their government; Andros's instructions specifically omitted a House of Deputies, and his council was appointed by the king.[52] Thus when Andros began assessing taxes, some colonists claimed they had not had the opportunity to consent to them and refused to pay. In August 1687, the Ipswich town meeting voted unanimously not to pay a tax the government had ordered, protesting that the tax "doth infringe their Liberty, as free born English Subjects of His Majesty, by interfering with the Statute Laws of the Land, by which it was Enacted that no Taxes should be Levied upon the Subjects without consent of an Assembly chosen by the Freeholders for assessing of the same." Ipswich's minister, John Wise, encouraged this resistance by declaring, "we had a good God, and a good King, and should do well to stand for our Privileges." Andros's Council, which promptly jailed a number of the protesters, took a more dim view of their opinions, with Joseph Dudley declaring that they "must not think the Laws of England follow [them] to the ends of the Earth, or whither [they] went." The argument Massachusetts leaders had once used—that the laws of Parliament were bounded by the four seas, so did not apply to them—was plainly a two-edged sword.[53] For their disobedience, Ipswich's protesters were fined twenty one pounds, imprisoned twenty-one days, and banned from holding any office, including, in the case of Mr. Wise, the ministry.[54]

Massachusetts colonists' resentment of Andros's arbitrary government was aggravated by the war that broke out with the Indians under his watch. King William's War—called the *Decennium Luctuosum* by Cotton Mather—lasted over ten years, from 1688 to 1699, and placed heavy demands for men and materials on the colony. These demands could only be met with taxes, and this double burden increased the deep resistance to Andros's administration. While rumors of Indian uprisings to the northeast had troubled New England colonists long before Andros's arrival as governor in 1686, many blamed him for the actual outbreak of hostilities in 1688.[55] In April of that year Andros had led an expedition to Penobscot, Maine—a region long in dispute between the French and English—to demand the submission of Baron Jean-Vincent d'Abbadie de Saint Castine, the Frenchman who had married the daughter of Penobscot sachem Madockawando and held significant influence with the local Indians. Arriving at Castine's fort, Andros and his men found him gone. They looted the fort of many belongings and sent word that they would return the goods only if Castine swore obedience to the English crown, an action that highly offended both Castine and his Wabanaki allies. Colonists later swore that Andros's attack on Castine had completely altered the Indians' relations with the local English. Before the attack, they had been on good terms of trade and friendship. Afterward, the Indians never approached the English "but in an hostile manner."[56] By August of 1688, Indians began attacking settlements in Maine, and rumors spread that hundreds of Indians and French had gathered at Pennacook to plot a war against the English.[57]

While many suspected that Castine had incited the Indians to attack the English to revenge Andros's actions, another conspicuous provocation was Maine resident Benjamin Blackman's unauthorized seizure and imprisonment of over twenty Saco Indians in the late summer of 1688. He acted in reponse to news of French-allied Indian attacks on the Massachusetts towns of Northfield and Springfield and fears that the violence would cascade throughout the region.[58] In retaliation for the seizure, the Wabanaki increased their attacks on English settlements and took captives of their own.[59] When Andros returned from New York, where he had been on government business, he was enraged to find Wabanaki Indians in prison in Boston. Fearing the consequences, he immediately released all the Indian captives, to the outcry of many in the colony.[60] Next he acted quickly and forcefully to quell the uprising in Maine, leading a troop of soldiers to the northeast and, once peace was settled, setting up a string of forts and garrisons housing over 700 soldiers to maintain peace through a strong, visible English presence. He also sent two royal ships, the *HMSS Speedwell* and *Mary*, and two provincial sloops to patrol the coast.[61]

Many Massachusetts colonists judged Andros's strengthening of forces to the northeast as both excessive and unnecessary, an example of his abuse of his office. (Massachusetts agents in London called his garrisons "trifling forts.")[62] They complained that the forts were an enormous expense in men and money that accomplished little beyond salvaging the property of a few wealthy merchants and traders. Indeed, impressing troops to go to the northeast left Massachusetts's own outlying towns dangerously exposed, leading to such complaints as this anonymous screed in January 1689: "The purport of the paper was to give notice to the people of the danger they were in being under the sad circumstances of an Arbitrary Government. Sir Edmund Andros having about One thousand of our Soldiers as I was informed pressed out of the Massachusetts Colony and carried with him to the Eastward under pretence of destroying our Enemy Indians (although not one Indian killed by them that I hear of, & at that time we had no watching nor warding at our Town by order of those that Sir Edmund put in Command there."[63]

The prolonged service of their sons, husbands, and fathers was another grievance to Massachusetts colonists, particularly when reports began coming in of the abuses being heaped on them by Andros's military officers. Few of the men impressed into service in the northeast had served under one of the king's regular officers before. In King Philip's War, men served in units organized in their towns, under officers well known to them. They were unused to the strict and sometimes cruel punishments Andros's officers administered, such as torture to force men to confess misdeeds or prolonged deprivation of food.[64] Resentment of these officers was also fueled by the disdain they showed for the Massachusetts recruits, referring to them as "Boston Dogs & Boars" and openly proclaiming that they would not be sorry if thousands of Indians attacked Boston itself.[65]

Some colonists went so far as to suspect that Andros's expedition to the northeast had a sinister purpose as part of a plot with the French to destroy New England.[66] Massachusetts soldiers serving in the northeast testified that Andros was supplying Indians with powder and ammunition: "*We did very much question amongst ourselves whether the said Sir E. did not intend the destruction of our Army, and brought us thither to be a Sacrifice to our Heathen Adversaries.*" Increase Mather proclaimed that Andros thought New Englanders were "fit to be rooted off the face of the Earth" and was conspiring with the French against them.[67] Some colonists claimed Andros's purpose in going to New York was to engage the Mohawks and French against the English, and they found several Indians willing to testify that Andros had "hired the Indians to kill the English" by sending them two bushels of wampum and several cartloads of trade goods.[68] If such wild but passionately believed tales were not the result of hysteria alone, they would also have served the purpose of undercutting Andros's authority as general governor of the Dominion of New England. Indeed, these charges would be dredged up in deposition after deposition immediately following the Glorious Revolution.[69]

Deep-seated suspicions of Andros and his officers, resentment of his "arbitrary government," and the burdens of a war viewed by many as a Catholic plot fueled the swift and decisive overthrow of the Dominion of New England after news of the Glorious Revolution in England reached Massachusetts. In England, the overthrown King James II was replaced with the Protestant rulers William and Mary. In Massachusetts, on April 18, 1689, colonists seized Andros, Randolph, and other officers of the Dominion and threw them into prison, and the colonies of Massachusetts, Plymouth, Connecticut, and Rhode Island quickly restored their former charter governments. Colonists rejoiced in the return of Protestant rulers to the throne and believed that the Glorious Revolution would safeguard their liberties. Those who believed Andros had persecuted them merely for "too boldly endeavour[ing] to persuade ourselves we were English Men, and under privileges" took heart from the change of government. They believed they were acting against "the Enemies of . . . our *English Liberties.*"[70]

While the fall of the Dominion government was celebrated "with such a Joy, Splendour, Appearance and Unanimity, as had never before been seen in these Territories," the same political uncertainty that had dogged Massachusetts in the years preceding the establishment of royal government persisted, increasing the turmoil within the colony and making it vulnerable to outside forces.[71] Of most immediate concern, the fall of Dominion government gave notice to the Wabanaki of English weakness, encouraging them to renew hostilities. One of Governor Bradstreet's first actions after resuming the government interrupted in 1686 was to recall military forces from Maine. With the return of the charter government, Andros's hated officers were arrested or turned out of their garrisons, and soldiers impressed from New England abandoned their posts for home.[72] Within weeks the war, which had been dormant since the preceding fall, resumed with a vengeance. On June 27, 1689, following the pattern the Indian Simon had established in his 1676 attack on Falmouth, two Indian women staying the night in two Cocheco garrisons opened the doors to their tribesmen. Falling upon the sleeping English, the Indians killed twenty-three and took twenty-nine others captive, later selling them to the French. Richard Waldron was among those killed. During his long years of trade with the Indians, he had gained a reputation for "sharpness," or unfair dealing, undoubtedly compounded by his participation in the deception at Cocheco during King Philip's War. He was reputed to have failed to cross out Indian debts when paid and to have used his fist as a pound measure when weighing Indians' furs. An English observer returned from captivity described Waldron's death: "Some gashed his breast with knives, saying, 'I cross out my account'; others cut off joints of his fingers, and said to him, 'Now will your fist weigh a pound?' "[73] The attack on Cocheco was followed by a string of Indian attacks in July and August that once more plunged the Maine and New Hampshire settlements into a siege existence.

Cries for help and protests at their being left vulnerable to attack by the provisional government in Massachusetts poured out of Maine and New Hampshire. A January 1690 petition to the king from the inhabitants of Maine and the county of Cornwall declared that Indian attacks had "ruinated and depopulated the whole County of Cornwall and great part of the Province of Maine, before any help or assistance was sent from Boston." The petitioners complained of the death or capture of 300 inhabitants and 40,000 pounds in property losses—a striking contrast to the peace they had enjoyed under the defenses Andros had established. Drawing on the comparison, they argued that Governor Andros's swift response to Wabanaki attacks in 1688 had been completely effective, "that in all appearance they [the Indians] would in a very short time have submitted at mercy or been wholly subdued and overcome. And during that time We suffered not the least Loss in our persons or Estates by them." In contrast, by May of 1690, colonists had abandoned all the towns north of Wells. Nearly four hundred refugees streamed into Essex County, leaving their homes and forts to be burned by the Indians. Many of them blamed Massachusetts's resumption of government for their misfortunes. "We Cannot but very justly Conclude," the petitioners wrote, "that all this misery, loss and Calamity which hath befallen us and this Country, hath been Continued and increased upon us by Occasion of the late Insurrection and alteration of the Government at Boston—and the irregular proceedings and management of affairs there since that time."[74]

Critics of the Massachusetts provisional government blamed it not only for ill management of the war but for the blatant advertisement of English weakness that its withdrawal of forces had sent to the Indians. Nicholas Shapleigh's claim that if royal authority were overthrown, Indians would attack the English as "rebels to his Majesty" had proven eerily prophetic. There was no question that the Indians knew of the change in government or that it influenced their renewal of hostilities. Writing of the withdrawal of forces, Andros claimed, "of which, and their actings at Boston, the Indians having notice . . . they were encouraged and enabled to renew and pursue the war."[75] The Wabanakis' eyewitness to the "actings at Boston" was the Penobscot sachem Madockawando, who, ironically enough, traveled there in late April 1689 to confer with Andros about settling a peace. Instead, he found Andros in prison and a new set of authorities set up in his place. Although the provisional leaders did their best to win Madockawando's friendship, loading him and his companions with presents, giving them passage on a boat back to Penobscot, and giving them a letter for Castine to smooth over the rough treatment he had received at Andros's hands, English weakness in the region spoke much louder than these friendly overtures.[76] Within two months, the cease-fire had collapsed, and Wabanaki Indians themselves testified that Andros's absence allowed them to renew the war. Indians sacking the fort at Pemaquid declared that Andros had nearly starved them by blockading the coast and preventing trade of ammunition, powder, and food, but now that he was in prison they would fight again. Confident of their success, they declared that they "no care for the New England people; they have all their country by and by."[77]

While the provisional government's withdrawal of forces significantly weakened the English presence in Maine, Indian success against the remaining English was also made possible by English violation of decrees established under Andros's authority. His ban on selling ammunition and provisions to the Indians had successfully prevented that trade for nearly a year, but Boston merchants seized the opportunity of the governor's extended stay in New York to renew the trade. According to Edward Randolph, the Boston merchants Foster and Waterhouse, who he claimed were leaders in the overthrow of the Dominion government, sent forty tons of ammunition and provisions to trade in the Penobscot River region during Andros's absence. Thus, by defying the authority of the royal governor, these Englishmen were largely responsible for the devastation the Wabanaki later visited on English settlements, allowing the Indians to "continue a war to this time which they have been & are enabled to do by the English themselves."[78]

Authority—its violation and its absence—played a critical role in the renewal of hostilities immediately following the Glorious Revolution, but authority also proved to be critical in the long duration of the war. The provisional government's weakness and questionable legitimacy not only emboldened Indians to attack but crippled the English ability to respond militarily, and this obvious impotence further undermined the authority of the colony. Massachusetts leaders responded to Indian attacks by sending out orders to impress troops, but their uncertain authority encouraged widespread resistance to their efforts. Many argued that the provisional government lacked the authority to impress men or complained about the low wages offered. One colonist reported, "We have many Impresses for men, but can get but few that will go by reason the Government [is] not Settled."[79] Although the newly crowned King William sent a letter in July 1689 authorizing the provisional government to continue until it received further direction, all knew that the magistrates were acting under the authority of a vacated charter, and resistance to impresses continued.[80] Captain Benjamin Church reported that fellow officer Captain Willard's "men will not Come" and complained, "if I had more men when we had the fight by God's blessing we might have Destroyed the enemy at once."[81] Edmund Quinsey of Braintree excused his failure in obtaining soldiers, explaining that "if they be impressed they will not take notice of it, some are so disobedient & others will escape."[82] The colony's authority had sunk so low by June 1691 that Thomas Noyes of Newbury wrote to the Council that he had not even attempted to carry out its order for a party of cavalry to go to Maine: "we did not move for mention to the people, because we find them very much discouraged by reason they can have no encouragement from the Council for any service they have done upon such occasions." The "encouragement" Noyes mentioned was pay for service and remuneration for supplies. Noyes complained that Newbury's costs had been "very great to the damage both in estate and otherwise." They had petitioned the Council for relief, "but could have none for their time nor yet for their ammunition." He added darkly, "Our Soldiers do think themselves much Wronged and can hardly be quieted."[83]

The problem of course was that the colony had no money. As during the period following the first news of legal proceedings against the charter, colonists uncertain where authority lay and not wishing to bow to "every pretender" delayed paying taxes or refused to pay them at all. Some, like Samuel Farlow of Billerica, openly declared the reason for their refusal: the illegitimacy of the government. Threatening to shoot the constables if they came to demand his taxes, Farlow proclaimed that "the Curse of God had followed us ever since they took sir Edmond down and that the Government was not worthy to kiss sir Edmond's arse."[84] The government had issued demands for ten single rates, but very little had come in. The author of *Further Quaries upon the Present State of the New-English Affairs* derided those who refused to pay taxes, demanding, "Whether it be not better to give a shilling to a public Account with our own consent in a general Assembly, than to have a penny forced from us without it, as in the late Arbitrary Government." Those who continued to undermine the government were "*Grumbletonians*," he asserted, and "the worst Enemies which the Country can have." Nevertheless, the treasury remained empty, and an empty treasury could supply neither pay nor provisions to soldiers. Soldiers showed their discontent by refusing to serve or, if already in service, threatening to desert.[85]

Not only was Massachusetts unable to exert its authority to compel colonists to serve as soldiers or to support them while in the field, but its unsettled authority, and that of its fellow English colonies, undercut its ability to secure assistance from longtime allies. As the war dragged on, Massachusetts authorities wrote to the governors of Plymouth, Rhode Island, and Connecticut to plead for assistance—troops and supplies. All three made it clear in their replies that they lacked the authority to compel assistance from their citizens. The Rhode Island Council wrote to commiserate with Massachusetts's troubles but declared that it could not help and that any attempt to collect taxes would result in "blood shed." They gave as the reason for this resistance the political uncertainty that reigned in that colony, too. People there were "Afraid to do Justly for fear or doubting that the french party [those sympathetic to the deposed James II] might prevail & that then it might be worse for them for so doing."[86]

Plymouth leaders, too, reported strong resistance to their authority, both because of the "confusion" of unsettled government and because of contradictory messages from authorities within and outside the colony:

Several of our Towns at least considerable numbers of their inhabitants do renounce and disclaim any authority that we have here—& forceably refuse to pay the Rates made for the payment of the soldiers heretofore sent forth . . . and are now also further animated to cast off the yoke of Government, not only by what they received from Governor Sloughter, but also by a Letter lately to them from the present Governor of New York, (as is credibly informed) directing them to pay no Rates till their Majesties' pleasure be known.

Plymouth officials lamented the resistance of the "perverse mutinous spirits" in their colony but believed nothing could be done: "Therefore in vain to call a General Court to advise [about] that affair: But must in the way of humbling our selves under [God's] mighty hand Commit our all to him, who will judge his people & repent himself concerning his servants when he sees their power is gone."[87]

Connecticut authorities also seemed to believe that their "power [was] gone." Meeting to confer on the Massachusetts request, the magistrates dismissed outright the idea of issuing a tax. Instead, they sent word to the towns that any who wished to make a voluntary contribution to the war effort could do so.[88] While these colonies had resumed their charter governments, they suffered from the same sense of illegitimacy as Massachusetts and could neither compel military service nor payment of taxes.

Another reason may also have contributed to these colonies' denial of Massachusetts's request. At the end of King Philip's War, Plymouth and Connecticut had both refused to assist Massachusetts in fighting the war in Maine, questioning the validity of the colony's claim to the region. Hesitancy to cast their lot with a colony in disfavor with the king persisted after the war. When Edward Randolph wrote urging King Charles II to vacate the Massachusetts charter in 1681, he argued, "The King cannot hope for a better opportunity than this for settling the country, for the other Colonies that were their confederates have now fallen off. . . . Nor do they find it reasonable to be involved in the mischief which may follow such repeated disloyalty."[89] As the New England colonies waited to learn "their Majesties' pleasure" regarding the form their government would take, that same desire to hold off from association with Massachusetts may have persisted.[90]

Uncertain authority not only weakened English leaders' command over their own people and allies, it also made them vulnerable to the aggressions of non-English colonies and interests. As we have seen, the Wabanaki Indians knew of the post-Revolution change in government and acted quickly to strike while the English were vulnerable. The Iroquois in the colony of New York were also aware of the political turmoil, at least partly through the instrumentality of "the common People of Albany, who are all Dutch, [and who] could not forbear giving the Indians some Ill Impressions of the English." In response to Dutch complaints, the Mohawks declared, "We hear a Dutch Prince reigns now in England. Why do you suffer the English Soldiers to remain in the Fort? Put all the English out of the Town." Like the Dutch, the Iroquois had grievances against the English, who forced them to sleep on the ground when they came to trade, while the Dutch had always welcomed them into their houses. The change to what the Iroquois perceived as Dutch government held out the promise of better treatment, and the fact that the Dutch had temporarily retaken New York as recently as 1673 and had fought yet another war with England from 1680 to 1684 made such a turnover entirely plausible.[91] Reports of the Iroquois demand that the Dutch "put all the English out" confirmed English suspicions that Indian loyalty to them was tenuous, and rumors flew throughout the northeast that the inconstant Five Nations would take the opportunity the unsettled state of the colonies offered to join with the French and conquer the English colonies of North America.[92]

Fears of French plots against New England ran rampant during this time of political instability. Randolph, writing from the "common jail" in which he was imprisoned following the Glorious Revolution, warned that the

French had 4,000 soldiers and he feared "that upon the news of the Bostoners reassuming their old government (no care being taken for the out towns and Provinces) they will join with the Indians, and in a short time swallow and be masters of that part of the Country."[93] French Canadian reaction to the events of the Glorious Revolution demonstrates that such fears were not unreasonable. The French and English were at war with each other for nearly twenty of the fifty years between 1675 and 1725.[94] Indeed, renewal of war between the two nations in May 1689 was a direct consequence of the Glorious Revolution, and the French sought alliances with the Wabanaki to assist them in the war—a conflict that served both Indian and French interests. French forces both supplied the Wabanaki and participated with them in raids on New England, including the January 1692 attack on York, Maine. Silvanus Davis, captured in that attack, spent several months in Canada before being ransomed and returned to New England. He met with Govenor Frontenac while there and heard him condemn the English for deposing a reigning Catholic king and replacing him with the "Prince of Orange" who was "but an Usurper." James II had taken refuge in France, and the French officers who captured Davis declared that "they did fight for King James as Being under the protection of the french King." It would be surprising if French officials did not share these accusations with their Wabanaki allies in order to undermine the legitimacy of the English who claimed authority over them. The desperate efforts of the English to bring the Wabanaki to submission would have been greatly hampered by French claims that the new colony governments were "all Rebels against our King [James II]."[95] Why should the Wabanaki yield obedience to rebellious governments under an illegitimate ruler? Resentment of English incursions on their land, of the seizure and imprisonment of twenty of their sachems and kin, and English failure to keep promises made in earlier agreements turned the Wabanaki toward the French. Their preference was so obvious to the few English venturing into Maine that some ship captains chose for their own safety to fly French colors. When sailors from one such vessel met Indians on shore, the Indians boasted that there were no more English left in the area. Forgetting himself, a sailor retorted in English, and the Indians attacked him.[96]

The ongoing conflict between the English and French—with each fighting to exert their authority over, and secure the alliance of, the region's native peoples—played a significant role in the tensions and uncertainty of this period. Securing the submission of the Indians to their authority was a way for each European power to ensure the safety of its colonists and to challenge the power of competitors for the continent. The English invoked this authority when they sent a message to the hostile Wabanaki chiding them for breaking faith, reminding them of their subjection to the English crown, and warning them of the consequences of violating that subjection: "Let them also understand the Regard which their Majesties of England &c.

our Sovereigns have for their Territory and good Subjects here, and their high Resentment of the Spoils and mischiefs that have been perpetrated upon them by the Indians, and their Instigators and Supporters the french, and that they may Expect their Majesties will sharply revenge it upon them." In addition, the English argued that the French were poor allies, "it being probable that the french will be incapacitated to afford them Succors, most of the Princes in Europe being joined in a confederacy against france."[97] But Wabanaki knowledge of Massachusetts's unsettled authority made this an empty threat. Madockawando, on returning from his April 1689 visit to Boston, expressed his sense that the English no longer held any true authority. He refused to treat for peace with the English he and his forces attacked, declaring: "They were not Sagamores."[98]

For the Indians, renewing the war with the English was not a decision based simply on opportunity. Rather, it was a considered response, a final recourse after repeated failures to achieve their demands and defend their sovereignty.[99] Wabanaki grievances against the English of New England had been building since the peace treaty of 1678. Their relations with local English had been severely damaged by the events of King Philip's War. The Indians' request that Massachusetts be excluded from the 1678 peace treaty offers stark testament to that fact. At the insistence of New York governor Edmund Andros, Massachusetts remained a party to the peace, but its local citizens were forced to pay a tribute of corn to local Indians, a requirement that appeared to make them subject to the Wabanaki. In the intervening years, English settlers had not only failed to pay the tribute, thus symbolically rejecting any such submission, but they had also expanded their settlement, in direct contradiction to Wabanaki demands.[100] The first Indian attacks in King William's War fell on North Yarmouth, Maine, a new English settlement that Indians believed infringed on their territory. Their attack on the town was a direct demonstration that the Wabanaki would defend their rights and that if the English refused to respect them, the Wabanaki would "have all their country by and by."[101] Defending their sovereignty meant not only protecting their land, but their authority, which they complained the English too frequently disregarded. The English found pliable sachems to sign away land when others would not, and they scoffed at the validity of past agreements with Indians: "what Ever Any indian did it was but as for A Raccoon to put his paw to it."[102] Repeated Wabanaki protests at previous English infringements and threats had been ignored. Thus recourse to war was a final option, made easier by the withdrawal of English forces in the immediate aftermath of the Glorious Revolution.

War was not the only arena in which the vacuum of authority created by the fall of the Dominion government was felt. Lack of authority also accen-

tuated divisions within the colony of Massachusetts and dissatisfaction with
its weak government. Despite the celebration that accompanied the capture and imprisonment of Governor Edmund Andros and his officers, the
Glorious Revolution was not welcomed by everyone in New England. The
pamphlet war that followed the revolution gives ample evidence of that.
Sticklers for royal authority such as Connecticut's Gershom Bulkeley complained that because New England governments' charters had been legally
vacated, there was no authority to resume. Disagreement over this issue
deepened divisions in the colonies, leading one New Englander to write,
"Nor can any thing be More ill boding to us & our all than the Cursed
Murmurings which the Almighty God hears in our Streets from day to day;
instead of praying to God for the direction of our Government at this
Extraordinary time, we Spend our time in Fretting & railing at them; Nothing they do can please."[103]

Ironically, some of the same charges that had been leveled at Andros
during his time as governor were hurled at the provisional government that
succeeded him: the war was fought to enrich a few, colony leaders
neglected their own subjects to fight in the northeast, and Massachusetts
merchants supplied the French and Indians with ammunition and provisions.[104] This transfer of hostility to their chosen leaders is evidence that
colonists were heartily weary of the prolonged instability. Their dissatisfaction and open distrust of colony authorities only undermined authority further, leading many to long for the stability royal government might offer.
Colonel Cuthburt Potter, sent north in the summer of 1690 by Virginia
leaders to assess the impact of the Glorious Revolution, reported on readiness for a change in government in Massachusetts: "The people [are] generally much dissatisfied with their present Government, and blame it very
much for all their sufferings, which have happened only through their ill
management of affairs and sending away Sir Edmond Andrews, that caused
all those great losses to the Eastward. I went over to Cambridge and Charles
Town . . . and having spent some time in discoursing several Gentlemen
and others, I generally observed that many who had been for, were now
inveterate enemies to the present Government." A Boston merchant
claimed that many in Massachusetts, as well as Maine and Rhode Island,
hoped for a royal governor, even the return of a general one over all the
colonies in the region.[105] Proving that such claims were not just talk, colonists representing a broad range of interests and political views petitioned
the king for his speedy settlement of royal government. In January 1690,
four groups sent such petitions: forty-four "gentlemen, merchants and others of Boston," the wardens of Boston's Anglican Church, twelve "sundry
inhabitants of Charlestown," and sixteen inhabitants of Maine. They noted
the chaos gripping the region, the devastation the withdrawal of military
forces had brought, and the "anarchy" that they claimed could only be
settled by having a royal governor over them.[106]

The growing openness to royal government that these petitions and statements reveal was also made possible by the simple passage of time. Many of the most ardent supporters of the old commonwealth party—including Daniel Gookin and John Eliot—had died by 1692. Taking their places as leaders in government and churches were such moderates as Boston Third Church's Samuel Willard, who helped shepherd the changes voted by the 1679 synod, and government leaders Simon Bradstreet and Joseph Dudley. Moderate political and religious approaches had become increasingly appealing to colonists whose prolonged snaring in a "time of trouble" had given them a longing for settled order.[107] A new generation had also come of age in New England, and they were struggling to begin their own families during a period of enormous anxiety and economic hardship. Renewed war with the Indians laid a heavy emotional and financial burden on a colony that had not yet recovered from King Philip's War. The expenses of that conflict had raised colony taxes, traditionally lower than local taxes, to double or triple their usual rate. They had remained at a higher than normal level for a decade after that conflict and soared again during King William's War.[108] This financial burden created resentments that helped destabilize the government, as the younger generation turned away from local authorities who had been in power throughout the devastation and before, hoping for better times under new leaders.[109]

The willingness of Massachusetts's new leaders to embrace royal government appears in their political actions. In striking contrast to the foot-dragging of the previous generation, the officers that served in Massachusetts from 1689 through 1691, when hopes for preservation of the original charter government would seem to have had the greatest chance of realization, took dramatic steps to align themselves with the secular model of government the king had been urging on them. During that period, "ex-moderates and Anglicans" such as Samuel Shrimpton—the same man who had declared "there was no Governor and Company" a few years earlier—were elected to the magistracy, and 738 men were admitted to freemanship, an increase of nearly 50 percent.[110] Religious freedoms, too, increased, along with a growing sense of religious tolerance and ecumenicalism. By 1694, both Anglican and Baptist church steeples graced the Boston skyline, and while non-Puritans were still expected to pay taxes to support the established Congregational Church, prosecutions of Quakers and other religious dissenters had long since ceased and protests had dwindled dramatically.[111]

The changes promised by the Glorious Revolution also made royal government less threatening to New Englanders. Andros's excesses—and those of his royal master—had blatantly contradicted the widely held convention that "the king's authority was always exercised for the good of his subjects." England's new monarchs agreed to a political settlement that bolstered parliamentary power and reined in arbitrary action by the crown.[112] Indeed, in both old and New England, the Glorious Revolution gave notice that monarchs and governors could no longer hide their misdeeds behind the traditional notion of the divine right of kings. Violation of their contract with the people would justify their removal.[113]

With this understanding firmly in place, most of Massachusetts was prepared to accept royal government. In 1691 the colony's provisional leaders joined their voices to those of the petitioners of 1690 in asking the king for a royal governor.[114] Even Increase Mather, who had doggedly defended the old charter for much of the previous decade, bowed in the face of the inevitable and helped to secure the most favorable terms possible for the new Massachusetts charter issued in October 1691, a "skillful compromise between the forces of consolidation and those of self-government." Massachusetts jurisdiction over Maine was at last acknowledged by the king, who placed Plymouth under the same government. The king also conceded to Massachusetts colonists the right to continue annual elections, to have their own elected officers appoint the royal council, and to have their royal governor selected by the king from among them rather than to have a stranger, like Andros, placed over them.[115]

While authority was finally settled in a new charter, its royal governor—the Maine-born Sir William Phips—did not arrive in Massachusetts until May 1692. In the interim, war continued to rage, and the provisional government continued to flounder. In the midst of this political limbo, a final blow fell on New England: the Salem witchcraft trials. A few witchcraft accusations in January 1692 snowballed into a major crisis by late spring, requiring a separate court, involving hundreds of witnesses, accused and accusers, and paralyzing much of the colony with fear and dismay. Some historians have suggested that the crisis was a response to both the instability of the times and the trauma of war. Those caught up in the witchcraft frenzy revealed their preoccupation with King William's War, and colony leaders' inept prosecution of it, by their frequent mention of Indians, the French, and colonists with connections to both in their accusations. Repeated Indian attacks, combined with the colony's inability to meet them with any kind of effectiveness, contributed dramatically to the sense of being beset by powerful, even sinister, outside forces.[116] The provisional government took little action to resolve the witchcraft crisis, which only increased the hysteria. As during King Philip's War, many English saw the witchcraft as a sign of God's wrath against New England—a perception that could only undermine leaders' authority further. And, as they had in the previous war, Indians targeted this spiritual insecurity. Noting that former Maine minister George Burroughs had been hanged by the Salem judges, Indians taunted, "[the French Catholic] *Priests are good Men, our Ministers are Devils, and hung for Witches.*"[117] The shocking explosion in accusations and executions in the witchcraft trials by the summer of 1692 gave another reason for the region to welcome the arrival of stable royal government. One of the few acts for which Massachusetts's new royal governor William Phips received general acclaim was his suspension of the witchcraft proceedings in the fall of 1692.

All these troubles make minister Samuel Willard's 1694 plea to "Look for Changes in a World of Mutability, and lay in, as far as innocent Prudence may direct, for your Own, and your People's Safety" resonate.[118] The years following King Philip's War had been an unbroken time of turmoil. Even the return of the old charter government in 1689 had not provided for the people's safety or peace. Instead, the colonists had been wracked by another devastating war with the Indians, burdened with heavy taxes to pay for it, beset by witches, and left in the care of governors who seemed helpless to protect or direct them. As Cuthbert Potter reported, such stresses had turned even those who once supported the provisional government into "inveterate enemies." Although he had been among the former stalwarts for the charter government, Joshua Scottow offered a remarkably positive judgment of the royal government that was finally settled in Massachusetts in 1692. Instead of the mourning that imbues Samuel Sewall's account of the royal government imposed in 1686, Scottow's assessment of the new Massachusetts charter rings with optimism: "Our prayers were heard, as appeareth by their Majesties' grant of a *Province Charter*, there declared, and here with great acclamation Proclaimed; this we looked at as a happy Omen of Halcyon days now come to this distressed, & wounded people."[119] John Pynchon, a long-time magistrate, shared Scottow's optimism about the new charter, writing, "I greatly rejoice, looking upon it as an answer of Prayers, and tendency to a hopeful good Settlement of the Country."[120]

The transformation of Massachusetts from a fiercely independent religious commonwealth to a royal colony with more widespread political franchise and religious freedom than its founders would ever have countenanced was a long, painful process. Many in the colony—men such as Elisha Cooke, Thomas Danforth, and Samuel Sewall—continued to bewail the loss of the charter and the increasingly secular turn of society and government.[121] Sewall's dream of a Christian Commonwealth, a place where even the Savior might wish to dwell, had not been realized, religiously or politically. Instead, the English had been forced to accept the full implications of their subjection to the king; they had submitted to the changes brought by an Atlantic world whose vast distances seemed to draw closer together every year. Faced with that rapidly changing world, most citizens of the Bay Colony countenanced the surrender of their charter authority in exchange for a "good Settlement of the Country," hoping that, in time, some liberties lost might be restored.[122] Phips's term as governor was a controversial one, but succeeding governors would help usher the province into a longstanding era of relative domestic stability and harmony.[123] Massachusetts had surrendered its authority, but remembrance of the sovereignty so ardently defended in seventeenth-century Massachusetts would revive in succeeding generations as both English and Indians confronted anew their subjection to authority.

Epilogue

Land. Where white pine giants once skimmed the sky, English fields now dot the shores of New England. Since the first English stranger set foot here, hundreds of thousands of trees have been felled, the tallest of them shipped to England to become masts for the king's navy. The trees feed the growing lumber industry, which supplies planks, shingles, and barrel staves, not only for New England, but for the Caribbean trade as well.[1] As the trees fall, colonists burn the stumps and clear the land to make way for the English plow. Well before the end of the century, English settlement has spread so far and so thickly that the children and grandchildren of English colonists have to leave the places of their birth to find land to farm for themselves, relentlessly pushing the remaining Indians further west and north.[2]

Natives. Nipmucks, Narragansetts, Wampanoags, and Mohegans still tend fields of maize, still fish and hunt the streams and forests of New England. But there are far fewer of them than at the century's start. Many have died of disease, of hunger, or in war. King Philip's War alone dramatically diminished the Indian presence in New England; 60 to 80 percent of the Indians who fought against the English are gone, as well as nearly half of those who sided with them.[3] Some, unwilling to bear continued domination, chose exile when colonial forces proved victorious in the war. But some Indians remain. They live and work in English towns as servants, dwell in the still vital Wampanoag communities on the sea coast and the islands of Nantucket and Martha's Vineyard, or gather in former praying towns, now set aside to supervise Indian habitation and soothe the fears of an English populace grown increasingly hostile to all Indians.[4]

Sea. The masted ships of European sailors are no longer a strange sight in the waters of New England. They have crossed the Atlantic in growing numbers from year to year, advancing the trade and swelling the population of the English settlements. Colonists themselves now build many of the ships that carry goods up and down the coast, to the Caribbean, and to England.[5] New England-built ketches and schooners supply the fishing industry as well as the carrying trade. In Essex County, particularly, fishing has boomed since King Philip's War, with sixty large ketches moored in Salem alone by 1689.[6] Indians from the native enclaves remaining on Cape Cod, the islands, and the Maine and New Hampshire coasts can now as easily be found as crewmen on a Nantucket whaling ship as in a canoe.[7] Where distance once shielded New England from royal influence, now the king's power is personified in the soldiers and sailors stationed in Boston. By 1696 the town is a base for the English navy, staging expeditions against the French that will bring as many as sixty ships and 5,000 royal soldiers at a time to Boston's harbor and shores.[8] A flourishing trade and the unmistakable royal presence have drawn New England more noticeably into the Atlantic world and more tightly under the wing of the empire to which it yielded subjection in 1692.

Subjection. By the end of the seventeenth century, the Indians remaining within the Anglo-defined borders of Massachusetts, Connecticut, and Rhode Island are completely subordinate to English authority, no longer sovereign peoples. Even their dealings with Indians outside the area are mediated through local English governors tied to the Five Nations of the Iroquois through the Covenant Chain.[9] New England Indians have little choice but to accept their subordination and remain peaceable, even as their numbers, land holdings, and status continue to decrease. There is evidence that a few hold to ideas of Indian autonomy and equal subject status that had motivated such men as Pessacus, Ninigret, and Philip in earlier years. From time to time, Indians still appeal directly to the king to protect his native subjects, hoping to trump local authority. But the crown's distance and the Indians' steadily diminishing numbers make these largely empty gestures.[10] In time, the Indians will learn, as had Ninigret and others before them, that the English only tout equal subject status when it serves their own interests, and that most English do not accept the idea that Indians are subjects with the same privileges as themselves.[11]

Through over seven decades, both Indians and English within New England had insisted on the finality of their own authority, and both had lost it. Local English colonists would not stand for the challenge from the Indians, and the crown would not stand for it from its subjects. War delivered the final blow, giving England the opportunity to tighten the reins on its English subjects that it had unsuccessfully attempted to draw in a generation earlier. In the end, New England's colonists acceded to royal authority, accepting the loss of the long-cherished dream of a colony governed by godly law, free from the contraints of a sometimes hostile crown. For Indians, too, war quelled their hopes, killing or driving them out of southern New England or into small, supervised reserves.

But there remained some in New England who had not yet bowed to an outside authority and who would continue to insist on their sovereignty with marked success for years to come—the Wabanakis of Maine and New Hampshire. In striking ways, the Wabanaki experience recapitulates that of the Wampanoags and Narragansetts in the earliest years of colonization, a time when the still-weak English were forced to treat Indians as equals, to recognize their sovereignty, even to adopt their models of negotiation and diplomacy. In southern New England, these patterns of reciprocity and respect fell away quickly as the English gained numbers and power and began requiring submission to their own governments, not just to the king. In Maine, Indians were able to defend their sovereignty longer, because English settlement was thin and scattered, and because the proximity of the French gave the Wabanakis a competing power to play off against the English. With these advantages, the Wabanakis were able to insist on their rights to land and respect, and that insistence appears in document after document—an explicit declaration that they were not subjects of the English, but free people. When English settlement pushed too far, the Wabanakis pushed back, insisting that "the English shall not repossess and enjoy the lands in the Province of Maine otherwise than by agreement with them."[12] When either English or French took land without "agreement" of the Wabanakis, or ordered them to fight for them, as if they were slaves, they protested. When their protests failed, the Wabanakis used force against trespassers—over 150 attacks against New England before 1763.[13] European powers that respected Wabanaki rights won their approval; those who did not lost it, creating a long-standing tug-of-war between the English and French to secure the alliance of the Wabanakis during the imperial wars that raged through much of the eighteenth century. Firm peace between Indians and English would not finally be settled until 1763, when the French were forced from the continent.[14] Thus, for nearly a century after New England governments had surrendered their authority, the Wabanakis, like the Iroquois, continued to defend themselves as sovereign people, to resist demands for subjection from either the French or the English.

The Wabanakis also defended their sovereignty by uniting their interests with other Indian peoples. Thomas Stevens, taken captive by Wabanaki Indians in King William's War, reported sachem Hope Hood's declaration, "if ever it were a war again, it would not be as it was formerly, for the Indians & the Mohawks were all agreed throughout the whole Country that they would not fight to kill one another, any more."[15] All were agreed, "throughout the whole Country." In the post-King Philip's War period many land deeds were in fact signed by representatives of more than one sachemship. Before the war, only one such deed exists, suggesting that in Maine, at least, Indians did combine to defend their interests at the end of the seventeenth century.[16]

The Wabanaki experience in the late seventeenth and eighteenth centuries deserves the kind of sustained attention not possible here. Nevertheless, this brief recounting illustrates that the patterns outlined—Indian expectations of equal treatment and defense of their own authority—were widespread and long-lasting. English colonization forced both natives and newcomers to grapple with the issue of who had the supreme power in New

England, and that conflict drew in other English and European colonies, the leaders of European empires, Indian nations, and divergent interests within each group. The struggle reverberated throughout the Atlantic world, drawing strength from clashes in other spheres. And adversaries in those spheres used Indian-English strife to further their own interests. In the end, the increasingly complex and far-reaching contest undermined both Indian and English authority in colonial New England.

The question of authority—or, in today's terms, sovereignty—emerged at the very beginning of sustained Indian-English contact and continued long after the seventeenth century ended. Sovereignty remains an issue critical to Native Americans and other first peoples worldwide.[17] Just as seventeenth-century Indians' protests over colonial infringements on their rights spurred intervention from across the Atlantic, the struggles and successes of today's Native Americans influence indigenous peoples and governments worldwide in their negotiations over rights and authority. During most of the past three hundred years, the position English and Indians occupied relative to each other has remained the same, but, just as in the seventeenth century, many Indians continue to challenge that subordination.[18] Today's Wampanoags, Narragansetts, Mohegans, Nipmucks, Wabanakis, and others still seek to claim the autonomy, authority, and respect due to a people whose ancestors possessed the land long before English settlement and whose generosity and friendship allowed the English to grow to power and authority themselves. They still look for the fulfillment of the promise of the 1621 league of peace, in which Indians were called the "ally" of the English king, Indians and English colonists named each other friends, and the question of subjection failed to arise at all.

Appendix: League of Peace Between Massasoit and Plymouth, March 21, 1621

1. That neither he nor any of his should injure or do hurt to any of our people.

2. And if any of his did hurt to any of ours, he should send the offender, that we might punish him.

3. That if any of our tools were taken away when our people were at work, he should cause them to be restored, and if ours did any harm to any of his, we would do the like to them.

4. If any did unjustly war against him, we would aid him; if any did war against us, he should aid us.

5. He should send to his neighbor confederates, to certify them of this, that they might not wrong us, but might be likewise comprised in the conditions of peace.

6. That when their men came to us, they should leave their bows and arrows behind them, as we should do our pieces when we came to them.

Lastly, that doing thus, King James would esteem of him as his friend and ally.[1]

Abbreviations

CCR   J. Hammond Trumbull, ed., *Public Records of the Colony of Connect-icut* (Hartford, Conn.: F.A. Brown, 1852)

CSPCS   W. Noel Sainsbury, ed., *Calendar of State Papers, Colonial Series, America and West Indies* (Vaduz: Kraus Reprint, 1964)

DCHNY   John Romeyn Brodhead, ed., *Documents Relative to the Colonial History of the State of New-York* (Albany: Weed, Parsons and Company, Printers, 1853)

DHSM   James Phinney Baxter, ed., *Documentary History of the State of Maine*, 2nd series (Portland, Maine: Thurston Print, 1900)

ECR   *Records and Files of the Quarterly Courts of Essex County* (Salem, Mass.: Essex Institute, 1911)

JA   Judicial Archives, at the Massachusetts State Archives, Boston, Massachusetts

JAH   *Journal of American History*

JJW   *The Journal of John Winthrop, 1630–1649*, ed. Richard S. Dunn, James Savage, and Laetitia Yeandle (Cambridge, Mass.: Harvard University Press, 1996)

MPCR   Charles Thornton Libby and Robert E. Moody, eds., *Maine Province and Court Records* (Portland, Maine: Maine Historical Society, 1928–47)

MA   Massachusetts State Archives, Boston, Massachusetts

MAC   Massachusetts Archives Collection (SC1/45x), Massachusetts State Archives, Columbia Point, Massachusetts

MCR   Nathaniel B. Shurtleff, ed., *Records of the Governor and Company of the Massachusetts Bay in New England* (Boston: William White, 1854)

MHS   Massachusetts Historical Society, Boston

MHSC   *Collections of the Massachusetts Historical Society*

NEHGR   *New England Historical and Genealogical Register*

NEQ   *New England Quarterly*

PCR   David Pulsifer, ed., *Records of Plymouth Colony* (Boston: William White, 1855–61)

RICR   *Records of the Colony of Rhode Island and Providence Plantations* (Providence, R.I.: A. Crawford Greene and Brother, 1856)

WMQ   *William and Mary Quarterly*

Notes

Introduction

1. Joshua Scottow, *Narrative of the Planting*, 49. For other primary accounts of the New England landscape, see William Wood, *New England's Prospect*; John Josselyn, *Colonial Traveler*; and Thomas Morton, *New English Canaan*.

2. My discussion of precontact landscape owes a debt to William Cronon, *Changes in the Land*, and Charles E. Clark, *The Eastern Frontier*, who powerfully evoke the land before European settlement, and to Edmund Morgan, who, though writing of Virginia, also beautifully imagines an earlier world in *American Slavery, American Freedom*.

3. Kathleen J. Bragdon's *Native People of Southern New England* offers the most recent and authoritative discussion of Indian settlement patterns in precontact New England, noting three, the estuarine or coastal dwellers, the riverine peoples, and the uplands dwellers, who may have included seasonal gatherings of coastal and river dwellers.

4. Bragdon calls distribution of "wreck goods" the responsibility of sachems. *Native People of Southern New England*, 145.

5. Roger Williams gives this definition in his 1643 *Key into the Language of America*, cited in William S. Simmons, *Spirit of the New England Tribes*, 65.

6. Simmons, *Spirit of the New England Tribes*, 65–72. It is interesting that Englishman Joshua Scottow used this same metaphor to describe the English migration, saying, "the Well-affected came over as Clouds, and like Doves to their Windows" (Scottow, *Narrative of the Planting*, 22). See also Increase Mather, "Phineas Pratt's Relation," 488. Pratt, who settled Massachusetts with Thomas Weston before the arrival of the Pilgrims, relates the Indians' first sight of a ship: "Some old Indians reported, that the first ship seemed to them to be a Floating Island, wrapped together with the limbs of trees, and broken off from the Land, which with their Canoes they went to see, but when they found men there and heard guns, they hasted to the shore again not a little amazed."

7. On trade, see Cronon, *Changes in the Land*, 82–84, and Christopher L. Miller and George R. Hamell, "New Perspective on Indian-White Contact."

8. William Bradford, *Of Plymouth Plantation*, 81, n.

9. For extended discussion of the impact of European diseases on the Indian population, see Alfred W. Crosby, *Columbian Exchange* and *Ecological Imperialism*; Neal Salisbury, *Manitou and Providence*; Cronon, *Changes in the Land*.

10. For discussions of Winthrop's use of this concept and its derivation, see Francis Jennings, *The Invasion of America*, 82–83, 136–38, and Salisbury, *Manitou and Providence*, 176–77, 197–98. Both authors also discuss the conflict, which arose quite quickly, between English and Indian notions of land use and ownership.

11. Bradford, *Of Plymouth Plantation*, 65–66.

12. Dwight B. Heath, ed., *Mourt's Relation*, 50–51.

Chapter 1. Models of Authority

1. Dwight B. Heath, ed., *Mourt's Relation*, 50; William Bradford, *Of Plymouth Plantation*, 81–82, 66.
2. Bradford, *Of Plymouth Plantation*, 79; Heath, *Mourt's Relation*, 20, 42, 43, 48–49.
3. Heath, *Mourt's Relation*, 50; Bradford, *Of Plymouth Plantation*, 81–82, 66.
4. Neal Salisbury, *Manitou and Providence*, 96, 101, 108. See also Nathaniel Morton, *New England's Memorial*, 40; and Bradford, *Of Plymouth Plantation*, 81.
5. Bradford, *Of Plymouth Plantation*, 79–80.
6. Ibid., xi, 77.
7. Heath, ed., *Mourt's Relation*, 50–57. For the full text of the treaty, see Appendix.
8. See Alfred W. Crosby, *Columbian Exchange* and *Ecological Imperialism*; Salisbury, *Manitou and Providence*; William Cronon, *Changes in the Land*.
9. Kathleen Bragdon in *Native People of Southern New England* argues that most Indian cultural patterns persisted after contact with Europeans, though that contact and the demographic catastrophe accompanying it may have accelerated some changes already in process. This book, which describes widespread Indian use of English political patterns, does not argue that those patterns replaced Indian patterns. In many cases, Indians used English and Indian tools of governance interchangeably, suiting them to the demands of particular circumstances.
10. See Salisbury, *Manitou and Providence*, 42–49. Kathleen Bragdon rejects the blanket application of such qualities as egalitarianism, consensus-building, and gender equality to all Indian groups. The "Ninnimissinuok," or natives of southern New England, had hierarchical government structures both before and after contact with Europeans, and sachems could use political power both to ensure the well being of their followers and to reinforce their own positions (*Native People of Southern New England*, 45).
11. Douglas Edward Leach, ed., *A Rhode Islander Reports*, 22.
12. See William Wood, *New England's Prospect*, 97–99. James Drake discusses English and Indian patterns of hierarchy and consensus in his "Symbol of a Failed Strategy," 111–41.
13. *PCR*, 10:44.
14. Ives Goddard and Kathleen Bragdon, *Native Writings in Massachusett*, 2:598. The Massachusett language also contains the word *mounnum*, or "he pays it as tribute" (2:651). For Massachusett versions of the words subject and subjection, see John Eliot, trans., *Mamusse wunneetupanatamwe Up-Biblum God*, Titus 3:1, 1 Peter 2:18, and 1 Peter 2:1; Roger Williams, *Key into the Language of America*, 141.
15. Denys Delage, *Bitter Feast*, 57, 62.
16. For Indian tribute practices, see *MCR*, 2:23–24; *RICR*, 2:269; Williams, *Key into the Language of America*, 140–45; Edward Winslow, *Good Newes from New England*, 61–62; *Lieutenant Lion Gardener*, 150; *JJW*, 459; see also Bragdon, *Native People of Southern New England*, 46, 141–55 and Alden T. Vaughan, *New England Frontier*, 221.
17. The Iroquois also used familial terms for political relationships, calling their subjects "children" and their allies "brethren"; see Lawrence H. Leder, ed., *Livingston Indian Records*, 33, 39; and William N. Fenton, "Structure, Continuity and Change," 6.
18. *Lieutenant Lion Gardener*, 153–55.
19. From William Strachey, "History of Travel into Virginia Britannia," 215.
20. On gift-giving to secure alliances, see Roger Williams to John Leverett, Jan. 14, 1675, *MHSC*, 4th ser., 6:307; *Relation of the Plott—Indian* (ND, probably August

1642), *MHSC*, 3rd ser., 3:162; Mary Pray to James Oliver, Oct. 20, 1675, *MHSC*, 5th ser., 1:105; *PCR*, 9:14–15, 85.

21. *PCR*, 10:222. See also *JJW*, 458–62.

22. For good discussions of competing views of English authority in this period, see Mary Beth Norton, *Founding Mothers and Fathers*, and Robert M. Bliss, *Revolution and Empire*.

23. John Davenport, "Sermon Preach'd at the Election of the Governour."

24. John Winthrop, quoted in Perry Miller, *New England Mind*, 1:416. James Drake uses a similar model of hierarchy in his *King Philip's War*, 37, 44, 78. For extensive discussions of the family model for government in Puritan New England, see Edmund Morgan, *Puritan Family*, and John Demos, *Little Commonwealth*.

25. Davenport, "Sermon Preach'd at the Election." See also William Hubbard, "Happiness of a People." For further discussion of Puritan concepts of government, see Stephen Foster, *Long Argument*, and T. H. Breen, *The Character of a Good Ruler*.

26. Morton, *New England's Memorial*, 23.

27. Sir Robert Carr to Colonel Nicolls, Feb. 2, 1665, *CSPCS*, 5:274, item 925.

28. Governor Cradock to John Endicott, Feb. 16, 1629, in Alexander Young, ed., *Chronicles of the First Planters*, 133–34. For an excellent discussion of English views of Indian status and civility, see Karen Ordahl Kupperman, *Indians and English*, especially chapters 1 and 2.

29. During the English conquest of Ireland, tribute—"black rent"—was imposed on Irish and even Anglo-Irish settlers (Brendan Bradshaw, "Native Reaction to the Westward Enterprise," 69).

30. Tzvetan Todorov, *Conquest of America*, 112–13, 136–37.

31. Richard Hakluyt the elder, "Reasons for Colonization," 31–32.

32. Governor Cradock's Letter to John Endicott, Feb. 16, 1629, in Young, *Chronicles of the First Planters*, 133–34.

33. The Massachusetts Bay Company's first general letter of instructions to Endicott and his council, April 17, 1629, in Young, *Chronicles of the First Planters*, 159. Colony leaders justified shipping Thomas Morton back to England in 1630 because of his "many injuries offered to the Indians, & other misdemeanors." The Puritans believed Morton set an example of licentious behavior for the Indians; he also sold them liquor and firearms (*JJW*, 39).

34. Thomas Shepard, *The Clear Sunshine of the Gospel*, *MHSC*, 3rd ser., 4:66, 38.

35. Heath, *Mourt's Relation*, 57.

36. Winslow, *Good Newes from New England*, 13–14.

37. Ibid., 38.

38. Bradford, *Of Plymouth Plantation*, 87.

39. Winslow, *Good Newes from New England*, 61–62.

40. *Lieutenant Lion Gardener*, 153–55.

41. Heath, *Mourt's Relation*, 66, 78, 83.

42. William Simmons, *Spirit of the New England Tribes*, 124.

43. Nathaniel Saltonstall, "Continuation of the State of New England," 71.

44. The Narragansetts would not be as fortunate in later epidemics (Salisbury, *Manitou and Providence*, 30, 191, 209; Heath, *Mourt's Relation*, 58; Bradford, *Of Plymouth Plantation*, 87).

45. Bradford, *Of Plymouth Plantation*, 96–97; Winslow, *Good Newes from New England*, 9–10; Paul A. Robinson, "Lost Opportunities," 19.

46. *JJW*, 47.

47. *JJW*, 54.

48. Robinson, "Lost Opportunities," 18–19.

49. *JJW*, 211.

50. *JJW*, 133, 213–21. For a description of the war, see *Lieutenant Lion Gardener* and Alfred A. Cave, *Pequot War*.

51. Morton, *New England's Memorial*, 127–28.

52. *JJW*, 220–21.

53. Gov. Winthrop to Gov. Bradford, May 20, 1637, in Bradford, *Of Plymouth Plantation*, 394. While the Long Island Indians paid tribute and expected protection, the United Colonies commissioners insisted that they "be no way engaged to protect" them (*PCR*, 9:18–19).

54. *JJW*, 256.

55. Bradford, *Of Plymouth Plantation*, 438.

56. *JJW*, 280.

57. *MCR*, 1:216.

58. Morton, *New England's Memorial*, 130.

59. *JJW*, 225, 259, 329.

60. Edward Johnson, cited in Robinson, "Lost Opportunities," 15, 21–23.

61. Francis Jennings, *Invasion of America*, 214, 257; John Underhill, "News from America," 84. Michael Leroy Oberg's recent article on Miantonomi's struggle for autonomy is particularly useful for its detailed discussion of the Dutch element of the contest ("We are all the Sachems").

62. Roger Williams to Gov. John Winthrop, Aug. 20, 1637, in Williams, *Correspondence*, 1:113–14.

63. *JJW*, 337.

64. *JJW*, 47, 410–11.

65. Massachusetts leaders described Gorton's misbehavior in their March 4, 1664–65, reply to his "invective petition," in *MCR*, 4, part 2, 255–65; Philip F. Gura, "Radical Ideology."

66. *MCR*, 4, part 2, 253–65; *JJW*, 458–62.

67. *JJW*, 472.

68. Morton, *New England's Memorial*, 127–28.

69. *Lieutenant Lion Gardener*, 153–55.

70. *JJW*, 472.

71. *JJW*, 431.

72. See the Aug. 27, 1645, treaty between the United Colonies and the Narragansett Indians, reprinted in Bradford, *Of Plymouth Plantation*, 437–40. Winslow, who had close contact with the Wampanoags and other tribes in the region, stated that the Indians' "sachems cannot be all called kings, but only some few of them, to whom the rest resort for protection, and pay homage unto them; neither may they war without their knowledge and approbation" (*Good Newes from New England*, 61–62).

73. *JJW*, 458–61.

74. Submission of the Massachusetts subtribes to the Massachusetts Bay Colony, March 8, 1644, in Vaughan, *New England Frontier*, appendix 3, 342. Passaconnaway, the Merrimack sachem, submitted "as Pumham, etc. had done before" in May 1644 (*JJW*, 509).

75. *JJW*, 509; MHS photostats, Oct. 1, 1675, MHS.

76. MAC, 30:140–42, 145–46.

77. *PCR*, 1:25; *JJW*, 432. Connecticut and New Haven, both of which drew their colonists largely from Massachusetts, followed a similar pattern in their own styling of authority, dropping the king from their oaths and summons during the Civil War years. However, Connecticut broke from this practice after the restoration of the king. Desiring their own charter, colony leaders sent John Winthrop, Jr., to England

for it. He obtained it (obliterating New Haven's separate existence in the process), and the colony was carefully deferential to royal authority afterward.

78. *JJW*, 481, 495.

79. Joseph Henry Smith, *Appeals to the Privy Council*, 45, 51–53.

80. *PCR*, 1:5.

81. *RICR*, 2:155, 198–99.

82. Randall Holden and John Greene to the Committee of Trade and Plantations (1679), *RICR*, 3:62.

83. Cited in Drake, *King Philip's War*, 36.

84. For an account of these events, see Salisbury, *Manitou and Providence*, 228–35.

85. *RICR*, 1:133.

86. *PCR*, 10:415–16.

87. *JJW*, 509.

88. *PCR*, 9:19.

89. *PCR*, 10:8, 23–42.

90. *PCR*, 9:21, 143, 148, 202.

91. *PCR*, 10:6–7.

92. *PCR*, 10:11–13, 23, 42–65.

93. *PCR*, 10:101.

94. *MCR*, 4, part 1, 143.

95. See *MCR*, 4, part 1, 141–44; see also 165–75.

96. Lion Gardiner, quoted in Ward, *United Colonies of New England*, 206.

97. *RICR*, 2:3–7.

98. *PCR*, 10:125.

99. *PCR*, 10:222.

100. Hakluyt the elder, *Reasons for Colonization*, 31–32.

101. *MCR*, 4, part 2, 175.

Chapter 2. Massachusetts Under Fire

1. A tug-of-war between local militias and the colony magistrates over who could select military officers had been going on since the settlement of the colony. Originally, magistrates selected the officers. When town deputies were added to the General Court in 1636, the Court changed its policy, allowing the town bands to nominate their own officers, pending Court approval. From there, voting became increasingly open, with Indians and African servants participating in the nomination vote in some towns. In 1656, the General Court tightened restrictions on voting and in 1668 rescinded the nomination right, allowing locals to vote only on the selection of the colony major general. See T. H. Breen, *Puritans and Adventurers*, chapter 2.

2. *ECR*, 3:139, 142–43. Samuel Hunt's role in this incident is described in Breen, *Puritans and Adventurers*, chapter 2.

In a manuscript written by Samuel Maverick sometime between 1660 and 1664, he mentions Massachusetts's response to a report that the king was sending over a general governor. Shortly afterward, another rumor spread that a large ship, accompanied by a smaller one, had entered Cape Ann Harbor. An alarm was given, town militias in Boston and all the adjacent towns were called out—to oppose their landing, Maverick opined—and continued in readiness until the report was found to be mistaken. This incident may have been the foundation for Tuttle's comment about the frigates being stopped. The royal commissioners were near their departure from England when Tuttle made his "seditious" speech (Samuel Maverick, "Briefe discription of New England," 240).

3. *ECR*, 3:139.

4. Charles M. Andrews, *Colonial Period of American History*, 1: chapter 21; G. L. Kittredge, "Dr. Robert Child the Remonstrant," 1.

5. See, for example, the 1658 response of the commissioners for foreign plantations to the complaint against Massachusetts lodged by Rhode Islanders Samuel Gorton and Randall Holden. While granting them some relief, the committee stated its unwillingness to believe wrong of Massachusetts: "We knowing well how much God hath honored [Massachusetts] government, and believing that [their] spirits and affairs are acted by principles of justice, prudence, and of zeal to God; and therefore cannot easily receive any evil impressions concerning [their] proceedings" (*RICR*, 1:367).

6. On the Sagadahoc colony, see James Axtell, "Exploration of Norumbega," 160–62.

7. *CSPCS*, 1:32, Aug. 10, 1622; 1:102, Nov. 7, 1629; 1:137, Dec. 2, 1631; 1:293, April 3, 1639.

8. To describe accurately the numerous changes in government in New Hampshire and Maine during this period goes beyond the scope of this work. I have omitted or only obliquely referred to several short-lived governments. Those readers who desire full details can find them in the prefaces to *MPCR*; Emerson Woods Baker, et al., eds., *American Beginnings*, particularly John G. Reid's "Political Definitions"; Charles E. Clark, *The Eastern Frontier*; John Reid, *Acadia, Maine and New Scotland*, and *Maine, Charles II and Massachusetts*. In addition, William D. Williamson, *History of the State of Maine*, is still valuable.

9. In his *Adjustment to Empire*, Richard E. Johnson argues that disputes over land titles played a chief role in bringing Massachusetts to the king's attention (22).

10. *CSPCS*, 1:392, Nov. 6, 1652. Edward Godfrey, appointed by Gorges as governor of the province of Maine, complained that Gorges's neglect had forced Maine residents to combine as the "Keepers of the liberties of England."

11. *MCR*, 4, part 1, 70.

12. *MCR*, 4, part 1, 70. See also *CSPCS*, 1:392, Oct. 28, 1652.

13. Kittery and York sent their submissions to the Massachusetts government on Nov. 20 and 22, 1652 (*MCR*, 4, part 1, 124–26, 128–29); *MCR*, 4, part 1, 161–65.

14. Black Point and Blue Point (renamed Scarborough by Massachusetts) and Spurwink and Casco Bay (renamed Falmouth) sent in their submissions on Oct. 19, 1658 (*MCR*, 4, part 1, 357–60).

15. J. M. Sosin, *English America and the Restoration Monarchy*, 87.

16. *MPCR*, 2:22–56.

17. *MPCR*, 2:63. This record calls the deputy governor Richard Bradstreet, confusing Richard Bellingham with Simon Bradstreet, another of the magistrates.

18. Phippeny, a seaman and blockmaker, was living in Boston in 1653. By 1658 he had become a neighbor of Richard Foxwell of Blue Point, Maine. Characterized as a "man of contention and strife ever since coming" to Maine, Phippeny did little to promote tolerance for Massachusetts immigrants among his new neighbors (Sybil Noyes, Charles Thornton Libby, and Walter Goodwin Davis, *Genealogical Dictionary*).

19. Emerson W. Baker, *Clarke & Lake Company*.

20. *MPCR*, 2:82.

21. Edwin A. Churchill, "Mid-Seventeenth-Century Maine," 242.

22. William Hubbard, *History of the Indian Wars*, 2:256–57. For a discussion of the lure of (and fear of) the Indian way of living, see James Axtell, "Scholastic Philosophy of the Wilderness"; and John Canup, *Out of the Wilderness*.

23. Increase Mather, "Earnest Exhortation," 99.

24. *JJW*, 285, 368–69, 421.

25. Gorges died in May 1647, and Mason died in 1635. Both left their holdings to their daughters' sons. Mason's heir, Robert Tufton Mason, was only nine months old at John Mason's death in 1635 (Noyes, Libby, and Davis, *Genealogical Dictionary*).

26. Gov. John Endicott to Charles II, Dec. 19, 1660, *MCR*, 4, part 1, 450–53.

27. *MPCR*, 2:197. In May 1658, the Massachusetts General Court complained that Quakers "do take upon them to change and alter the received laudable customs of our nation in giving civil respect to equals or reverence to superiors, whose actions tend to undermine the authority of civil government" (*MCR*, 4, part 1, 345).

28. *MCR*, 4, part 1, 345.

29. For the evolution of the Quakers' public character, see Carla Gardina Pestana, "The Quaker Executions as Myth and History."

30. *MCR*, 4, part 1, 384–90.

31. *MPCR*, 1:295.

32. *MCR*, 3:415–16.

33. *MCR*, 4, part 2, 69.

34. *MCR*, 4, part 1, 383–90, 419.

35. *MCR*, 4, part 1, 450–53.

36. *ECR*, 3:95, 110; 4·41

37. This, of course, would have required Massachusetts to recognize the right of people to appeal to England, which it had no intention of doing. References to Quaker petitions appear in *CPSCS*, 5:31, items 89 and 90; and 5:34–35, item 97. See also Samuel Shattock's letter in *MHSC*, 4th ser., 9:160–62. The king's request to Massachusetts is in *CSPCS*, 5:55, item 168. Joseph Henry Smith notes the king's request that there be no further legal prosecution of Quakers and that they instead be sent to England. By obeying, however, the colony would have been acknowledging the Quakers' right to appeal to the king, in direct contradiction to the colony's interpretation of its charter rights. Through "inaction" against Quaker protests, the colony avoided highlighting the conflict between their own and the king's authority (*Appeals to the Privy Council*, 54).

While Massachusetts's execution of Quakers was universally condemned, corporal and other punishments of Quakers were practised in other colonies as well as in England. Massachusetts merchant Thomas Temple reported that he was in the king's presence when he received Massachusetts's letter proclaiming the colony's intention to cease prosecuting the Quakers. "The King hearing this clapped his hand on his breast said that he intended not so, but that they should not hang them" (J. Curwine letter, 1663–64, *MHSC*, 1st ser., 1:398–99). Charles II's June 28, 1662, letter to the colony acknowledged that the Quakers, "being inconsistent with any kind of goverment," had had to be prosecuted and punished in England (*MCR*, 4, part 2, 164–66).

38. *MCR*, 4, part 2, 59.

39. Middlesex County Court Records, Pulsifer transcript, 1:287, JA.

40. It is clear from the king's letter to the colonies and from George Cartwright's 1665 report to him that he had received petitions from "neighbor princes," and his later gift of two scarlet coats to two Narragansett sachems was in explicit recognition of their expressions of affection to him at the time of the granting of Rhode Island's charter (*CSPCS*, 5:201, item 715; 5:203, item 721; 5:341–48, item 1103; *MCR*, 4, part 2, 158–61).

41. *DCHNY*, 3:39–41.

42. *MCR*, 4, part 2, 31. On the day before the proclamation, the Court posted an order forbidding the kind of revelry "wicked & prophane persons" were prone to on such days. Lest some think that this damper on celebration signified the

court's disapproval of the king, rather than of "disorderly carriage," the declaration notes that the king had himself "signified his pleasure for suppressing such excesses & profaneness," in particular the drinking of the king's health.

43. MHS photostats, June 19, 1661. Thirty-six men signed the petition, "in the name of many other freemen." Signers included Joshua Scottow, John Hull, Hezekiah Usher, John Wilson, Sr., and William Davis, members of a moderate group who would increasingly urge colony leaders to accommodate both royal demands and religious adjustments in the maturing colony (Mark A. Peterson, *Price of Redemption*, 29–30).

44. *MCR*, 4, part 2, 26–31.

45. Tensions also existed within the Court between magistrates and deputies. For an excellent discussion of the political divisions that crystallized in the wake of the Restoration, see Paul R. Lucas, "Colony or Commonwealth."

46. *MCR*, 4, part 1, 452.

47. *MCR*, 4, part 1, 452.

48. The magistrates' styling of their authority appears in an order to a committee to bring the county of Yorkshire, in Maine, back into obedience to Massachusetts: "By the authority of the king's most excellent majesty derived to us by patent" (*MCR*, 4, part 2, 77).

49. Massachusetts leaders had substituted an oath of fidelity to the colony for the oath of allegiance to the king. To their way of thinking, this accomplished the same purpose because the colony was subject to the king. The oath did not, however, mention the king's name (Maverick, "Briefe discription," 241). *MCR*, 4, part 1, 79–80 gives a shortened version of the oath for strangers. See also Harry M. Ward, *United Colonies of New England*, 77, concerning the removal of the king's name from the governor's and magistrates' oaths.

50. *MCR*, 4, part 2, 58.

51. *CSPCS*, 5:55, item 168. The Quaker executions had given the colony very bad press and were linked to talk of Massachusetts's desire for independence from the king. For example, someone eager to highlight the colony's misbehavior sent the royal government an account of magistrate Daniel Denison's declaration to Quakers brought to court before him: "You will go to England to complain this year, the next year they will send to see if it be true, and by the next year the government in England will be changed; so speaking in a scoffing manner, rejecting the thing" (*CSPCS*, 1:495–96, Dec. 19, 1660).

52. *MCR*, 4, part 2, 164–66.

53. Robert M. Bliss, *Revolution and Empire*, 131–37.

54. In October 1663, the Court disfranchised Quakers because of their influence on the outcome of elections in areas where their numbers were substantial (*MCR*, 4, part 2, 88).

55. Charles II to Massachusetts governor and magistrates, April 25, 1664, in *MCR*, 4, part 2, 158–61.

56. *MCR*, 4, part 2, 74.

57. *MPCR*, 1:181–210. For other reports, see *MCR*, 4, part 2, 158; *CSPCS*, 5:127, item 432.

58. John Gorham Palfrey, *Compendious History of New England*, 2:58–60; Sosin, *English America and the Restoration Monarchy*, 110–11.

59. Suffolk Files, #633, vol. 5, JA. Similar anxiety in Connecticut led to the hiding of its charter; as the story goes, it was secured for years in a hollow tree, the "charter oak."

60. The General Court received petitions from Boston, Cambridge, Woburn, Dorchester, Reading, Chelmsford, Concord, Billerica, Dedham, Medfield, Roxbury,

Northampton, and Hadley. Many of these petitions appear in the Massachusetts Archives Collection, vol. 106. Well over 1300 men signed them. The petitioners from Hadley declared: "Our liberty and privilege herein, as men we prize and would hold as our lives: this makes us Freemen and not slaves. . . . Nor is it our own portion only that we trade with in this Case; but our children's Stock also: even their advantages as men, & Christians to Serve the Lord, & be accounted to him for a generation, for evermore" (MAC, 106:107).

61. *MCR*, 4, part 2, 161–62.

62. *MCR*, 4, part 2, 161–62. Surprisingly, these instructions, which give great latitude to the commissioners to hear appeals, directly contradict the king's particular instructions for the commissioners' visit to Massachusetts, written two days earlier, on April 23, 1664: "You shall not receive any complaint of any thing done amiss by any Magistrate, except it appears to be against their Charter . . . nor shall you interrupt the proceedings in justice, by taking upon you the hearing and determining any particular right between party and party, but shall leave all matters of that nature to the usual proceedings in the several judicatories of the country" (*DCHNY*, 3:53).

63. *MCR*, 4, part 2, 25.

64. Robert Carr, George Cartwright, and Samuel Maverick to Sir Henry Bennet, secretary of state, May 27, 1665, in *DCHNY*, 3:96–97; Palfrey, *Compendious History of New England*, 2:69–72.

65. *MCR*, 4, part 2, 166–68, 158–61.

66. The General Court's October 19, 1664, letter to the king reflects its effort to both satisfy the king and adhere to its interpretation of its charter rights, something which many believed undergirded their religious way of life: "As for such particulars of a civil & religious nature . . . we have applied ourselves to the utmost to satisfy your majesty, so far as doth consist with conscience of our duty towards God, & the just liberties & privileges of our patent" (*MCR*, 4, part 2, 130).

67. MHS photostats, Sept. 6, 1664.

68. *MCR*, 4, part 2, 168–73, also 129–33; *CSPCS*, 5:247, item 832; 301, item 1002.

69. *MCR*, 4, part 2, 129, 133.

70. *CSPCS*, 5:282, item 945.

71. *MHSC*, 2nd ser., 8:49–51.

72. See *MCR*, 4, part 2, 274–75; *CSPCS*, 5:291–92, item 978.

73. *MCR*, 4, part 2, 161, 182–83, 252, 274; *DCHNY*, 3:52–53, 57.

74. *CSPCS*, 5:178, item 623. Maverick's "Briefe discription," a manuscript describing the towns and resources of New England and railing against the government of Massachusetts Bay Colony, was written sometime between 1660 and early 1664. It is held by the British Museum, which suggests that Maverick wrote it during his three years in London. It is nearly certain that the king read the manuscript. Not only did he appoint Maverick to his royal commission, but the charges and language in his April 1664 letter to Massachusetts echo Maverick's (see especially Maverick, "Brief discription," 240).

75. *CSPCS*, 5:288, item 963.

76. *CSPCS*, 5:178, item 623; 5:288, item 963; 5:316, item 1031. Maverick refers to Carr as "tumbling in plunder" in Delaware rather than returning to the commission as ordered. Richard Nicolls was forced to break off his business to fetch Carr back (Samuel Maverick to John Winthrop, Jr., Nov. 9, 1664, *MHSC*, 4th ser., 7:309).

77. *CSPCS*, 5:300, item 999. In this letter, Cartwright promises Gorton that on his return to England he will "truly represent their sufferings and loyalty." Here again, Cartwright disregards the king's private instructions that the commissioners avoid dealings with those with "a great prejudice against the form of Religion there

professed" and that they guard against any actions that may make them seem to "incline to a party, or to be yourselves engaged in their passions and appetite" (*DCHNY*, 3:59).

78. *CSPCS*, 5:291, item 978.

79. *DCHNY*, 3:270, gives Bredon's version of this affair. Bredon's fine is mentioned in *MCR*, 4, part 2, 69.

80. Suffolk Files, #791, vol. 8, JA. Those present when treason was charged were Robert Carr, Samuel Maverick, Sir Thomas Temple, and Nicholas Paige; the latter two were prominent merchants.

81. *DCHNY*, 3:57.

82. *DCHNY*, 3:88–89, 93.

83. *CSPCS*, 5:275, item 931. For the commissioners' attitude toward Massachusetts, see letters, chiefly from George Cartwright, in *CSPCS*, 5: 271, item 918; 272, item 921; 275, item 931; 277, item 933; 300, item 999; and in *DCHNY*, 3:101–2.

84. A glance through the pages and index of *CSPCS*, vols. 1 and 5, makes this clear immediately. In addition, the vast majority of records concerning Maine relate to its resistance to Massachusetts jurisdiction.

85. *MCR*, 4, part 2, 172.

86. Nadhorth to Mr. Secretary Morrice, Oct. 26, 1666, *DCHNY*, 3:140. "Nadhorth" is either a pseudonym or a garbled version of Danforth. The political opinions of either Samuel or Thomas Danforth resemble those of the writer of this letter.

87. *CSPCS*, 1:478–9, item 79, endorsed, "This was after Richard Cromwell was out."

88. *CSPCS*, 5:16–17, item 49, petition of sufferers in New England to the Council for Foreign Plantation, for themselves and "thousands there," signed John Gifford, Archibald Henderson, Edw. Chapman, James Bate, Henry Wilson, Robert Seymor, Edward Godfree [Godfrey], Theophilus Salter, John Dand, George Baxter, John Baker, Arch. Crowder, John Baxe. See also *CSPCS*, 5:18–19, item 53, letters from Edward Godfrey, sometime governor of Maine.

89. *MPCR*, 1:181–210.

90. *MPCR*, 1:182–83.

91. *MPCR*, 1:181–210. This language echoes that in the Simon Tuttle case and is a likely source of the news that reached Ipswich by 1664.

92. *MPCR*, 1:181–210.

93. *MPCR*, 1:181–210.

94. *MPCR*, 2:142. See also 139.

95. *CSPCS*, 5:142, item 489.

96. *CSPCS*, 5:417, item 1297. By 1671, England had reduced the power of the governor of another Caribbean island, Jamaica, ordering him to send first to England for orders in case of an attack. Massachusetts hoped to ward off similar constraints through its continued insistence that it reserved final authority in its charter and that appeal to England could not be allowed (Winthrop Family Papers, Oct. 1671, Reel 10, MHS).

97. *MCR*, 4, part 2, 164.

98. *DCHNY*, 3:110.

99. For example, the commissioners told Plymouth leaders that if they would agree in the future to select their governor from three names presented by the royal commissioners, the commissioners would see the colony's charter through the process of confirmation. For the king's instructions on presenting this proposal, see *DCHNY*, 3:58.

100. Address of Connecticut to Charles II, July 15, 1665, Winthrop Family Papers, Reel 8, MHS.

101. Palfrey, *Compendious History of New England*, 2:68. See also Samuel Maverick to John Winthrop, Jr., Aug. 29, 1666, in which he says the king "resents as ill the Massachusetts standing out, or rather Rebellion," *MHSC*, 4th ser., 7:313.

102. *CSPCS*, 5:342, item 1103. This charge reflects the conflation of Massachusetts and the United Colonies in both the Narragansetts' and the royal commissioners' eyes. The commissioners seemed to view the United Colonies as Massachusetts's creature, further evidence of the aspiration to be a "free state." The United Colonies took the liberty of negotiating with other colonies, including Dutch New Netherland, and joining with its sister colonies in defensive wars, actions that the royal commissioners believed went beyond the rights of English colonies or the directives of colony charters. Under the disapproval of the royal commissioners, the "so-called" United Colonies effectively ceased functioning until King Philip's War, when its military arm was revived. See Ward, *United Colonies of New England*.

103. *PCR*, 9:34–45.

104. *RICR*, 2:60.

105. *CSPCS*, 5:341–50, item 1103. See *DCHNY*, 3:56, in which the king instructs his commissioners to investigate the Narragansetts' 1644 submission of their lands to the king.

106. *RICR*, 2:59; *CSPCS*, 5:342, item 1103.

107. *CSPCS*, 5:274, item 925.

108. Thomas Lechford protested this practice as early as 1642 (*Plain Dealing*, 84).

109. *MCR*, 4, part 2, 233.

110. *MCR*, 4, part 2, 234, 274.

111. Roger Williams, *Correspondence*, 2:577–79, note 4.

112. *MHSC*, 4th ser., 7:556.

113. MAC, 30:131–32, 72, 73, 275a.

114. *CSPCS*, 5:347, item 1103.

115. *CSPCS*, 5:380, item 1197. As the commissioners of the United Colonies did not meet from 1664 to 1667 and then met on a drastically limited scale, the commissioners referred to are probably royal. Carr and Maverick were still in Boston until March 1666. See also Williams, *Correspondence*, 2:599, note 4.

116. *DCHNY*, 3:56; *RICR*, 2:93.

117. *RICR*, 2:94–95.

118. *MCR*, 4, part 2, 253. Evidence that Massachusetts did in fact use this phrasing appears in the Court's declaration in 1671, that "acts of this honored Court, being the supreme authority, are not liable to question by any" (*MCR*, 4, part 2, 493).

119. *MCR*, 4, part 2, 177, 194, 216–19; *CSPCS*, 5:339–340, item 1100. For a detailed discussion of the Porter case, see Jane Kamensky, *Governing the Tongue*, chapter 4.

120. *MCR*, 4, part 2, 216.

121. *MCR*, 4, part 2, 234.

122. *CSPCS*, 5:200, item 713 contains the king's "secret instructions" to his royal commissioners in which he suggests that men favorable to the king be urged on the colony, ideally, Nicolls for governor and Cartwright for major-general. By this time, the commissioners had no doubt given up the hope that the governor and major general would be chosen from their number.

123. *MCR*, 4, part 2, 173.

124. MHS photostats, April 19, 1665. The Court's official record of the royal commissioners' visit complained that the king's agents entered town "in an obscure manner, thereby preventing that respect & honorable reception, not only intended,

but actually prepared for them." While they did not blame the commissioners for this, the Court members noted it in order to shield themselves from "the reflection of disrespect & incivillity by them often cast upon us" (*MCR*, 4, part 2, 177).

125. *MCR*, 4, part 2, 177, 186.

126. *MCR*, 4, part 2, 188–89, 198. The General Court denied any wrongdoing toward the Narragansetts, but was not surprised to have been accused: "It is not [a] strange thing to us that have been so long acquainted with the falsehood & barbarous practices of the Indians, Narragansets & others, to hear them make complaints, when themselves have done the injury." It referred the commissioners to the Records of the United Colonies for all its proceedings with the Indians and explanations of its actions.

127. *MCR*, 4, part 2, 204–6.

128. The irreconcilable views the magistrates and royal commissioners held of what the charter demanded are reflected in the commissioners' argument that "the limits of that obligation [the charter] are too narrow to circumscribe all that duty & allegiance, which, from natural born subjects, is due to his majesty" (*MCR*, 4, part 2, 189). The magistrates saw anything beyond what the charter prescribed as a violation of their rights.

129. *MCR*, 4, part 2, 207–8.

130. *MCR*, 4, part 2, 150, 209–10. Samuel Maverick's daughter would recall the trumpets and declaration twenty-two years later in a petition to Sir Edmund Andros, newly appointed governor of the Dominion of New England (*DHSM*, 6:329).

131. *MCR*, 4, part 2, 210–11, May 24, 1665. We "do assure you," the commissioners wrote to the General Court, "that we shall not represent your denying of his [majesty's] commission in any other words than yourselves have expressed it in your several papers."

132. *MCR*, 4, part 2, 211–13.

133. Massachusetts claimed to have been complying with the order on acting in the king's name since receiving the king's letter requesting it in June 1662, a claim supported by Bredon's statement in his 1662 trial that he was "glad to see that we acted in his majesty's name as by the warrant he had received & which he gladly did obey." He then added, however, that "he never saw any before" (Suffolk Files, #516, vol. 4, JA). The Middlesex County Court records document the changeover; before 1662, the king is unmentioned in warrants, summons, etc. In 1662, scattered orders contain the words "in his Majesty's name." By 1663, virtually all orders use the prescribed form (Middlesex County Court, Folio Collection, JA).

134. A number of documents in the British State Papers refer to Massachusetts's commonwealth leanings, for example, Cartwright to Nicolls, Feb. 4, 1664, says Massachusetts is "inclinable to a commonwealth" (*CSPCS*, 5: 275, item 931). Cartwright to Secretary Sir Henry Bennet, Feb. 7, 1664, notes the town petitions in support of the present government and says they "have given ground for fear that the fancy of a commonwealth is yet in some of their brains" (*CSPCS*, 5:277, item 933).

135. *MCR*, 4, part 2, 211–13.

136. Minister William Gilbert, a Scottish immigrant, spoke for those who thought any yielding to the king's religious directives was immoral: "I came hither to N. E. (said he) to keep myself from perjury, from prelates, from Common-prayer-book: & shall we now yield to these, to please princes, great men, to get a Living, & belly Timber[?]" (*ECR*, 3:312).

137. Here, too, the commissioners failed the king's expectations. He had directed that they "not give any umbrage or jealousy to them in matters of religion, as if you were at least enemies to forms observed amongst them, you shall do well to frequent their churches and to be present at their devotion." They were, however,

encouraged to keep their own "learned and discreet" chaplain to direct their private, Anglican, devotional services (*DCHNY*, 3:58).

138. *CSPCS*, 5:292, item 978.

139. *CSPCS*, 5:286, item 957.

140. *CSPCS*, 5:272, item 921.

141. *RICR*, 1:293.

142. *DCHNY*, 3:112.

143. Oddly, the king had specifically directed that the first item of business, rather than the last, be the settlement of boundary disputes, indicating that all else would go smoothly if that were settled first.

144. *MCR*, 4, part 2, 186–88, 214–15, 240.

145. John Josselyn, *Colonial Traveler*, 145.

146. See *MCR*, 4, part 2, 248–51.

147. MHS photostats, July 10, 1665.

148. *MCR*, 4, part 2, 278–79, 370–73.

149. *DCHNY*, 3:99–100. The commissioners were probably referring to Barbados, the site of recent resistance to efforts to impose stricter royal authority. See *CSPCS*, 5:142, item 489.

150. *DCHNY*, 3:99–102.

151. *CSPCS*, 5:372–73, item 1171. In his report to the king, Cartwright charged Hathorne with making "a seditious speech at the head of his company" and Bellingham with "another at the meeting-house at Boston" (*CSPCS*, 5:344, item 1103). On May 3, 1665, William Hathorne made a public acknowledgment of his offense to the royal commissioners. They had charged him with specific offensive speeches in General Court, "which words," Hathorne said, "I never spake." He admitted, however, that he had spoken "many words rashly, foolishly, & unadvisedly" at one time or another. For these statements, he said he was very sorry and sought the forgiveness of the Court. The commissioners had, he alleged, already forgiven him (*MCR*, 4, part 2, 149). The commissioners' pointing Hathorne out as a chief offender before the king suggests that they had changed their minds.

152. *MCR*, 4, part 2, 171–72, 132.

153. *MCR*, 4, part 2, 233.

154. *DCHNY*, 3:112–13.

155. *CSPCS*, 5:282, item 945 (printed in full in *DCHNY*, 3:90–91). It is unclear from this letter what specific offenses of Endicott had turned the king against him. The governor had a reputation for rash action. He had ripped the cross from Salem's flag back in 1634, which caused a minor uproar (see Andrews, *Colonial Period of American History*, 361–62 [note], 414). Several discontented persons who had the king's ear in the early 1660s, such as Samuel Gorton and Samuel Maverick, could have recounted this and other tales.

156. *DCHNY*, 3:142.

157. Suffolk Files, #625, vol. 5, JA; the New Hampshire petition is discussed in *MCR*, 4, part 2, 272, Dec. 8, 1665; MHS photostats, July 20, Oct. 9, 1665.

158. MHS photostats, Sept. 6, 1664.

159. *CSPCS*, 5:341–48, item 1103.

160. *ECR*, 3:377.

161. *MCR*, 4, part 2, 291.

162. Suffolk Files, #904, vol. 9, JA.

163. John Hull, *Diary of Public Occurrences*, 219; Suffolk Files, #744a, vol. 7, JA.

164. *ECR*, 3:310–12.

165. *DHSM*, 6:34–36.

166. Cited in Bliss, *Revolution and Empire*, 159–60.

167. *MHSC*, 2nd ser., 8:110.

168. Cited in Bliss, *Revolution and Empire*, 159–60. Daniel Denison asked that his dissent be entered into the record (*MHSC*, 2nd ser., 8:109). By King Philip's War, Denison was serving again as the colony's major general. Other dissenters such as Edmund Batter and John Appleton suffered temporary loss of office but were soon serving again and seemed not to lose the esteem of their fellow colonists.

169. MHS photostats, Oct. 16–17, 1666. Based on his analysis of the 25 signatories from Boston, Bernard Bailyn argues that "outspoken support of the commissioners in Boston centered in the recently arrived merchants without church affiliation or the franchise" (*New England Merchants*, 123–24).

170. MHS photostats, Oct. 17, 1666.

171. *MHSC*, 2nd ser., 8:111.

172. Palfrey, *Compendious History of New England*, 2:78–81, 93; David S. Lovejoy, *Glorious Revolution*, 135.

173. Bliss, *Revolution and Empire*, 153.

174. *CSPCS*, 7:20, item 58. Evidence suggests that these masts were cut from Mason's patent in New Hampshire (see *CSPCS*, 5:468, item 1485). Nicholas Shapleigh, assigned to oversee the patent by the royal commissioners, forwarded to London the testimonies of several local justices of the peace that Richard Waldron and Peter Coffin had cut the masts. Even in sending the presents that helped win its reprieve, Massachusetts was crossing the line drawn for it by the king and royal commissioners, placing its own interpretations of charter and boundary limits above those of Charles II. For Massachusetts's provision of supplies to the Caribbean, see MHS photostats, Oct. 30, 1667.

175. For example, John Hull noted in his diary that the attack on Cartwright's ship (and the safety of the ship bearing letters from Bay Colony magistrates) was "one thing remarkable in the summer past" (*Diary of Public Occurrences*, 221).

Chapter 3. Years of Uncertainty

1. *MCR*, 4, part 2, 233.

2. Roger Williams, *Correspondence*, 2:579, note 4; Paul A. Robinson, "Lost Opportunities," 20.

3. See *RICR*, 2:193, 264–65, 267, 370.

4. Neal Salisbury, "Social Relationships on a Moving Frontier," 89–99.

5. For laws on Indian land sales, see William H. Whitmore, ed., *Colonial Laws of Massachusetts*, 161; *MCR*, 4, part 2, 282. Jeremy Bangs argues that English land use, "including enclosing fields and felling timber," increased markedly in the 1660s (*Indian Deeds*, 162).

6. See Lincoln A. Dexter, *Maps of Early Massachusetts*, 89, 71; Evarts B. Greene and Virginia D. Harrington, *American Population*, 9, 13; Alison Games, *Migration and the Origins of the English Atlantic World*, 173. On Indian population see James D. Drake, *King Philip's War*, 169; and James Axtell, *Invasion Within*, 219–20.

7. William Hubbard, *History of the Indian Wars*, 1:169.

8. Increase Mather, "Earnest Exhortation," 196. In Marlborough, founded in 1656, the church was not officially gathered or the minister called until 1664 (Levi A. Field, *Historical Sketch*). See also Richard Bushman, *From Puritan to Yankee*, chapter 4.

9. Mathew Cradock, governor of the Company of the Massachusetts Bay in New England, to John Endicott, Feb. 16, 1628, *MCR*, 1:383–85.

10. Passaconnaway's 1644 submission included the words "according to such

articles as Cutshamekin and others formerly accepted" (Nathaniel Bouton, ed., *Provincial Papers*, 174); *MCR*, 2:55.

11. Henry W. Bowden and James P. Ronda, eds., *John Eliot's Indian Dialogues*, 27–28.

12. Thomas Shepard, "Cleare Sunshine," *MHSC*, 3rd ser., 4:38.

13. Alden T. Vaughan, *New England Frontier*, 260. See also Ives Goddard and Kathleen Bragdon, *Native Writings in Massachusett*, 1:4–13.

14. Daniel Gookin, *Historical Collections*, chapter 7.

15. Gookin, *Historical Collections*, 194–200; Vaughan, *New England Frontier*, 303–4. Henry W. Bowden and James P. Ronda argue for the much smaller figure of 10 percent, but they exclude the Indians on Martha's Vineyard and Nantucket (*John Eliot's Indian Dialogues*, 40). Vaughan's *New England Frontier* was first published in 1965. In response to the book, which gave Eliot's idealism as the motivation for his work, an entire historiographic tradition sprang up, with an opposing materialistic interpretation. See Francis Jennings, "Goals and Functions of Puritan Missions to the Indians," and his following book *Invasion of America*; Neal Salisbury, "Red Puritans"; Elise Brenner, "To Pray or Be Prey"; James Ronda, "We Are Well as We Are"; and Harold Van Lonkhuyzen, "A Reappraisal of the Praying Indians." Richard W. Cogley reasserts idealism, specifically millenarianism, as the motive for Eliot's work and makes the point that for seventeenth-century Puritans religion was inseparable from political, social, and economic life. Thus studies that focus exclusively on material motives reflect the twentieth century's separation of religion from everyday life ("Idealism vs. Materialism"). Cogley's book, *John Eliot's Mission*, expands on the issues raised in the article and includes a strong rebuttal of Francis Jennings's assertions. Other studies that assert the validity of Indian conversions and compare English and Indian conversions include Charles L. Cohen, "Conversion Among Puritans and Amerindians"; James Axtell, "Were Indian Conversions *Bona Fide*?"; and James Ronda, "Generations of Faith."

16. Vaughan, *New England Frontier*, 261–79.

17. Virginia DeJohn Anderson, "King Philip's Herds."

18. *MCR*, 3:985. All the court decisions and documents associated with English and Indian complaints are reprinted in *Early Records of the Town of Dedham*, 4:235–92.

19. *Early Records of the Town of Dedham*, 4:279.

20. For a detailed discussion of the division of Sudbury and the settlement of Marlborough, see Sumner Chilton Powell, *Puritan Village*, especially 116–38.

21. Powell, *Puritan Village*, 136–37.

22. Hubbard, *History of the Indian Wars*, 1:208, note.

23. Daniel Gookin, cited in Anderson, "King Philip's Herds," 611. Anderson provides a very insightful discussion of the clash between English and Indian subsistence patterns.

24. Gookin, *Historical Collections*, 185.

25. Greene and Harrington, *American Population*, 9.

26. Neal Salisbury notes that since 1630 the policy of the Narragansetts had been to have multiple political alliances, rather than depending on one ally as the English encouraged ("Toward the Covenant Chain," 63).

27. *PCR*, 4:164–66.

28. Salisbury, "Toward the Covenant Chain," 66; Drake, *King Philip's War*, 54. For a description of Mohawk attacks, see Gookin, *Historical Collections*, chapter 4. For a detailed account of the Mohawks and other Iroquois in this period, see Daniel K. Richter, *Ordeal of the Longhouse*.

29. Gookin, *Historical Collections*, 162.

30. Ibid., chapter 4.
31. *MCR*, 4, part 2, 360–61.
32. Harald E. L. Prins, "Turmoil on the Wabanaki Frontier," 113–14. See also Salisbury, "Toward the Covenant Chain," 68. For English opposition to the attack, see Gookin, *Historical Collections*, 166. On Massachusett Indian population, see James Axtell, *Invasion Within*, 219–20.
33. Gookin, *Historical Collections*, 162.
34. Winthrop Family Papers, Sept. 8, 1665, reel 8, 17:6, MHS.
35. Joshua Micah Marshall, "Indian Laborers."
36. Ibid.
37. Suffolk Files, #868, vol. 9, JA.
38. Criminal cases involving both Indians and English made the English suspicious of English-Indian association. For one example of such a case, the murder of an Englishman by an Indian during a drunken brawl at a New Hampshire trading house, see MAC, 30:154–64a, July 30–Nov. 5, 1668.
39. *RICR*, 2:270. The Council had called Ninigret to answer for the report that he was planning to draw other Indian nations into a combination to cut off the English and that seven of sachem Philip of the Wampanoags' ancient men had been in council with him for over a week. Ninigret denied any such plot, supplied acceptable excuses, and pledged his loyalty, doing so according to the line of submission he had insisted on since the royal commissioners' visit.
40. *DCHNY*, 3:182.
41. Samuel Gorton, Jr., to Josiah Winslow, late June 1675, Miscellaneous Bound Manuscripts, MHS.
42. MAC, 30:129–129a, 150; Middlesex County Court, Folio Collection, 1663, folio 34, group 6, JA; see also Anderson, "King Philip's Herds."
43. Massachusetts government to the Narragansett sachems, Sept. 5, 1668, MHS photostats, emphasis added.
44. *PCR*, 10:96.
45. *PCR*, 10:236.
46. Robert M. Bliss, *Revolution and Empire*, 159–60. The phrase "sacrifice, not obedience," refers to the biblical story in 1 Samuel, chapter 15. Through his prophet Samuel, God commanded Saul, the king of Israel, to kill every living thing when he went to war against the Amalekites. Instead, Saul saved the best of the oxen and sheep and offered them to the priests as a sacrifice. Samuel condemned Saul for this action, declaring, "to obey is better than sacrifice."
47. *DCHNY*, 3:183.
48. *MCR*, 4, part 2, 464. Thanksgiving Day proclamations that mention the continuation of Massachusetts's liberties occurred on Nov. 8, 1665, Nov. 8, 1666, Oct. 12, 1670, and Oct. 8, 1672. On Nov. 22, 1666, following the General Court's decision against sending agents in response to the king's demand, the Court appointed a day of humiliation to pray for the continuation of their liberties (*MCR*, 4, part 2, 280–81, 320, 464, 534). See also W. DeLoss Love, Jr., *Fast and Thanksgiving Days*.
49. John Davenport, "Sermon Preach'd at the Election of the Governour," 4.
50. See *MCR*, 4, part 2, 305, 534. Notably, the state of Massachusetts preserves this terminology today, using as its official title, "The Commonwealth of Massachusetts."
51. Charles II to the Colonies of New England, April 10, 1666, in *CSPCS*, 5:372–73, item 1171.
52. Thomas Hutchinson, *History of the Colony*, 1:224–30. Henry Jocelyn, Francis Hooke, Francis Champernowne, Edward Rishworth, John Wincoll, and Edward Johnson sent a description of and complaint about these proceedings to Colonel

Richard Nicolls on Sept. 29, 1668 (*CSPCS*, 5:614, item 1848). They noted that when Leverett arrived, the royal justices displayed their commission as well as the king's "mandamus" of April 10, 1666, confirming the commissioners' order. Leverett was openly surprised and declared that he did not think they had such a letter, "which had the General Court seen, I am persuaded at present it might have stopped our voyage." The Court had received the same letter from Samuel Maverick, but Maverick's reputation with the Court was such that many dismissed it as a forgery (*MCR*, 4, part 2, 314–15, 317; *CSPCS*, 5:509–10, item 1611). Leverett acknowledged that the Maine officers' letter was in the king's hand, but since it lacked a royal seal, he and his fellow agents determined to proceed with their errand.

53. *DHSM*, 6:23–26.

54. Rishworth's adept adjustment to succeeding governments is clear in his letter to the General Court justifying his service on the royal government (*DHSM*, 6:33–34).

55. Richard Nicolls to the Council of Massachusetts, June 12, 1668, in *DCHNY*, 3:170–71.

56. *CSPCS*, 5:609, item 1835.

57. *DHSM*, 6:29–32.

58. Such substantial penalties were handed down only by the highest Massachusetts courts, and only rarely. In Maine, on the other hand, punishment was more likely to consist of a much lighter fine, setting the offender in the stocks or requiring him to swear the oath of fidelity. Those such as William Phillips and John Bonithon whose behavior was obnoxious enough to get the attention of the Massachusetts Court of Assistants drop from the records after finally appearing before the magistrates in Boston, chastened in spirit and pocketbook.

59. *MPCR*, 2:142, 176, 193. Bonithon was fined 20 pounds by the county court in Maine and referred to the Massachusetts Court of Assistants.

60. These included Walter Gendall and Nathan Bedford, of whom we will hear more later (*MPCR*, 2:193).

61. *MPCR*, 2:177.

62. *MPCR*, 2:183.

63. MHS photostats, Sept. 9, 1671. After Bonithon pledged his good behavior, with himself and his estate as security for the performance, the court charged him 20 pounds and returned him to prison "till this sentence be performed."

64. *DCHNY*, 3:184.

65. *DCHNY*, 3:183.

66. Town petitions exist for Northampton, Hadley, Dedham, Boston (3), Roxbury, Concord, Cambridge, Woburn, Reading, Chelmsford, Dorchester, Billerica, Medfield, and one unidentified town. See MAC, 106:97, 104–5, 107, 110, 111; MHS photostats, Oct. 1664, Oct. 24–26, 1664; Ruth Wheeler, *Concord: Climate for Freedom*, 199; Samuel G. Drake, *History and Antiquities of Boston*, 393–95; *MCR*, 4, part 2, 136–37. Complete copies with signatures are available for only 9 of the 17 extant petitions, totaling 710 signatures. The average number of signatures on these petitions is 79. Because frontier towns are as well represented in the known as the unknown numbers, I have used the average of 79 for all remaining petitions. Population estimates are from Greene and Harrington, *American Population*, 13. See also William Pencak, *War, Politics, & Revolution*, 11.

67. Frederick William Gookin, *Daniel Gookin*, 119–22. This passage includes a 1673 letter of Governor John Leverett et al. to Robert Boyle denying the charge that Massachusetts was a "divided people." Apart from some "petty differences," he wrote, "we bless God, we have much peace and tranquility in church and state."

68. Paul R. Lucas, "Colony or Commonwealth."

69. For Maverick's complaints, see *DCHNY*, 3:160–61.

70. *CSPCS*, 9:456, item 1037.

71. MHS photostats, Oct. 17, 1666.

72. In a 1672 meeting of the king's Council, Ferdinando Gorges presented a report of the number of militia in Maine. The same report claimed Massachusetts could raise a force of 15,000 men, 9000 of whom were of the "disaffected party" who could neither vote nor have their children baptized (*CSPCS*, 7:332, item 762). Gorges clearly shared Maverick's bias, and both that bias and his highly inflated population numbers reflect the difficulty of obtaining accurate information from the distant colony. The royal government had nothing to base decisions on but the claims and counterclaims of those with the motivation and resources to send or travel to London. It is not at all surprising under the circumstances that border disputes and other colonial conflicts dragged on as long as they did and underwent the number of reversals they did.

73. *CSPCS*, 7:171, item 439.

74. *CSPCS*, 7:244, item 598.

75. Samuel Sewall, *Diary*, 1:xiii. Sewall's father-in-law, John Hull, recorded in his diary the deaths of many ministers and colony leaders in this period, including Rev. John Norton (1663), Rev. Mr. Thompson (1666–67), Rev. John Wilson (Aug. 1667), Rev. Samuel Shepherd (April 8, 1668), church teacher Henry Flynt (1668), Rev. Jonathan Mitchell (July 9, 1668), Rev. John Eliot, Jr., (Dec. 9, 1668), Rev. Richard Mather (April 23, 1669), Revs. John Davenport, William Woodward, Benjamin Bunker, Zachariah Symmes, and Deputy Governor Francis Willoughby (March 1670), Rev. John Allin of Dedham (Aug. 26, 1670) (*Diary of Public Occurrences*, 207, 223, 226–31).

76. Cited in Michael G. Hall, *Last American Puritan*, 98.

77. Middlesex County Court, Folio Collection, 1668, folio 49, group 4, JA.

78. *MPCR*, 2:202, emphasis added.

79. *ECR*, 5:306–8; *MCR*, 4, part 2, 394.

80. "To the Elders and Ministers."

81. *MCR*, 4, part 2, 394, 449–51.

82. *DCHNY*, 3:184.

83. Mark Peterson describes this episode in his *Price of Redemption*, 165.

84. *MCR*, 4, part 2, 489–93.

85. Francis J. Bremer, *Puritan Experiment*, 165.

86. *MCR*, 4, part 2, 489–93. Signers included Edmund Brown, John Ward, Samuel Whiting, John Allin, Thomas Thatcher, Sr., John Higginson, John Sherman, Thomas Cobbet, Seaborn Cotton, Thomas Shepherd, Samuel Phillips, William Hubbard, Antipas Newman, Samuel Torrey, and Samuell Whiting, Jr.

87. *MCR*, 4, part 2, 290–91.

88. *MCR*, 4, part 2, 373–75.

89. Middlesex County Court Records, Pulsifer transcript, 3:16–17, 1671, JA.

90. *MCR*, 4, part 1, 383–90. Walter Barefoot and others like him may have provided the incentive for such guards. When Quakers Anna Colman, Mary Tompkins, and Alice Ambrose were sentenced to be whipped through the towns of the colony, Barefoot volunteered to convey them between Salisbury and Newbury. Instead, he spirited them out of the colony altogether, sparing the women beatings in eight more towns (Bouton, *Provincial Papers*, 1:243–44, Dec. 22, 1662).

91. MHS photostats, Nov. [?] 1668. English Puritan John Westgate's May 8, 1677, letter to Increase Mather pleads for latitude in the treatment of religious dissidents such as Baptists and Quakers (*MHSC*, 4th ser., 8:577–81).

92. MHS photostats, Nov. [?] 1668. Signers included James Oliver, Richard Way,

Thomas Temple, Elisha Hutchinson, Thomas Clarke, Edward Hutchinson, Edward Wilson, Samuel Shrimpton, John Usher, Henry Taylor, Nathaniel Wiswall, and Jonathan Shrimpton.

93. *MCR*, 4, part 2, 413. See also the petition of James Oliver, Richard Way, Randall Nicolls, and others, apologizing for their petition in behalf of the Anabaptists (MHS photostats, Oct. 22, 1668).

94. MHS photostats, June 3, 1671.

95. MHS photostats, Oct. 22, 1670.

96. MHS photostats, June 3, 1671. The biblical reference is to Matthew 12:25.

97. *MCR*, 4, part 2, 211–13.

98. John Eliot mentions the capture and execution of the murderer by Massachusetts officials in a letter to Gov. Thomas Prince of Plymouth, June 16, 1671, John Davis Papers, MHS.

99. Josiah Winslow to Gov. Thomas Prince, written in a March 24, 1670, letter from Richard Bellingham to Prince, Winslow Family II Papers, MHS.

100. This "squaw sachem" was undoubtedly either Awashonks of the Saconets or Weetamoo of the Pocassets, both Wampanoags owing allegiance to Philip (Thomas Hinckley and Nathan Bacon to Gov. Prince, April 6, 1671, Winslow Family II Papers, MHS).

101. Ibid.

102. Ibid.

103. *PCR*, 5:59–63.

104. Gov. Prince to Gov. Bellingham of Massachusetts, May 8, 1671, Winslow Family II Papers, MHS.

105. *PCR*, 5:70–72.

106. James Walker to Governor Prince, Sept. 1, 1671, Winslow Family II Papers, MHS. This letter notes that Philip "exclaimed much against Sausiman for reporting that any of the Narragansett sachems were there." Sausimon would lose his life for relaying similar tales to the English four years later, just before the outbreak of King Philip's War.

107. See Carla Gardina Pestana, *Quakers and Baptists in Colonial Massachusetts*, 27.

108. James Walker to Governor Prince, Sept. 1, 1671, Winslow Family II Papers, MHS (reprinted in *MHSC*, 1st ser., 6:197).

109. For evidence of this "hopeful progress," see *PCR*, 10:383–86. Eliot's belief that this was so is evident not only in this incident, but in his inclusion of Philip in his semifictional account of Indian conversion dialogues, published in 1671 (Bowden and Ronda, *John Eliot's Indian Dialogues*).

110. Instructions from the church at Natick to William and Anthony, signed by John Eliot, "with the consent of the church," Aug. 1, 1671, *MHSC*, 1st ser., 6:201–3.

111. There is no proof that Philip did stop, but the instructions are interesting evidence of the continuing interchange between Christian Indians and Philip's people. Another example of this continuing interaction is Christian Indian Sarah Ahhaton's flight to Philip's people after she was charged with adultery (MHS photostats, Oct. 24, 1668). For an extended discussion of Sarah Ahhaton's case, see Ann Marie Plane, "Examination of Sarah Ahhaton."

112. Plymouth complained that, since the Treaty of Taunton, Philip had violated several articles and had refused to treat with them further (*PCR*, 5:63).

113. *PCR*, 5:77–79.

114. *PCR*, 10:416.

115. Nathaniel Saltonstall's "Continuation of the State of New-England" contains a letter on the rebellion of African slaves in Barbados. The unidentified writer refers to this claim, made by Philip before the governor in Boston. As Philip never

appeared before the governor during King Philip's War, Charles Lincoln attributes this phrase to his 1671 visit (*Narratives of the Indian Wars*, 73).

116. See Philip's complaint in John Easton, "Relacion of the Indyan Warre," 10–11.

117. *PCR*, 5:76–100.

118. *PCR*, 5:79.

Chapter 4. Allies Fall Away

1. The Sassamon murder trial, which was the immediate pretext for the war, has been examined in depth by many historians, most recently James Drake, "Symbol of a Failed Strategy," and Jill Lepore, "Dead Men Tell No Tales," and also chapter 1 in her *Name of War*. See also James P. and Jeanne Ronda, "Death of John Sassamon," as well as Douglas Leach's account in *Flintlock and Tomahawk*.

2. John Brown to Governor Josiah Winslow, June 15, 1675, Winslow Family II Papers, MHS.

3. Samuel Gorton, Jr., to Josiah Winslow, late June 1675, Miscellaneous Bound Manuscripts, MHS.

4. See copy of John Brown to Weetamoo and Ben, sachems of Pocasset, June 15, 1675, Winslow Family II Papers, MHS.

5. MAC, 67:202, Governor Winslow to Governor Leverett, June 21, 1675.

6. MAC, 67:200–200a, Instructions to Seth Perry, June 21, 1675; MAC, 30:169–70, Report of Ephraim Curtis, June 24–26, 1675.

7. Benjamin Batten to Thomas Allin, June 29–July 6, 1675, in Douglas Edward Leach, "Benjamin Batten and the London Gazette Report," 508. Notably, all three of these men had been signers of either the petition in favor of leniency toward the Baptists or the 1666 petition to send royal agents to the king. Clearly, those actions had not undermined their trustworthiness in the eyes of the governor. Batten referred to these Massachusetts messengers as "three plenipotentiaries with three attendants." The reference clearly belittles Massachusetts's exaggerated claims of authority. Batten was critical of Massachusetts's antagonistic relationship with royal authority, as he made clear in later letters highlighting the colony's failure to use the king's name in official papers and its continued repression of Quakers (Leach, "Benjamin Batten," 507; Benjamin Batten, Oct. 26, 1676, in *CSPCS*, 9:299, item 700).

8. John Easton, "Relacion of the Indyan Warre," 12.

9. For contemporary comment on this, see Samuel Gorton, Jr., to John Winthrop, Jr., Sept. 11, 1675, in *MHSC*, 4th ser., 7:627. Gorton mentions the king's charge not to take any Indian lands without giving due satisfaction, adding his fear that "the not observing this charge, is a great and universal grudge among the Indians at this day, while men take up lands and plant upon them as their own, without any retribution, at the least not to the chief Sachems, if any small thing at all to some base inferior fellow; which makes the Sachems afraid, lest by this means in short time they shall be spewed out of the country, for want of land to reside upon." This letter provides contemporary criticism of English disregard for structures of Indian authority, dealing with "some base inferior fellow" (such as Narragansett subsachem Pomham) rather than "the chief Sachems"; Petition of Monaquo Woaoksunt [?] sachem of Coisset [Cowesit], ND, John Davis Papers, MHS.

10. Benjamin Tompson, in his verse narrative of King Philip's War, gives a disdainful version of such Indian complaints, proclaimed by an Indian "Lout" on a rotten stump of a throne ("Sad and Deplorable News from New-England," 7). For

secondary discussions of Easton's conference with Philip's delegation, see Leach, *Flintlock and Tomahawk*, 42–43; Jill Lepore, *Name of War*, 23–25, 42.

11. Increase Mather, *Brief History of the War*, 152.

12. Jeremy Dupertuis Bangs, *Indian Deeds*, 98, 164.

13. Ibid., 173.

14. Easton, "Relacion of the Indyan Warre," 11.

15. Ibid., 10.

16. Nathaniel Saltonstall, "Present State of New-England," 25; Rev. John Cotton, Jr., noted that Indians frequently attended Plymouth Colony Court sessions, at which he was often asked to act as interpreter. As a result, Cotton made a practice of preaching in his home on court days to as many as 100 Indians at once (Len Travers, ed., "Missionary Journal of John Cotton, Jr.," 82).

17. Report of King's Commissioners concerning Massachusetts, in *DCHNY*, 3:112.

18. Easton, "Relacion of the Indyan Warre," 10. Claims of Philip's antipathy toward Christian Indians appear in another contemporary account as well. The author of "News from New England" noted the "Coals of Dissension which had a long time lain hid under the ashes of a secret envy; contracted by the Heathen Indians of New-England, against the English; and Christian Natives of that Country" ("News from New-England," 5–6).

19. Christian Indians themselves testified to this situation. Black James, ruler of the praying town of Chabanakongkomun in 1675, said "he no loves Pilep for he said that since he is become a Praying indian the sachems they no love. We asked him why he they no love. He said because he pray to god" (MAC, 30:169–70, Report of Ephraim Curtis, June 24–26, 1675).

20. I thank Richard Cogley for pointing out to me the connection between Philip's disdain for the Christian Indians and his 1671 experience. He details this connection in *John Eliot's Mission to the Indian*, 200–6.

21. Nantucket Court Records, page 3, Aug. 5, 1675, cited in Ann Marie Plane, *Colonial Intimacies*, 213.

22. Easton, "Relacion of the Indyan Warre," 10.

23. Easton, "Relacion of the Indyan Warre," 9. This phrase, from an authentically contemporary document, is as close as anything comes to Philip's famous but unverifiable statement, "I am determined not to live until I have no country."

24. Massachusetts Council to Major John Pynchon, July 10, 1675, Winthrop Family Papers, MHS.

25. MAC, 30:170, Report of Ephraim Curtis, June 24–26, 1675. Douglas Leach notes that initially Philip made a point of preventing harm to Massachusetts citizens who came his way, wanting to limit the fight to himself and Plymouth (*Flintlock and Tomahawk*, 49).

26. Massachusetts's Dec. 7, 1675, declaration justifying its involvement in the war appears in Nathaniel Saltonstall, "Continuation," 62–64. See also Massachusetts Council to the Secretary of State, April 5, 1676, in *DHSM*, 6:109–13.

27. MAC, 69:169, Massachusetts Council to Connecticut Council, Sept. 3, 1677; *PCR*, 10:462. Jill Lepore discusses English efforts to justify their engagement in the war in *Name of War*, 105–15.

28. MAC, 69:169, Massachusetts Council to Connecticut Council, Sept. 3, 1677; *PCR*, 10:462–64. In an April 1676 letter from James Printer, scribe to the Indian sachems, to Governor Leverett, Printer confirmed that Indians originally saw Plymouth as their only English enemy: "I am sorrow that I have done much to wrong you and yet I say the fault is lay upon you, for when we began quarrel at first with Plimouth men I did not think that you should have so much trouble as now is" (in

Mary Rowlandson, *The Sovereignty and Goodness of God*, 136). According to Printer, the Massachusetts English were at fault for their own sufferings by joining a quarrel that was only with "Plimouth men."

29. Harry M. Ward offers an extended discussion of the history of the United Colonies in his *United Colonies of New England.*

30. Ibid., 201, 261.

31. Massachusetts Council to Plymouth Council, Aug. 23, 1677, Winslow Family II Papers, MHS.

32. Evidence that Massachusetts helped prod Connecticut into joining the war effort appears in a letter from John Leverett to John Winthrop, Jr., July 31, 1675, Winthrop Family II Papers, MHS.

33. MAC, 30:169–70, Report of Ephraim Curtis, June 24–26, 1675.

34. Roger Williams to John Winthrop, Jr., July 25, 1675, in *MHSC*, 4th ser., 6:299–302; John Pynchon to John Winthrop, Jr., July 2, 1675, in Carl Bridenbaugh, ed., *Pynchon Papers*, 1:137.

35. MAC, 30:169, Report of Ephraim Curtis, June 24–26, 1675. Curtis received confirmations of continued subjection to the Massachusetts government from sachems of the Nipmuck towns of Hassanamesit, Manchage, Chabanakongkomun, Maanexit, Quantisset, Wabquisset, and Pakachoog, all of which had become praying towns within the last several years, as well as from Quabaug.

36. In a strikingly similar exchange between French trader Pierre Charles Le Sueur and a group of Sioux Indian allies in 1700, the Sioux chief gave the trader presents, confirming their alliance, and then declared, "No longer regard us as Sioux, but as Frenchmen" (Brett Rushforth, "A Little Flesh We Offer You," 789). Here, in a similar time period, but far distant locale, Indians asserted common identity—even kinship—through political alliance. While the Nipmucks had no contact with the Sioux, they did with the Iroquois, who traditionally defined relationships through assertions of kinship. Richard White describes the close contacts between Sioux Indians and the French, who also maintained ties with the Iroquois, in his *Middle Ground.* Whatever the origin of these ideas and practices, they were clearly operating among many Indian societies in this period.

37. Saltonstall, "Present State of New-England," 26.

38. Ibid., 27. See also the copy of John Brown's letter to "Weetamoo, and Ben her husband, Sachems of Pocasset, Freinds and Neighbrs" in Mr. Brown to Governor Winslow, June 15, 1675, Winslow Family II Papers, MHS.

39. Roger Williams to Governor John Winthrop, Jr., June 25, 1675, in Roger Williams, *Correspondence*, 2:693–95.

40. Easton, "Relacion of the Indyan Warre," 10.

41. Roger Williams to Robert Williams, April 1, 1676 (disputed), in Williams, *Correspondence*, 2:720–24. It is odd that the veracity of this letter is disputed. Irrefutable evidence exists that such a letter was written. It is quoted, citing the same location and participants, in a letter between Noah Newman and John Cotton, written two weeks later (Noah Newman to John Cotton, April 19, 1676, in Richard LeBaron Bowen, *Early Rehoboth*, 15–19).

42. MAC, 30: 169–70, Report of Ephraim Curtis, June 24–26, 1675.

43. The uniting of all the English colonies against the Indians may have been a defining moment in the emergence of racism in early New England. Rhode Islanders, long in enmity with the other colonies, chose to join with Plymouth, Massachusetts, and Connecticut out of the apparent belief that they, too, were threatened, that the Indians would rise to cut off all English. For other discussions of the emergence of racism in this period, see Neal Salisbury's Introduction to Rowlandson, *Sovereignty and Goodness of God*, 48; and Lepore, *Name of War*, 166.

44. Mather, *Brief History*, 94–98.

45. Thomas Stanton and Thomas Minor to the Council at Hartford, June 30, 1675, Winthrop Family Papers, MHS. Niantic sachem Ninigret used the same gesture to manifest his loyalty to the English, sending the head of one of Philip's men to Connecticut's Major FitzJohn Winthrop "as a testimony of his faithfulness to the English." At the same time, he asked Major Winthrop to write to the governor and Council at Hartford to tell them of the gift and that he had sent out 120 men to subdue the enemy (*MHSC*, 6th ser., 3:447).

46. Thomas Stanton and Thomas Minor to the Council at Hartford, June 30, 1675, Winthrop Family Papers, MHS.

47. Richard Smith to John Winthrop, Jr., Sept. 4, 1675, Winthrop Family Papers, MHS. Evidence that Philip's message as well as his messengers were reaching surrounding Indians is clear in the declaration of some counselors to Narragansett sachem Canonchet after the Great Swamp Fight in December. Rejecting the English invitation to come and parley, the counselors said it was only to entrap the sachems, "as they had done Phillip many times, who when he was in their hand made him yield to what they pleased" (Roger Williams to John Leverett, Jan. 14, 1675, in *MHSC*, 4th ser., 6:307).

48. Massachusetts Council to Major Pynchon, July 10, 1675, in Winthrop Family Papers, MHS.

49. Tobias Saunders to Captain Wait Winthrop, July 7, 1675, Winthrop Family Papers, MHS.

50. John Pynchon to John Winthrop, Jr., July 2, 1675 in Bridenbaugh, *Pynchon Papers*, 1:137; Nathaniel Thomas to Governor Winslow, June 25, 1675, in *MHSC*, 1st ser., 6:86.

51. On July 10, 1675, Edward Rawson wrote to John Pynchon that "there is cause to fear this Ind[ian] Plot is more general than we formerly expected" (Winthrop Family Papers, MHS). The first attack by non-Wampanoags outside of Plymouth Colony occurred four days after this letter; Nipmucks attacked Mendon on July 14, 1675.

52. Uncas, accompanied by 61 of his warriors, made the offer on June 26, 1675. See John Leverett to Honoured Sir [John Winthrop, Jr.], July 31, 1675, Winthrop Family Papers, MHS; and Benjamin Batten to Sir Thomas Allin, June 29–July 6, 1675, in Leach, "Benjamin Batten," 514.

53. Job, a Christian Indian, accompanied Curtis on this expedition (MHS photostats, June 27, 1675).

54. William Hubbard, *History of the Indian Wars*, 1:105.

55. Leaders included Sagamore Sam and Mattaump, both later executed at Boston.

56. MAC, 67:214–17, Report of Ephraim Curtis, July 16, 1675.

57. MAC, 67:222–23, Report of Ephraim Curtis, July 24, 1675.

58. See Chapter 6 for a more detailed discussion of the conflict between Massachusetts's Indian policy and the colony's treatment of allied and Christian Indians.

59. For details on this treaty and attempts to treat with Indians, see Roger Williams to Captain Wait Winthrop, July 7, 1675, in Williams, *Correspondence*, 2:701–2; Thomas Stanton, Sr., to Captain Wait Winthrop, July 9, 1675, Winthrop Family Papers, MHS.

60. Hubbard includes the July 15, 1675, treaty in *History of the Indian Wars*, 1:75–79.

61. John Winthrop, Jr., to Major Savage and other officers, Hartford, July 12, 1675, *MHSC*, 5th ser., 8:172–74.

62. John Leverett to Josiah Winslow, July 17, 1675, and John Freeman to Gover-

nor Winslow, July 18, 1675, Winslow Family II Papers, MHS. On Narragansett hostages, see a letter from William Harris, which claims four hostages were given (Douglas Edward Leach, ed., *Rhode Islander Reports*, 88); this figure was seconded by William Hubbard (*History of the Indian Wars*, 1:75). The letter from Massachusetts Governor John Leverett to Plymouth Governor Josiah Winslow lists 21 hostages arriving in Boston (July 17, 1675, Winslow Family II Papers, MHS). On at least one occasion, the English offered hostages to the Indians as well. Captain Richard Smith of Rhode Island offered himself, his wife, and children as hostages for the safe return of Ninigret's son (Saltonstall, "Present State of New-England," 44).

63. "Military instructions for Cornet Thomas Brattle and Lieut. Thomas Henchman," Sept. 8, 1675, in Samuel A. Green, M.D., *Groton During the Indian Wars*, 17. See Chapter 6 for details on the Wamesits in the remainder of the war.

64. On Pocumtuck hostages, see Hubbard, *History of the Indian Wars*, 1:120.

65. Written from [Winslow's?] house, July 1675, Winslow Family II Papers, MHS.

66. Patrick M. Malone discusses Indian tactics and use of weaponry in his *Skulking Way of War*.

67. John Pynchon to John Winthrop, Jr., Aug. 7, 1675, in Bridenbaugh, *Pynchon Papers*, 1:142.

68. Massachusetts Council to John Pynchon, Sept. 15, 1675, MHS Photostats. Turning down his request, the Council acknowledged that "that spirit in Opposing Rulers which too much shows it self among us . . . is a matter of grief and discouragement; but yet it is no other than moses & aaron & david divers others of the servant of God have met with."

69. Massachusetts Council to John Pynchon, Sept. 15, 1675; John Pynchon to John Winthrop, Jr., Aug. 19, 1675, and John Pynchon to John Allyn, Aug. 25, 1675, in Bridenbaugh, *Pynchon Papers*, 1:146.

70. Hubbard, *History of the Indian Wars*, 1:108–9.

71. Mather, *Brief History*, 94–95.

72. John Pynchon to John Allyn, Aug. 25, 1675, in Bridenbaugh, *Pynchon Papers*, 1:149.

73. Hubbard, *History of the Indian Wars*, 1:109.

74. Evan Haefeli and Kevin Sweeney, "Revisiting *The Redeemed Captive*"; Leach, *Flintlock and Tomahawk*, 86–87.

75. Captain Allyn to John Winthrop, Jr., Sept. 10, 1675, Winthrop Family Papers, MHS.

76. James Fitch to "Right Worshipful," Aug. 30, 1675, Winthrop Family Papers, MHS.

77. Hubbard, *History of the Indian Wars*, 1:109.

78. James D. Drake, *King Philip's War*, 40.

79. Leach, *Flintlock and Tomahawk*, 142.

80. For rumors about Uncas's infidelity, see Nathaniel Thomas to Governor Winslow, June 25, 1675, *MHSC*, 1st ser., 6:86.

81. James Quanapaug [Quannapohit]'s information, *MHSC*, 1st ser., 6:205.

82. Saltonstall, "Present State of New-England," 26.

Chapter 5. The "Narragansett War"

1. Mary Pray to James Oliver, Oct. 20, 1675, *MHSC*, 5th ser., 1:105.

2. Richard Smith to John Winthrop, Jr., Sept. 4, 1675, Winthrop Family Papers, MHS.

3. Massachusetts Council to John Pynchon, Sept. 15, 1675, MHS photostats.

4. Wait Winthrop to dear brother (probably Fitz-John Winthrop), from Mr. Richardson's [house], ND, Winthrop Family Papers, MHS.

5. Roger Williams to Captain Wait Winthrop, July 7, 1675, in Roger Williams, *Correspondence*, 2:701–2.

6. William Hubbard, *History of the Indian Wars*, 1:136; Roger Williams to Captain Wait Winthrop, July 7, 1675, in Williams, *Correspondence*, 2:701–2.

7. Richard Smith to John Winthrop, Jr., Sept. 4, 1675, Winthrop Family Papers, MHS.

8. Depositions concerning William Smith's abuse of Corman, Ninigret's counselor brought in to speak with the Council, Sept. 29, 1675, MHS photostats. Smith was found guilty and sentenced to pay 10 shillings to Corman for his damages, plus 40 shillings to the country or to be whipped.

9. Douglas Edward Leach, ed., *Rhode Islander Reports*, 36.

10. Hubbard includes the July 15, 1675, treaty in *History of the Indian Wars*, 1:75–79. On the October treaty, see Williams, *Correspondence*, 2:707, note 20. Although the new treaty was not signed until October 18, 1675, the sachems who signed may have been in Boston by late September, when William Smith was called to court for abusing Ninigret's aged counselor Corman (MHS photostats, Sept. 29, 1675).

11. Douglas Edward Leach, *Flintlock and Tomahawk*, 115.

12. Roger Williams to Governor John Winthrop, Jr., June 27, 1675, in Williams, *Correspondence*, 2:698.

13. Ibid. Canonicus was the name Miantonomi's brother Pessacus took after the death of his uncle, Canonicus.

14. Richard Smith to John Winthrop, Jr., Sept. 4, 1675, Winthrop Family Papers, MHS.

15. Roger Williams to Governor John Winthrop, Jr., June 13, 1675, in Williams, *Correspondence*, 2:691.

16. Men who used the phrase "young sachems" include Englishmen Roger Williams, William Hubbard, and Richard Hutchinson, as well as Christian Indian Peter Ephraim. See Roger Williams to John Leverett, Jan. 14, 1675, *MHSC*, 4th ser., 6:307; Hubbard, *History of the Indian Wars*, 1:101; Richard Hutchinson, "Warr in New-England Visibly Ended," 105; MAC, 30:202, Report of Peter Ephraim, June 1, 1676. Glenn LaFantasie notes that a Connecticut court tried Tatuphosuit, found little evidence against him, and released him, bidding the Mohegans to avoid such acts in the future. The Narragansetts could easily have judged this decision as "partiality," further undermining their trust in English authority and justice. This case, which must have heightened the animosity between the Narragansetts and Mohegans, was further reason for the Mohegans to ally with the English in the war, rather than with the Narragansetts and Wampanoags (Williams, *Correspondence*, 2:697, note 13).

17. Hubbard, *History of the Indian Wars*, 1:98. See also Saltonstall, "Continuation of the State of New-England," 62–64.

18. Hubbard, *History of the Indian Wars*, 1:109.

19. John Allyn, for the Connecticut Council, to the Massachusetts Council, on the bottom of John Mason to Fitz-John Winthrop, Sept. 6, 1675, Winthrop Family Papers, MHS.

20. "The Examination and Relation of James Quannapoaquait," in Mary Rowlandson, *The Sovereignty and Goodness of God*, 124.

21. John Brown to Gov. Winslow, June 11, 1675, Winslow Family II Papers, MHS; copy of John Brown "To Weetamoo, and Ben her husband, Sachems of Pocasset, Freinds and Neighbrs," in John Brown to Gov. Winslow, June 15, 1675, Winslow Family II Papers, MHS.

22. Benjamin Church, *Diary of King Philip's War*, 73–74.

23. Hubbard, *History of the Indian Wars*, 2:220.

24. Increase Mather, "Earnest Exhortation," 181.

25. Roger Williams to Governor John Winthrop, Jr., June 25, 1675, in Williams, *Correspondence*, 2:694.

26. John Easton, "Relacion of the Indyan Warre," 14.

27. The name given in the manuscript is "pucquach." Because of the similarity in sound and the wide range of spellings used for all Indian names in this period, I believe this name is Pessacus, another name for Canonicus (Richard Smith to "Much Honored" [John Winthrop, Jr.?], Aug. 5, 1675, Winthrop Family Papers, MHS).

28. Ibid.; *PCR*, 5:173.

29. Roger Williams to John Leverett, Jan. 14, 1675, *MHSC*, 4th ser., 6:307. Not only Indians, but several English protested the "mercy" that consigned hundreds of Indians to slavery in foreign lands. See John Eliot to the United Colonies commissioners, August 6, 1675, *PCR*, 10:451; Thomas Walley to Rev. John Cotton, April 17, 1676, John Davis Papers, MHS; William Leete to John Winthrop, Jr., Sept. 23, 1675, *MHSC*, 4th ser., 7:578; William Leete to John Winthrop, Jr., Oct. 21, 1675, *MHSC*, 4th ser., vol. 7:580. For a detailed discussion of Indian slavery in early America, see Almon Lauber, *Indian Slavery*. Margaret Newell previews her forthcoming book on Indian slavery in her "Changing Nature of Indian Slavery in New England."

30. "Examination and Relation of James Quannapoaquait," 125.

31. James Fitch to "Right Worshipful," August 30, 1675, Winthrop Family Papers, MHS.

32. William Leete to John Winthrop, Jr., Sept. 23, 1675, *MHSC*, 4th ser., 7:578; William Leete to John Winthrop, Jr., Oct. 21, 1675, *MHSC*, 4th ser., 7:580.

33. William Leete to John Winthrop, Jr., Sept. 23, 1675, *MHSC*, 4th ser., 7:578.

34. William Leete to John Winthrop, Jr., Oct. 21, 1675, *MHSC*, 4th ser., 7:580.

35. Leach, *Flintlock and Tomahawk*, 118–19. See also Douglas Edward Leach, "A New View of the Declaration of War," 33–41.

36. MAC, 30:188, Massachusetts General Court to Richard Smith, November 21, 1675. See also Massachusetts Council to Richard Smith, November 21, 1675, MHS photostats.

37. "Examination and Relation of James Quannapoaquait," 126.

38. Saltonstall, "Continuation of the State of New-England," 58.

39. Church offers the most extended account of the fight in his *Diary of King Philip's War*. See also the account in George M. Bodge, *Soldiers in King Philip's War*, 185–90.

40. Leach, *Flintlock and Tomahawk*, 128–35.

41. William S. Simmons, *Spirit of the New England Tribes*, 149.

42. Hamilton B. Tompkins, "Great Swamp Fight," 12.

43. Jill Lepore discusses the naming of the war in *Name of War*, introduction. See James Drake's discussion of the same in his *King Philip's War*, 91.

44. Not one of the over twenty contemporary accounts of the war calls it "King Philip's War." Eleven call it "The Indian War," the "Late" war, or some version of a war between the Indians and the English. The closest contemporary phrase to "King Philip's War" is Roger Williams's call for the "quenching of this Phillipian Fire in the beginning of it" (Roger Williams to Gov. John Winthrop, Jr., in Williams, *Correspondence*, 2:693). The first use of the term "King Philip's War" may have been in 1716, when Benjamin Church's son Thomas used it for his account of his father's military exploits.

45. Joshua Scottow, *Narrative of the Planting*, 38–39, 42, 43–45, 72.

46. R. Wharton to John Winsley, Feb. 10, 1675–76, *CSPCS*, 9:350–51, item 816.
47. Mr. Brown to Gov. Winslow, June 15, 1675, Winslow Family II Papers, MHS.
48. *DHSM*, 6:177–79.
49. In this sense, King Philip's War was a civil war rather than a rebellion, as James Drake argues in his *King Philip's War.*
50. *Court Martial held at Newport, Rhode Island.* Plymouth and Massachusetts viewed Rhode Island's trial and execution of these war criminals as a presumptuous infringement on the authority those colonies had long claimed over the Wampanoags and Narragansetts. Plymouth demanded that all war criminals be sent to them for trial, to which Massachusetts added its second (Edward Rawson to Josiah Winslow, Aug. 20, 1676, Winslow Family II Papers, MHS). Rhode Island officials undoubtedly thought that their claim to authority over the Indians, confirmed by the royal commissioners in 1665, superseded that of both colonies. While they agreed to return Plymouth Indians who fled to Rhode Island, they refused to send Narragansetts to Massachusetts, trying and executing them themselves.
51. Plymouth Commissioners for the United Colonies Narrative, *PCR*, 10:362–65.
52. Easton, "Relacion of the Indyan Warre," 10.
53. For Philip's refusal to meet with Plymouth, see Samuel Gorton, Jr., to Josiah Winslow, late June 1675, Miscellaneous Bound Manuscripts, MHS; and Benjamin Batten to Sir Thomas Allin, June 29–July 6, 1675, *CSPCS*, 9:251–53, item 614. Batten notes that on June 23, 1675, Plymouth sent three "plenipotentiaries with three attendants" to treat with Philip, who refused to see them.
54. MHS photostats, Nov. 5, 1675.
55. Thomas Stanton, Sr., to [Waite?] Winthrop, July 11, 1675, Winthrop Family Papers, MHS.
56. Samuel Symonds to John Winthrop, Jr., July 14, 1675, *MHSC*, 4th ser., 7:136.
57. Order of the Connecticut Council, July 10, 1675, *PCR*, 2:260–62.
58. Sir John Werden to Major Andros, Aug. 31, 1676, *CSPCS*, 9:445, 1024.
59. See MAC, 68:17, Edmund Andros to Gov. Leverett, Oct. 16, 1675. Andros claims the Mohawks would not assist Philip and his allies. Leverett's answer is in shorthand (see also *PCR*, 10:453).
60. Hubbard, *History of the Indian Wars*, 1:282; Mather, *Brief History*, 141.
61. John Pynchon to John Leverett, Aug. 15, 1676, in Carl Bridenbaugh, ed., *Pynchon Papers*, 1:168.
62. Mather, *Brief History*, 132. Stephen Saunders Webb argues that Andros encouraged Philip to remove to New York permanently in order to increase the population of the duke of York's dominions (*1676*, 370).
63. MAC, 68:17, Edmund Andros to Governor Leverett, Oct. 16, 1675.
64. Samuel Symonds, by order of the Council, to Secretary Sir Joseph Williamson, April 6, 1676, *CSPCS*, 9:371–73, item 876; an April 5, 1676, draft is reprinted in full in *DHSM*, 6:109–13.
65. Massachusetts's Dec. 7, 1675, declaration justifying its involvement in the war appears in Saltonstall, "Continuation of the State of New-England," 62–64.
66. Mather, *Brief History*, 114.
67. Massachusetts Council to the king, Sept. 3, 1676, MHS photostats; Edward Randolph to Secretary Coventry, June 17, 1676, *CSPCS*, 9:406–9, item 953.
68. Edmund Andros's report on his assistance to New England during the Indian War, April 18, 1678, *DCHNY*, 3:264–65. See also Church, *Diary of King Philip's War*, 105. Stephen Saunders Webb notes that the London papers publishing reports of the war claimed the Mohawks, not the English, were responsible for Philip's defeat (*1676*, 222, 367).

69. There is evidence that some of Ninigret's warriors joined with Philip against his will, a situation that damned the Narragansett sachems in English eyes. However, because Ninigret dealt almost exclusively with the more tolerant messengers from Connecticut, he escaped similar condemnation (Wait Winthrop to John Winthrop, Jr., July 4, 1675, *MHSC*, 5th ser., 8:401).

70. Josiah Winslow, July 28, 1675, MHS photostats; Roger Williams to John Leverett, Jan. 14, 1675, *MHSC*, 4th ser., vol. 6:307–12.

71. John Winthrop to Wait Winthrop, July 8, 1675, Winthrop Family Papers, MHS.

72. See Ninigret's warning about Uncas in *MHSC*, 5th ser., 1:426–27, and Tobias Sanders to Fitz-John Winthrop, July 3, 1675, *MHSC*, 4th ser., 8:426. It is important to note that Ninigret and Uncas and their peoples were long-standing enemies. Ninigret may have been trying, as Uncas was, to ensure his own position of trust among the English following the war and to discredit his opponent.

73. Hubbard, *History of the Indian Wars*, 1:287.

74. Tobias Sanders to Fitz-John Winthrop, July 3, 1675, *MHSC*, 5th ser., 1:426.

75. Ibid.

76. Daniel Gookin wrote to Richard Smith, "You write that Ninnigret hath delivered nine wompanogues to major winthrop. If it is [true] . . . then there is good reason he could be distinguished from the rest of the Narragansetts" (MAC, 30:188, Nov. 21, 1675).

77. Tobias Sanders to Fitz-John Winthrop, July 3, 1675, *MHSC*, 5th ser., 1:426.

78. James Quanapaug [Quannapohit]'s information, Jan. 24, 1675, *MHSC*, 1st ser., 6:205.

79. See Daniel Gookin's complaint that the colony deprived itself of a valuable ally by not using the Christian Indians as soldiers (Daniel Gookin, *Historical Account*, 456).

80. Roger Williams to Robert Williams, April 1, 1676 (disputed), in Williams, *Correspondence*, 2:720. See Chapter 4, note 41 on the disputed nature of this letter.

81. See Chapter 6.

82. Saltonstall, "Present State of New-England," 46. This phrase echoes two passages from the Old Testament. In Judges 2:3, an angel declares to the Israelites that, because of their disobedience, the Caananites will be "as thorns in your sides" rather than being driven out of the land. In the second, from 1 Samuel 25:16, Israelite soldiers protect the servants of Nabal, acting as "a wall unto" them. Both illustrate the way Puritans saw their experience through a providential lens. To them, the Indians were Caananites. Because of Puritan disobedience, God had made the Indians a "thorn in [their] sides." Puritans believed that, unlike the Israelites, they should convert and befriend, rather than destroy, the natives of the land. Had they done so, the Indians could have been "a wall unto" them. Ironically, in the aftermath of the Massacre of 1622, Virginia's Governor Wyatt used the same scripture not to condemn the sinful English, but to justify waging a war of extermination against the Indians, declaring, "It is infinitely better to have no heathen among us, who at best were but as thornes in our sides, then to be at peace and league with them" (cited in Alden T. Vaughan, *American Genesis*, 163).

Chapter 6. A Perilous Middle Ground

1. Daniel Gookin, *Historical Account*, 513–14.

2. On the life of Daniel Hoar, see Gary Boyd Roberts, ed., *English Origins of New England Families*, 2nd ser., 2:365, 358; William Richard Cutter, *New England Families*, 4:1732. On Daniel Goble, see James Savage, *Genealogical Dictionary*, 2:263–64; Goble

Papers, Concord Public Library Special Collections, Concord, Mass.; Thomas Bellows Wyman, *Genealogies and Estates of Charlestown*, 1:411; Middlesex County Probate Records, #9234, #9235, JA. On Nathaniel Wilder, see Henry S. Nourse, *Early Records of Lancaster*, 299, 318–19, 321; Wyman, *Genealogies and Estates of Charlestown*, 2:1030.

3. MAC, 30:214a, Report of Thomas Danforth, Sept. 4, 1676; John Noble, ed., *Records of the Court of Assistants*, 1:71–72; *MCR*, 5:117.

4. Witnesses included Thomas and John Wilder, the junior and senior Thomas Gobles, and Concord resident Daniel Deane. William Keene, Stephen Mattock, Philip Negro and two other illegible names are also listed. John Hoar is mentioned in testimony, and may have served as a witness as well (MAC, 30:210a, Aug. 10–11, 1676; Lemuel Shattuck, *History of the Town of Concord*, 369).

5. Gookin, *Historical Account*, 514.

6. This petition is reprinted in Roberts, *English Origins of New England Families*, 2d ser., 2:363.

7. MAC, 30:214a, Report of Thomas Danforth, Sept. 4, 1676.

8. MAC, 30:214a, Report of Thomas Danforth, Sept. 4, 1676; Noble, *Records of the Court of Assistants*, 1:71–72; *MCR*, 5:117.

9. MAC, 30:221a, Deposition of John Woodcock, Sept. 12, 1676.

10. Nathaniel Wilder and Daniel Hoar appealed their death sentence and were pardoned on Oct. 12, 1676 (*MCR*, 5:117). Nathaniel returned to Sudbury afterwards, where he and his wife had four more children before returning to Lancaster in 1681. He was killed while commanding his garrison during an Indian attack on July 31, 1704 (Nourse, *Early Records of Lancaster*, 324–25, 329; Middlesex County Probate Records, #24881, JA; Henry S. Nourse, *Birth, Marriage, and Death Register of Lancaster*, 17). Daniel Hoar appealed his fine on October 13, the day following his pardon, but was denied. Daniel's crime seems to have cast a very small shadow: From Daniel and Mary Stratton Hoar's eleven children came a succession of Hoar lawyers and statesmen that, by the nineteenth century, would earn them the title of Concord's "royal family" (Suffolk Files, #1506, vol. 17, JA; Roberts, *English Origins of New England Families*, 2d ser., 2:363–65; Ruth R. Wheeler, *Concord: Climate for Freedom*, 181).

11. On the Christian Indians, see Richard Cogley, *John Eliot's Mission*; Dane Morrison, *A Praying People*; and Kristina Bross, *Dry Bones*.

12. Additional mention of Christian Indians' "subject" status appears in Gookin, *Historical Account*, 459.

13. From the settlement of the Massachusetts Bay Colony until the outbreak of war in 1675, Puritans followed a legal policy toward Indians that Yasuhide Kawashima called "clearly distinguishable from that of other English colonies," which practiced "legal imperialism": "Equal application of law was in general the rule rather than the exception. The colonial court, in theory and practice, largely succeeded in treating the natives fairly." Although Kawashima traces a post-King Philip's War shift to "special" minority treatment of Indians, rarely equal to English legal status, he states that until 1676 procedural rights were identical for English and Indians, Indian testimony was generally as valid as English, and punishment for crimes was nearly identical for both races. While policy and law were consistently just, English prejudice and ignorance of Indian beliefs sometimes interfered with the application of law (*Puritan Justice and the Indian*, 236–37, 9, 150).

14. See, for instance, Pomham's submission in *JJW*, 458–61.

15. John Easton, "A Relacion of the Indyan Warre," 9–10.

16. Henry Whitfield, *The Light Appearing*, 131, 139–41; Cogley, *John Eliot's Mission*, 76.

17. Thomas Shepard, *The Clear Sun-shine of the Gospel*, 64–65.

18. *The Day-Breaking*, 19. In his *John Eliot's Mission to the Indians before King Philip's War*, Richard Cogley also notes that the introduction of religious authority allowed converted Indians to pull back from sachems' authority that had become artificially inflated in the presence of English hierarchical models, and to insist on a more consensual approach to governance (55).

19. Ibid., 442.

20. *MCR*, 2:55–56.

21. Massachusetts Council to Major Pynchon, July 10, 1675, Winthrop Family Papers, MHS.

22. Gookin, *An Historical Account*, 444.

23. MAC, 30:171, Examination of "Old Tom," July 8, 1675; MAC, vol. 67:218–19, Deposition of Isaac Johnson, July 10, 1675. It is unclear whether Tom was actually executed or not.

24. MHS photostats, July 19, 1675.

25. Gookin, *Historical Account*.

26. *MCR*, 5:45. One of the first laws enacted in the colony banned the sale of firearms to Indians, obviously as a measure of self-protection. This restriction was dropped and reenacted many times during the century. Christian Indians, as subjects of the colony, legally bore arms before the crisis of the war (*MCR*, 1:76, Sept. 28, 1630; Kawashima, *Puritan Justice and the Indian*, 81).

27. George M. Bodge, *Soldiers in King Philip's War*, 394–95.

28. *MCR*, 2:55–56.

29. Gookin, *An Historical Account*, 450.

30. Ibid.

31. Ibid., 468. No author is given for this paper, but Gookin's extensive description of it, as well as his habit of referring to himself in the third person, makes it likely to have been his own.

32. Ibid., 471–72. Plymouth, too, exiled some of its friendly Indians during the war, sending them to Clark's Island (Douglas Edward Leach, *Flintlock and Tomahawk*, 161).

33. *MCR*, 5:64.

34. Gookin, *Historical Account*, 481; Bodge, *Soldiers in King Philip's War*, 398. This same scout later proved his loyalty by giving Gookin warning of the Lancaster attack (Gookin, *Historical Account*, 490).

35. Gookin, *Historical Account*, 507.

36. Bodge, *Soldiers in King Philip's War*, 76; Gookin, *Historical Account*, 496–97.

37. Bodge, *Soldiers in King Philip's War*, 67.

38. Gookin, *Historical Account*, 475.

39. In his *Genealogical Dictionary*, James Savage said that Mosely "showed gallant spirit, [and] had great success in destroying the Indian," though "by some [he] was thought to take too great delight in that exercise" (3:179).

40. Gookin, *Historical Account*, 501.

41. Ibid., 509, 512, 533.

42. *MCR*, 5:86–87.

43. Leach, *Flintlock and Tomahawk*, 154–75.

44. The life of Daniel Goble's wife Hannah illustrates the reorganization of homes and families brought on by the Indian wars. Hannah remarried in 1677. Her second husband was Ephraim Roper, a refugee from Lancaster. Ephraim was the only person to escape capture or death in the Indian attack on the Rowlandson garrison in February 1676. His first wife Priscilla died in that attack. Hannah and Ephraim moved to Lancaster when it was resettled and added several children to

their combined family. During the Indian attacks of King William's War in 1697, both Hannah and Ephraim were killed, along with their fourteen-year-old daughter Elizabeth. Their twelve-year-old son, Ephraim, was captured in that attack but later returned to Lancaster. The administration of Ephraim Roper's estate was assigned to his fellow townsman, Nathaniel Wilder, Daniel Goble's companion in crime twenty-one years before (Nourse, *Early Records of Lancaster*, 135–36, 282, 321).

45. MAC, 113:193, transcribed in Charles H. Walcott, *Concord in the Colonial Period*, 118.

46. Huntington Library Manuscripts, item #8389, photostat, Concord Public Library Special Collections, Concord, Mass.; Nourse, *Early Records of Lancaster*, 111.

47. Suffolk Files Calendar Index, items 24370, 26055, JA; Middlesex County Court, Folio Collection, 1672, folio 59, group 3; 1672, folio 62, group 7; 1668, folio 45, group 6; 1668, folio 48, group 2; 1670, folio 53, group 1, JA; *MCR*, 4:291 (see also 4:301, 387); Noble, *Records of the Court of Assistants*, 3:195; petition reprinted in Roberts, *English Origins of New England Families*, 2d ser., 2:363. John Hoar's fractiousness apparently earned him the enmity of his neighbors. He was forced to drop one land dispute against Concord resident Edward Wright because other townspeople refused to testify on his behalf (Middlesex County Court, Folio Collection, 1672, folio 59, group 3, JA).

48. Gookin, *Historical Account*, 529.

49. Ibid.

50. Ibid., 484, 530.

51. Ibid., 531.

52. Mosely's reputation for harshness against Indians traveled as far as Albany. There, a rumor that Mosely was in the town started a panic among Wampanoags in winter refuge (Donna Merwick, "Becoming English").

53. Gookin, *Historical Account*, 495–97.

54. Bodge, *Soldiers in King Philip's War*, 62–63.

55. Gookin, *Historical Account*, 530.

56. Mary Rowlandson, *The Sovereignty and Goodness of God*, 71.

57. Gookin, *Historical Account*, 456–57.

58. Ibid., 458.

59. *MCR*, 5:57.

60. Gookin, *Historical Account*, 471–72.

61. *MCR*, 5:57.

62. Gookin, *Historical Account*, 471.

63. Ibid., 475.

64. Ibid., 482.

65. Ibid., 483.

66. Ibid., 477. For additional sources on this incident, see Leach, *Flintlock and Tomahawk*, 258, note 56.

67. Gookin, *Historical Account*, 476.

68. Ibid., 474, 449.

69. Daniel Gookin to Richard Smith, Nov. 1675 [indexed as 1676], MHS photostats. See also Magistrates and Deputies to Richard Smith, Nov. 1675, MHS photostats.

70. See Noble, *Records of the Court of Assistants*, 1:52–53, 86, 88, and *MCR*, 5:57; and Gookin, *Historical Account*, 497–500.

71. See, for example, Massachusetts colony treasurer John Hull's account of nearly 200 Indian slaves sold from August to September, 1676 ("Account of Captives sold by Mass. Colony," in Bodge, *Soldiers in King Philip's War*, 479–80).

72. "James Quanapaug's [Quannapohit] information," Jan. 24, 1675, *MHSC*, 1st ser., 6:205.

73. MAC, 30:193a, Copies of placard threatening Gookin and Danforth, Feb. 28, 1675/76; Saltonstall, "The Present State of New-England," 40.

74. Daniel Goble was paid under the service of Capt. Nicholas Manning in February 1676, and his family was later assigned wages on August 24, 1676, while he sat in a jail cell. Stephen served under Concord's own Capt. Thomas Wheeler in February 1676, and, like Daniel, was assigned wages during his imprisonment (Bodge, *Soldiers in King Philip's War*, 114, 277, 373). In late April, 1676, the General Court released soldiers from the frontier towns of Medfield, Sudbury, Concord, Chelmsford, Andover, Haverhill, and Exeter, and ordered them to return home to defend their towns (*MCR*, 5: 79–80). From then on, local soldiers patrolled their town borders, watching for Indians, listening for sounds of attack. Nathaniel Wilder may have regularly gone on these scouting expeditions, often enough, at least, to become familiar with Daniel and Stephen Goble and Daniel Hoar of Concord. All four rode out with the troops on August 7, 1676, a day when they found what they were looking for.

75. Goble Papers, Concord Public Library, Concord, Mass.

76. Gookin, *Historical Account*, 503.

77. See *MCR*, 5:72.

78. James Axtell, ed., "Vengeful Women of Marblehead," 652.

79. Gookin, *Historical Account*, 494.

80. See footnote 2 above.

81. Saltonstall, "The Present State of New England," 40–41.

82. Gookin, *Historical Account*, 494. This mob gathered after news came of the attack on Medfield. The Council prevented action against the Deer Islanders by calling in several plotters and warning them "at their peril" to desist.

83. Bodge, *Soldiers in King Philip's War*, 59. Samuel Mosely was born in Braintree on June 14, 1641, making him thirty-five at the outbreak of Philip's War. For the others mentioned in this section who committed anti-Indian violence, I have been unable to find birth records. Given the fact that adults arriving in the first wave of New England migration would be in their sixties or older by 1676, the likelihood that rank and file military men would be of the second or later generations is high.

84. See Gookin, *Historical Account*, 501, 506–7, 524–25; Roberts, *English Origins of New England Families*, 2d ser., 2:52; Bodge, *Soldiers in King Philip's War*, 87, 47–48.

85. Cited in Bernard Bailyn, *Education in the Forming of American Society*, 79.

86. Increase Mather, *Brief History*, 86.

87. *MCR*, 5:59.

88. Joseph Eliot to Increase Mather, July 17, 1678, *MHSC*, 4th ser., 8:374.

89. *MHSC*, 5th ser., 8:69, cited in David Cressy, *Coming Over*, 209.

90. Increase Mather's Diary, June 2, 1666, cited in Cressy, *Coming Over*, 210; Suffolk County Wills, 62, cited in Cressy, *Coming Over*, 212.

91. Suffolk Files, #1506, vol. 17, JA.

92. The diminishing supply of land in New England is discussed in Kenneth Lockridge, "Land, Population and the Evolution of New England Society," and Linda Auwers Bissel, "From One Generation to Another."

93. Gookin, *Historical Account*, 455; Bodge, *Soldiers in King Philip's War*, 209.

94. Noble, *Records of the Court of Assistants*, 1:53; see also Gookin, *Historical Account*, 455–60 for his account of the trial.

95. Saltonstall, "The Present State of New England," 40–41.

96. Ibid.

97. Ibid., 41.

98. Gookin, *Historical Account*, 497–500.

99. Ibid., 475.

100. Poet Benjamin Tompson's "New England's Crisis" gives clear evidence of the wartime view of Indians among the populace, attitudes which must have underlain both accusations and jury findings: "Let crawl these fiends with brands and fired poles, / Paint here the house & there the barn on fire, / With holocausts ascending in a spire. / Here granaries, yonder the Churches smoke / Which vengeance on the actors doth invoke" (24).

101. Gookin, *Historical Account*, 483.

102. Noble, *Records of the Court of Assistants*, 1:57.

103. Gookin, *Historical Account*, 475.

104. Axtell, "The Vengeful Women of Marblehead," 652.

105. Saltonstall, "The Present State of New England," 40.

106. Gookin, *Historical Account*, 481.

107. MAC, 30:193a, Copies of placard threatening Gookin and Danforth, Feb. 28, 1675/76.

108. Bodge, *Soldiers in King Philip's War*, 71, 100, 264, 277, 374.

109. MAC, 30:192, Deposition of Elizabeth Belcher and others, March 4, 1675/76.

110. Noble, *Records of the Court of Assistants*, 1:60–61.

111. MAC, 30:193b, Warrant for Richard Scott's arrest, March 11, 1675/76.

112. From Rev. John Eliot's Records of the First Church, *NEHGR* 33 (July 1879): 297–98.

113. *MCR*, 5:77; Huntington Library Manuscripts, item #8400, photostat, Concord Public Library, Concord, Mass.; John Eliot recorded: "Election day, the people in their distemper, left out Capt. Gookins, & put him off the Bench" (Eliot's Records of the First Church, *NEHGR* 33 [July 1879]: 298). In the same month, Gookin was nominated by the magistrates as major of the Middlesex militia, to replace Simon Willard, who had died. The deputies rejected the nomination, proposing Hugh Mason instead. The magistrates refused their consent for that change, and, on the vote of the entire General Court, Gookin was confirmed as major (Suffolk Files, #1443, vol. 17, JA).

114. Samuel Sewall, *Diary*, 1:21–22.

115. *MCR*, 5:115; Sewall, *Diary*, 1:21–22.

116. Increase Mather, *Historical Discourse Concerning the Prevalency of Prayer*, in Samuel G. Drake, ed., *Early History of New England*, 257.

117. MAC, 39:455, 455a.

118. Suffolk Files, #1505, vol. 17, JA.

119. *MCR*, 5:117.

120. Jenny Hale Pulsipher, "Our Sages are Sageles."

121. MAC, 30:210, Warrant for Joshua Assatt and others, Aug. 11, 1676.

122. Gookin, *An Historical Account*, 509, 512, 533.

123. For an example of this attitude and its consequences, see Pulsipher, "'Our Sages are Sageles.'"

Chapter 7. Massachusett's Authority Undermined

1. MAC, 68:130.

2. MHS photostats, Jan. 14, 1675.

3. Edmund Browne to the Massachusetts governor and Council, July 3, 1677, MAC, 69:147.

4. Thomas Hutchinson, *Hutchinson Papers*, 2:228.

5. MAC, 68:70. "Mr.," a completely nondistinguishing form of address today, was an honorific in seventeenth-century Massachusetts, indicating that the man so addressed was a person of wealth and/or status.

6. MAC, 68:75a.

7. MAC, 68:86–86a. Not all elite men were able to remain out of the fighting. MAC, 68:81 includes a list of impressed men, with "Mr Eliakim Hutchinson" listed as one, not an officer.

8. *DHSM*, 6:105–6.

9. MAC, 68:81.

10. MAC, 68:248. He begged to be released "so his urgent occasions be not impeded; and friends greatly damnified." The Council's verdict was not recorded.

11. Massachusetts Council to Committee of Militia at Woburn, March 14, 1675/76, MAC, 68:159a. An example of a complaint of partiality in impressment is Stephen Haskett's against his commanding officer George Corwin. Haskett, impressed by Corwin, who thought him both "worthy" and fit to serve, disagreed vigorously. In fact, he charged Corwin with making the impressment for "mercenary ends" to destroy his business, "thinking thereby to raise [himself] out of [Haskett's] Ruins" (MAC, 68:34).

12. MHS photostats, June 24, 1675.

13. MAC, 68:130.

14. *PCR*, 5:182–83.

15. Magistrates acknowledged the existence of "disorderly" soldiers in the ranks, but urged officers to go lightly on them (*CCR*, 2:394–95, 487–88).

16. Resistance to impressment did not, of course, emerge with King Philip's War. Bitter anti-army sentiment, accompanied by long-standing disagreements over how much power the king or Parliament could exert in behalf of the army, had raged for most of the seventeenth century in England, with impressment and billeting of soldiers one of the issues in debate. One pamphleteer argued that both be strictly limited to times of invasion (anonymous author, *The Peaceable Militia*, cited in Lois G. Schwoerer, *"No Standing Armies!"* 55). King Philip's War met that requirement, but that did not deter resistance.

17. MAC, 68:7a. It is interesting that the constable and the Council describe these miscreants with a word traditionally reserved for Indians: "skulking." Several historians have speculated that colonists on the frontier were particularly susceptible to the lure of the Indian way of life and that the wilderness in fact began to transform them into Indians (James Axtell, "Scholastic Philosophy"; John Canup, *Out of the Wilderness*). Contemporary leaders' fear of such consequences is clearly evident in William Hubbard's and Increase Mather's condemnations of the settlers living in "scattering" towns on the frontier (see Chapter 9).

18. MAC, 68:21, 70–71, 82a–86, 92a–94.

19. MAC, 68:64. Originally, the order had imposed a five-pound fine on anyone refusing service. The magistrates reviewing the order differed on whether five pounds was too little or too much and put punishment at the court's discretion.

20. MAC, 68:106.

21. MAC, 68:186, 243.

22. *MCR*, 5:78.

23. *ECR*, 6:132–33.

24. MAC, 68:80.

25. MAC, 68:139b.

26. MAC, 69:159.

27. MAC, 68:71. See also *ECR*, 6:212, in which Henry Green is bound over to answer the complaint of John Smith and Henry Dow for resisting them as they went to his house to impress his son, Jacob Green.

28. MAC, 69:150.

29. See Douglas Edward Leach, *Flintlock and Tomahawk*, 94.

30. MAC, 67:259.

31. MAC, 68:86–86a.

32. Petition of Capt. William Davis, Lt. Thomas Brattle, Cornet Jacob Eliot, of Boston Troop, Feb. 26, 1676, MAC, 68:145a.

33. Many examples of this appear in MAC, vols. 67–69.

34. Then again, three of the four fined had no money to pay their fines. Instead, the constables distrained their marsh lands for payment. Land could not, however, be locked away like pigs and cows. Those distrained may have hoped to continue harvesting the hay on their marsh lands without being caught (MAC, 68:71).

35. For example, John Hoar was fined 50 pounds in May 1666 for contempt of authority. Richard Scott was fined 150 pounds for his abuse of magistrate Daniel Gookin in March 1676 (John Noble, ed., *Records of the Court of Assistants*, 3:195–96; 1:60–61).

36. Some might claim Joshua Tefft as a contrary example. His crime was, however, clearly stated to be treason—joining with the Indians to fight against the English (Nathaniel Saltonstall, "Continuation of the State of New-England," 67). For a detailed account of the Tefft case, see Colin G. Calloway, "Rhode Island Renegade." Deserters were tried and imprisoned, however. MAC, 68:151a, gives an order regarding three deserters, Henry Bartlet, William Marsh, and George (Pike?), who had been ordered to guard provisions to Quabaug but took that opportunity to desert. William Marsh may well be the same man who threatened to break Nathaniel Wilder, Daniel and Stephen Goble, and Daniel Hoar from prison. If it was he, his later offense makes it clear that any punishment he suffered for desertion did not last very long.

37. Laws and Ordinances of war passed by the General Court of Massachusetts, Oct. 26, 1675, in *CSPCS*, 9:299, item 700.

38. *MCR*, 5:90, 104. Other men charged with similar crimes appear in MAC, 68:54 and *MCR*, 5:68–69.

39. Massachusetts magistrates to Charles II, Dec. 19, 1660, in *MCR*, 4:1:450–53.

40. *DHSM*, 6:113.

41. Laws and Ordinances of war passed by the General Court of Massachusetts, subscribed by Benjamin Batten, Oct. 26, 1676, in *CSPCS*, 299, 700.

42. William Hubbard, *History of the Indian Wars*, 1:208.

43. Increase Mather, "Earnest Exhortation," 179–80. See also Richard Bushman, *From Puritan to Yankee*, chapter 4.

44. Mather, "Earnest Exhoration," 189.

45. In one intriguing example, men who were charged with abusive carriage and sentenced to public correction appealed their sentence on the grounds that a parent had been killed while defending the country in the Indian war. Apparently, they wanted to have their cake and eat it too, claiming that their parents' dutiful behavior made up for their own misbehavior (Suffolk Files, #1549, vol. 18, JA).

46. Edward Wharton, *New-England's Present sufferings*, 7; Hubbard, *History of the Indian Wars*, 2:198. Richard Melvoin discusses this Indian strategy in his *New England Outpost*.

47. *MCR*, 5:65.

48. The General Court issued additional orders to prevent the desertion of frontier towns on Dec. 9, 1675 (*DHSM*, 6:103–4), Feb. 21, 1676 (*MCR*, 5:73), March 22, 1676 (MAC, 68:139a), and May 3, 1676 (*MCR*, 5:79–81).

49. See Suffolk Files, #1445, vol. 17, JA. Acknowledging the perilous condition of many of the frontier towns, in April 1676 the Massachusetts government advised residents of the weakest towns to remove themselves to safer quarters (Leach, *Flintlock and Tomahawk*, 168).

50. MAC, 68:168.

51. Leach, *Flintlock and Tomahawk*, 184; see *MCR*, 5:54.

52. MAC, 68:4.

53. Leach, *Flintlock and Tomahawk*, 88. This attack took place on Sept. 18, 1675.

54. Samuel A. Green, M.D., *Groton During the Indian Wars*, 21.

55. Like the coastal towns of Maine, Weymouth was built in a "scattering" manner difficult to defend against Indian attacks and requiring numerous garrisons.

56. William Torrey to the General Court, April 28, 1676, MAC, 68:226.

57. Nathaniel Saltonstall, "New and Further Narrative," 94. An Indian woman reported a similar threat during the first Dutch war, telling her English neighbors that Indians and their Dutch allies would attack Wethersfield on election day, "the strength of the English colonies being gathered from the several towns" (*PCR*, 10:11).

58. MAC, 68:213b.

59. Mary Rowlandson, *The Sovereignty and Goodness of God*, 104, 97–98.

60. Increase Mather, *Brief History*, 143.

61. Middlesex County Court Records, Pulsifer transcript, 3:143, 219, JA.

62. Punishment of seditious speech was not enough to quash grumblings in the area. Captain Waite of nearby Reading was heard objecting to the colony's irregular sending of orders. Waite complained that the Council's actions obstructed "the Army in the vigorous [pursuit] of the enemy," a statement the Council considered defamation and charged accordingly (Middlesex County Court, Folio Collection, Warrant to Lt. Danforth of Billerica to summon Capt. Waite to appear before the governor or some of the magistrates, June 16, 1676, folio 72, group 4, JA).

63. R. Wharton to John Winsley, Feb. 10, 1675/76, *CSPCS*, 9:350–51, item 816.

64. Middlesex County Court, Folio Collection, Edmund Browne to Worthy Sirs, 1677, folio 78, JA.

65. John Cotton to Thomas Walley, April 16, 1676, Cotton Family Papers, MHS.

66. MHS photostats, June 7–8, 1676. A groat was the equivalent of four pence, or one-third of a shilling. Compare this with the one shilling and six pence per day wage set for impressed laborers by the General Court in 1675 (*MCR*, 5:65).

67. Joshua Micah Marshall, "Indian Laborers," 199.

68. Petition of Rachel Clinton, approximately 1665, in John Demos, *Entertaining Satan*, 30. Writing of English hostility toward Daniel Gookin, Louise A. Breen argues that in late seventeenth-century Massachusetts, "the coveted status of landed 'independency,' connoting full 'manhood,' increasingly eluded the best efforts of many English colonists. Gookin, by protecting Indian claims to land, appeared to be extending hopes of economic 'competency' to 'savages' while depriving his own people of the same benefit" ("Praying with the enemy," 105).

69. MAC, 68:174, reprinted in Green, *Groton During the Indian Wars*, 41.

70. Hugh Mason, Richard Lowden, Jonathan Danforth, committee from Middlesex appointed by the Council to report on the "best means of the preservation of our outtowns remote houses and farms, for their planting and security from the common enemy," March 28, 1676, Shattuck manuscripts, New England Historical and Genealogical Society, Boston, Mass., reprinted in Green, *Groton During the Indian Wars*, 39.

71. Further evidence of division between center and periphery appears in disagreements between the deputies and magistrates over General Court orders for increased taxes to support the war effort. On several occasions, the deputies reduced the number of rates proposed by the magistrates. On at least one occasion, the deputies refused to concur with the magistrates' vote that frontier towns be taxed (Suffolk Files, #1528, vol. 18, JA; MAC, 69:8a). The deputies represented the

towns, including frontier towns. Most of the magistrates lived in, or spent much of their time in, central towns such as Boston, Cambridge, and Charlestown.

72. Opinions of officers expressed in a council at Quabaug, April 27, 1676, MAC, 68:235.

73. Hubbard, *History of the Indian War,* 1:228–34.

74. Ibid., 1:122.

75. Ibid., 1:234 (note by Samuel Drake).

76. The increasing turn to individualism, the "independent yeoman farmer," is traced in such books as Richard Bushman's *From Puritan to Yankee,* and Richard P. Gildrie's *The Profane, the Civil, & the Godly.*

77. *MCR,* 5:71.

78. *CCR,* 2:431.

79. R. Wharton to John Winsley, Feb. 10, 1675/76, *CSPCS,* 9:350–51, item 816.

Chapter 8. A Crisis of Spirit

1. Thomas Hutchinson, *History of the Colony,* 1:262.

2. John Bishop to Increase Mather, July 8, 1676, *MHSC,* 4th ser., 8:299.

3. William Hubbard, *History of the Indian Wars,* 1:56.

4. Reprinted in Nathaniel Saltonstall, "Continuation of the State of New-England," 62–64.

5. John Bishop to Increase Mather, July 8, 1676, *MHSC,* 4th ser., 8:299.

6. Increase Mather, *Brief History,* 89. Mather used several other arguments to support the justice of the war in his *Brief History,* including the fact that the "young Indians were earnest for a War" (149), Philip's violation of the 1671 Treaty of Taunton (151), and Plymouth's careful avoidance of offence: "The Governors of that Colony have been as careful to prevent injuries to him as unto any others; yea, they kept his Land not from him but for him" (152). Arguments over the justifiability of the war extended beyond the bounds of Massachusetts and Plymouth. Rhode Islander William Harris acknowledged that some claimed the war was an "unJust war," but he then went on to argue otherwise (Douglas Edward Leach, ed., *Rhode Islander Reports,* 18–22).

7. John Pynchon to Joseph Pynchon, Oct. 20, 1675, in *Pynchon Papers,* ed. Carl Bridenbaugh, 1:166.

8. Order of Plymouth Council, Nathaniel Morton, Sec., June 22, 1675 [transcript], Cotton Family Papers, MHS.

9. Thomas Walley to John Cotton, July 25, 1675 [transcript], Cotton Family Papers, MHS.

10. *MCR,* 5:59. See also Mather, *Brief History,* 105. In striking contrast to Massachusetts, Connecticut suspended penalties against Quakers during the war, "provided they do not gather into assemblies in this Colony nor make any disturbance" (*CCR,* 2:264).

11. Richard P. Gildrie, *The Profane, the Civil, & the Godly.*

12. Samuel Sewall, *Diary,* Dec. 18, 1676, 1:30.

13. See Carla Gardina Pestana, *Quakers and Baptists in Colonial Massachusetts,* 131–33. William McLaughlin also mentions Puritan laxity toward Baptists in his *Soul Liberty,* 180.

14. Increase Mather, quoted in Gildrie, *The Profane, the Civil, & the Godly,* 195.

15. Joshua Scottow, *Narrative of the Planting of the Massachusets Colony,* 43–45.

16. For an insightful discussion of this reformation process, see Gildrie, *The Profane, the Civil, & the Godly,* chapter 1.

17. Josiah Winslow to Capt. Cudworth, July 6, 1675, Winslow Family II Papers, MHS.

18. Thomas Walley to John Cotton, ND [transcript], Cotton Family Papers, MHS.

19. N Phepps[?] to Honored Sir [Josiah Winslow?], Aug. 11, 1675, Winslow Family II Papers, MHS.

20. William Leete to John Winthrop, Jr., Jan. 5, 1675, *MHSC*, 4th ser., 7:582. "Achan" was an Israelite who, against the direction of Joshua, took and tried to hide spoils from a war. As a result of his disobedience, God punished all the Israelites, sending them defeat in their next battle. Joshua 22:20 summarizes the story and the Puritans' sense that all would suffer for individual sin: "Did not Achan the son of Zerah commit a trespass in the accursed thing, and wrath fell on all the congregation of Israel?" (King James version).

21. Capt. Joshua Scottow to Gov. Leverett, Nov. 6, 1675, *DHSM*, 6:101.

22. Mather, *Brief History*, 89.

23. Ibid., 143.

24. Leach, *A Rhode Islander Reports*, 34.

25. Mary Rowlandson, *The Sovereignty and Goodness of God*, 105.

26. Massachusetts Council declaration, Aug. 30, 1675, reprinted in Nathaniel Saltonstall, "Present State of New-England," 33.

27. Thomas Walley to John Cotton, July 25, 1675 [transcript], Cotton Family Papers, MHS. Walley replied that he thought it more likely that God was provoked by Plymouth leaders' allowing Quaker worship within their colony.

28. MAC, 241:284–86, Edward Perry, "Sermon warning," April 4, 1676.

29. Pestana, *Quakers and Baptists*, 94 (note 41), 151.

30. Sewall, *Diary*, July 8, 1677, 1:43.

31. Perry, "Sermon Warning"; "Testimony from us in scorne called Quakers but are the children of ye light," Aug. 24, 1675, Winthrop Papers, Reel 11, MHS; *MCR*, 5:153; *ECR*, 6:191–92; Edward Wharton, *New-England's Present sufferings*, 7; Sewall, *Diary*, July 15, 1676, 1:15.

32. Mather, *Brief History*, 90.

33. *MCR*, 5:134.

34. *MCR*, 4, part 1, 345, 348.

35. Nathaniel Saltonstall reported that "Several Men, some whereof are Quakers, will not go out on Command, and for their Disobedience thereunto, are forced to run the Gauntlet" ("Present State of New-England," 44). Meredith Baldwin Weddle notes that some Quakers participated to a degree in the war and that this did not jeopardize their church membership. She cites this as an example of the latitude given to personal interpretation of the obligation to the peace testimony at this point in the development of the Quaker religion, a time when individual salvation, rather than influence on the world, was paramount ("Conscience or Compromise"). William Harris claimed that Baptists, too, refused to bear arms (*CSPCS*, 9:221, item 543). In another letter, however, he allowed that Baptist Captain William Turner and his company of volunteers served well in the war (Leach, *Rhode Islander Reports*, 76–80).

36. John Easton, "Relacion of the Indyan Warre," 13; Nathaniel Saltonstall, "New and Further Narrative," 79.

37. "Testimony from us in scorne called Quakers."

38. Perry, "Sermon warning."

39. Wharton, *New-England's Present Sufferings*, 1, postscript, 4–5, 6–7.

40. Ibid., 5.

41. *CSPCS*, 9:377, item 889.

42. Benjamin Batten to Sir Thomas Allin, July 6, 1675, reprinted in Douglas E. Leach, "Benjamin Batten and the London Gazette Report on King Philip's War."

43. Richard Hutchinson, "Warr in New-England Visibly Ended"; Wharton, *New-England's Present Sufferings*; Easton, "A Relacion of the Indyan Warre"; Perry, "Sermon warning"; "Testimony from us in scorne called Quakers"; Peter Folger, "Looking Glass for the Times"; George Joy, "Innocency's Complaint." While *Early Massachusetts Broadsides* lists Joy's narrative as being printed in 1677 in Boston, it was probably printed later in England. The typeface is more elaborate than other contemporary prints in Massachusetts. More significantly, the content, highly critical of the Massachusetts government, would almost certainly have prevented the document's being printed in either of the colony's two licensed presses in 1677. On John Easton's account being sent to Governor Andros, see Jill Lepore, *Name of War*, 267, note 3.

44. *ECR*, 6:101.

45. *MCR*, 5:80.

46. William Hubbard, "Happiness of a People"; John Davenport, "Sermon Preach'd at the Election of the Governour," 1–6.

47. *MCR*, 5:67. James Savage notes that after a vote of the church in April 1676, Nicholet was dismissed and returned to London (*Genealogical Dictionary*, 3:278).

48. *ECR*, 6:267.

49. "News from New-England," 16; Hubbard, *History of the Indian Wars*, 1:71.

50. Saltonstall, "New and Further Narrative," 86. See Jill Lepore's discussion of this incident in *Name of War*, 105. Edward Gray also discusses it in his *New World Babel*, 79–80.

51. Mather, *Brief History*, 126.

52. Easton, "Relacion of the Indyan Warre," 10.

53. Thomas Wheeler, "A thankefull remembrance of Gods mercy," 574.

54. Hubbard, *History of the Indian Wars*, 1:198; see also Mather, *Brief History*, 113.

55. Emphasis added. "Farther Brief and True Narration," 4; see also "True Account," 2.

56. Mather, *Brief History*, 109.

57. To Honored Sir, July 18, 1675, Winslow Family II Papers, MHS.

58. Leach, *Rhode Islander Reports*, 18.

59. Roger Williams to Robert Williams, April 1, 1676 [disputed, see Chapter 4, note 41], in Roger Williams, *Correspondence*, 2:720.

60. Hubbard, *History of the Indian Wars*, 2:203. Karen Kupperman discusses the importance of names in New England Indian cultures, noting that both Squanto and Hobbamock, Indian men who assisted the English at Plymouth, shared the names of powerful Indian dieties, which they may have adopted "as they took up English association to indicate that they were entering a liminal state with all the power and danger that that entailed" (*Indians and English*, 185). Squando may have done the same thing.

61. William Simmons, *Spirit of the New England Tribes*, 51–52.

62. See Leach, "Benjamin Batten"; James D. Drake, *King Philip's War*, 91.

63. Berkeley to Thomas Ludwell, Feb. 16, 1676, in Wilcomb E. Washburn, "Governor Berkeley and King Philip's War."

64. Berkeley to Thomas Ludwell, April 1, 1676, in Washburn, "Governor Berkeley and King Philip's War."

65. Berkeley to Sec. Henry Coventry, in Washburn, "Governor Berkeley and King Philip's War."

66. John Burk, *History of Virginia*, vol. 2, Appendix, L, "Series of documents relating to mission to procure a more perfect charter (1674–76)." This document is

"Notes, explanatory of some of the heads annexed to the petition of the Virginean agents, referred to mr. attorney and solicitor, with somewhat of answer to some things objected," written after Nov. 27, 1675.

67. Several of these sources were quite critical of Massachusetts, undoubtedly helping to stoke the fires burning against the colony. Two accounts of the war published in England were written by Quakers, Richard Hutchinson and Edward Wharton. Governor Berkeley of Virginia sent more information about New England's war than did Massachusetts's Governor Leverett, much of it critical of Massachusetts (Washburn, "Governor Berkeley and King Philip's War").

68. Hutchinson, *History of the Colony*, 1:262.

69. Easton, "Relacion of the Indyan Warre," 17. Massachusetts minister John Eliot seems to confirm this belief in a letter to Governor Winthrop, July 24, 1675, in which he writes "one effect of this trouble may be to humble the English, to do the Indians justice, & no wrong about their lands" (*MHSC*, 5th ser., 1:424).

70. Samuel Nowell to Jonathan Bull of Hartford, Sept. 25, 1676, *MHSC*, 4th ser., 8:572.

71. John Cotton to Thomas Walley, April 17, 1676 [transcript], Cotton Family Papers, MHS.

72. See MHS photostats, Jan. 19–29, 1674.

73. Samuel Symonds, by order of the Council, to Sec. Sir Joseph Williamson, April 5, 1676, *DHSM*, 6:113.

74. King Charles II to the governor and magistrates "of our town of Boston in New England," March 10, 1676, *CSPCS*, 9:358, item 838.

75. Aid was, however, sent through church channels. See Jane Hook to Increase Mather, Aug. 8, 1677, *MHSC*, 4th ser., 8:261. See also MAC, 69:180, Dec. 13, 1677. Ironically, during the same time period, the king sent two ships with troops in response to Governor Berkeley's call for assistance against Bacon's Rebellion in Virginia. Unlike Massachusetts's rulers, Berkeley did not narrowly prescribe the kinds of assistance that would be acceptable to him. He welcomed the king's troops. Berkeley's fate is evidence that Massachusetts's fears of the consequences of direct military assistance were well founded. Soon after the troops—accompanied by royal commissioners—arrived and quelled the rebellion, Berkeley was relieved of office and shipped to London to answer the charges raised by many of those who had fomented the crisis. Berkeley died while awaiting trial. For detailed accounts of this contemporary colonial crisis, see Stephen Saunders Webb, *1676*, and Wilcomb Washburn, *Governor and the Rebel.*

76. *CSPCS*, 9:455, item 1037; Thomas Hutchinson, *Hutchinson Papers*, 2:241.

77. That old issues were still unsettled is evidenced by Randolph's resurrection of the charge of Massachusetts's aiding and abetting men implicated in the murder of Charles I (*CSPCS*, 9:463, item 1067).

78. Given the Committee on Plantation's directive that men "of great sobriety and discretion" be selected as commissioners to the colonies, it is ironic that the king selected Edward Randolph as his agent (*CSPCS*, 7:244, item 598). Like the royal commissioners a decade before him, Randolph soon made it abundantly clear that he had an axe to grind (*CSPCS*, 9:224, item 546; 9:455, item 1037).

79. Hutchinson, *Hutchinson Papers*, 2:243. Some colonists indulged in wishful thinking. Royal distractions had kept the king from pursuing his course against them before. Now, they told Randolph, there were reports that the duke of York had broken with the king and aligned himself with the rebellious City of London and that the kingdom was in disarray. Randolph quickly squelched the rumor (*CSPCS*, 9:455, item 1037).

80. *CSPCS*, 9:455, item 1037; Edward Randolph to Sec. Coventry, June 17, 1676, *CSPCS*, 9:407, item 953.

81. *CSPCS*, 9:494, item 1138, Nov. 17, 1676.

82. Edward Randolph's report to King Charles II, Sept. 20, 1676, Hutchinson, *Hutchinson Papers*, 2:245.

83. Ibid., 2:248.

84. Ibid., 2:243, 248.

85. Edward Randolph to Sec. Coventry, June 17, 1676, *CSPCS*, 9:409, item 953.

86. Part of the royal government's justification for sending an agent to demand that Massachusetts respond to complaints was the fact that the colony was ostensibly under the king's protection. The king promised to defend the colony from attacks by hostile powers. It was only right that in return for this protection Massachusetts be under the same obligations as other English subjects. Ironically, however, the king did not defend New England in King Philip's War. In spite of receiving regular updates on the status of the war, the king sent neither troops, materiel, nor money to assist his colonies (*CSPCS*, 9:222–24, item 545).

87. Michael G. Hall, *Last American Puritan*, 188. See also William D. Williamson, *History of the State of Maine*, 560.

88. *CSPCS*, 9:308, item 723.

89. See, for instance, *CSPCS*, 9:288, item 681. In these minutes of the Committee of Trade and Plantations, the minutes of past meetings were read in which the committee had discussed addressing Mason's and Gorges's claims to lands in New England. The committee decided to put further discussion of the issue off until "a time of more leisure."

90. Hutchinson, *Hutchinson Papers*, 2:235–36. On the claim that most inhabitants desired a royal governor, Hutchinson said, "Not one man in a hundred throughout the governments then desired it."

91. Hutchinson, *Hutchinson Papers*, 2:219, 238. Many negative reports on Massachusetts claimed that the "better sort" were not church members. See *CSPCS*, 9:306, item 721.

92. Edward Randolph to Sec. Coventry, June 17, 1676, in *CSPCS*, 9:408, item 953.

93. Hutchinson, *Hutchinson Papers*, 2:247. I have found no evidence that any of the signers suffered any lasting tangible consequences.

94. *CSPCS*, 9:307–8, item 721; Hutchinson, *Hutchinson Papers*, 2:226.

95. Hutchinson, *Hutchinson Papers*, 2:227.

96. *MCR*, 5:99–100.

97. One of the boys was Joseph, son of Annawekin (deceased), assigned to Captain Thomas Prentice: "This boy was after taken from Capt. Prentice and sent wth mr Stoughton for England" ("Indian Children Put to Service," 272). The chosen boys were none too eager for their mission. Daniel Gookin warned their caretaker to keep close watch on them, "[lest they] may slip away being [possibly] afraid to go for England. But I pray let them not be put in prison for now [they] are clean & free from vermin" (MAC, 30:224a, Oct. 18, 1676).

98. Sewall, *Diary*, 1:30.

99. Mather, *Brief History*, 102–3.

100. Kathleen J. Bragdon, *Native People of Southern New England*, 45–47, chapter 5.

101. Hubbard, *History of the Indian Wars*, 1:105.

102. Cited in *Leach, Flintlock and Tomahawk*, 222.

103. James Quanapaug's [Quannapohit] information, Jan. 24, 1675, *MHSC*, 1st ser., 6:205–11.

104. Rowlandson, *Sovereignty and Goodness of God*, 84, 106.

105. MAC, 67:285, Council of Connecticut to Council of Massachusetts, Oct. 7, 1675. The concept of losing heart occurs in several Indian speeches in this period. For instance, when his gun fell into the water as he fled a pursuing Pequot, Canon-

chet said "his heart turned within him, and he became as a rotten stick, void of strength" (George M. Bodge, *Soldiers in King Philip's War*, 383). For another example, see MAC, 30:242, 242a, 1677.

106. "True Account," 5.

107. Roger Williams to John Leverett, Jan. 14, 1675, *MHSC*, 4th ser., 6:307.

108. "News from New-England," 16–17; Saltonstall, "New and Further Narrative," 91–92; Hubbard, *History of the Indian Wars*, 1:182.

109. "True Account," 2.

110. Ibid., 4.

111. Mattamuck et al. to John Leverett et al., in Rowlandson, *Sovereignty and Goodness of God*, 141.

112. Hubbard, *History of the Indian Wars*, 2:131.

113. Ibid., 1:269

114. "True Account," 5.

115. Ibid., 2.

116. Thomas Cobbet, "Narrative of New England's Deliverances."

117. Ibid. The older sachems were not always overruled. James Oliver, an English officer in the Great Swamp Fight, described the "signal mercy" that the Indians did not pursue the exhausted and ill-supplied English troops departing the swamp fort, "which the young men would have done but the Sachems would not consent" (James Oliver letter, Feb. 26, 1675/76 [transcript], Cotton Family Papers, MHS).

118. Saltonstall, "New and Further Narrative," 97–98.

119. On Schagticoke, see Gordon M. Day, *Identity of the Saint Francis Indians*.

120. "True Account," 4–5.

121. The English did not seem to recognize the irony of condemning Indian attacks on, for instance, the Clark garrison in Rhode Island as murder while commending Captain William Turner's attack on slumbering Indians at Turner's Falls as heroic. In both instances, those attacked were exceptionally vulnerable. Most of the men of the Clark garrison had gone to worship services, leaving several women and children behind unguarded. All of the Indians at Turner's Falls were sleeping when Turner attacked. Both attacks cost the lives of women and children, but there is no evidence that the English recognized a parallel between English homes and Indian encampments. In their eyes, women and children traveling with warriors were at war; women and children living within garrisons were at home. Hence one attack could be seen as good strategy, the other as criminal.

122. Bodge, *Soldiers in King Philip's War*, 382–85.

123. Simmons, *Spirit of the New England Tribes*, 52.

124. MAC, 69:41a, Aug. 10, 1676.

125. On July 25, 1676, the English easily captured fifty Indians, plus twelve pounds of powder they claimed had come from Albany two days earlier (Mather, *Brief History*, 134; see also 139, 182–83).

126. Saltonstall, "New and Further Narrative," 97.

127. Edward Rawson to Josiah Winslow, Aug. 20, 1676, Winslow Family II Papers, MHS.

Chapter 9. Massachusetts Fights Alone

1. Daniel Meade and Hannah Meade depositions, Oct. 8, 1677, Collection 77, Autographs of Special Note, Box 1, Collections of Maine Historical Society, Portland, Maine.

2. Suffolk Files, #1642, vol. 19, JA.

3. Meade depositions, Collections of Maine Historical Society. Wompas was committed to prison in Cambridge for his reproachful speeches, threatening the life of Mrs. [Thomas?] Oliver, and trying to sell land—English and Indian—he had no legal right to. He escaped from prison on Oct. 1, 1677, and died not long thereafter (Middlesex County Court Records, Pulsifer transcript, 3:192, JA). The courts were dealing with the tangled aftermath of Wompas's land sales as late as 1681, when a group of Christian Indians petitioned to have Wompas's sales revoked (MAC, 30:260a, Sept. 14, 1681).

4. When he returned to Massachusetts, Wompas bore the king's own letter to Governor John Leverett, informing him that Wompas, "our subject," had taken the oaths of allegiance and supremacy and urging Leverett to see justice done to Wompas in the matter of some disputed lands (*MHSC*, 5th ser., 9:123–40).

5. Most histories of King Philip's War have ignored the conflict in Maine and New Hampshire after 1676. For a contemporary account, see William Hubbard, *History of the Indian Wars*, vol. 2. Modern accounts appear in John O. Noble, Jr., "King Philip's War in Maine"; Russell Bourne, *The Red King's Rebellion*; and Emerson Woods Baker, II, "Trouble to the Eastward." On Indians in Maine, see Kenneth M. Morrison, *Embattled Northeast*.

6. Hubbard, *History of the Indian Wars*, 2:70.

7. Ibid., 2:85.

8. Ibid., 2:56–57.

9. Increase Mather, *Brief History*, 99.

10. *DHSM*, vol. 6; William Willis, *History of Portland*, 211–12.

11. Hubbard, *History of the Indian Wars*, 2:257.

12. Increase Mather, too, noted English provocation of the Indians in Maine, declaring, "It is greatly to be lamented that the heathen should have any ground for such allegations, or that they should be scandalized by men that call themselves Christians" (Mather, *Brief History*, 117).

13. For instance, in *The Name of War*, Jill Lepore argues that the English "utterly failed to consider . . . that the war might not only be an obscure message from a distant but reproachful God but also a loud shout from extremely disgruntled but very nearby neighbors" (119). David Lovejoy takes a similar stance, claiming that John Eliot was the only Englishman who acknowledged any provocation for war (*The Glorious Revolution in America*, 133).

14. Willis, *History of Portland*, 210.

15. *DHSM*, 6:91–93.

16. Hubbard, *History of the Indian Wars*, 2:148–49.

17. *DHSM*, 6:92.

18. Hubbard, *History of the Indian Wars*, 2:152.

19. Mather, *Brief History*, 117.

20. *DHSM*, 6:177–79. Emerson W. Baker notes that by this point in the seventeenth century, many Maine Indians had become dependent on European weapons and powder in their hunting, which led to abandonment of and loss of skill in the making of traditional weapons. Thus, when the English seized Indians' weapons and denied them powder, many Indians lacked any means to obtain food ("Trouble to the Eastward," 193).

21. Hubbard, *History of the Indian Wars*, 2:156.

22. *DHSM*, 6:92.

23. Samuel G. Drake, *History of the Early Discovery*, 299.

24. Hubbard, *History of the Indian Wars*, 2:100, note.

25. Hubbard, *History of the Indian Wars*, 2:99–100. While Hubbard believed the Falmouth attackers were the Kennebec Indians, Gardiner thought they were most

likely "some straggling persons from the Southwards," the war in the south spilling over into Maine (*DHSM*, 6:91–93).

26. Thomas Hutchinson, *Hutchinson Papers*, 2:245–46.

27. *DHSM*, 6:91.

28. Willis, *History of Portland*, 217. Concerning Maine, the Massachusetts Council wrote that in spite of its utmost effort, "by reason of their remote living, one from another & the incommodious situation of their Towns they could not be preserved: but are mostly destroyed, many of the people being slain, and the rest retired to places of better security" (Massachusetts Council to the secretary of state, April 5, 1676, in *DHSM*, 6:111).

29. MAC, 69:128b, June 6, 1677.

30. *DHSM*, 6:93–96.

31. *DHSM*, 6:198.

32. MHS photostats, Oct. 3, 1676.

33. Hubbard, *History of the Indian Wars*, 2:169–70.

34. *DHSM*, 6:98–99, Oct. 21, 1675. See also MAC, 68:28, 1675.

35. Testimony of John Wilson, Aug. 23, 1676, Collection 77, Autographs of Special Note, Box 2, Collections of Maine Historical Society. Wilson claimed that Gardiner and Oliver did "buy & sell & truck with the Indians" and with Frenchmen too, for all he knew.

36. Hubbard, *History of the Indian Wars*, 2:255.

37. *DHSM*, 6:106–8, 122.

38. Willis, *History of Portland*, 222–23, cites Richard Martin complaining that the army from the Bay had devoured all their supplies: "Sir please to give notice to the Council that supply be sent to the army from the Bay for they have eaten us out of bread, and here is little wheat to be gotten and less money to pay for it."

39. Joshua Scottow, Diary.

40. *DHSM*, 6:101.

41. MAC, 68:125b, 1675.

42. A measure of Maine's resistance to Massachusetts's authority is that the names several Maine towns held before Massachusetts renamed them in the 1650s, including Black Point and Blue Point, have persisted to the present day.

43. MHS photostats, Aug. 1, 1671, June 19, 1672; William S. Southgate Collection, Box 1/4, Misc. Papers, Collections of Maine Historical Society.

44. Southgate, *History of Scarborough*, 80.

45. James Savage, *Genealogical Dictionary*, 4:40. *Old Men's Tears* was published "by some of Boston's old Planters" in 1691. It was reprinted several times over the next century. In 1694 Scottow's *Narrative of the Planting* was published.

46. Scottow was finally elected as town commissioner for Scarborough in 1676 but served only one year. In 1679 he served a one-year term as an associate (*MPCR*, 2:330, 346). That Scottow was elected at all shows that there was some support for Massachusetts. Significantly, however, both elections followed the depopulation of King Philip's War, when many of Scottow's chief opponents fled the region or were killed. Arthur and Andrew Alger were killed in an attack on Scarborough in October 1676 (Willis, *History of Portland*, 212).

47. *MPCR*, 2:289.

48. Deposition of John Edgecom, Suffolk Files, #1828:10, reprinted in *Records of the Suffolk County Court*, 2:1110. See also Scottow, Diary; George M. Bodge, *Soldiers in King Philip's War*, 332.

49. Petition against Joshua Scottow by Richard Foxwell, Rol: Allanson, William Sheldon, Giles Barge, Joseph Oliver, John Cocke, and John Tinney, in Bodge, *Soldiers in King Philip's War*, 332.

50. Deposition of Richard Foxwell, Oct. 1676, Suffolk Files, #1828:15, reprinted in *Records of the Suffolk County Court*, 2:1108–9.

51. Deposition of John Jackson, July 1676, in Hubbard, *History of the Indian Wars*, 2:127, note.

52. Southgate, *History of Scarborough*, 103–6.

53. Deposition of Thomas Cousens, Jan. 16, 1679, reprinted in *Records of the Suffolk County Court*, 2:1110.

54. Suffolk Files, #1828:14, reprinted in ibid., 2:1110.

55. Scottow, Diary.

56. *MCR*, 5:102–3.

57. Brian Pendleton and George Munjoy to Honored Friends, July 12, 1676, Collection 77, Autographs of Special Note, Box 2, Collections of Maine Historical Society.

58. Petition of Inhabitants of Scarborough, in Bodge, *Soldiers in King Philip's War*, 335.

59. Additional Favourable Testimony, in ibid., 334–35.

60. Richard Foxwell deposition, Suffolk Files, #1828:15, reprinted in *Records of Suffolk County Court*, 2:1108–09.

61. *DHSM*, 6:115.

62. Scottow, Diary. The fact that this removal occurred in October raises the strong possibility that it came in the aftermath of the Saco Sands disaster. Foxwell, with fewer men, had come to the assistance of the English there. His criticism of Scottow's failure to send speedy aid may have prompted Scottow to revoke his authority.

63. Deposition of John Jackson, July 1676, in Hubbard, *History of the Indian Wars*, 2:127, note; for more depositions in this case, see also 2:126–27, note; *Records of Suffolk County Court*, 2:1108–16; Bodge, *Soldiers in King Philip's War*; Brian Pendleton and George Munjoy letter, July 13, 1676, Collection 77, Autographs of Special Note, Box 2, Collections of Maine Historical Society.

64. That one man was Henry Jocelyn who, remarkably, seems to have organized the two petitions in Scottow's favor. Why he set himself apart from his former allies, Rishworth and Shapleigh, is unclear. He may have developed a friendship with Scottow, who seems to have had no trouble securing the regard of his former neighbors in Boston. He may, on the other hand, have supported Scottow in order to remain in the good graces of the Massachusetts government, which dismissed all charges against Scottow and ordered York County to reimburse Scottow's wartime expenses. Jocelyn's signature appears first on the petition, and, as acting commander of the garrison while Scottow was in Boston to stand trial, he took the depositions of the men signing the testimony as well. See Bodge, *Soldiers in King Philip's War*, 332–35.

65. Jocelyn was one of several men in Maine who had over the years of turnovers in government become adept at judging which way the wind was blowing and either ending up on the winning side or, if the other side succeeded, being abject enough in apologies that they were accepted into the new government. Chameleons were most successful in holding power over the course of the century. Those who ardently and inflexibly maintained their pro- or anti-Massachusetts positions lost power and influence.

66. Richard Waldron to John Leverett, "about 1676," *DHSM*, 6:108.

67. Henry Jocelyn and Joshua Scottow to Gov. John Leverett, Sept. 15, 1676, Collection S-888, Misc. Box 33/21, Collections of Maine Historical Society.

68. Willis, *History of Portland*, 217.

69. Henry Jocelyn and Walter Gendall to Joshua Scottow, Aug. 9, 1676, MHS photostats.

70. Major William Hathorne to Massachusetts governor and General Court, Oct. 2, 1676, *DHSM*, 6:129.

71. Bodge, *Soldiers in King Philip's War*, 307.

72. Hubbard, *History of the Indian Wars*, 2:172–73. The garrison inhabitants would have needed sufficient time to gather their families and go to their boats. Presumably, they would have had to do this out of sight of the Indians. Jocelyn must have met the Indians to parley at a considerable distance from the garrison gates. The discussions with Mogg, who spoke good English, would not have been slowed by the need for interpretation. One wonders if Jocelyn purposely delayed the parley to give the garrison residents time to escape, not knowing the outcome of his discussion with Heigon beforehand. In the end, any such ruse was unnecessary. Both parties got what they wanted.

The final phrase comes from one of several depositions in support of Scottow and echoes his own claims. Deposition of Anthony Row, Suffolk Files, #1828:20, reprinted in *Records of Suffolk County Court*, 2:1111.

73. Bodge, *Soldiers in King Philip's War*, 336–37.

74. Hubbard, *History of the Indian Wars*, 2:173–76.

75. Suffolk Files, #1573:103, vol. 18, JA. It seems unlikely that the Indians would have discussed their plans in English, unless they wished to alarm their captives (certainly a possibility). Gendall later served as an agent to the Indians. It is possible that he spoke some of their language at this point.

76. See also Suffolk Files, #1573, vol. 18, JA, in which soldiers complaining against Gendall said "he was with [the Indians] when they came to . . . summons their garrison."

77. Hubbard, *History of the Indian Wars*, 2:196 notes Heigon's kind treatment of captive Thomas Cobbett.

78. Suffolk Files, #1573, vol. 18, JA. A transcription of this document appears at the end of Horatio Hight, "Mogg Heigon."

79. Brian Pendleton to Governor and Council, Oct. (or later) 1676, *DHSM*, 6:141.

80. Suffolk Files, #1573, vol. 18, JA.

81. Ibid.; Daniel Denison to Massachusetts Council, Dec. 14, 1676, *DHSM*, 6:145–46.

82. For primary accounts of Tefft, see Roger Williams to John Leverett, Jan. 14, 1675, *MHSC*, 4th ser., 6:307–11; and James Oliver letter, Feb. 26, 1675/76, Cotton Family Papers, MHS. See also Colin G. Calloway, "Rhode Island Renegade."

83. Gendall later served as a deputy to the Massachusetts General Court, a justice of the peace, and an Indian agent. For an account of his life, see Charles E. Banks, "Captain Walter Gendall."

84. Daniel Denison to Massachusetts Council, Dec. 14, 1676, *DHSM*, 6:145–46.

85. Deposition of Jno Layton, Jr., Benjamin Turstrum, and Robert Booth, all of Winter Harbor, Nov. 14, 1676, *DHSM*, 6:143.

86. Brian Pendleton to Governor and Council, Oct. (or later) 1676, *DHSM*, 6:141–42.

87. Daniel Denison to Massachusetts Council, Dec. 14, 1676, *DHSM*, 6:145–46.

88. Ibid.; Daniel Meade and Hannah Meade depositions, Oct. 8, 1677, Collection 77, Autographs of Special Note, Box 1, Collections of Maine Historical Society; Report from Silvanus Davis, commander, et al., *DHSM*, 6:164–65.

89. Mather, *Brief History*, 100.

90. Joshua Scottow's diary describes one instance in which English and Indians agreed to meet to discuss peace. Misunderstanding the time of the meeting, the English failed to appear, and the disappointed Indians immediately fell to burning English barns and haystacks in retaliation.

91. Bodge, *Soldiers in King Philip's War*, 303.

92. Deogenes and Madoasquarbet to Massachusetts Governor, *DHSM*, 6:177–79; Hubbard, *History of the Indian Wars*, 2:129–32.

93. MAC, 30:207, Order of the Massachusetts Council to Major Gookin, July 3, 1676.

94. *DHSM*, 6:92–93.

95. Hubbard, *The History of the Indian Wars*, 2:135; see also Francis Card's declaration, Jan. 22, 1676/77, *DHSM*, 6:149–51.

96. William Hubbard, cited in Emerson W. Baker, *The Clarke & Lake Company*, 84, note 56.

97. Testimonies of John Wilson, John Lountedanson, John Haughton, Aug. 23, 1676, Collection 77, Autographs of Special Note, Box 2, Collections of Maine Historical Society. See also Suffolk Files, #1592, vol. 18, JA; MAC, 30:227a, petition of John Horton [Haughton], committed to prison for stealing and conveying away Indians, Nov. 20, 1676; John Noble, ed., *Records of the Court of Assistants*, 1:86–87; *DHSM*, 6:119–20.

98. Hubbard, *History of the Indian Wars*, 2:136.

99. Ibid., 2:155.

100. Meeting of Massachusetts Governor and Council, July 10, 1677, *DHSM*, 6:186–88.

101. Hubbard, *History of the Indian Wars*, 2:137.

102. Brian Pendleton to Governor and Council, Oct. (or later) 1676, *DHSM*, 6:141.

103. John Cotton to Thomas Walley (includes transcription of letter from Mr. Moodey), April 17, 1676 (transcript), Cotton Family Papers, MHS.

104. Hubbard, *History of the Indian Wars*, 2:141–45.

105. Edward Rishworth, George Munjoy, John Tenny, Job Alcocke, and Nathaniel Fryer to the Massachusetts General Court, Sept. 2, 1676, MHS photostats.

106. As usual, the General Court acted with more severity against the Indians than the Council acting alone did.

107. Philip complained of this type of English tactic in his conference with Rhode Island's John Easton: "some being given to drunkenness the English made them drunk and then cheated them in bargains" (John Easton, "Relacion of the Indyan Warre," 11). Deogenes's and Madoasquarbet's complaint against Waldron is similar: "he gave us drink & when we were drunk killed us" (*DHSM*, 6:179).

108. Richard Waldron to Governor Leverett, Sept. 6, 1676, Collection 77, Autographs of Special Note, Box 2, Collections of Maine Historical Society.

109. Bodge, *Soldiers in King Philip's War*, 479–80.

110. *DHSM*, 6:179. In a letter written at the same time, Deogenes and Madoasquarbet explained that, to their people, captivity was the equivalent of death: "we count it killed with us whenever we are bound and thrown in the cellar" (*DHSM*, 6:178).

111. MAC, 30:228a, Nov. 23, 1676. Documents from the Massachusetts Archives Collection indicate that a number of the Indians sold at this time were later redeemed and returned to their homes, some from as far away as Fayal in the Azores (30:226, 228, 228a, 229, 492).

112. Richard Waldron to Governor Leverett, Sept. 6, 1676, and Nicholas Shapleigh and Thomas Daniel to Massachusetts Governor and Council, Collection 77, Autographs of Special Note, Box 2, Collections of Maine Historical Society.

113. *DHSM*, 6:179.

114. John Williams, Deerfield's minister captured in the attack, heard this justification from a French priest in Canada (cited in Evan Haefeli and Kevin Sweeney, "Revisiting *The Redeemed Captive*," 23).

115. Historians have disagreed, not over the degree of French involvement in the war but whether it occurred at all. Richard Slotkin and Kenneth Morrison deny it altogether, attributing reports of seeing Frenchmen among the Indians to English panic under duress. Morrison further supports his contention by arguing that French Governor Frontenac gave orders against any French assistance to the Indians; therefore, it could not have happened ("Bias of Colonial Law"). The logical fallacy of such a claim is clearly evident, something Massachusetts tried to point out to Governor Andros when he objected to a similar charge. Douglas Leach and Emerson W. Baker both argue that the French were involved in the war, and a wide range of reports from Indians and English offer ample verification of their position (Douglas Leach, "Question of French Involvement"; Emerson W. Baker, "New Evidence on the French Involvement").

116. Francis Card's declaration, Jan. 22, 1676/77, *DHSM*, 6:149–51. Others who reported French assistance to the English included Joshua Tefft, a captive of the Narragansetts, and James Quannapohit, who spent several weeks spying among the Nipmucks and Wampanoags under Philip. See James Quanapaug [Quannapohit]'s information, Jan. 24, 1675, *MHSC*, 1st ser., 6:205; Roger Williams to John Leverett, Jan. 14, 1675, *MHSC*, 4th ser., 6:307. See also R. [Richard?] Wharton to John Winsley, Feb. 10, 1675/76, *CSPCS*, 9:350–51, item 816; and *MCR*, 5:123.

117. *MCR*, 5:123.

118. Willis, *History of Portland*, 228.

119. MHS photostats, Oct. 19, 1676.

120. The Massachusetts governor's letter assuring Mogg Heigon of safe conduct contains an alteration that highlights English distrust of Indian professions of peace. Mogg had earlier assured Leverett that English captives in Indian hands were safe and well. In response, the governor wrote, "I give you thanks for saving the living of such as fall into your hands." Then, reconsidering, Leverett crossed out his thanks to Mogg and instead gave them to God: "I acknowledge God's goodness in your saving the living of such as fall into your hands for whom we will give you ransom or exchange of persons." It was not Mogg's goodness, but God's, that explained any honorable dealings from the Indians (Draft of Gov. Leverett to Capt. [crossed out] Mog, Oct. 19, 1676, MHS photostats).

James Drake notes that Maine Indian groups were more autonomous from each other than many Indian groups in southern New England, following a "band" structure of organization rather than a regional "chiefdom" organization. As a result, it may have been even more difficult for such men as Mogg Heigon to secure compliance with treaties from surrounding sachems and their people than it was for sachems to the south (*King Philip's War*, 27).

121. Hubbard, *History of the Indian Wars*, 2:190–92.

122. Francis Card's Declaration, *DHSM*, 6:149–51.

123. To be fair to Waldron, the order for the surprisal had come from the Massachusetts General Court, not from him. By carrying it out, he became the focus for Indian (and some English) enmity. While the surprise was not Waldron's idea, he embraced it with enthusiasm, showing none of the resistance to the plan that other men who were present, such as Shapleigh and Daniel, did. In many other interactions with Indians, Waldron manifested a contempt for them and disregard for fair dealing that might have earned him almost as much antipathy had Cocheco never occurred.

124. Suffolk Files, #1508, vol. 17, JA; Plymouth Colony (Nathaniel Morton, Sec.) to John Leverett, Governor of Massachusetts, June 8, 1677, John Davis Papers, MHS. For an earlier effort to recruit Captain Church's assistance, see Edward Rawson to Josiah Winslow, Aug. 20, 1676, Winslow Family II Papers, MHS.

125. *DHSM*, 6:154–55.

126. Plymouth Colony (Nathaniel Morton, Sec.) to John Leverett, Gov. of Massachusetts, June 8, 1677, John Davis Papers, MHS.

127. Commission for 200 troops, including 80 Natick Indians, to be impressed by Daniel Gookin, Jan. 29, 1676, *DHSM*, 6:153–54.

128. Richard Waldron to Massachusetts Council, April 18, 1677, in *DHSM*, 6:162–63.

129. Blind Will had been a subject of discussion between Governor Leverett and Mogg Heigon the previous October (MHS photostats, Oct. 19, 1676). Leverett stated that Will had been "received formerly to Mercy." Therefore, he could not "without further proofs proceed against him," implying that Blind Will was in English captivity, but would not be executed. What became of him is unclear. Under the definition of mercy the English applied to their summer call for submission, Blind Will could have been sold into slavery.

130. Waldron gives no reason for the recall. Although Waldron retained the office of major to the end of his life, this expedition was his last active military command (Richard Waldron's account of his expedition, in Hubbard, *History of the Indian Wars*, 2:212–25).

131. *MCR*, 5:140–42.

132. Hubbard, *History of the Indian Wars*, 2:234.

133. For an account of this battle, see Hubbard, *History of the Indian Wars*, 2:234–36; Southgate, *History of Scarborough*, 113–14. See also the petition of Thomas Dutton, Jr., in MAC, 69: 209–10, Oct. 2, 1678.

134. For a detailed account of these attacks, see James Axtell, "The Vengeful Women of Marblehead." See also Samuel G. Drake's extensive note on this event in Hubbard, *History of the Indian Wars*, 2:237.

135. Council of Massachusetts to Plymouth, Aug. 23, 1677, Winslow Family II Papers, MHS.

136. Massachusetts Council to Connecticut Council, MHS photostats. The letter is indexed "1676?" but was most likely written in July or August 1677. The letter is noted in *CCR*, 2:503, and is assigned the date Aug. 16. The letter from the Connecticut Council to the Massachusetts Council, Sept. 3, 1677, in MAC, 69:169, is in direct response to this letter.

137. Plymouth Colony [Nathaniel Morton, Sec.] to John Leverett, Gov. of Massachusetts, June 8, 1677, John Davis Papers, MHS; MAC, vol. 69:169, Connecticut Council to Massachusetts Council, Sept. 3, 1677.

138. Plymouth Colony [Nathaniel Morton, Sec.] to John Leverett, Gov. of Massachusetts, June 8, 1677, John Davis Papers, MHS.

139. Report of Edward Randolph to King Charles II, Sept. 20, 1676, *CSPCS*, 9:455–56, item 1037.

140. Samuel Symonds to John Winthrop, Jr., July 14, 1675, *MHSC*, 4th ser., 7:136; Connecticut General Court to [?], July 9, 1675, MHS photostats.

141. Petition of Sir Edmond Andros, governor of New York, to king, April 9, 1678, *MHSC*, 4th ser., 2:279–304. While many documents point to the fact that powder and guns were issuing from New York, no evidence supports Andros's acquiescence in the sales. In fact, John Pynchon wrote Governor John Leverett that Indians returning from Albany in September 1675 said that Indians at war with the English could get no powder or ammunition there and that the English even refused to sell to Mohegans until "the fall of the leaf when they hunt," by which time they would have proved their loyalty to the English (Carl Bridenbaugh, ed., *Pynchon Papers*, 152). Massachusetts had not blamed Andros personally, however, and most reports of supplies from Albany pinned blame on Andros's Dutch subjects.

142. Suffolk Files, #1510, vol. 17, JA; *DCHNY*, 3:255.

143. Massachusetts Council to Major Daniel Dennison, May 5, 1677, *DHSM*, 6:166–67. The Council engaged John Pynchon to make arrangements. See also MAC, 69:7, Edmund Andros to Massachusetts Council, May 22, 1677, and MAC, 69:126a, John Leverett to Edmund Andros, May 28, 1677.

144. *DCHNY*, 3:248–49. There is no evidence that any Mohawks joined New York troops on this expedition.

145. *MCR*, 5:161–69.

146. *MCR*, 5:169.

147. Edmund Andros, "A short Accompt," *DCHNY*, 3:254–57.

148. Report of Sir Edmund Andros to the Committee on Trade and Plantations, April 8, 1678, *DCHNY*, 3:257.

149. John Evelyn diary, June 6, 1671, cited in *MPCR*, 1:194.

150. *DCHNY*, 3:255, 265.

151. Anthony Brockhollt, Ceasar Knapton, Mattias Nicolls to Hon Gentlmn [Council], Aug. 18, 1677, *DHSM*, 6:191–93.

152. Petition of Joshua Scottow to Massachusetts Governor and Council, Oct. 18, 1677., *DHSM*, 6:199.

153. Suffolk Files, #1642, vol. 19, JA.

154. Emerson W. Baker, et al., eds., *American Beginnings*, 188; Willis, *History of Portland*, 230.

155. Hubbard, *History of the Indian Wars*, 2:257.

Chapter 10. Surrendering Authority

1. Samuel Sewall, *Diary*, Jan. 2, 1685/86–May 26, 1686, 1:115–41; *CSPCS*, 11:718–19, item 1928.

2. For a detailed discussion of this time period, see Richard E. Johnson, *Adjustment to Empire*.

3. Sewall, *Diary*, Jan. 10, 1677, 1:33.

4. Ibid., Jan. 24–25, 1676/77, 1:34; MHS photostats, Oct. 10, 1677.

5. Charles II to Governor and Council of Massachusetts Colony, April 27, 1678, in Thomas Hutchinson, *Hutchinson Papers*, 2:253–54. See also *MCR*, 5:192–93.

6. James David Drake, *King Philip's War*, 4, 169, 182; Sherburne F. Cook, *MCR*, 5:106.

7. *MCR*, 5:136–37; *CCR*, 2:481–82.

8. Suffolk Files, #1654, vol. 19, JA; *MCR*, 5:327–28. Kathleen Bragdon discusses the lessening of Indian legal autonomy in the aftermath of King Philip's War ("Crime and Punishment").

9. MAC, 30: 313, July 2 and 6, 1689.

10. Jill Lepore argues that the war increased the imperative to preserve English identity as a civilized society against the threat of Indian savagery and that the large numbers of Indians sold into slavery or long-term servitude following the war hastened the "racialization" of relations between the English and Indians (*Name of War*, 166). On the breakdown of "what had once been neighborly ties between the two peoples," see Neal Salisbury's introduction to Mary Rowlandson, *Sovereignty and Goodness of God*, vii; and Drake, *King Philip's War*.

11. Edmund Browne to Massachusetts Magistrates, [1677?], Middlesex County Court, Folio Collection, 1677, Folio 78, JA; Jenny Hale Pulsipher, "Our Sages are Sageles," 435; Rowlandson, *Sovereignty and Goodness of God*, 50, 71, 75, 99–100.

12. Even Indian champion Daniel Gookin confessed that "'tis very difficult,

unless upon long knowledge, to distinguish Indians from one another" (*Historical Account*, 492).

13. Postwar legislation was designed both to protect the wary English from any possibility of Indian threat and to shield the drastically reduced Indian population from English aggression (Yasuhide Kawashima, *Puritan Justice and the Indian*, chapter 8, 239).

14. *MCR*, 5:216. For an extended discussion of this synod, see Richard P. Gildrie, *The Profane, the Civil, & the Godly*, chapter 1.

15. Ironically, in listing these concerns, the Court used the phrase "the Lord hath of late made awful breaches, both upon the common wealth & upon the churches," using the very word the royal commissioners had expressly denounced and which the Lords of the Council for Trade and Plantation had objected to as recently as 1677 (*MCR*, 5:198; CSPCS, 5:139–142, items 378–381).

16. *MCR*, 5:222.

17. Gildrie, *The Profane, the Civil, & the Godly*, 34–38.

18. *CSPCS*, 11:103–5, item 211. William Pencak argues that despite continuing dissension between conservatives and moderates in Massachusetts, the colony enjoyed almost complete unison in its opposition to Edward Randolph (*War, Politics, & Revolution*, 12).

19. Edward Randolph to Governor Winslow, Jan. 29, 1679, *MHSC*, 1st ser., 6:92.

20. Johnson, *Adjustment to Empire*, 43.

21. Harry M. Ward, *United Colonies of New England*, 325.

22. *CSPCS*, 11:288–89, item 670; *MCR*, 5:270; *MCR*, 5:333.

23. *MPCR*, 3:xiii.

24. *DHSM*, 4:392–93.

25. *Maine Historical Society Collections*, 1st ser., 1:400–2; *DHSM*, 4:391.

26. *MPCR*, 3:xiii.

27. *MPCR*, 3:xv; *DHSM*, 4:397.

28. *CSPCS*, 11:27, item 69; 11:38, item 7; 11:45, item 98; 11:46, item 99; 11:49–52, item 106.

29. *CSPCS*, 11:234–35, item 512.

30. Charles II to Governor and Council of Plymouth, June 5, 1682, *MHSC*, 4th ser., 5:71.

31. *CSPCS*, 11:373–74, item 906; 11:387–88, item 952; 11:449–50, item 1129; Bernard Bailyn, *New England Merchants*, 169; *MHSC*, 1st ser., 10:37.

32. *CSPCS*, 11:373–74, item 906. Cranfield exercised far greater severity in his office than the king would have approved. Locked in the Tower of London, Gove petitioned the king for release. Not only was it granted, but James II later pardoned him and, after receiving a number of petitions and protests over Cranfield's high-handed government, relieved the governor of office (J. M. Sosin, *English America*, 268–71).

33. On the response to Monmouth's Rebellion in the English colonies, see *CSPCS*, 12:41–42, item 183; 12:95, item 371.

34. *CSPCS*, 11:240, item 529.

35. *CSPCS*, 11:240, item 529.

36. *CSPCS*, 11:296, item 697.

37. *CSPCS*, 11:447, item 1124.

38. *CSPCS*, 11:454, item 1151.

39. *CSPCS*, 11:587–88, item 1541; 11:599–600, item 1566.

40. *CSPCS*, 11:563, item 1445.

41. *CSPCS*, 11:587–88, item 1541; 11:599–600, item 1566; 11:606–7, item 1589; 11:456, item 1159. See also Kenneth M. Morrison, *Embattled Northeast*, 112.

328 Notes to Pages 248–255

42. *MCR*, 5:436–37; *CSPCS*, 11:606–7, item 1589; 11:669, item 1808.

43. Middlesex County Court, Folio Collection, 1684, folio 107, group 4; 1684, folio 110, group 3; 1684, folio 116, group 3; 1685, folio 116, group 1, JA.

44. Richard Bushman, *King and People in Provincial Massachusetts*, 21–24.

45. Sewall, *Diary*, April 16, 1685, 1:69–70.

46. Ibid., Dec. 4, 1685–April 1, 1686, 1:110–31.

47. Dudley received 666 votes for magistrate. Samuel Sewall noted that the votes were counted twice, some thinking that the ominous number 666 (the mark of the "beast," or Satan, in the Book of Revelation) might be a mistake (Sewall, *Diary*, April 16, 1685, 1:69–70).

48. Philip S. Haffenden, "The Crown and the Colonial Charters."

49. *CSPCS*, 12:233, item 832.

50. *DHSM*, 5:147.

51. *CSPCS*, 12:582–83, item 1868; William D. Williamson, *History of the State of Maine*, 581–85; Pencak, *War, Politics, & Revolution*, 15; Gildrie, *The Profane, the Civil, & the Godly*, 194.

52. *CSPCS*, 12:xii–xiii; 12:242, item 856.

53. Charles McLean Andrews, *Colonial Period of American History*, 3:141.

54. *Revolution in New England Justified*, in *Andros Tracts*, Part 1:83.

55. On fears of Indians plotting war with the English, see *DHSM*, 6:325, 327.

56. Emerson W. Baker and John G. Reid, *New England Knight*, 91–92; *DHSM*, 5:38. See also *A Narrative of the Proceedings of Sir Edmond Androsse and his Complices*, in *Andros Tracts*, Part 1:145.

57. Williamson, *History of the State of Maine*, 587–88; *DHSM*, 5:38; *CSPCS*, 12:592, item 1877:IV; 12:582–83, item 1868.

58. *A Narrative of the Proceedings of Sir Edmond Androsse and his Complices*, in *Andros Tracts*, Part 1:145; Samuel Adams Drake, *The Border Wars of New England*, 11; C. D. [possibly Captain Joseph Dudley], *New England's Faction Discovered, or a brief and true account of their persecution of the Church of England*, in *Andros Tracts*, Part 2: 207; *CSPCS*, 12:582–83, item 1868.

59. *DHSM*, 6:421.

60. *Revolution in New England Justified*, in *Andros Tracts*, Part 1:110–11; *A Narrative of the Proceedings of Sir Edmond Androsse and his Complices*, in *Andros Tracts*, Part 1:146–47; *DHSM*, 6:144.

61. *CSPCS*, 13:273–74, item 912.

62. *CSPCS*, 13:274–75, item 913.

63. *DHSM*, 5:28–29.

64. T. H. Breen, *Puritans and Adventurers*, 42–43; *DHSM*, 5:38. Fred Anderson discusses the clash between Massachusetts soldiers' expectations of their officers and the brutal treatment they witnessed from regular British officers during the French and Indian War. The clash led to resentment of the British officers and supported the creation of a separate, proto-American identity, a process visible during this time period as well (*A People's Army*).

65. *DHSM*, 5:40, 35, 20–21.

66. *DHSM*, 5:142–53.

67. *Revolution in New England Justified*, in *Andros Tracts*, Part 1:101–13; Increase Mather, *A Vindication of New England*, in *Andros Tracts*, Part 2:50–51.

68. *Revoluton in New England Justified*, in *Andros Tracts*, Part 1:103–5. See also *CSPCS*, 13:756, item 2741.

69. *CSPCS*, 13:121, item 338; *Andros Tracts*, Parts 1–2.

70. *Revolution in New England Justified*, in *Andros Tracts*, Part 1: 83–101; *An Account of the Late Revolutions in New-England by A. B.*, in *Andros Tracts*, Part 2:198.

71. *An Account of the Late Revolutions in New-England,* in *Andros Tracts,* Part 2:201.

72. "An Answer to Sir Edmund Andros's Account, May 30, 1690," in *Andros Tracts,* Part 3:34–35.

73. Samuel G. Drake, *History of the Early Discovery,* 299–302.

74. *DHSM,* 5:101–4; Petition of the Inhabitants of Maine to the King, Jan. 25, 1689/90, in *Andros Tracts,* Part 1:176–78. See also *CSPCS,* 13:120, item 336; 13:263, item 884. See also *DHSM,* 5:108

75. C. D., *New England's Faction Discovered,* in Andros Tracts, Part 2:213; Sir Edmund Andros's Report of his Administration, in *Andros Tracts,* Part 3:24.

76. Williamson, *History of the State of Maine,* 594; Sir Edmund Andros's Report of his Administration, in *Andros Tracts,* part 3:24.

77. *CSPCS,* 13:115, item 316.

78. *CSPCS,* 13:46, item 152; *DHSM,* 10:1.

79. *CSPCS,* 13:310, item 111; 13:120, item 336; *DHSM,* 5:1; see also Baker and Reid, *New England Knight,* 95–97.

80. *Further Quaries upon the Present State of the New-English Affairs,* in *Andros Tracts,* Part 1:197, *DHSM,* 4:107.

81. *DHSM,* 4:459.

82. *DHSM,* 5:107; see also *DHSM,* 5:101.

83. *DHSM,* 5:257–58. On Indian soldiers' dissatisfaction with the colony's pay, provisions, and management of the war, see *DHSM,* 4:459. Officers over garrisons in Maine feared soldiers would desert if they did not receive supplies of clothing before winter (*DHSM,* 4:295–96, 299).

84. Middlesex County Court, Folio Collection, Sept. 19, 1690, Folio 131, group 3, JA.

85. Williamson, *History of the State of Maine,* 599; *DHSM,* 5:1, 10.

86. *DHSM,* 5:304–7.

87. *DHSM,* 5:307–8.

88. *DHSM,* 5:309.

89. *CSPCS,* 11:35, item 91.

90. Plymouth leaders wrote the King in November 1683, declaring their joy in his escape from a plot against him and requesting his favorable consideration of a charter for their colony. The timing of the letter—immediately after Edward Randolph delivered the *Quo Warranto* to Massachusetts—and its submissive, loyal wording shows their desire to set themselves apart from their disgraced neighbor colony in order to preserve their own privileges (*CSPCS,* 11:545–46, item 1389).

91. Cadwallader Colden, *History of the Five Indian Nations,* 83–84.

92. *CSPCS,* 13:38–39, item 121; "The People's Right to Election or Alteration of Government in Connecticutt Argued in a Letter by Gershom Bulkeley," in *Andros Tracts,* 2:103.

93. Randolph's letter to the Lords of Trade, in *Andros Tracts,* 3:226–32.

94. Baker and Reid, *New England Knight,* 100.

95. *DHSM,* 5:145–46.

96. *CSPCS,* 13:163–64, item 509.

97. *DHSM,* 5:321–23. See also *DHSM,* 5:231–32.

98. *DHSM,* 5:255.

99. Emerson W. Baker and John G. Reid provide a nuanced discussion of Wabanaki efforts to use diplomacy as well as the threat of violence to defend their sovereignty in "Amerindian Power in the Early Modern Northeast."

100. Williamson, *History of the State of Maine,* 606; See also Alice N. Nash, "Abiding Frontier," 188–89.

101. North Yarmouth was also called Westcustogo and was founded in 1680 next to a large Wabanaki village (Baker and Reid, *New England Knight,* 140–41).

102. *DHSM*, 5:304–7.

103. "The People's Right to Election or Alteration of Government in Connecti-cutt," in Andros Tracts, Part 2:83–109; *DHSM*, 5:189.

104. *DHSM*, 5:304–7.

105. "Mr. Potter's Journal," 8; *CSPCS*, 13:40, item 129.

106. Baker and Reid, *New England Knight*, 78; *CSPCS*, 13:212–13, items 740–743. See also *CSPCS*, 13:263, item 884.

107. Pencak, *War, Politics, & Revolution*, 13.

108. Breen, *Puritans and Adventurers*, 84–86, 88–89, 103.

109. Ibid., chapter 5, 93, note 45. For an extended discussion of the physical and spiritual aftermath of King Philip's War, see Michael J. Puglisi, *Puritans Besieged*.

110. Pencak, *War, Politics, & Revolution*, 17–18.

111. Joshua Scottow, *A Narrative of the Planting*, 40; Francis J. Bremer, *The Puritan Experiment*, 217–18; Carla Gardina Pestana, *Quakers and Baptists in Colonial Massachusetts*, 137–39, 152.

112. Bushman, *King and People in Provincial Massachusetts*, 22.

113. Robert M. Bliss, *Revolution and Empire*, 223, and Chapter 9.

114. Pencak, *War, Politics, & Revolution*, 13.

115. Ward, *United Colonies of New England*, 362.

116. Breen, *Puritans and Adventurers*, 105. James Kences notes the fact that association with Indians was a common characteristic among many accused of witchcraft in the 1692 Salem witchcraft trials and may have contributed to their being accused ("Some Unexplored Relationships.") Mary Beth Norton expands on both Breen's and Kences's findings in *In the Devil's Snare*. Insightful discussions of the witchcraft crisis and its connections to war with the Indians and the political instability of the times also appear in Baker and Reid, *New England Knight*, chapter 7; and Louise A. Breen, *Transgressing the Bounds*, 213–19. Indian attacks fell hardest on Maine, but the costs of the destruction burdened Massachusetts residents as well and may have contributed to the hysteria. For a discussion of connections between Massachusetts colonists' Indian land speculation and the witchcraft crisis, see Emerson W. Baker and James Kences, "Maine, Indian Land Speculation, and the Essex County Witchcraft Outbreak."

117. Scottow, *Narrative of the Planting*, 54. The fact that many Maine Indians began converting to Catholicism would have further heightened antipathy against them in New England.

118. Samuel Willard, "Character of a Good Ruler," 27.

119. Scottow, *Narrative of the Planting*, 55.

120. Cited in Baker and Reid, *New England Knight*, 134.

121. On Cooke and Danforth, see Baker and Reid, *New England Knight*, 76–78, 112, 181, 191; on Sewall's regret over secularization, see Sewall, *Diary*, June 11, 1696, 1:428.

122. Pencak, *War, Politics & Revolution*, 28. Baker and Reid's *New England Knight* gives a detailed description of Massachusetts colonists' reconciliation to the new charter and its governor and of the factions opposing both (chapter 9).

123. On William Phips's life, see Baker and Reid, *New England Knight*.

Epilogue

1. William Cronon, *Changes in the Land*, 110–13; Allan Kulikoff, *From British Peasants to Colonial American Farmers*, 80.

2. Evarts B. Greene and Virginia D. Harrington estimate that by the end of the seventeenth century the population of New England approached 100,000, with

80,000 in Massachusetts alone. Adult Indians comprised perhaps 3,000 of this number (*American Population*, 9–14). Massachusetts officials counted 4,168 Indians in the province in 1698 (Daniel Mandell, *Behind the Frontier*, 165).

3. James D. Drake, *King Philip's War*, 172; Sherburne F. Cook, "Interracial Warfare and Population Decline Among the New England Indians."

4. On the status of Indians in New England during the post-King Philip's War period, see Colin Calloway, *After King Philip's War*; Ann Marie Plane, *Colonial Intimacies*; Jean M. O'Brien, *Dispossession by Degrees*; and Mandell, *Behind the Frontier*.

5. Samuel E. Morison, *Maritime History of Massachusetts*, 14–15; Robert G. Albion et al., *New England and the Sea*, 23–29.

6. Daniel Vickers, *Farmers and Fishermen*, 145–49.

7. Daniel Vickers, "The First Whalemen of Nantucket."

8. Michael G. Hall, *Last American Puritan*, 338, 326.

9. Drake, *King Philip's War*, 184; after 1675, the Iroquois were tied to the English through the "covenant chain," an alliance that, given the kinship term "brother" used by both sides, was far more equal than the subordinate/superior position of Indians and English in Massachusetts. Francis Jennings discusses the beginning of the covenant chain in his *Ambiguous Iroquois Empire*.

10. See, for example, Reuben Cognehew's 1760 journey to England to appeal to the king, in Francis G. Hutchins, *Mashpee*, 73; and Mohegan appeals to the king to settle land disputes in Connecticut, in John W. DeForest, *History of the Indians of Connecticut*, 323.

11. Gregory Dowd argues that the eighteenth-century English did not consider Indians true subjects of the king, with all the privileges such status entailed in the period following the Glorious Revolution. Rather, they saw them as inferiors entitled to royal protection, a status that paved the way for Indians to be seen as "domestic, dependent nations" in the early national period (*War Under Heaven*, chapter 6).

12. Quoted in Emerson W. Baker and John G. Reid, "Amerindian Power in the Early Modern Northeast," 89. Baker and Reid's article is an outstanding discussion of Wabanaki power in the late seventeenth- and early eighteenth-century European imperial world. See also Kenneth M. Morrison, *The Embattled Northeast*; Olive Patricia Dickason, "The French and the Abenaki"; and David L. Ghere, "Mistranslations and Misinformation."

13. Alice N. Nash, "The Abiding Frontier," 258.

14. Emerson W. Baker, "Trouble to the Eastward," chapter 7.

15. Deposition of Thomas Stevens, Sept. 4, 1688, *DHSM*, 6:421–31.

16. Baker, "Trouble to the Eastward," 223.

17. For an excellent historical overview and discussion of Indian sovereignty, see Wilcomb E. Washburn, *Red Man's Land, White Man's Law*.

18. See, for example, "Five Hundred Years of Indigenous Resistance."

Appendix

1. From Dwight B. Heath, ed., *Mourt's Relation*, 56–57.

Bibliography

Manuscript Collections

Concord Public Library Special Collections
   Goble Papers
   Huntington Library Manuscripts (photostats)
Maine Historical Society Archives
   Collection 77, Autographs of Special Note
   Collection S-888
   William S. Southgate Collection
Massachusetts Historical Society
   Broadsides
   Cotton Family Papers
   John Davis Papers
   Massachusetts Historical Society Photostats
   Miscellaneous Bound Manuscripts
   Winslow Family II Papers
   Winthrop Family Papers
Massachusetts State Archives
   Massachusetts Archives Collection
Massachusetts State Judicial Archives
   Middlesex Court Folios
   Middlesex County Court Record Book, 4 volumes (vol. 2 missing) (David Pulsifer
     transcript)
   Suffolk Court Files

Primary Published Sources

Andros, Edmund. "A Short Accompt of late passages at New York, Rec'd from Sir
   Edmund Andross, in March 1678, Concerning the Indians. *DCHNY*, 3:254–57.
The Andros Tracts. Publications of the Prince Society, vols. 5–7. New York: Burt
   Franklin, 1868–1874.
Baxter, James Phinney, ed. *Documentary History of the State of Maine*. Series 2, vol. 6.
   Portland, Maine: Thurston Print, 1900.
Bouton, Nathaniel, ed. *Provincial Papers: Documents and Records Relating to the Province
   of New-Hampshire*. Vol. 1, *1623–1686*. Concord, N.H.: George E. Jenks, State
   Printer, 1867.
Bowden, Henry W. and James P. Ronda, eds. *John Eliot's Indian Dialogues: A Study in
   Cultural Interaction*. Westport, Conn.: Greenwood Press, 1980.
Bowen, Richard LeBaron. *Early Rehoboth*. Vols. 1–3. Rehoboth, Mass.: privately
   printed, 1945–48.

Bradford, William. *Of Plymouth Plantation, 1620–1647.* Ed. Samuel Eliot Morison. New York: Alfred A. Knopf, 1952.

Bridenbaugh, Carl, ed. *The Pynchon Papers.* Boston: Colonial Society of Massachusetts, 1982.

"A Brief and True Narration of the Late Wars Risen in New-England: Occasioned by the Quarrelsome disposition, and Perfidious Carriage of the Barbarous, Savage and Heathenish NATIVES There." London, 1675.

Brodhead, John Romeyn, ed. *Documents Relative to the Colonial History of the State of New-York.* Albany, N.Y.: Weed, Parsons, 1853.

Church, Benjamin. *Diary of King Philip's War, 1675–76.* Ed. Alan Simpson and Mary Simpson. Chester, Conn.: Pequot Press, 1975.

Cobbet, Thomas. "A Narrative of New England's Deliverances." In *NEHGR* 7:209–19.

Collections of the Massachusetts Historical Society. Various years. Boston: The Society.

Collections of the New-York Historical Society. Various years. New York: Trow and Smith for the Society.

A Court Martial held at Newport, Rhode Island, In August and September, 1676, for the trial of Indians, charged with being engaged in King Philip's War. Albany, N.Y.: J. Munsell, 1858.

Davenport, John. "A Sermon Preach'd at the Election of the Governour, at Boston in New-England, May 19th 1669." *Transactions of the Colonial Society of Massachusetts* 10 (1904–6): 1–6.

The Day-Breaking, if not The Sun-Rising of the Gospell With the Indians in New-England. London: Rich. Cotes for Fulk Clifton, 1647. Reprinted in *MHSC*, 3rd ser., 4:1–23.

Early Records of the Town of Dedham, Massachusetts. Vol. 4, *1659–1673.* Ed. D. G. Hill. Dedham, Mass.: Dedham Transcript Press, 1894.

Easton, John. "A Relacion of the Indyan Warre, by Mr. Easton, of Roade Isld., 1675." In *Narratives of the Indian Wars, 1675–1699*, ed. Charles H. Lincoln, 7–17. New York: Barnes and Noble, 1913.

Eliot, John, trans. *Mamusse wunneetupanatamwe Up-Biblum God.* 1685.

"The Examination and Relation of James Quannapoaquait." In Mary Rowlandson, *The Sovereignty and Goodness of God, by Mary Rowlandson, with Related Documents*, ed. Neal Salisbury. Boston: Bedford Books, 1997.

"A Farther Brief and True Narration of the Late Wars Risen in New-England." Reprinted in *A farther Brief and True Narration of the Great Swamp Fight in the Narragansett Country December 19, 1675.* Providence, R.I.: Society of Colonial Wars, 1912.

Folger, Peter. "A Looking Glasse for the Times, or, The Former Spirit of New-England revived in this generation." April 23, 1676. In *Rhode Island Historical Tracts*, no. 16. Providence, R.I.: Bidney S. Rider, 1883.

Goddard, Ives and Kathleen J. Bragdon. *Native Writings in Massachusett.* Philadelphia: American Philosophical Society, 1988.

Gookin, Daniel. *An Historical Account of the Doings and Sufferings of the Christian Indians in New England, in the Years 1675, 1676, 1677.* New York: Arno Press, 1972.

———. *Historical Collections of the Indians in New England.* MHSC, 1st ser., 1:141–227.

Greene, Evarts B. and Virginia D. Harrington, *American Population Before the Federal Census of 1790.* New York, 1932.

Green, Samuel A., M.D. *Groton During the Indian Wars.* Cambridge, Mass.: John Wilson and Son, University Press, 1883.

Hakluyt, Richard, the Elder. "Reasons for Colonization." 1585. In *The Elizabethans' America*, ed. Louis B. Wright. Cambridge, Mass.: Harvard University Press, 1965.

Hammond, Isaac and Albert S. Batchellor. *Provincial and State Papers of New Hampshire.* Concord, N.H.: 1868–91.

Harris, William to Sir Joseph Williamson, August 1676. *Rhode Island Historical Society Collections* 10:162–79.

Heath, Dwight B., ed. *Mourt's Relation: A Journal of the Pilgrims at Plymouth.* Bedford, Mass.: Applewood Books, 1963.

Hubbard, William. *The Happiness of a People in the Wisdome of their Rulers Directing And in the Obedience of their Brethren Attending Unto what Israel ough[t] to do.* Election sermon preached at Boston, May 3, 1676. Boston: John Foster, 1676.

——. *The History of the Indian Wars in New England from the First Settlement to the Termination of the War with King Philip, in 1677.* Ed. Samuel G. Drake. 1677. New York: Kraus Reprint, 1969.

Hull, John. *Diary of Public Occurrences.* In vol. 7 of *Puritan Personal Writings: Diaries.* New York: AMS Press, 1982.

Hutchinson, Richard. "The Warr in New-England Visibly Ended." In *Narratives of the Indian Wars, 1675–1699*, ed. Charles H. Lincoln, 103–6. New York: Barnes and Noble, 1913.

Hutchinson, Thomas. *The Hutchinson Papers.* 2 vols. Publications of the Prince Society. Albany, N.Y.: The Society, 1865.

"Indian Children Put to Service. 1676." *NEHGR* 8 (1854): 270–73.

Josselyn, John. *Colonial Traveler: A Critical Edition of Two Voyages to New-England.* London, 1674. Ed. Paul J. Lindholt. Hanover, N.H.: University Press of New England, 1988.

Joy, George. "Innocency's Complaint against Tyrannical Court Faction in Newengland." Boston, 1677. In *More Early Massachusetts Broadsides: The First Century, 1639–1739.* Boston: MHS, 1981.

Leach, Douglas Edward. "A New View of the Declaration of War Against the Narragansetts, November, 1675." *Rhode Island History* 15, 2 (April 1956): 33–41.

——, ed. *A Rhode Islander Reports on King Philip's War: The Second William Harris Letter of August, 1676.* Providence: Rhode Island Historical Society, 1963.

Lechford, Thomas. *Plain Dealing: Or, Newes from New-England.* London: W.E. and I.G. for Nath: Butter, 1642. Reprinted in *MHSC*, 3rd ser., 3:54–128.

Leder, Lawrence H., ed. *The Livingston Indian Records, 1666–1723.* Gettysburg: Pennsylvania Historical Association, 1956. Reprint Stanfordville, N.Y.: Earl M. Coleman, 1979.

Libby, Charles Thornton and Robert E. Moody, eds. *Province and Court Records of Maine.* Portland: Maine Historical Society, 1928–47.

Lieutenant Lion Gardener His Relation of the Pequot Warres. 1660. Reprinted in *MHSC*, 3rd ser., 3:150.

Mather, Increase. *A Brief History of the War with the Indians in New-England.* Reprinted in *So Dreadfull a Judgment: Puritan Responses to King Philip's War, 1676–1677*, ed. Richard Slotkin and James K. Folsom. Middletown, Conn.: Wesleyan University Press, 1978.

——. "An Earnest Exhortation to the Inhabitants of New-England." Boston: John Foster, 1676. Reprinted in *So Dreadfull a Judgment: Puritan Responses to King Philip's War, 1676–1677*, ed. Richard Slotkin and James K. Folsom. Middletown, Conn.: Wesleyan University Press, 1978.

——. *An Historical Discourse Concerning the Prevalency of Prayer.* In *Early History of New England*, ed. Samuel G. Drake. Boston: County of Suffolk, 1901.

——. "Phineas Pratt's Relation of the first settlement at Massachusetts." *MHSC*, 4th ser., 4:488.

Maverick, Samuel. "A Briefe discription of New England and the Severall Townes therein, together with the present Government thereof." *Proceedings of the Massachusetts Historical Society* 2:1:231–49.

Morton, Nathaniel. *New England's Memorial.* In *Chronicles of the Pilgrim Fathers,* ed. John Masefield. New York: E.P. Dutton, 1936.

Morton, Thomas. *New English Canaan, or, New Canaan: containing an abstract of New England.* Amsterdam: Printed by Jacob Frederick Stam, 1637.

"Mr. Potter's Journal from Virginia to N. England." In Newton D. Mereness, *Travels in the American Colonies.* New York: Macmillan, 1916.

"News from New-England, Being A True and Last Accompt of the Present Bloody Wars caried on betwixt the Infidel natives and the English Christians and converted Indians of New-England." London: J Coniers, at the Sign of the Black Raven in Duck-Lane, 1676. Boston: S.G. Drake, 1850.

Noble, John, ed. *Records of the Court of Assistants of the Colony of the Massachusetts Bay, 1630–1692.* Boston: County of Suffolk, 1901.

Nourse, Henry S., ed. *Birth, Marriage, and Death Register, Church Records and Epitaphs of Lancaster, Massachusetts, 1643–1850.* Clinton, Mass.: W.J. Coulter, 1890.

———, ed. *Early Records of Lancaster, Massachusetts 1643–1725.* Lancaster, Mass.: W.J. Coulter, 1884.

Pulsifer, David, ed. *Records of Plymouth Colony.* Boston: William White, 1855–61.

Records and Files of the Quarterly Courts of Essex County, Massachusetts. Salem, Mass.: Essex Institute, 1914.

Records of the Colony of Rhode Island and Providence Plantations. Providence, R.I.: A. Crawford Greene and Brother, 1856.

Records of the Suffolk County Court, 1671–1680, Part I. Publications of the Colonial Society of Massachusetts. Boston: The Society, 1933.

Rev. John Eliot's Records of the First Church in Roxbury, Mass. *NEHGR* 33 (July 1879).

Rowlandson, Mary. *The Sovereignty and Goodness of God, by Mary Rowlandson, with Related Documents,* ed. Neil Salisbury. Boston: Bedford Books, 1997.

Sainsbury, W. Noel, ed. *Calendar of State Papers, Colonial Series, America and West Indies.* Vaduz: Kraus Reprint, 1964.

Saltonstall, Nathaniel. "The Present State of New-England with Respect to the Indian War," "A Continuation of the State of New-England," and "A New and Further Narrative of the State of New-England." In *Narratives of the Indian Wars, 1675–1699,* ed. Charles H. Lincoln, 24–99. New York: Barnes and Noble, 1913.

Scottow, Joshua. Diary, October 1675-May 1676. In William S. Southgate, *The History of Scarborough, from 1633 to 1783.* In *Maine Historical Society Collections,* 1st ser., 3 (1853): chapter 7.

———. *A Narrative of the Planting of the Massachusets Colony Anno 1628. Published by Old Planters, the Authors of the Old Mens Tears.* Boston: Benjamin [Harris?], 1694.

———. *Old Men's Tears for their own Declensions, mixed with Fears of their and posterities further falling off from New England's Primitive Constitution.* Boston: Benjamin Harris and John Allen, 1691.

Sewall, Samuel. *The Diary of Samuel Sewall, 1674–1729.* 2 vols. *MHSC,* 5th ser., 5–6.

Shepard, Thomas. *The Cleare Sunshine of the Gospell Breaking Forth upon the Indians in New-England.* London: R. Cotes for John Bellamy, 1648. Reprinted in *MHSC,* 3rd ser., 4:64–65.

Shurtleff, Nathaniel B., ed. *Records of the Governor and Company of the Massachusetts Bay in New England.* Boston: William White, 1854.

Slotkin, Richard and James K. Folsom, eds. *So Dreadfull a Judgment, Puritan Responses to King Philip's War, 1676–1677.* Middletown, Conn.: Wesleyan University Press, 1978.

Strachey, William. "The History of Travel into Virginia Britannia." In *The Elizabethans' America,* ed. Louis B. Wright. Cambridge, Mass.: Harvard University Press, 1965.

Strength out of Weaknesse; or a Glorious Manifestation of the further progresse of the Gospel among the Indians in New-England. London: M. Simmons for John Blague and Samuel Howes, 1652. Reprinted in *MHSC*, 3rd ser., 4:171.

"To the Elders and Ministers of every Town within the Jurisdiction of the Massachusets in New-England." In *More Early Massachusetts Broadsides: The First Century, 1639–1739.* Boston: Massachusetts Historical Society, 1981. No. 2: March 10, 1668.

Tompson, Benjamin. *New England's Crisis.* 1676. Boston: Club of Odd Volumes, 1896.

———. "Sad and Deplorable News from New-England . . . Occasioned by many unheard of Cruelties, Practised upon the Persons and Estates of its United Colonies, without Respect of Sex, Age or Quality of Persons by the barbarous Heathen thereof." London: H.J., 1676.

Travers, Len, ed. "The Missionary Journal of John Cotton, Jr., 1666–1678." *Proceedings of the Massachusetts Historical Society* 109 (1997): 52–101.

"A True Account of the most Considerable Occurrences that have hapned in the Warre between the English and the Indians in New-England, From the Fifth of may, 1676, to the Fourth of August last; as also of the Successes it hath pleased God to give the English against them." London, Oct. 11, 1676. Reprinted Salem, Mass.: New England & Virginia Co.

Trumbull, J. Hammond, ed. *Public Records of the Colony of Connecticut.* Hartford, Conn.: Brown & Parsons, 1850.

Underhill, John. "News from America, or a late and experimental discovery of New England." In *History of the Pequot War,* ed. Charles Orr, 49–86. Cleveland: Halman-Taylor, 1897.

Wharton, Edward. *New-England's Present sufferings under Their Cruel Neighboring Indians. Represented in two Letters, lately Written from Boston to London.* London, 1675.

Wheeler, Thomas. "A thankefull remembrance of Gods mercy to several persons at Quabaug or Brookfield . . ." Cambridge, Mass.: Printed and sold by Samuel Green, 1676. Reprinted in *History of Middlesex County, Massachusetts,* vol. 2, ed. D. Hamilton Hurd. Philadelphia: J.W. Lewis & Col., 1890.

Whitfield, Henry. *The Light Appearing more and more towards the perfect Day.* London: T.R. & E.M. for John Bartlet, 1651. Reprinted in *MHSC,* 3rd ser., 4:139–41.

Whitmore, William H., ed. *The Colonial Laws of Massachusetts, 1672–1686.* Boston: Rockwell and Churchill, 1887.

Willard, Samuel. "The Character of a Good Ruler." Election sermon given May 30, 1694. Boston: Benjamin Harris, 1694. Reprinted in *Election Day Sermons: Massachusetts,* ed. Sacvan Bercovitch. New York: AMS Press, 1984.

Williams, Roger. *The Correspondence of Roger Williams.* Ed. Glenn W. LaFantasie. 2 vols. Hanover, N.H.: University Press of New England, 1988.

———. *A Key into the Language of America.* London: Gregory Dexter, 1643. Bedford, Mass.: Applewood Books, 1997.

Winslow, Edward. *Good Newes from New England: A True relation of things very remarkable at the plantation of Plimoth in New England.* 1624. Bedford, Mass.: Applewood Books, 1996.

Winthrop, John. *The Journal of John Winthrop, 1630–1649.* Ed. Richard S. Dunn, James Savage, and Laetitia Yeandle. Cambridge, Mass.: Harvard University Press, 1996.

Wood, William. *New England's Prospect.* 1634. Ed. Alden T. Vaughan. Amherst: University of Massachusetts Press, 1977.

Wright, Louis B., ed. *The Elizabethans' America.* Cambridge, Mass.: Harvard University Press, 1965.

Wyman, Thomas Bellows, ed. *The Genealogies and Estates of Charlestown, 1629–1818.* Boston: David Clapp and Son, 1879.

Young, Alexander, ed. *Chronicles of the First Planters of the Colony of Massachusetts Bay, from 1623 to 1636.* Boston: Charles C. Little and James Brown, 1846.

Secondary Sources

Albion, Robert G., Willam A. Baker, and Benjamin W. Labaree. *New England and the Sea.* Middletown, Conn.: Wesleyan University Press, 1972.

Anderson, Fred. *A People's Army: Massachusetts Soldiers and Society in the Seven Years' War.* Chapel Hill: University of North Carolina Press, 1984.

Anderson, Virginia DeJohn. "King Philip's Herds: Indians, Colonists, and the Problem of Livestock in Early New England." *WMQ* 3rd ser. 51, 4 (October 1994): 601–24.

Andrews, Charles M. *The Colonial Period of American History.* 4 vols. New Haven, Conn.: Yale University Press, 1934.

Axtell, James. "The Exploration of Norumbega." In *American Beginnings: Exploration, Culture, and Cartography in the Land of Norumbega,* ed. Emerson W. Baker et al. Lincoln: University of Nebraska Press, 1994.

———. *The Invasion Within: The Contest of Cultures in Colonial North America.* New York: Oxford University Press, 1985.

———. "The Scholastic Philosophy of the Wilderness." *WMQ* 3rd ser. 29, 3 (July 1972): 335–66.

———, ed. "The Vengeful Women of Marblehead: Robert Roules' Deposition of 1677." *WMQ* 3rd ser. 31, 4 (October 1974): 652.

———. "Were Indian Conversions *Bona Fide?*" In *After Columbus: Essays in the Ethnohistory of Colonial North America.* New York: Oxford University Press, 1988.

Bailyn, Bernard. *Education in the Forming of American Society: Needs and Opportunities for Study.* Chapel Hill: University of North Carolina Press, 1960.

———. *The New England Merchants in the Seventeenth Century.* New York: Harper Torchbooks, 1955.

Baker, Emerson W. *The Clarke & Lake Company: The Historical Archaeology of a Seventeenth-Century Maine Settlement.* Occasional Publications in Maine Archaeology, no. 4. Augusta, Maine: Maine Historic Preservation Commission, 1985.

———. "New Evidence on the French Involvement in King Philip's War." *Maine Historical Society Quarterly* 27 (Fall 1988): 85–91.

———. "Trouble to the Eastward: The Failure of Anglo-Indian Relations in Early Maine." Ph.D. dissertation, College of William and Mary, 1986.

Baker, Emerson W., Edwin A. Churchill, Richard D'Abate, Kristine L. Jones, Victor A. Konrad, and Harald E. L. Prins, eds. *American Beginnings: Exploration, Culture, and Cartography in the Land of Norumbega.* Lincoln: University of Nebraska Press, 1994.

Baker, Emerson W. and James Kences. "Maine, Indian Land Speculation, and the Essex County Witchcraft Outbreak of 1692." *Maine History* 40, 3 (Fall 2001): 159–89.

Baker, Emerson W. and John G. Reid. "Amerindian Power in the Early Modern Northeast: A Reappraisal." *WMQ,* 3rd ser. 61, 1 (January 2004): 77–106.

———. *The New England Knight: Sir William Phips, 1651–1695.* Toronto: University of Toronto Press, 1998.

Bangs, Jeremy Dupertuis. *Indian Deeds: Land Transactions in Plymouth Colony, 1620–1691.* Boston: New England Historical and Genealogical Society, 2002.

Banks, Charles E. "Captain Walter Gendall, of North Yarmouth, Maine." *Old Times in North Yarmouth, Maine* 3, 4 (July 1880): 511–37.

Berkhofer, Robert F., Jr. *The White Man's Indian: Images of the American Indian from Columbus to the Present.* New York: Alfred A. Knopf, 1978.

Bissel, Linda Auwers. "From One Generation to Another: Mobility in Seventeenth-Century Windsor, Connecticut." *WMQ* 3rd ser. 31, 1 (January 1974): 79–110.

Bliss, Robert M. *Revolution and Empire: English Politics and the American Colonies in the Seventeenth Century.* Manchester: Manchester University Press, 1990.

Bodge, George M. *Soldiers in King Philip's War.* Boston, 1906. Baltimore: Genealogical Publishing Company, 1967.

Bourne, Russell. *The Red King's Rebellion: Racial Politics in New England, 1675–1678.* New York: Atheneum, 1990.

Bradshaw, Brendan. "Native Reaction to the Westward Enterprise: A Case-Study in Gaelic Ideology." In *The Westward Enterprise: English activities in Ireland, the Atlantic, and America, 1480–1650*, ed. K. R. Andres, N. P. Canny, and P. E. H. Hair. Liverpool: Liverpool University Press, 1978.

Bragdon, Kathleen Joan. "Crime and Punishment Among the Indians of Massachusetts, 1675–1750." *Ethnohistory* 28, 1 (Winter 1981): 23–32.

———. *Native People of Southern New England, 1500–1650.* Norman: University of Oklahoma Press, 1996.

Breen, Louise A. "Praying with the Enemy: Daniel Gookin, King Philip's War, and the Dangers of Intercultural Mediatorship." In *Empire and Others: British Encounters with Indigenous Peoples, 1600–1850*, ed. Martin Daunton and Rich Halpern, 101–22. Philadelphia: University of Pennsylvania Press, 1999.

———. *Transgressing the Bounds: Subversive Enterprises Among the Puritan Elite in Massachusetts, 1630–1692.* New York: Oxford University Press, 2001.

Breen, T. H. *The Character of a Good Ruler: A Study of Puritan Political Ideas in New England, 1630–1730.* New Haven, Conn.: Yale University Press, 1970.

———. *Puritans and Adventurers: Change and Persistence in Early America.* New York: Oxford University Press, 1980.

Bremer, Francis J. *The Puritan Experiment: New England Society from Bradford to Edwards.* Hanover, N.H.: University Press of New England, 1995.

Brenner, Elise. "To Pray or Be Prey: That is the Question. Strategies for Cultural Autonomy of Massachusetts Praying Indians." *Ethnohistory* 27 (Spring 1980): 135–52.

Bross, Kristina. *Dry Bones and Indian Sermons: Praying Indians in Colonial American Identity.* Ithaca, N.Y., Cornell University Press, 2004.

Burk, John. *The History of Virginia, from its first settlement to the present day.* Petersburg, Va.: Dickson and Pescud, 1805.

Bushman, Richard L. *From Puritan to Yankee: Character and the Social Order in Connecticut, 1690–1765.* Cambridge, Mass.: Harvard University Press, 1967.

———. *King and People in Provincial Massachusetts.* Chapel Hill: University of North Carolina Press, 1985.

Calloway, Colin G., ed. *After King Philip's War: Presence and Persistence in Indian New England.* Hanover, N.H.: University Press of New England, 1997.

———. *The American Revolution in Indian Country: Crisis and Diversity in Native American Communities.* New York: Cambridge University Press, 1995.

———. "Rhode Island Renegade: The Enigma of Joshua Tefft." *Rhode Island History* 43 (November 1984): 137–45.

Canup, John. *Out of the Wilderness: The Emergence of an American Identity in Colonial New England.* Middletown, Conn.: Wesleyan University Press, 1990.

Cave, Alfred A. *The Pequot War.* Amherst: University of Massachusetts Press, 1996.

Churchill, Edwin A. "Mid-Seventeenth-Century Maine: A World on the Edge." In *American Beginnings: Exploration, Culture, and Cartography in the Land of Norumbega*, ed. Emerson W. Baker et al., 241–60. Lincoln: University of Nebraska Press, 1994.

Clark, Charles E. *The Eastern Frontier: The Settlement of Northern New England, 1610–1763*. New York: Alfred A. Knopf, 1970.

Cogley, Richard W. "Idealism vs. Materialism in the Study of Puritan Missions to the Indians." *Method & Theory in the Study of Religion* 3, 2 (1991): 165–82.

——. *John Eliot's Mission to the Indians Before King Philip's War*. Cambridge, Mass.: Harvard University Press, 1999.

Cohen, Charles L. "Conversion Among Puritans and Amerindians: A Theological and Cultural Perspective." In *Puritanism: Transatlantic Perspectives on a Seventeenth Century Anglo-American Faith*, ed. Francis J. Bremer. Boston: Massachusetts Historical Society, 1993.

Colden, Cadwallader. *The History of the Five Indian Nations Depending on the Province of New-York in America*. 1727, 1747. Ithaca, N.Y.: Great Seal Books, a division of Cornell University Press, 1958.

Cook, Sherburne F. "Interracial Warfare and Population Decline among the New England Indians." *Ethnohistory* 20, 1 (1973): 1–24.

Cressy, David. *Coming Over: Migration and Communication Between England and New England in the Seventeenth Century*. New York: Cambridge University Press, 1987.

Cronon, William. *Changes in the Land: Indians, Colonists, and the Ecology of New England*. New York: Hill and Wang, 1983.

Crosby, Alfred W. *The Columbian Exchange: Biological and Cultural Consequences of 1492*. Westport, Conn.: Greenwood Press, 1972.

——. *Ecological Imperialism: The Biological Expansion of Europe, 900–1900*. Cambridge: Cambridge University Press, 1986.

Cutter, William Richard, ed. *New England Families, Genealogical and Memorial*. New York: Lewis Historical Publishing Company, 1915.

Day, Gordon M. *The Identity of the Saint Francis Indians*. Canadian Ethnology Service, Paper 71. Ottawa: National Museums of Canada, 1981.

DeForest, John W. *History of the Indians of Connecticut from the Earliest Known Period to 1850*. Hartford, Conn.: William James Hammersley, 1851.

Delage, Denys. *Bitter Feast: Amerindians and Europeans in Northeastern North America, 1600–64*. Trans. Jane Brierly. Vancouver: UBC Press, 1993.

Demos, John. *Entertaining Satan: Witchcraft and the Culture of Early New England*. New York: Oxford University Press, 1982.

——. *A Little Commonwealth: Family Life in Plymouth Colony*. New York: Oxford University Press, 1970.

Dexter, Lincoln A. *Maps of Early Massachusetts: Pre-History Through the Seventeenth Century*. Springfield, Mass.: Dexter, 1979.

Dickason, Olive Patricia. "The French and the Abenaki: A Study in Frontier Politics." *Vermont History* 58, 2 (1990): 82–98.

Dowd, Gregory Evans. *War Under Heaven: Pontiac, the Indian Nations, & the British Empire*. Baltimore: Johns Hopkins University Press, 2002.

Drake, James David. *King Philip's War: Civil War in New England*. Amherst: University of Massachusetts Press, 1999.

——. "Symbol of a Failed Strategy: The Sassamon Trial, Political Culture, and the Outbreak of King Philip's War." *American Indian Culture and Research Journal* 19, 2 (1995): 111–41.

Drake, Samuel Adams. *The Border Wars of New England*. New York: Charles Scribner's Sons, 1910.

Drake, Samuel G. *History of the Early Discovery of America, and Landing of the Pilgrims, with a Biography of the Indians of North America.* Boston: L.P. Crown, 1854.

————. *The History and Antiquities of Boston.* Boston: Luther Stevens, 1856.

Fenton, William N. "Structure, Continuity and Change in the Process of Iroquois Treaty Making." In *The History and Culture of Iroquois Diplomacy: An Interdisciplinary Guide to the Treaties of the Six Nations and Their League,* ed. Francis Jennings. Syracuse, N.Y.: Syracuse University Press, 1985.

Field, Levi A. *An Historical Sketch of the First Congregational Church in Marlborough, Mass.* Worcester, Mass.: Henry J. Howland, Printer, 1859.

"Five Hundred Years of Indigenous Resistance." *Oh-Toh-Kin,* 1, 1 (Winter/Spring 1992). http://sisis.nativeweb.org/sov/oh11500.html.

Foster, Stephen. *The Long Argument: English Puritanism and the Shaping of New England Culture, 1570–1700.* Chapel Hill: University of North Carolina Press, 1991.

Games, Alison. *Migration and the Origins of the English Atlantic World.* Cambridge, Mass.: Harvard University Press, 1999.

Ghere, David L. "Mistranslations and Misinformation: Diplomacy on the Maine Frontier, 1725 to 1755." *American Indian Culture and Research Journal* 8, 4 (1984): 3–26.

Gildrie, Richard P. *The Profane, the Civil, & the Godly: The Reformation of Manners in Orthodox New England, 1679–1749.* University Park: Pennsylvania State University Press, 1994.

Goddard, Ives and Kathleen Bragdon, eds. *Native Writings in Massachusett.* 2 vols. Philadelphia: American Philosophical Society, 1988.

Gookin, Frederick William. *Daniel Gookin, 1612–1687: Assistant and Major General of the Massachusetts Bay Colony, His Life and Letters and Some Account of His Ancestry.* Chicago: Private, 1912.

Gray, Edward. *New World Babel: Languages and Nations in Early America.* Princeton, N.J.: Princeton University Press, 1999.

Greene, Evarts B., and Virginia D. Harrington. *American Population Before the Federal Census of 1790.* 1932. Baltimore: Genealogical Publishing Co., 1993.

Gura, Philip F. "The Radical Ideology of Samuel Gorton: New Light on the Relation of English to American Puritanism," *WMQ* 3rd ser. 36, 1 (1979): 78–100.

Haefeli, Evan, and Kevin Sweeney. "Revisiting *The Redeemed Captive:* New Perspectives on the 1704 Attack on Deerfield." *WMQ* 3rd ser. 52, 1 (January 1995): 3–46.

Haffenden, Philip S. "The Crown and the Colonial Charters, 1675–1688: Part I." *WMQ* 3rd ser. 15, 3 (July 1958): 297–311.

Hall, Michael G. *The Last American Puritan: The Life of Increase Mather.* Middletown, Conn.: Wesleyan University Press, 1988.

Hannaford, Ivan. *Race: The History of an Idea in the West.* Baltimore: Johns Hopkins University Press, 1996.

Hauptman, Laurence M. and James D. Wherry, eds. *The Pequots in Southern New England: The Fall and Rise of an American Indian Nation.* Norman: University of Oklahoma Press: 1990.

Hight, Horatio. "Mogg Heigon—His Life, His Death, and its Sequel." *Maine Historical Society Collections,* 2nd ser. 5:345–60, 6:256–80.

Hirsch, Adam J. "The Collision of Military Cultures in Seventeenth-Century New England." *JAH* 74, 4 (March 1988): 1187–1212.

Hutchins, Francis G. *Mashpee: The Story of Cape Cod's Indian Town.* West Franklin, N.H.: Amarta Press, 1979.

Hutchinson, Thomas. *The History of the Colony and Province of Massachusetts-Bay.* Ed. Lawrence Shaw Mayo. Cambridge, Mass.: Harvard University Press, 1936.

Jennings, Francis. *The Ambiguous Iroquois Empire: The Covenant Chain Confederation of Indian Tribes with English Colonies from Its Beginnings to the Lancaster Treaty of 1744.* New York: W.W. Norton, 1984.

———. "Goals and Functions of Puritan Missions to the Indians." *Ethnohistory* 18, 3 (Summer 1971): 197–212.

———. *The Invasion of America: Indians, Colonialism, and the Cant of Conquest.* New York: W.W. Norton, 1976.

Johnson, Richard E. *Adjustment to Empire: The New England Colonies, 1675–1715.* New Brunswick, N.J.: Rutgers University Press, 1981.

Judd, Richard W., Edwin A. Churchill, and Joel W. Eastman, eds. *Maine: The Pine Tree State from Prehistory to Present.* Orono: University of Maine Press, 1995.

Kamensky, Jane. *Governing the Tongue: The Politics of Speech in Early New England.* New York: Oxford University Press, 1997.

Kawashima, Yasuhide. *Puritan Justice and the Indian: White Man's Law in Massachusetts, 1630–1763.* Middletown, Conn.: Wesleyan University Press, 1986.

Kences, James. "Some Unexplored Relationships of Essex County Witchcraft to the Indian Wars of 1675 and 1689." *Essex Institute Historical Collections* 120, 3 (1984): 179–212.

Kittredge, G. L. "Dr. Robert Child the Remonstrant." *Colonial Society of Massachusetts Publications* 21, 1.

Kulikoff, Allan. *From British Peasants to Colonial American Farmers.* Chapel Hill: University of North Carolina Press, 2000.

Kupperman, Karen Ordahl. *Indians and English: Facing Off in Early America.* Ithaca, N.Y.: Cornell University Press, 2000.

———. *Settling with the Indians: The Meeting of English and Indian Cultures in America, 1580–1640.* Totowa, N.J.: Rowman and Littlefield, 1980.

Lauber, Almon W. *Indian Slavery in Colonial Times Within the Present Limits of the United States.* New York: Columbia University Press, 1913.

Leach, Douglas Edward. "Benjamin Batten and the London Gazette Report on King Philip's War." *NEQ* 36, 4 (December 1963): 502–17.

———. *Flintlock and Tomahawk: New England in King Philip's War.* 1958. Hyannis, Mass.: Parnassus Imprints, 1995.

———. "The Question of French Involvement in King Philip's War." *Publications of the Colonial Society of Massachusetts* 38 (1953): 414–21.

Lepore, Jill. "Dead Men Tell No Tales: John Sassamon and the Fatal Consequences of Literacy." *American Quarterly* 46, 4 (December 1994): 479–512.

———. *The Name of War: King Philip's War and the Origins of American Identity.* New York: Alfred A. Knopf, 1998.

Lockridge, Kenneth. "Land, Population and the Evolution of New England Society 1630–1790." *Past & Present* 39 (April 1968): 62–80.

Love, W. DeLoss, Jr. *The Fast and Thanksgiving Days of New England.* Boston: Houghton, Mifflin, 1895.

Lovejoy, David S. *The Glorious Revolution in America.* New York: Harper and Row, 1972.

Lucas, Paul. "Colony or Commonwealth: Massachusetts Bay, 1661–1666." *WMQ* 3rd ser. 24, 1 (1967): 88–107.

Malone, Patrick M. *The Skulking Way of War: Technology and Tactics Among the New England Indians.* Baltimore: Johns Hopkins University Press, 1991.

Mandell, Daniel. *Behind the Frontier: Indians in Eighteenth-Century Eastern Massachusetts.* Lincoln: University of Nebraska Press, 1996.

Marshall, Joshua Micah. "Indian Laborers in the Early New England Settlements." Seminar Paper for the American Seminar at the John Nicholas Brown Center for the Study of American Civilization, Providence, R.I., 1996.

————. "Settling Down: Labor, Violence and Land Exchange in the Anglo-Indian Settlement Society of 17th Century New England, 1630–1692." Ph.D dissertation, Brown University, 2003.

McLaughlin, William. *Soul Liberty: The Baptists' Struggle in New England, 1630–1833.* Hanover, N.H.: University Press of New England, 1991.

Melvoin, Richard. *New England Outpost: War and Society in Colonial Deerfield.* New York: W.W. Norton, 1989.

Merwick, Donna. "Becoming English: Anglo-Dutch Conflict in the 1670s in Albany, New York." *New York History* 62, 4 (1981): 389–414.

Miller, Christopher L. and George R. Hamell. "A New Perspective on Indian-White Contact: Cultural Symbols and Colonial Trade." *JAH* 73 (1986): 311–28.

Miller, Perry. *The New England Mind.* 2 vols. 1939. Cambridge, Mass.: Harvard University Press, 1967.

Morison, Samuel Eliot. *The Maritime History of Massachusetts.* 1921. Boston: Houghton Mifflin, 1961.

Morgan, Edmund S. *American Slavery, American Freedom: The Ordeal of Colonial Virginia.* New York: W.W. Norton, 1975.

————. *The Puritan Family: Religion and Domestic Relations in 17th Century New England.* New York: Harper and Row, 1966.

————. *Visible Saints: The History of a Puritan Idea.* New York: New York University Press, 1963.

Morrison, Dane. *A Praying People: Massachusett Acculturation and the Failure of the Puritan Mission, 1600–1690.* American Indian Studies Series 2. New York: Peter Lang, 1995.

Morrison, Kenneth M. "The Bias of Colonial Law: English Paranoia and the Abenaki Arena of King Philip's War, 1675–1678." *NEQ* 53 (September 1980): 363–87.

————. *The Embattled Northeast: The Elusive Ideal of Alliance in Abenaki-Euroamerican Relations.* Berkeley: University of California Press, 1984.

Murray, David. *Indian Giving: Economies of Power in Indian-White Exchanges.* Amherst: University of Massachusetts Press, 2000.

Nash, Alice N. "The Abiding Frontier: Family, Gender and Religion in Wabanaki History, 1600–1763." Ph.D. dissertation, Columbia University, 1997.

Newell, Margaret Ellen. "The Changing Nature of Indian Slavery in New England, 1670–1720." In *Reinterpreting New England Indians and the Colonial Experience,* ed. Colin G. Calloway and Neil Salisbury. Boston: Colonial Society of Massachusetts, 2003.

Noble, John O., Jr. "King Philip's War in Maine." Master's thesis, University of Maine, 1970.

Norton, Mary Beth. *Founding Mothers and Fathers: Gendered Power and the Forming of American Society.* New York: Alfred A. Knopf, 1996.

————. *In the Devil's Snare: The Salem Witchcraft Crisis of 1692.* New York: Alfred A. Knopf, 2002.

Noyes, Sybil, Charles Thornton Libby, and Walter Goodwin Davis, eds. *Genealogical Dictionary of Maine and New Hampshire.* Baltimore: Genealogical Publishing, 1996.

Oberg, Michael Leroy. *Dominion & Civility: English Imperialism & Native America, 1585–1685.* Ithaca, N.Y.: Cornell University Press, 1999.

————. "'We are all the Sachems from East to West': A New Look at Miantonomi's Campaign of Resistance." *NEQ* 77 (2004): 478–99.

O'Brien, Jean M. *Dispossession by Degrees: Indian Land and Identity in Natick, Massachusetts.* New York: Cambridge University Press, 1997.

Palfrey, John Gorham. *A Compendious History of New England.* Boston: Houghton Mifflin, 1873.

Pencak, William. *War, Politics, & Revolution in Provincial Massachusetts.* Boston: Northeastern University Press, 1981.

Pestana, Carla Gardina. *Quakers and Baptists in Colonial Massachusetts.* New York: Cambridge University Press, 1991.

———. "The Quaker Executions as Myth and History." *JAH* 80, 2 (September 1993): 441–69.

Peterson, Mark A. *The Price of Redemption: The Spiritual Economy of Puritan New England.* Stanford, Calif.: Stanford University Press: 1997.

Plane, Ann Marie. *Colonial Intimacies: Indian Marriage in Early New England.* Ithaca, N.Y.: Cornell University Press, 2000.

———. " 'The Examination of Sarah Ahhaton': The Politics of 'Adultery' in an Indian Town of Seventeenth-Century Massachusetts." In *Algonkians of New England, Past and Present: Proceedings of the Dublin Seminar for New England Folklife,* ed. Peter C. Benes, 14–25. Boston: Boston University Press, 1993.

Powell, Sumner Chilton. *Puritan Village: The Formation of a New England Town.* Middletown, Conn.: Wesleyan University Press, 1963.

Prins, Harald E. L. "Turmoil on the Wabanaki Frontier, 1524–1678." In *Maine: The Pine Tree State from Prehistory to Present,* ed. Richard W. Judd, Edwin A. Churchill, and Joel W. Eastman. Orono: University of Maine Press, 1995.

Puglisi, Michael J. *Puritans Besieged: The Legacies of King Philip's War in the Massachusetts Bay Colony.* Lanham, Md.: University Press of America, 1991.

Pulsipher, Jenny Hale. "Massacre at Hurtleberry Hill: Christian Indians and English Authority in Metacom's War." *WMQ* 3rd ser. 53, 3 (July 1996): 459–86.

———. " 'Our Sages are Sageles': A Letter on Massachusetts Indian Policy After King Philip's War." *WMQ* 3rd ser. 58, 2 (April 2001): 431–48.

Reid, John S. *Acadia, Maine, and New Scotland: Marginal Colonies in the Seventeenth Century.* Toronto: University of Toronto Press, 1981.

———. *Maine, Charles II, and Massachusetts: Government Relations in Early Northern New England.* Portland, Maine: Maine Historical Society, 1977.

Richter, Daniel K. *Facing East from Indian Country: A Native History of Early America.* Cambridge, Mass.: Harvard University Press, 2001.

———. *Ordeal of the Longhouse: The Peoples of the Iroquois League in the Era of European Colonization.* Chapel Hill: University of North Carolina Press, 1992.

Richter, Daniel K. and James H. Merrell, eds. *Beyond the Covenant Chain: The Iroquois and Their Neighbors in Indian North America, 600–1800.* Syracuse, N.Y.: Syracuse University Press, 1987.

Roberts, Gary Boyd, ed. *English Origins of New England Families.* 2nd ser., vol. 2. Baltimore: Genealogical Publishing, 1985.

Robinson, Paul A. "Lost Opportunities: Miantonomi and the English in Seventeenth-Century Narragansett Country." In *Northeastern Indian Lives, 1632–1816,* ed. Ralph Grumet. Amherst: University of Massachusetts Press, 1996.

Ronda, James P. "Generations of Faith: The Christian Indians of Martha's Vineyard." *WMQ* 3rd ser. 38 (July 1981): 369–94.

———. "We Are Well as We Are: An Indian Critique of Seventeenth-Century Christian Missions." *WMQ* 3rd ser. 34 (January 1977): 67–82.

Ronda, James P. and Jeanne Ronda. "The Death of John Sassamon: An Exploration in Writing New England Indian History." *American Indian Quarterly* 1 (Summer 1974): 91–102.

Rushforth, Brett. " 'A Little Flesh We Offer You': Captive Exchange, Alliance, and the Origins of Indian Slavery in New France." *WMQ* 3rd ser. 60, 4 (October 2003): 777–808.

Salisbury, Neal. "Indians and Colonists in Southern New England After the Pequot

War: An Uneasy Balance." In *The Pequots in Southern New England: The Fall and Rise of an American Indian Nation*, ed. L. M. Hauptman and J. D. Wherry, 81–95. Norman: University of Oklahoma Press, 1990.

———. *Manitou and Providence: Indians, Europeans, and the Making of New England, 1500–1643*. New York: Oxford University Press, 1982.

———. "Red Puritans: The 'Praying Indians' of Massachusetts Bay and John Eliot." *WMQ* 3rd ser. 31 (January 1974): 27–54.

———. "Social Relationships on a Moving Frontier: Natives and Settlers in Southern New England, 1638–1675." *Man in the Northeast* 33 (1987): 89–99.

———. "Toward the Covenant Chain: Iroquois and Southern New England Algonquians, 1637–1684." In *Beyond the Covenant Chain: The Iroquois and Their Neighbors in Indian North America, 1600–1800*, ed. Daniel K. Richter and James H. Merrell. Syracuse, N.Y.: Syracuse University Press, 1987.

Savage, James. *Genealogical Dictionary of the First Settlers of New England*. Baltimore: Genealogical Publishing, 1965.

Schwoerer, Lois G. *"No Standing Armies!": The Antiarmy Ideology in Seventeenth-Century England*. Baltimore: Johns Hopkins University Press, 1974.

Segal, Charles M. and David C. Stineback. *Puritans, Indians & Manifest Destiny*. New York: G. P. Putnam's Sons, 1977.

Shattuck, Lemuel. *A History of the Town of Concord*. Boston: Russell, Odiorne, 1835.

Simmons, William S. *Spirit of the New England Tribes: Indian History and Folklore, 1620–1984*. Hanover, N.H.: University Press of New England, 1986.

Smith, Joseph Henry. *Appeals to the Privy Council from the American Plantations*. New York: Columbia University Press, 1950.

Sosin, J. M. *English America and the Restoration Monarchy of Charles II: Transatlantic Politics, Commerce, and Kinship*. Lincoln: University of Nebraska Press, 1980.

Southgate, William S. *The History of Scarbrough, from 1633 to 1783*. Maine Historical Society Collections, 1st ser. 3 (1853).

Todorov, Tzvetan. *The Conquest of America*. 1982. Norman: University of Oklahoma Press, 1999.

Tompkins, Hamilton B. "The Great Swamp Fight 19th of December 1675." Paper read before the New York Chapter of the Colonial Order, April 11, 1906. Printed by the Chapter, 1906.

Van Lonkhuyzen, Harold. "A Reappraisal of the Praying Indians: Acculturation, Conversion, and Identity at Natick, Massachusetts, 1646–1730." *NEQ* 63 (September 1990): 396–428.

Vaughan, Alden T. *American Genesis: Captain John Smith and the Founding of Virginia*. Boston: Little, Brown, 1975.

———. *New England Frontier: Puritans and Indians 1620–1675*. 3rd ed. Norman: University of Oklahoma Press, 1995.

———. *Roots of American Racism: Essays on the Colonial Experience*. New York: Oxford University Press, 1995.

Vickers, Daniel. *Farmers and Fishermen: Two Centuries of Work in Essex County, Massachusetts, 1630–1850*. Chapel Hill: University of North Carolina Press, 1994.

———. "The First Whalemen of Nantucket." In *After King Philip's War: Presence and Persistence in Indian New England*, ed. Colin G. Calloway. Hanover, N.H.: University Press of New England, 1997.

Walcott, Charles H. *Concord in the Colonial Period*. Boston: Estes and Lauriat, 1884.

Ward, Harry M. *The United Colonies of New England—1643–90*. New York: Vantage Press, 1961.

Washburn, Wilcomb E. *The Governor and the Rebel: A History of Bacon's Rebellion in Virginia*. New York: W.W. Norton, 1972.

———. "Governor Berkeley and King Philip's War." *NEQ* 30, 3 (September 1957): 363–77.

———. *Red Man's Land, White Man's Law: The Past and Present Status of the American Indian.* 2nd ed. Norman: University of Oklahoma Press, 1995.

Webb, Stephen Saunders. *1676: The End of American Independence.* New York: Alfred A. Knopf, 1984.

Weddle, Meredith Baldwin. "Conscience or Compromise: The Meaning of the Peace Testimony in Early New England." *Quaker History* 81, 2 (1992): 73–86.

Wheeler, Ruth R. *Concord: Climate for Freedom.* Concord, Mass.: Concord Antiquarian Society, 1967.

White, Richard. "'Although I am dead, I am not entirely dead. I have left a second of myself': Constructing Self and Persons on the Middle Ground of Early America." In *Through a Glass Darkly: Reflections on Personal Identity in Early America,* ed. Ronald Hoffman et al. Chapel Hill: University of North Carolina Press, 1977.

———. *The Middle Ground: Indians, Empires, and Republics in the Great Lakes Region, 1650–1815.* New York: Cambridge University Press, 1991.

Williamson, William D. *The History of the State of Maine.* 2 vols. Hallowell, Maine: Glazier, Master, 1832.

Willis, William. *History of Portland, Part 1.* In *Maine Historical Society Collections* 1st ser., vol. 1.

Index

Alexander (Wamsutta), 98

Algonquian Indians, of New England. *See* Androscoggins; Kennebecs; Mahicans; Massachusetts; Mohegans; Montauks; Narragansetts; Niantics; Nipmucks; Pennacooks; Penobscots; Pequots; Pocassets; Pocumtucks; Quabaugs, Wabanakis, Wampanoags

Algonquian Indians, of Chesapeake. *See* Chickahominies

alliances: breakdown of Indian-English, 117, 119–34; breakdown of inter-Indian, 203–4, 278 n. 20; Dutch-Indian, 33–34, 77, 312 n. 57; Indian-English, 19, 20, 115–16, 126, 132, 301 n. 16; Indian patterns, 12, 14; Mohegans-United Colonies, 22; Pequots-Massachusetts Bay Colony, 21

Anderson, Fred, 328 n. 64

Anderson, Virginia DeJohn, 291 n. 23

Andros, Edmund, 106, 129–32, 194, 204–5, 228, 250, 254, 257, 262, 265; accusations against, 255, 325 n. 141; arbitrary government of, 253–54, 264; King Philip's War and, 303 n. 59, 303 n. 62, 303 n. 68; King William's War and, 253–55; Maine and, 233–35, 245–46; Massachusetts's resistance to, 254; overthrow of, 255, 258, 263; siege of Saybrook and, 130

Androscoggins, 210, 230

Anglesey, Lord (Arthur Annesley), 179, 194–95

Anglican Church, 239, 246, 251, 263–64

Anglo-Dutch wars, 32, 48, 240, 260

Annesley, Arthur. *See* Anglesey, Lord

appeals to king, 28; Indian, 28–32, 57–58, 207–8, 269, 319 n. 4, 331 n. 10; John Wompas and, 207–8; Josiah Wampatuck and, 58; Massachusetts's refusal to allow, 60–61, 65; Narragansetts and, 28–32, 55–57, 80; Philip and, 5; Rhode Island and, 29–32; right of, 283 n. 378; Wabanakis and, 58. *See also* petitions to king.

Appleton, Captain John, 68, 290 n. 168

Arlington, Lord (Henry Bennet), 51, 64, 87

authority: divine, 179, 190–91, 199, 205; English styling of, 29, 280 n. 77, 284 n. 48; English views of, 14–18, 279 n. 22; Indian views of, 11–14. *See also* government; politics

Awashonks, 95, 123, 205, 295 n. 100

Axtell, James, 282 n. 22, 290 n. 6, 291 n. 15, 292 n. 32, 325 n. 134

Bacon's Rebellion, 316 n. 75

Bailyn, Bernard, 290 n. 169

Baker, Emerson W., 319 nn. 5, 20, 324 n. 115, 329 n. 99, 330 nn. 116, 122–23, 331 n. 10

Bangs, Jeremy Dupertuis, 290 n. 5

banishment from Massachusetts, 39, 93, 182, 221

Banks, Charles E., 322 n. 83

Baptists, 39, 44–45, 66–67, 92, 182, 264; laws against, 182, 199; organization of church, 67, 92; refusal to bear arms, 314 n. 35; resistance to Massachusetts, 43; supporters of, 294 n. 92, 296 n. 7; tolerance by Massachusetts, 313 n. 13

Barbados, 54, 289 n. 149; slave rebellion in, 295 n. 115

Barefoot, Walter, 294 n. 90

Batten, Benjamin, 168, 188, 192, 296 n. 7

Batter, Edmund, 68, 86, 290 n. 168

battles: of Black Point, 231, 235; "Bloody Brook," 116; Brookfield, 114, 191; Casco Bay, 225; Cocheco (Dover), 256; Deerfield, 116, 227; Falmouth, 208, 218, 223, 225; Great Swamp Fight, 127, 132, 164, 184, 187, 199–202; Groton, 191, 195; Hatfield, 116; Kennebeck, 225; Lancaster, 142, 148, 152; Marlborough, 195; Mendon, 113, 170, 299 n. 51; Northfield, 254; North Yarmouth, 262; Pemaquid, 257; Providence, 191, 195; Richmond Island, 219, 228; Saco, 191; Saco Sands, 215–16;

Acknowledgments

I first began thinking and writing about Indians and English in seventeenth-century New England in the fall of 1993. I write this more than ten years later, a decade during which I have run up countless debts to institutions, mentors, friends, and family. Brandeis University's Crown Fellowship provided financial support during the initial stages of researching and writing this book. The Society of Colonial Wars of Massachusetts granted me a fellowship at the Massachusetts Historical Society, and the Society of Colonial Wars of Washington, D.C., gave me an award that helped with research expenses. My department and college at Brigham Young University have been very generous in funding travel and research in the final stages of completing this book.

I am grateful to the staffs of many research libraries and archives: the Brandeis University Library, the Houghton and Weidner Libraries at Harvard University, the New England Historical and Genealogical Society, the Concord, Massachusetts, and Belmont, Massachusetts Public Libraries and Special Collections, the Marlborough Town Historian's Office, and the Maine Historical Society. I spent many fruitful days at the Massachusetts State Archives, where I particularly thank Elizabeth Bouvier of the Supreme Judicial Archives for her guidance. My fellowship at the Massachusetts Historical Society in the summer of 1996 was enriched by the company and assistance of fellow researchers and staff, particularly Peter Drumy, Conrad Wright, Len Travers, and Ben Mutschler. Brigham Young University's librarians, especially Mike Hunter, made my life easier by finding numerous articles and books I needed.

I thank the archivists, staff, and owners of collections I drew on for the illustrations in this book: the American Antiquarian Society, the Annenberg Rare Book and Manuscript Library at the University of Pennsylvania (especially John Pollack), the Boston Public Library, the John Carter Brown Library at Brown University, the Henry E. Huntington Library and Art Gallery, the J. Willard Marriott Library at the University of Utah, the Library of Congress, the Massachusetts Archives (especially Michael Comeau), the Massachusetts Historical Society, the Museum of Fine Arts, Boston; the National Museum of the American Indian, the New England Historical and Genealogical Society, Plimoth Plantation and the Plymouth County Registry of Deeds, and the Winterthur Museum. Thanks particularly to Alan Pensler of the Pensler Galleries in Washington, D.C., for permission to reproduce the lovely painting on the cover of this book.

I have benefited greatly from the association and wisdom of fellow scholars and mentors, who have been careful readers, great role models, good friends, and frequently all of the above. I thank Tona Hangen, Martha Gardner, Chad Cover, Jennifer Ratner, and Matthew Hale of my writing group at Brandeis University; the participants and commentors at many conferences who shared their ideas with me, particularly Karen Kupperman, Alan Taylor, Alice Nash, Neil Salisbury, James Drake, and the organizers and audiences of the Ray L. Ginger lecture at Brandeis University and the Atlantic Seminar at the University of Pennsylvania; fellow early Americanists whose ideas and work have strengthened my own: Ann Marie Plane, Benjamin Irvin, Richard Cogley, David Silverman, Jill Lepore, Ben Mutschler, Michael Fickes, Emerson Woods Baker, Alice Nash, Neal Salisbury, Mary Beth Norton, and especially Anne Lombard and James Drake; Richard Cogley, James Drake, Neal Salisbury, and Laurel Thatcher Ulrich, who all read and generously commented on early versions of this book; and FREAC (the Front-Range Early Americanists Consortium), founded by Gloria and Jackson Turner Main, which has been a delightful place to share ideas and good company each year. I will always be grateful for the superb education I received at Brandeis University, where I learned what it is to be a historian from Jane Kamensky, David Hackett Fischer, Jacqueline Jones, Morton Keller, and James Kloppenberg. Neal Salisbury, Laurel Thatcher Ulrich, and Thomas Buckley were valued mentors as well. My greatest debt is to Jane Kamensky and David Hackett Fischer—model historians, peerless editors, generous mentors and friends.

The history department at Brigham Young University has provided a wonderfully collegial environment in which to research, write and teach. Thanks particularly to Mark Choate, who read and commented helpfully on a late draft, to Susan Sessions Rugh and Neil York, who read all or parts of the manuscript, and to Gary Daynes and Don Harreld for ideas and encouragement. My efficient research assistant Lisa Thurston Brown helped me sort through an earlier draft and keep all my notes in place.

I am grateful to many at the University of Pennsylvania Press who saw this book through its final stages. Ann Marie Plane, Brendan McConville, and Peter Mancall gave insightful feedback on my book proposal. Peter Mancall and Daniel Richter provided detailed, incisive comments on the manuscript. My editor, Dan Richter, encouraged me to take a little longer to make this book what I had originally conceived it to be—a study of the contest of authority in New England—rather than simply a narrative of King Philip's War. I am grateful for his unflagging enthusiasm and for the high standards he held me to. Robert Lockhart was a pleasure to work with, generous with suggestions, quick to respond. I also thank Peter Agree, Alison Anderson, and Ellie Goldberg for prompt answers to all my questions and helpful suggestions. All remaining faults are, of course, my own.

For my husband, Michael, and my children, Katie, Jon, Annie, and Sam, this book has been a permanent fixture in our whirlwind life. Mike was always willing to read or listen to draft after draft of my evolving manuscript. Katie accompanied me around the rocks on Black Point and let me try out word choices on her. Jon, Annie, and Sam were patient and pitched in when needed. I thank them all for helping me complete something I have loved, though not nearly as much as I love them.